Brotherhoods of Color

Brotherhoods of Color

*Black Railroad Workers
and the Struggle for Equality*

ERIC ARNESEN

HARVARD UNIVERSITY PRESS

Cambridge, Massachusetts, and London, England │ 2001

Library of Congress Cataloging-in-Publication Data

Arnesen, Eric.
    Brotherhoods of color : black railroad workers and the struggle for
equality / Eric Arnesen.
        p.   cm.
    Includes bibliographical references and index.
    ISBN 0-674-00319-5 (alk. paper)
    1. Railroads—United States—Employees—History.   2. Afro-Americans—
Employment—United States—History.   3. Discrimination in employment—
United States—History.   4. Race discrimination—United States—History.
I. Title.
HD8039.R12 U612 2001
331.6'396073—dc21   00-057515

Contents

Illustrations follow page 150.

Prologue

The railroad loomed large in the lives of Wynetta Frazier and Tony Berry, as well as in the lives of many other black children who grew up in Jackson, Tennessee, in the 1940s. Both Frazier's and Berry's grandfathers worked for the Illinois Central (IC) for most of their working lives, Frazier's as a freight brakeman and Berry's as a shop laborer. In their youth, Wynetta and Tony were regular visitors to the IC yards, bringing their relatives lunch or just watching the trains. Occasionally Dillon Berry would allow his grandson Tony to sit in the engineer's chair. In those years, growing up in Jackson, as in the rest of the South, meant living in a highly segregated world, one where the written and unwritten rules of Jim Crow defined proper behavior for blacks and circumscribed their access to jobs and other resources. For Frazier and Berry, it meant growing up in a community composed overwhelmingly of railroad employees and their families, one that nurtured and provided well for its children. Railroad employment allowed for "a very good living," Frazier recalled decades later. Her neighbors "were all homeowners. All of them aspired to send their children to college and did." Their families and neighbors were churchgoers, and they "bought us practically everything we could have wanted as children . . . Some of them even had businesses." For these black children growing up in the era of Jim Crow, the railroad was a source of excitement, pride, relative economic comfort, and even dreams.[1]

What was true for Frazier and Berry was true for countless black families in the nineteenth and twentieth centuries. Railroad employment provided income to literally tens of thousands of black men (and a much smaller number of women) at any given time, making a vital contribution to the economic health of African-American communities in the North and the South. Railroad employment often provided blacks with a higher social status in their own communities, allowing many black railroaders to assume important leadership positions within those communities. The "rank and file of the black railway men represent . . . the bone and sinew of the race in the cities," remarked one observer in 1918. "Their occupation has been a stepping

1

stone upon which a majority of the business and professional men of the race have started."[2] For some, railroad employment in the service sector constituted a temporary occupational stage in a life of social advancement: jurist Thurgood Marshall, communist leader Harry Haywood, singer Taylor Gordon, educator Benjamin Mays, writers Claude McKay and Langston Hughes, civil rights activist Roy Wilkins, and Nation of Islam and nationalist leader Malcolm X, for example, all secured jobs as porters or waiters early in their adult lives. For others, employment in the operating trades on southern railroads was not a way station en route to greater economic or social advancement, but the achievement of what they hoped would be occupational stability and security.

Yet for all of the opportunities the railroad provided, it was an industry whose pronounced discriminatory policies sharply limited black occupational advancement and restricted blacks to specified positions only. "Like no other industry in America," concluded Equal Employment Opportunity Commission officer Samuel C. Jackson in 1966, "railroads have been allowed a free hand in writing their own traditions and prejudices into the laws of our land, been allowed to apply those laws themselves, and been allowed to interpret and reinterpret those laws by their own experiences. The result is, in racial terms, one of the most highly institutionalized forms of industrial segregation in our land."[3] By the early twentieth century, however, growing numbers of black workers began challenging their subordinate position in the labor market. Decades before the rise of the modern civil rights movement in the mid-1950s, black railroaders forged their own brand of civil rights activism that targeted discrimination in the workplace, in white unions, in the application of labor law, and at times in their broader communities.

From the origins of the industry in the early nineteenth century, black railroaders were members of a labor force stratified sharply by race. Their on-the-job experiences were structured by a pervasive system of employment discrimination that defined appropriate work for blacks, relegating them to some job categories and barring them from others. "As every traveler knows," one observer remarked in 1956, "Negroes have been conspicuous for their absence in railroad trains, offices and yards—except for waiters and porters in dining, parlor and sleeping cars—and through no wish of their own."[4] Everywhere, they dominated the service sector as porters, dining car attendants, and station red caps, and in many regions they dominated freight handling, track laying, and maintenance-of-way crews as well. Excluded from the most highly skilled and better-paid positions as engineers and conductors, African-American men could work as locomotive firemen and brakemen only in the South. By the early twentieth century, their hold on even those positions grew tenuous.

Employment discrimination on the railroads was never a static, impersonal, or passive process that inexorably restricted blacks' access to work and eroded their position in the labor market. Rather, it was a dynamic process propelled by human and institutional actors. The agents of employment discrimination included railroad company managers, powerful white railroad union (brotherhood) leaders, and government officials who debated, negotiated, and implemented strategies designed to advance the interests of whites at blacks' expense. Drawing on nineteenth-century racial assumptions common to whites, railroad managers assigned blacks to subordinate service positions on trains and in railway stations and barred them from positions of authority as engineers and conductors. White railroaders reinforced and deepened the racial division of labor. Prohibiting black membership in their brotherhoods until the late 1950s and 1960s, white railroad firemen and brakemen not only denigrated their black counterparts but also campaigned for their elimination from these occupations. They were assisted by a variety of federal agencies, including the U.S. Railroad Administration in the World War I era and the National Mediation Board and National Railroad Adjustment Board in the 1930s, 1940s, and 1950s. American railway labor law, although hardly designed with racial discrimination as a goal, often served as an important weapon in white labor's arsenal against blacks, while the federal agencies responsible for implementing it legitimized and sometimes encouraged discriminatory employment and union practices.

African Americans' responses to persistent employer discrimination, white union hostility, and the federally sanctioned system of labor relations that enforced black subordination were complex, distinctive, and substantial. During and after the 1910s, black railroaders launched campaigns for economic equality by organizing their own associations, seeking pragmatic accommodations with managers, challenging white trade unions, and pursuing legal redress through state and federal courts. Notwithstanding the shared opposition to discrimination, no unified approach to challenging it emerged. Sharp differences of opinion divided black proponents of a racially autonomous movement from those advocating affiliation with the broader labor movement. While many black railroaders were swept up in labor's organizational crusades during World War I and the 1930s and 1940s, the forms assumed by their organizations and protests do not always correspond to conventional expectations.

Many black railroaders were pioneer labor and civil rights supporters and labor activists. With a few exceptions, however, the narratives of labor and African-American history have not accorded their struggles a prominent place, for the histories of black railroaders' associations cross disciplinary subfields and rest uncomfortably within reigning historiographical approaches. Only within the past two decades have labor historians begun to address the distinctive experiences of the black working class and to examine the contours of white racial ideology and its institutional manifestations. Within African-American history, the labor movement's exclusionary role has received disproportionate attention, and there remains a degree of discomfort with exploring black demands that do not resemble those on today's political agenda. In short, until recently both labor and black history managed to neglect entire areas of black thought, experience, and protest that fell outside of their historiographical field of vision.[5]

Today it is recognized that the struggle for workplace rights was never restricted to white labor alone, nor was the struggle for civil rights the sole province of such prominent and heavily middle-class protest organizations as the NAACP. Black railroaders left a legacy of more than a half-century of organized resistance to their economic subordination and an even longer legacy of individual resistance. Their successes were long in the making and ultimately incomplete. They never spoke with one voice; they never pursued a single strategy against discrimination. But collectively they offered a moral, political, and economic critique of racial inequality in the workplace, the labor market, and the labor movement far more powerful than any emanating from either the ranks of organized white labor or the black civil rights establishment. *Brotherhoods of Color* seeks to reconstruct this world of black working-class activism. It does so in part by listening to the voices of black railroaders themselves, preserved incompletely in the pages of the black press, in the records of companies, federal agencies, and the courts, in the papers of black and white unions, and in oral histories. In recapturing and understanding their voices, aspirations, and challenges, it helps us to recast the history of black protest and American labor in the twentieth century.

1

Race in the First Century
of American Railroading

"The history of the Negro in America and the history of American railroad-ing are inseparable," argued Leon R. Harris, an employee of the Rock Island System's Silvis Shops and a future NAACP leader, in 1925. "Negroes helped grade the roadbed and lay the ties and rails for America's first railroad . . . [and] furnished most of the brawn that built every mile of track from the tip end of Florida on the South, to the Mason-Dixon line on the north, and from the Atlantic on the east, to the deserts of Arizona on the west." In addi-tion to constructing and maintaining the tracks, blacks had worked as south-ern firemen and brakemen since the first days of southern railroading and as porters and dining car waiters since the mid-nineteenth century. Americans in the early twentieth century had forgotten or consciously ignored the role played by African Americans in the construction and operation of the rail-roads. In 1923 the chief engineer of the St. Louis–San Francisco lines had omitted any reference to blacks when he declared, "Our railroads have been built and maintained largely with the labor that has immigrated from foreign countries"—first the British Isles, then Germany and Scandinavia, and finally southern and eastern Europe.[1]

Harris offered a corrective, advocating the inclusion of blacks in the broader narrative of American railroading. But adding blacks to the story is only one small step, for African Americans, and other minority workers, oc-cupied distinct places in the railroad labor hierarchy. Not only were the histo-ries of the "Negro in America" and railroading inseparable, but so too was the history of railroading predicated upon racial divisions of labor. From its beginnings in the late 1820s and early 1830s, the American railway labor force was sharply segmented along ethnic and racial lines. African Americans found employment as common laborers, service workers, and skilled workers in sharply defined job categories. While the racial classifications of labor in the nineteenth century were not wholly unchanging, railroad managers tended to assign certain positions only to blacks while denying them access to others.

Twentieth-century black railroad activists who sought to dissolve racial barriers to employment were battling a century-long racial division of labor.

Construction and maintenance of railroad tracks was the sector of the industry that employed the greatest number of workers. This "section" work was often arduous, unpleasant, and dangerous. Wages were usually low, and contractors sometimes paid them intermittently or not at all. Bouts of unemployment were frequent and discipline was often harsh. Life in mobile and isolated work camps was primitive and violent; the outdoor work exposed laborers to harsh temperatures and inclement weather; and mortality from accidents and disease was high. Because native-born white workers avoided section work at all costs, railroad companies and their contractors were forced to seek out other sources of available low-wage labor. Those who accepted the jobs usually had few alternatives. Thus, for much of the nineteenth century, it was African Americans and immigrants from Europe, Asia, and Mexico who graded the roadbeds, laid the track, and ensured their upkeep over rail networks that extended tens of thousands of miles.[2]

The ethnic or racial composition of construction or section gangs varied by geographical region and reflected the sources of available labor. What these gang members shared was their expendability in the eyes of their employers; they could be worked to death without raising serious public concern. In the North and some border states, Irish and to a lesser extent German immigrants constituted the mid-nineteenth-century construction labor force. In the 1830s through the 1850s and beyond, contractors responsible for building the Baltimore and Ohio railroad (B&O) drew heavily on Irish newcomers, Germans, and, briefly, a small number of slaves to excavate and lay track across Maryland and western Virginia. The Illinois Central addressed its serious construction labor shortages in the 1850s by extensively recruiting recently arrived Irish and German immigrants from eastern cities and the Midwest, and its section-gang shortages in southern Illinois in 1880 by employing blacks. By the turn of the century, Italians and other new immigrants from eastern and southern Europe, along with blacks and Mexicans, made up the section gangs on many northern and midwestern railroads. Immediately following World War I, the Pennsylvania Railroad's maintenance department employed immigrants from forty-seven different nations.[3]

A far different racial and ethnic division of labor prevailed in the western and southwestern states. The construction of the transcontinental railroad, completed in 1869 by the Union Pacific and Central Pacific railroads, required the assembly of an army of imported laborers, including a very small number of blacks, a much larger group of Irish, and as many as 12,000 Chinese immigrants.[4] In the Northwest, 15,000 Chinese immigrants labored in construction gangs for the Northern Pacific in Washington Territory and another 6,000 in Montana and Idaho in the early 1880s. But by the end of the century, northwestern railroads were relying on Greeks, Italians, Bulgarians, Austrians, and especially Japanese contract laborers. The Great Northern and the Oregon Short Line, for instance, utilized Japanese labor contracting firms to procure track workers and supervise their labor, providing only boxcars or sheds for housing. Roughly 10,000 Japanese section hands served in the employ of western railroad companies in 1909.[5] Mexican immigrants and Mexican Americans dominated the track crews of the Southwest and the Plains states by the end of the nineteenth century, replacing the Chinese, Irish, and southern and eastern Europeans. Often recruited by labor agents in Mexico or in El Paso, a primary distribution point of Mexican immigrant labor, Mexican men in the United States found more work on railroads than in any other industry. Railroads, including the Atchison, Topeka, and Santa Fe, the Missouri, Kansas, and Texas, and the Chicago, Rock Island, and Pacific, depended heavily on Mexican workers and competed sharply with local farmers and mine owners to retain them, though turnover rates remained high.[6]

In the American South, railroad construction and maintenance labor usually meant black labor. The relatively small southern railroad systems in the antebellum era depended almost exclusively on slave labor to lay and repair track. "Altogether, southern railroads probably employed more than 20,000 slaves" on the eve of the Civil war, historian Robert Starobin has estimated. Railroads occasionally offered company stock to farmers whose land the railroad passed through in exchange for grading performed by the farmers' slaves. Far more often, railroads or their contractors hired slaves from local plantations. Employers paid slaves' owners a stipulated fee, anywhere from $60 to $250 a year per slave in the 1860s, depending on the slave's availability and skill, and promised to provide medical care, food, and clothing to the slave employee. While most hired slaves lived in isolated and mobile camps, some were allowed to live on their own, forming small occupational communities like the one around the Central railroad's yard in East Macon, Georgia. For slaveowners, the possibility of getting remunerative employment for their bondsmen during periods of low cotton prices proved financially tempting. Much to the railroads' dismay, high cotton prices, especially during the 1850s, enabled slaveowners to raise even higher the cost of hiring their human property.[7]

In such times, southern railroads had two alternatives: hire whites or purchase their own slaves. Irish immigrants became the focus of employers' attention, particularly in the border and northern states, and even at times in the South. Beginning in 1850, the Virginia and Tennessee railroad's grading was done by Irish laborers and hired slaves as it pushed into southwestern Virginia. In much of the South, however, efforts at employing immigrants proved unsatisfactory. Forced to hire white men temporarily when slaves were unavailable, the Wilmington and Raleigh railroad was quickly disappointed, finding "the class of white men secured was less reliable than the slaves." At other times, clashes between Irish and slave workers, or between different groups of Irish immigrants, contributed to the railroads' decision to purchase their own bondsmen. By the Civil War, the South Carolina railroad owned 103 slaves, the Mississippi railroad 62, the Montgomery and West Point railroads 67, the New Orleans, Jackson, and Great Northern 106. Toward the end of the Civil War, the North Carolina Railroad hired 318 slaves and, when further hiring became difficult, finally purchased 28 slaves. "This is the way to build railroads," a New Orleans newspaper concluded in 1859, when some 88 slaves were put to work on an Alabama construction project. These men would "probably do more work, and for one-fourth the cost, than double the number of hired laborers."[8]

During the Civil War, enlistment and conscription of southern white skilled railroaders caused widespread labor shortages. At the same time, the flight and forcible relocation of slaves, as well as raids by Union troops, disrupted local supplies of black workers. As the war progressed, Confederate impressment of the railroads' slave laborers only exacerbated the problem. Railroads, however, were essential to the Confederate war effort, and maintaining the rolling stock and tracks, as well as repairing the often extensive damage inflicted by Union troops, required a small army of workers, both skilled and unskilled. Occasionally, the Quartermaster Department of the Confederate army provided hundreds of slaves or black prison inmates for the completion of rail projects in Virginia and Mississippi, but rail lines and their contractors largely relied on market forces, advertising extensively in daily newspapers and offering slaveholders higher prices for their bondsmen. When they could, railroads increased their slave purchases. Shortages grew so severe that the Virginia legislature authorized the state's governor to obtain slave labor for the Virginia Central through impressment. When that proved insufficient, the governor sought legislative approval for a plan to impress free blacks into railroad service as well. Despite these efforts, southern railroads failed to halt the deterioration of roadbeds, tracks, and locomotives.[9]

Union forces too found black labor at times indispensable. By late 1862 and early 1863, northern army officials were putting runaway slaves or blacks declared to be "contraband of war" to work on a variety of war-related jobs. Charged with rebuilding damaged rail lines or constructing new ones to transport supplies and troops to the Army of the Potomac in Maryland and Virginia in 1862, Herman Haupt initially relied on the untrained white "refuse" of three volunteer regiments. Their inexperience and inefficiency prompted Haupt to form a Construction Corps made up largely of hundreds of contrabands who had fled Confederate lines by escaping to Washington, D.C. The corps, headquartered in Union-controlled Alexandria, Virginia, quickly repaired rail lines damaged by southern troops and guerilla fights and destroyed Confederate-operated rail lines. "These Africans worked with enthusiasm," Haupt recalled decades later in his memoirs, "and each gang with a laudable emulation [sought] to excel others in the progress made in a given time." No "other class of men would have exhibited so much patience and endurance under days and nights of continued and sleepless labor," he asserted. (In fact, during Reconstruction, Haupt did find another class of men who worked as hard or even harder: convict laborers. As chief engineer of the Atlanta and Richmond Air Line in 1871, Haupt relied on cheap convict labor for his program of regrading and relaying track, praising the black prisoners, whose death rate from poor food and harsh conditions was high, for their "cheerfulness and industry.")[10]

The defeat of the Confederacy did nothing to alter the South's long-term reliance on black labor. What changed was simply the legal status of the laborers. The war had inflicted tremendous physical damage on the South's rail systems. The spate of postbellum southern railroad building begun under Republican administrations during Reconstruction and continued by their Democratic successors following "Redemption" drew upon the labor of former slaves. Yet emancipation caused considerable concern among rail managers over the availability and reliability of black labor. "The change in the labor system of the country, brought about by the war, was a source of much anxiety for some time, as it was believed the negroes would not labor," confessed chief engineer G. Jordan of the Mobile and Great Northern in 1867.[11]

In the late 1860s, the Central of Georgia railroad proved unable to retain a stable workforce of 400 to 450 freedmen to repair its tracks, while managers of the Atlantic and Gulf railroad in Georgia complained of an unwillingness on the part of freedmen to remain with the road for more than a month. (This proved to be a temporary problem; within a decade, black railroaders were again "well regarded.") Not just availability but reliability plagued southern railroads. The Selma & Meridian railroad initially had "great difficulty controlling the labor of the freedmen." Sometimes more than a little coercion was required to ensure adequate labor supplies: the provost marshal in Macon, Georgia, for instance, cracked down on alleged "vagrants" by rounding up black men and assigning them to railroad repair work, arresting those who refused to comply. Some southern railroad companies even went so far as to experiment with the racial composition of their track labor force. Immediately following emancipation, the North Carolina railroad's black la bor force shrank to virtually nothing, while hundreds of whites found work on its track gangs. By 1867, however, the railroad no longer employed any white section hands at all, and by 1868, the number of its black workers had reached 70 percent of its prewar level.[12]

Despite the arduousness of the work and the occasional coercion involved in labor recruitment, freedmen voluntarily sought out construction and track crew jobs, finding wage labor in the railroad industry an attractive alternative to gang labor or sharecropping on plantations. For one thing, it paid cash wages higher than anything they might earn in agriculture; daily rates ranged from 60 cents to $1.50. Black men seeking to supplement their families' income might take seasonal leave of the plantation in search of more remunerative employment, often returning home only at harvest time. White planters, government officials, and independent observers alike noted the destabilizing effect of railroad work on the South's agricultural labor supply well into the twentieth century. At times, the ostensible defenders of free labor, the officials of the Freedmen's Bureau, worked hard to prevent a "mass exodus" of freedmen from cotton production to railroad construction. Just six years after the Civil War, Robert Somers attributed a shortage of agricultural black labor in Alabama to the freedpeople's "spirit of roving" and to the "demand for labour on the railways." Yet the planters' lament was the railroad managers' dream, as the railroads gained what rural agricultural districts lost.[13]

The related problems of labor supply, turnover, and tractability, however, persisted in some places, leaving many southern rail managers frustrated with their reliance on local black labor. One solution seized upon by Georgia railroad contractors and quickly emulated in other states of the former Confederacy was the convict lease. Supporters of the lease included not only railroad contractors, but also Georgia's leading Republican officials, who fervently believed in state-sponsored economic development and the vanguard role of railroads in advancing the region's industrialization and economic diversification. The vast wartime destruction of Georgia's railroads and the state's own dire financial straits further informed Reconstruction-era politicians' commitment to accommodating contractors' requests to use convict labor. With the obvious exception of the convicts themselves, everyone stood to gain from the arrangement: contractors got cheap labor, and the state government freed itself of the financial burden of maintaining a penitentiary, instead making money on each individual leased.[14]

The convict lease system in Georgia first took shape in 1866. Within two years, the state was providing a contractor for the Georgia and Alabama railroad with a hundred "able bodied and healthy Negro convicts," formerly housed in the penitentiary, for a year's work in exchange for a $2,500 fee and all expenses of maintaining the convicts. Shortly thereafter, another contractor leased a hundred convicts for the Selma, Rome, and Dalton railroad. Contractors found a friend in Republican governor Rufus B. Bullock, an avid railroad booster and convict-lease supporter elected in 1868. In November 1868, the governor expanded the system dramatically, leasing virtually the entire state penitentiary to a single contracting firm, Grant, Alexander, and Company, at $10 per convict. By 1870, the firm had leased some 60 whites and 320 blacks. The state no longer had to support the penitentiary financially, but the company nonetheless made use of its facilities to house its leased convicts at night. For its building efforts farther afield, the company constructed makeshift stockades along the lines of the Macon and Brunswick and the Macon and Augusta railroads, whose tracks it was responsible for grading. Under Grant, Alexander, and Company's control, historian Alex Lichtenstein has written, "the Georgia 'penitentiary' soon became nothing more than mobile squads of forced laborers."[15]

The convicts themselves, who were predominantly black, found penal labor on the railroads little more than slavery. Although the terms of the lease stipulated that prisoners should work ten hours in winter and twelve in summer, convicts complained of being made to work sixteen-hour days. They also denounced their living and working conditions: food was supplied in inadequate quantities, their clothing wore thin and was rarely washed, they worked and slept while shackled, and guards were swift to mete out brutal punishment. From 1868 to 1870 at least five prisoners were shot while allegedly attempting to escape, and beatings were common. Twenty-year-old Hubbard Cureton, a black waiter from Atlanta who found himself assigned to a railroad chain gang for twelve months for sleeping with a white woman, testified that for telling his overseer he was too tired to throw the dirt he was shoveling any higher, he was forced to lie on his belly over a log. "Stripped stark naked," he testified, he was whipped twenty-five to thirty times with a two-foot piece of leather with holes in it attached to a wooden paddle "from the neck to the knees." Other prisoners were whipped while on their knees or stretched down on the ground. The only advantage over slavery that the convict lease offered its victims was the opportunity to escape. Railroad gangs were "porous as a sieve," Lichtenstein argues; by 1878, "555 convicts made their escape, one-sixth of the entire number sent to the penitentiary during those years."[16]

Neither the widespread physical abuse of convicts nor numerous escapes troubled southern legislatures sufficiently to curb the convict lease system, for it served too many powerful interests. The "gospel of prosperity" rested in part on railroad building; and the "railroad mania" fostered by southern Republicans, and to a lesser extent by their Democratic successors, involved state aid in the form of financial loans and subsidies, bonds, land, and service labor. Convicts continued to grade tracks well into the 1880s before other industries began to compete successfully with railroads for state prisoners. By the 1890s, however, coal mines were effectively supplanting railroad camps as the principal destination of leased convicts.[17] Railroad construction and maintenance reverted largely to free black labor, though many of these workers were themselves hardly "free" in any meaningful sense. In its labor recruiting in the early twentieth century, agents for the Louisville and Nashville (L&N) railroad, for instance, found that planters around Selma, Alabama, had a "sort of claim or mortgage on the negro community," requiring them to petition the planters to release black men into their employ when the planters had completed their work.[18]

Perpetually frustrated with inadequate supplies of common labor and the apparent reluctance of many blacks to work steadily for more than a few days, rail contractors in the late nineteenth and early twentieth centuries often invoked racist explanations for the behavior and character of their labor force. "I have had experience with negro labor on railroads for many years," an officer of the Norfolk and Southern railroad declared in 1905. "Many negroes are admirable as unskilled laborers, being hardworking and very willing when they have good foremen; but they are not as good as they were a few years ago." A Missouri railroad official did "not believe that the negro is improving in efficiency as a laborer," instead noticing "positive signs of his retrograding." To a labor contractor in Alabama and Mississippi, there was little that could be done to improve the situation, for "innately and naturally, the negro is a simple, tractable, lazy, shiftless and irresponsible being, with little or no proper ambition." Southern rail contractors encouraged, with little success, the immigration of Italians as a replacement labor force, and opposed any effort to improve working conditions or raise wages for blacks. Some went so far as to call for wage reductions, arguing that increasing blacks' economic need would promote their working more steadily.[19] Hardly unique to railroad managers and their contractors, these beliefs reflected the southern employers' deeply rooted sense of racial superiority. Like their planter counterparts following emancipation, they refused to believe that African Americans would work without compulsion. Simply by behaving as free laborers in a labor market that was itself only partially free, black workers confirmed their employers' racist views of them. Few rail contractors ever acknowledged that abusive treatment, the physical arduousness of the job, and the unpredictability and seasonality of the work contributed to blacks' inclination to avoid dead-end track work when possible or to seek out more attractive alternatives.

By the late nineteenth century, one example of black common labor stood in sharp contrast to the racialized images preferred by railroad officials. The details of the life of John Henry remain elusive, but it is likely that he was born a slave in the 1830s or 1840s in Virginia or North Carolina. As one of thousands of freedmen who secured employment in railroad construction following emancipation, Henry worked for a Chesapeake and Ohio (C&O) railroad contractor who was excavating Big Bend Tunnel in West Virginia between 1870 and 1872. The work was hard and dangerous, and with few safety measures in place, numerous tunnel workers lost their lives from cave-ins, rock slides, and explosions. As a hammer man, John Henry's job was to bore holes in rock for the setting of explosives. His legendary claim to fame was his race with a steam drill, a contest that pitted "de flesh ag'in de steam." In one version of the ballad that bears his name, Henry informed his captain, "A man ain't nothing but a man. An' before I'll let your steam drill beat me down, [I'll] die with the hammer in my hand." With a thirty-pound hammer, he managed to beat the steam drill, then died, either from "a rollin' or a roarin' in his head" (perhaps a stroke) or "because he busted his 'intrels' out or simply hammered himself to death," according to musicologist Brett Williams.[20]

Of the countless African-American workers who suffered serious injury or death with a hammer in their hand while performing common labor, John Henry's is the only name that has been widely memorialized in black folklore and white American popular culture. His legendary physical feats, hard work, and commitment to outperforming technology did nothing to alter white managers' views of black inferiority. But they contributed to Henry's popularity as a "steel-driving hero" among African-American laborers, who were among the first to immortalize him in song. Leon Harris recalled that "none honor and revere the memory of John Henry" more than black laborers. As a crew member in black track grading camps from the Great Lakes to Florida, Harris heard the "Ballad of John Henry" sung wherever he worked.[21] To those men, Henry served as a potent symbol of their own contribution to the building of the nation and a testament to physical strength, courage, and determination in an era that denied them any such recognition.

Often working in isolated labor camps or rural areas, the men who laid or maintained railroad track were a diverse but largely invisible group. Throughout much of the first century of American railroading, and even beyond, the public face of the African-American railroader has been that of the service worker—the Pullman porter and maid, the dining car cook and waiter, and the railroad station red cap. By the mid- to late nineteenth century, these jobs had emerged as occupations within the hierarchy of railroad labor that were invariably dominated by African Americans and, to a lesser extent, other non-whites.

The association of race and service proved remarkably strong and enduring. Like track workers, native-born whites tended to avoid railroad service if they could. "White Americans maintain that they are no good at being servants," concluded Russian writer Vladimir Bogoroz upon discovering during his American journey in the 1890s that the "help in the dining car and the other cars were almost exclusively Negroes." He noted that "Americans gladly leave this kind of work to others—Negroes, Chinese, or greenhorns from Europe who are too naïve to find any other means of making a living." With few employment alternatives open to them, African Americans quickly dominated railroad service work. "This business" of dining car service, a Southern Pacific superintendent informed the *Chicago Defender*'s black readership in 1914, "belongs to your race." (The Southern Pacific employed roughly a thousand black cooks and waiters that year.) For one French traveler, it was appropriate that blacks dominate railroad service. "The negro is the only servant who smiles in America," he concluded in 1891, "the only one who is sometimes polite and attentive, and the only one who speaks English with a pleasant accent."[22]

Not all service workers were African Americans or other minorities. Although no whites served as Pullman porters, they occasionally accepted positions as dining car cooks and red caps, at least in some parts of the North and the Pacific Northwest. In the white public imagination, however, blacks were expected to be servants, while whites were not. By the middle of the nineteenth century their expectations were reinforced by the broader racial divisions of labor firmly inscribed in the railroad industry and the larger American economy. Englishwoman Ethel Alec-Tweedie put the matter bluntly: "I never saw a darky except in some subservient post—as railway porter, restaurant waiter, domestic servant, boot-cleaner, [or] street-sweeper," she recalled of her experiences in the United States in 1900. What she saw made perfect sense, given her racial frame of reference: "What a strange person the negro really is. He makes a first-class servant."[23] Many, perhaps most, white Americans would have agreed.

Yet before black workers could take their place as servants on American railroads, the railroads had to provide service. In their first decades, they were hardly known for the provision of service beyond the basic transport of passengers to their destinations. The unpleasantness of rail travel was widely recognized; this included poor ventilation, inadequate or excessive heat, weak illumination, overcrowded and uncomfortable day coaches, the risk of onboard fires, dilapidated stations, unreliable schedules, and frequent stops. A lack of toilet facilities sometimes constituted another passenger inconvenience. Arriving and departing passengers found it necessary to hoist and haul their own luggage when station janitors or immigrant hack carriage drivers could not be found to assist them. Though the fact of long-distance and increasingly speedy travel was a marvel to nineteenth-century observers, the physical hardships involved in that travel were hardly appreciated.[24]

Among the necessities for which railroad companies initially made few arrangements were eating and sleeping. Well into the nineteenth century, independent vendors catered to travelers by selling food at rail stations. "Every fifteen miles . . . the car stops," noted one observer in 1838, "all the doors are thrown open, and out rush all the passengers like boys out of school, and crowd around the tables to solace themselves with pies, patties, cakes, hard-cooked eggs, hams," and the like. At a number of stops in Virginia immediately after the Civil War, northerner Whitelaw Reid found that his train "was besieged by an outgrowth of the peculiar institution" when a "score or two of negro women, bearing trays on which were rudely arrayed what they called 'snacks,' surrounded us, loudly announcing the merits of their various preparations." When stops were too brief for passengers to disembark, vendors would pass their goods through open train windows and "newsbutchers" would board the train, wandering its aisles to hawk not just reading material, but food as well. Through the end of the nineteenth century, young "waterboys" would walk through passenger cars selling ice water, jugs of lemonade, candy, fruit, and cigars. Between 1850 and 1900 "eating houses" sprang up around rail stations to provide meals to passengers. A few were elegant and served good food; most were, in railroad historian Stewart Holbrook's words, "dismal places" that served terrible food. Quality, or lack of it, was not necessarily passengers' first complaint, however: the brevity of station stops elicited widespread criticism from passengers, who resented having twenty minutes or less to dine.[25]

Two developments transformed the dining experience of American railroad passengers in the late nineteenth century. The first was pioneered by English immigrant and restaurateur Fred Harvey, who established a chain of "Harvey House" restaurants for the Atchison, Topeka, and Santa Fe railroad. Beginning in 1876 in the Santa Fe's Topeka station, Harvey quickly expanded his dining empire across the railroad line's western routes. Within a decade, every hundred miles of the Santa Fe route had an eating establishment run by Harvey. At his death in 1901, Fred Harvey owned and operated forty-seven restaurants, fifteen hotels, and thirty dining cars. Well-prepared, good-quality food was one part of Harvey's trademark, his labor force the other. By one estimate, 100,000 young white women migrated west between 1883 and the late 1950s to become waitresses known as "Harvey Girls." Living in company dormitories and dressing in company uniforms, many of these women remained in the West, marrying railroad workers, miners, or farmers. By design, they put a highly respectable white face on the Harvey system. Out of sight in the kitchens, however, Harvey sometimes employed black, Hispanic, and Native American men and women as cooks, janitors, maids, and bus boys, at least through the 1940s.[26]

The second development to transform the railway dining experience was the spread of the dining car. Although some companies sporadically experimented with buffet, "refectory," or dining car service as early as the 1840s, it was not until the 1870s and 1880s that the dining car became an established and popular feature on American railroads. George Mortimer Pullman, whose fame eventually would be based on his sleeping car empire, helped launch dining car service when he incorporated kitchens, pantries, wine cellars, and removable tables, along with black porters and waiters, into his luxury "hotel cars" in the 1860s and 1870s. To reduce crowding and eliminate lingering food smells, dining and sleeping spaces were soon separated, with food preparation and consumption relegated to a so-called dining car. Pullman's first luxury dining car, the Delmonico, began operation in 1868, and by the 1870s and 1880s, railroads generally were providing their own dining car services. One disadvantage of on-train food provision remained constant for railroads well into the twentieth century: it was an expensive service. The advantages, however, outweighed the disadvantages: dining car service was attractive to passengers (over time, companies without it risked losing patronage), and it reduced the need for more frequent stops.[27]

Even more than the dining car, the Pullman sleeping car addressed not merely passengers' need for comfort but their desire for luxury as well. Decades before Pullman began his long march toward monopoly in the sleeping car business, railroads experimented with a variety of sleepers that never seemed to catch on. It was Pullman who perfected the sleeping car and came to dominate its manufacture and operation. Handcrafted walnut woodwork, plush carpets, silver-plated metalwork, French glass mirrors, and heavy ornamentation marked the interior of the Pullman car, which was filled with upper and lower sleeping berths. "As much care was spent in decorating them as is expended in decorating the dwellings of the rich," observed an English traveler to the American West in 1871.[28]

Cultivating the aura and feel of luxury involved the provision of service—and those who did the actual providing were largely African Americans. For his "hotels on wheels," Pullman assembled a small army of servants to attend to the needs of passengers. The Pullman porter would arrive up to several hours before a train's departure to set up his car, checking the linen and other supplies, ensuring overall cleanliness, putting combs, brushes, and water glasses in their places, making beds, and otherwise guarding the car until departure. He would assist passengers for the trip's duration, while at night he would shine their shoes with high-quality polish he had purchased himself.[29]

From the introduction of portering service in 1867, the Pullman porter was an African American, drawn from the ranks of newly emancipated southern freedmen. The company quickly became the single largest employer of African-American labor in the United States, carrying roughly 6,000 blacks on its payroll in 1914 and perhaps double that two decades later. The black porter soon emerged as "one of the most distinctive institutions of America," one journalist observed in 1918. It was a job unlikely to be usurped, for Pullman had established a veritable caste of black servants. What inspired Pullman to create an occupational category that was strictly defined by race is not known, but the freedmen's availability and cheapness as a labor supply, the white traveling public's association of blacks with servile labor, and some blacks' own prior training as servants under slavery undoubtedly contributed to his decision. "Trained as a race by years of personal service in various capacities," Pullman associate Joseph Husband observed in 1917, "and by nature adapted faithfully to perform their duties under circumstances which necessitate unfailing good nature, solicitude, and faithfulness, the Pullman porters occupy a unique place in the great fields of employment."[30]

The Pullman Company's association of servility and race, like that of many whites, remained intact well into the twentieth century. On the eve of the Great Migration of southern blacks to northern cities during World War I, Pullman company president L. S. Hungerford admitted that he preferred southern to northern blacks for positions as porters: their training in the South, he admitted to the U.S. Commission on Industrial Relations, "better fits them for service on the car."[31] Although the Pullman Company preferred to hire former house servants, it recognized that relying on a decades-long tradition of assumed southern black docility and service was a poor substitute for modern training in the art of portering. The Pullman Company left little to chance, insisting that its newly hired black porters undergo two or three days of unpaid training before commencing work. Over time, that training became longer and more formal, until by the 1940s it consisted of a rigorous course to instill the "highest standards of cleanliness and personalized service" and to ensure that those standards were "religiously adhered to" by employees. Ironically, before the twentieth century, the higher-paid white supervisor of the porter, the Pullman conductor, received no formal training at all. "It is a custom, almost universal in the observance, that the breaking in of a new conductor is left to some old porter," explained attorney William Houston on behalf of a group of black railroaders.[32]

If Pullman executive Hungerford did not intend his remarks about southern blacks as a compliment, some porters could invert his logic and insist on a degree of respect based on the skill that southern porters possessed. Explained George Young, a Pullman porter on the New York Central, "I say there is a training, that you cannot go out and pick up a man off the street or out of a pool room or off of a section [gang] and make a private car man out of him."[33] But porters' best efforts at portraying themselves as trained, even skilled, workers made little impression either on the Pullman Company or the traveling public. Of course, passengers appreciated—or, more likely, expected—prompt, efficient, courteous, and obsequious service from their porters, but this in no way acknowledged the porter as a skilled worker, much less one worthy of passengers' respect. The generic appellation "George"— attached to porters generally by their white customers—signified both whites' refusal to recognize the porters' individuality and their expectations of stereotyped servile behavior.[34]

The larger racial discourse of black servility and the actual relegation of African Americans to the service rungs on the occupation ladder did not fully account for whites' expectations of stereotyped behavior. The compensation system utilized by Pullman for his porters and all railroads for their waiters virtually guaranteed that black workers had to fulfill white expectations if they wanted to earn a decent living. By the early twentieth century, the Pullman Company's base monthly salary for a porter who worked for the company less than fifteen years was $27.50, which the porter made if he worked all but four days a month. Every trip "was a sort of gamble as to the financial results it would bring to the employee," the *New York Age,* a black weekly, concluded in 1918. Although some porters claimed gratuities of up to $80 a month, an impressive amount, others brought in as little as fifty cents a trip. "[I]n these days," one porter complained during the Great Depression, "tips sometimes run far below the most modest living standard."[35]

The ubiquity of tipping allowed railroads to rationalize low salaries for their service workers. Those same low salaries also required blacks to work extremely hard for supplementary tips, often forcing them to assume a persona that was at once cautious, cheerful, even obsequious before their white patrons. To a considerable extent, the financially successful porter or waiter had to be both a keen student of human behavior (assessing his customer accurately) and an actor (playing the required part properly). What this meant in everyday practice was that the porter had to "cater to the vanity" of his passengers, for the average American "is not indifferent to flattery. He gives a substantial tip to the porter, who senses this and makes a fuss over him." While porters recognized the performative nature of their job, few white observers did, instead finding humorous what they perceived to be porters' innate or acquired abilities to collect money from whites. "Most of them have the faculty of eliciting tips, whether you feel you can afford to pay it or not," offered W. H. Morse, vice chair of the World War I-era Board of Railroad

Wages and Working Conditions. "The colored's [*sic*] man's smile goes a long way" in opening passengers' wallets or purses, white railroad executive L. S. Taylor concurred.[36]

What company officials considered amusing racial abilities, critics found demeaning. Tipping transformed the porter into a "beggar, a soft-soaping, coin-coaxing creature, instead of an upright, honorable, manly man, who is paid an honest wage for an honest service," *Financial America* editorialized in 1917. "From every angle the tipping system is unjust," concurred a scholar of black St. Louis in 1914. "It is unjust to the Negro because in accepting tips he feels himself less a free man, and because necessity forces him to perpetuate the system." Collectively, service workers expressed ambivalence about the tipping system: many preferred a substantially higher salary, but few advocated the outright abolition of tipping. "We are seeking a living wage," one black union leader argued during World War I, but "nothing should be done to wipe out that tip." Decades later, station red caps, who expected their new minimum wage under the Fair Labor Standards Act to be augmented by their traditional tips, protested angrily when rail stations required them to report and submit all gratuities to management to defray their wages. Asked by a member of the pre–World War I Commission on Industrial Relations if he felt that in receiving tips he was "disgraced or humiliated in any way," veteran Pullman porter G. H. Sylvester responded in the negative. The "degredation [*sic*]," he testified, "would be if we did not get them."[37]

With a large staff, railway dining cars entailed a complex division of labor. At the top stood the dining car steward—invariably a white man who usually, but not always, boasted a background in hotel or restaurant service—who was responsible for enforcing company rules and maintaining supplies and the condition of the car. As a railroad's "ambassador" at the "court of public opinion," the steward greeted passengers as they entered the dining car, escorted them to their seats, provided them with menus, and sought to anticipate, detect, and resolve any signs of customer dissatisfaction.[38] The steward's job also involved overseeing the food service crew, and, in theory, training the wait staff. Few black waiters or cooks, however, credited the steward with providing much, if any, training. Instead, they recognized the role of experienced waiters, cooks, and chefs in "breaking in" new workers on the job, teaching them the tricks of the trade, and, in some cases, ribbing them mercilessly until they learned the ropes. "The men, they put their arms around me and trained me," recalled Jimmy Clark, who first began railroading as a dishwasher in 1918 and eventually worked his way up to chef on the Southern Pacific.[39]

Below the position of steward, most if not all dining car workers were black. In a four-by-fourteen-foot kitchen, the chef was in command of the cooking staff. Chefs and cooks tended to be black in the South and East, while western railroads sometimes employed whites. (One 1921 survey of dining car superintendents revealed that white cooks worked exclusively on twelve railroads, while black cooks worked on fifty-one). Answering to the chef in the small kitchen were the second cook (who worked the broiler and fryer), the third (or vegetable) cook, and the fourth cook, who washed the dishes. While chefs and cooks prepared soups, baked rolls, cooked meat, and the like, by the early twentieth century much of the food had been prepared before being loaded on the train. Given the lack of space, portions of meat would have been already carved and wrapped, steaks cut and weighed, and chicken breasts split. Once on board, much of the food was stored in the adjoining pantry, which was under the jurisdiction of a waiter designated as the "pantryman." Between four and six waiters—"each with a big tray and balancing himself against the twists and turns of a train flying at sixty miles an hour"—served tables in the dining car itself, leaving their orders with the kitchen and getting them "when they are ready as easily as if they had been rehearsed." "They're one-stepping," a white steward explained to Edward Hungerford, who had observed waiters' "shuffling way of sliding" along the pantry counter of a New York Central train in 1914.[40] If whites saw a "shuffle," blacks had other words for the motion dining car waiters adopted to carry out their job. "We worked like house slaves on roller skates," recalled future NAACP leader Roy Wilkins, who had secured a summer dining car job shortly after World War I, "serving breakfast, lunch, and dinner, cleaning up, then starting all over again, seven meals in all."[41]

In the pre-union era (in general, before the 1930s) railroad service workers' satisfaction with their jobs was tempered by their resentment of its blatant inequities. All held their positions at the sufferance of their supervisors, possessing few if any rights before management. The white dining car steward "is absolutely in power. He is the monarch of all he surveys," complained Charles A. Reid, a Pennsylvania railroad waiter, in 1919. Penalties for rules infractions could range from five- or ten-day suspensions to outright dismissal.[42] In many cases, the passengers' word was gospel; if a complaint was lodged against a waiter or porter and management chose to believe it, there was literally nothing the accused employee could do.

Bars to promotion also rankled black railroaders well into the twentieth century. Railroad company policies prohibited African Americans from officially becoming stewards or, in the case of the Pullman Company, conductors. "These men could be stewards if they were white," the *Chicago Defender* complained in 1914.[43] As an economy measure, however, companies did permit blacks to serve as "waiters-in-charge" or "porters-in-charge" on specified runs. With the same responsibilities and authority as a white steward or Pullman conductor, the black waiter-in-charge or porter-in-charge received a substantially lower salary than his white counterpart. Only in the 1940s and 1950s did railroads relent, under legal and political pressure, and begin to employ black dining car stewards, and only in the 1960s did the Pullman Company, on the eve of its dissolution, consent to promote porters to conductors' jobs.

Black service workers' weak and subordinate status vis-à-vis their white managers was revealed in the multitude of rules governing their on-the-job performance and in the conditions they endured during their nonworking hours both on and off the train. For decades, company rules held waiters and cooks (but not stewards) collectively responsible at the end of the month for any breakage of glasses or plates or theft of silverware on their cars, regardless of fault. "Every piece of crockery that is broken by the movement of the train, not on account of any carelessness on the waiter's part, they have to pay for out of their own pockets," a white steward testified. Pullman porters were also responsible for replacing any missing blankets, linen, combs, pillows, and the like. Railroad companies distrusted their black dining car crews to the extent of having detectives periodically stop black crew members disembarking with suitcases or parcels, demanding that they open them for inspection, while exempting from examination the baggage of stewards and other whites.[44]

Sleeping accommodations long remained a sore spot with porters and especially dining car workers. Not infrequently, porters got no sleep at all on a trip lasting twenty-four hours or more; when they did, they often had to sleep sitting up in a smoking room. Even then, they remained on call if passengers required assistance. Dining car men had it worse: Although white stewards were provided with upper berths, through the 1920s black men were often required to sleep on dining car tables, with companies providing only pillows, sheets, and blankets. In other instances, they were relegated to the baggage car and "allowed the use of old discarded blankets that were never fumigated or washed," surrounded by "trunks and baggage and a big electric dynamo going at full blast all night to disturb the little sleep" they might get, as one former waiter put it. "I have never seen dining car quarters in my life that you would want to sleep in in warm weather," waiter and union leader Rienzi Lemus declared in 1919.[45]

Racial discrimination not only dictated unpleasant working conditions for black employees, it also made Pullman and dining cars sites of potential or actual racial discord. Considerable conflict would arise between white passengers or crew members and black passengers who questioned racially designated seating or sleeping arrangements. As early as 1842, Charles Dickens reported that a "black man never travels with a white one," instead being consigned to a "negro car; which is a great, blundering, clumsy chest."[46] By the 1890s, custom and increasingly Jim Crow laws prohibited blacks from riding in first-class railroad cars and often denied them berths on Pullmans. Instead, African Americans were relegated to the Jim Crow car, which prevailed throughout much of the South. Journalist T. Thomas Fortune reported in 1890 that it was "usually a half car, the other half of which is used as a smoker, a drinking den, profanity generator and escape, and general cussedness." Enforced segregation in unequal facilities did not sit well with many African Americans, particularly those who desired, and could afford, first-class or Pullman accommodations. In their personal behavior and in court, black women holding first-class tickets challenged the railroads' refusal to allow them to take their seats in the first-class "ladies' car," while black men blocked from regular first-class seating or Pullman berths lodged similar protests. Ida B. Wells and Homer Plessy are the best known of the numerous African Americans who objected to their forced assignment to the Jim Crow car and sought legal redress.[47]

For their part, black service workers were silent witnesses to the successful efforts of white stewards, trainmen, and conductors to eject blacks from dining cars and first-class seats. Occasionally, company policy required black workers to enforce rules mandating segregation. The *Chicago Defender* wasted few words in 1930 when it denounced some black railroaders as Uncle Toms for complying with segregation statutes or insulting black passengers. The paper also condemned black waiters at Baltimore's Union Station who refused to serve a black journalist until several whites had finished eating as "unfit for the association of self-respecting Race people," a "disgrace to present-day humanity and a real curse and detriment to all of our group." When it came to racial etiquette, the *Defender* expected not only defiance of Jim Crow norms and laws but of managerial authority as well.[48]

More charitably, and perhaps realistically, the Oklahoma *Black Dispatch* reminded its readers of the importance of context. The "Negro porter is not to blame," it concluded in 1920, "for the reason that he labors under a certain degree of intimidation"—that is, he "STANDS SUBJECT TO BE FIRED" for failing to follow a conductor's orders regarding black passengers. When the stationmaster in Washington, D.C.'s Union Station insisted on the segregation of even the baggage of white and black passengers headed south, he did not invite debate on the subject. As a very condition of their employment, black service workers were expected to follow their white supervisors' orders promptly and obediently. "We are not approving the law" of segregation, an angry Atlanta red cap responded to black attorney Elmer Carter's harsh criticism of their manner; "and neither do we feel called upon to break it. Not even for you."[49]

Whatever their role in maintaining segregation, black service workers were themselves hardly immune to conflicts over race that raged on and off railway trains. A dining car crew on the New Orleans Meridian Line quit their jobs in 1919 when their steward failed to protect a waiter from a fatal attack by a white flagman, and in 1926 Pullman porters at the Texas and Pacific station in New Orleans were mobbed by drunken white national guardsmen en route to their training camp in Alexandria, Louisiana. In an altercation with an Albany, New York, councilman in 1923, a porter was slapped and retaliated by hitting the politician, whereupon he was arrested and charged with assault with intent to murder. Five members of a Pennsylvania railroad dining car crew in 1920 were charged with disorderly conduct in Baltimore after fighting with two verbally abusive white southerners who objected to the presence of a black porter dining near them.[50]

Black railroad workers' travels to distant cities could be difficult, especially when negotiating the particularities of Jim Crow in unknown places. On his first trip to San Francisco in 1920, porter Robert Turner ended a day of sightseeing by trying to buy dinner. "We don't feed niggers here" was the response he received from white waiters and waitresses at a variety of restaurants. Ultimately, he dined on canned goods for the duration of his stay in the city. He had the same experience in Los Angeles, a city where he found "nearly all southern people" who had "brought their southern tradition along with them." In dangerous times, black service workers had to take even greater care. "Traveling from city to city and unable to gauge the attitude and temper of each one," Claude McKay recalled of the World War I years, "we Negro railroad men were nervous. We were less light-hearted. We did not separate from one another . . . We stuck together, some of us armed, going from the railroad station to our quarters . . . for we never knew what was going to happen."[51]

Given the countless drawbacks of railroad service work, why did so many African Americans accept and even remain in railroad service jobs? Primarily because railroad service jobs were relatively remunerative and secure. When asked what kept him in his waiter's job for thirty-two years, Altamont F. Bolt responded: "Money! Money kept me there." For decades—in the 1930s, 1940s, and beyond, "that was one of the best jobs you could get" outside of the post office. Although Bolt spent much of his working life in the union era, many pre-union porters and waiters also praised aspects of their respective jobs. "It was grueling work," Roy Wilkins recalled, "but it offered me my first sense of the sweep and expanse of the country. For the first time I began to look beyond the comfort and safety of St. Paul to the larger, harder world beyond." As one Pullman porter put it in 1931, the "chance to meet people and see the country, and the opportunity to make a living in a pleasant way are all magnets that draw us" to the work.[52]

Before and during the union era, wages and tips allowed railway service workers to occupy something of a middle-class stratum within black communities in New York, Boston, Chicago, St. Louis, Minneapolis, Oakland, and countless other cities. In the eyes of many African Americans, porters and waiters constituted a kind of "aristocracy of Negro labor" who occupied prominent positions in their communities, fraternal orders, and churches.[53] Short-term stints on board a sleeping or dining car allowed young black men to earn money to put themselves through college. Every summer the Pullman Company hired hundreds of temporary porters to cover the busy travel season, and southern black college students annually enlarged the Pullman summer payroll. "It seems that every railroad train is a sort of traveling black college," concluded Russian writer Vladimir Bogoraz upon learning that three black service workers on his cross-country trip in the 1890s were medical students. Just before and after World War I, future educator Benjamin E. Mays worked as a Pullman porter before matriculating at the University of Chicago, while during and after the war, communist leader Harry Haywood worked as a waiter on the Chicago Northwestern, the New York Central, and the Michigan Central. (Both men lost their jobs as a result of run-ins with supervisors.) The list of onetime railway service employees among distinguished blacks of the twentieth century is a long one. Even for those not intent on pursuing professional or political careers, service work could enable blacks to realize entrepreneurial ambitions. Tennessee native Richard Smith Bryan, for example, spent eight years in the service of the Pullman Company in the 1880s until he had saved enough to found the Estella Café in Chicago, an establishment that eventually commanded a large and lucrative black patronage and allowed him to become a leader in black Chicago's fraternal and labor societies. In a labor market that closed higher-paying industrial or craft jobs to African Americans, portering, cooking, and waiting offered real, if limited, financial opportunity to young black men seeking to climb the occupational ladder into the middle class.[54]

Beyond the visible realms of service and common labor on the tracks, African Americans made up a portion of the more skilled operating trades. Antebellum southern railroads employed either rented or purchased slaves as locomotive firemen, who rode in the engine alongside the engineer and were responsible for feeding coal into the engine's boiler, and brakemen, who performed the dangerous work of setting hand brakes (before the introduction of air brakes in the 1890s) and coupling rail cars with a link and pin.[55] After the Civil War, blacks retained and even increased their hold on these positions. By the beginning of the twentieth century, blacks constituted the vast majority of firemen, brakemen, and yard switchmen on the Gulf Coast lines;

they made up some 90 percent of the firemen on the Seaboard Air line and the majority of such positions on some divisions of the Illinois Central, the Southern, and the L&N railroads in the South. "It is an every-day occurrence in the South," one observer noted in 1900, "to see white locomotive engineers and colored firemen seated in the same cabs." From the 1890s to roughly 1930, blacks outnumbered whites as locomotive firemen on Georgia's railroads, holding 60 percent or more of these positions.[56]

Southern railroad companies had good reasons for employing blacks as firemen and brakemen. Most important, African-American men were a source of cheap labor. Black firemen and trainmen generally received lower rates of compensation than their white counterparts; until World War I, rates for southern blacks were 10 to 20 percent below white rates.[57] Beyond cost, railroads saw other advantages to employing black operating craft men. Despite white workers' constant complaints about blacks' supposed inability to perform their jobs, rail managers found blacks to be efficient workers. In 1886, James C. Clarke, the president of the Illinois Central and a former slaveholder, described his railroad's black firemen and brakemen in Kentucky, Mississippi, Tennessee, and Louisiana as "smart active men" who "show skill in learning quickly the duties they are to perform." Clarke considered black workers to be "generally amiable, docile and obedient." Disavowing any prejudice on the part of his railroad, Clark concluded that there "is no better labor among any race in the world." Given the tradition of black subordination, railroad companies could extract a greater amount and a wider range of labor out of their black workforce. Blacks often worked longer hours than whites, putting in "more preparatory time before a train starts than white employees," found the Eight-Hour Commission, a federal body studying the standard workday of railroad employees. "In these ways an extra hour may be added to their shifts, for which they get no pay."[58]

Railroad managers similarly found that they could use black labor to ensure control over their white labor force and as a bulwark against trade unions. White union members often correctly traced their inability to organize to the deterrent effect of black competition and attributed their loss of southern strikes to black strikebreakers. Following the defeat of white firemen and switchmen in the mid-1890s in strikes against the L&N railroad, the company installed nonunion blacks in most of the positions of brakemen, switchmen, and firemen on its Birmingham division to forestall renewed union agitation. Subsequent efforts by the white brotherhoods to remove blacks from train crews failed.[59] Few roads in the Southeast employed any new white firemen at all in the immediate aftermath of the failed 1909 strike by white Georgia firemen, perhaps as punishment, but more likely as a form of insurance against future union trouble. Harvard economist William Z.

Ripley, in a 1918 study, attributed the L&N's success in crushing workers' strikes to its financial strength, the "resolute antibrotherhood attitude of its president," and "its ample supply of negroes for firemen."[60]

African Americans' access to skilled positions was limited, however, by geography and by the existence of inflexible bars to promotion. From the time of railroading's origins through the mid-twentieth century, railroads in the North and West employed only white workers as firemen and brakemen (although in some states, blacks sometimes performed brakemen's work as "porter brakemen"—a distinct occupational category that combined on-board service with brakemen's tasks). In the nineteenth century, this in part reflected the character of the available labor supply. With few skilled African Americans in the North, it was not surprising that the ranks of firemen and brakemen would be filled mostly by American-born whites and immigrants from Germany and Ireland. But even with the migration of increasing numbers of blacks to the North by the century's end, no railroad relaxed its all-white policy. With management's apparent approval, white workers left nothing to chance and erected their own color lines, refusing to work with African Americans.

The two most coveted positions in the running trades—locomotive engineers and train conductors—remained off-limits to African Americans everywhere in the United States until the late 1960s and early 1970s. The prospective black worker "presents himself to the proper authorities as a person qualified for the work," complained AME Reverend R. C. Ransom in 1888, "but he is informed that he may not hope to enter there, that upon their engines white men hold the throttle, lift the tickets and manage the trains."[61] Representing something of a labor aristocracy, engineers and conductors were the highest paid and most autonomous of railroad workers. Engineers needed considerable technical knowledge, experience, and strength to direct the physical operation of the train, while conductors supervised train personnel, including brakemen and porters, acting as a kind of "traveling clerk who combines with his book work sufficient mechanical knowledge," as railroader turned sociologist W. Fred Cottrell put it in 1940. Railroad managers never proposed placing blacks in positions of such authority, respect, and prestige. Prevailing white notions about black workers' character, intelligence, and appropriate place in the economic hierarchy disqualified African Americans from assuming such roles. The practice of excluding blacks from conductors' and engineers' jobs long antedated the rise of trade unionism on the railroads; later, even where unions were weak or nonexistent, managers kept the top positions an all-white preserve.[62]

White workers concurred that no black should ever assume the top positions in the operating trades. The brotherhoods of engineers and conductors barred blacks from membership, and their members would undoubtedly have refused to work with any blacks in such positions had management had the audacity to promote them. It was virtually inconceivable to whites that that day would ever come. In the mainstream of late-nineteenth-century racial thinking, white workers, like white managers, defined blacks as wholly un-qualified to fill any job requiring "moral stamina and mental quickness."[63] It was not whites' color prejudice but the racial characteristics of blacks that kept them out of the engineer's position, the president of the Brotherhood of Locomotive Engineers explained in 1914. "There may come a time in the evolution of the centuries when the nego [sic] will make an engineer, but the time has not arrived yet" for two reasons: "you cannot keep him awake, the other is when you get him in close quarters he always loses his head . . . That is why the negro has never been a success as an engine man, and why he has never been promoted."[64]

Engineers and conductors may have faced no competition from African-American railroaders, but southern white firemen and brakemen did. In re-sponse, they contended that the jobs required character, deportment, and even skills that only whites, not blacks, possessed. Once "the calling of the lo-comotive fireman was considered low," reflected M. J. Boling, of Wilming-ton, North Carolina, in 1893, but "to-day it is looked upon as being worthy and honorable." He attributed this improvement to his union's success in raising "the standard of morality; no drunkard or person of dissipated habits can gain admission to the order." The growth of the firemen's association and the spread of its "conservative principles" in the South, one Nashville man reported in 1887, is "enabling every white born fireman to do justice to himself and family."[65] Brotherhood lodges not only provided insurance plans and entertainment, but also encouraged moral and personal uplift, emphasiz-ing the importance of both individual character and collective comportment. Through their brotherhoods, southern white railroaders promoted an ideol-ogy of self-improvement and intense craft pride.

The work of braking or firing an engine remained dangerous, dirty, and hard, but whites insisted that their jobs required a level of skill and command of scientific knowledge unobtainable by African Americans. "Railroading is rapidly advancing into the dignity of a profession," noted veteran conductor Charles B. George in 1887, "requiring a knowledge of many branches of sci-ence, training of a high order, and careful application as well as unselfish de-votion to public and corporate interests." Large sections of monthly union journals were devoted to explaining railroad technology and the latest inno-vations and to preparing workers to pass qualifying exams. Self-improvement, sobriety, and technical education, repeatedly promoted by white firemen and brakemen, were not merely abstract virtues. They were also requirements for advancement up the railroads' occupational ladder. A brakeman might eventually rise to become a conductor, while the locomotive fireman, as one nineteenth-century biographer put it, "was the engineer in embryo."[66] The positions of conductor and engineer were more prestigious, often physically less strenuous, and substantially better paid. (Engineers, for example, earned roughly twice firemen's wages.) To admit that African Americans possessed the qualifications to be firemen and brakemen would have required whites either to alter drastically their stereotypes of black inferiority or to acknowledge that these jobs were strictly of a manual nature requiring no higher training, knowledge, or even character traits.

Neither of these options proved palatable. Instead, white railroaders subjected their black counterparts to denigration, repeatedly resorting to stock racial caricatures in articulating their case against black advancement. Missouri railroader M. E. Dowdy concluded that the black fireman was a "person almost devoid of ambition, energy, business ability, and manly qualities, who knows nothing but [how to] shovel coal, shine brass (and the engineer's shoes if necessary) . . . [H]is clouded intellect, degeneracy, and dormant perceptive powers are as unyielding to modern education as the tax is heavy on the white people who pay for negro schools." Whites' list of damning attributes was lengthy: the black fireman was "indolent, untrustworthy, shiftless," "without honor, principle, pride, or fair intelligence"; he was "totally unfit, both socially and mentally."[67]

Notions of racial hierarchy were inscribed not only onto white railroad workers' ideological outlook but onto their personal and occupational identities and onto the organizations they constructed and joined as well. Known informally as the "Big Four," the largest white railroad brotherhoods—the Brotherhood of Locomotive Engineers, the Order of Railway Conductors of America, the Brotherhood of Locomotive Firemen and Enginemen, and the Brotherhood of Railroad Trainmen—were organized in the 1860s and 1870s. From their inception, race was written into the very definition of their unions' membership. Representing the industry's overwhelmingly white, native-born male constituency, the brotherhoods adopted explicit provisions in their constitutions to ensure continued racial, ethnic, and gender homogeneity. All four organizations officially restricted their membership to white men; any applicant for membership had to be "white born, of good moral character, sober and industrious, sound in body and limb, not less than eighteen nor more than forty-five years of age, and able to read and write the English language."[68] Exclusionary provisions in brotherhood constitutions remained standard well into the 1950s and 1960s, when federal and state courts, responding to and helping to forge a gradual revolution in labor and civil rights law, declared them unconstitutional.

Racial membership clauses were not attributable solely to the conservatism of the Big Four brotherhoods, for they were adopted by other, more radical white railroaders as well. In 1893, dissident railroad unionists formed the industrially organized American Railway Union (ARU) as a more radical alternative to the established brotherhoods. They too drew the color line and restricted membership. Copying a page out of their predecessor's rule book in 1894, the ARU's committee on legislation authored a constitution whose preamble defined "all railroad employes born of white parents" as "entitled to membership." Some delegates to the ARU's convention, including President Eugene V. Debs, objected to the constitutional narrowing of the ARU's base on the grounds of race. "It is not the colored man's fault that he is black," Debs argued before the assembled delegates. It "is not the fault of six million Negroes that they are here. They were brought by the avarice, cupidity [and] inhumanity of the white race. If we do not admit the colored man to membership the fact will be used against us." Adopting a variant of the "industrial equality" argument advanced by some proponents of biracial unionism, Debs drew a distinction between economic and social equality: "I am not here to advocate association with the Negro but I will stand side by side with him, take his hand in mine and help him whatever [*sic*] it is in my power." L. W. Rogers, a Southern ARU organizer and editor of the *Railway Times,* recommended adoption of the classic biracial formula of giving blacks who were loyal to the union cause "a separate organization as was the case in many churches in the South." Debs and his allies encountered strong opposition from the convention floor. Denver delegate Samuel A. Heberling not only blamed blacks for assuming the strikebreaker's role in past conflicts, but predicted that the ARU "would lose 5,000 members in the West if colored men were allowed to become members." Heberling, not Debs, carried the day when the convention narrowly upheld the racial restrictions on ARU membership. The best the ARU could do was to recommend the creation of an auxiliary for blacks, which, given its subordinate status, would likely have attracted few African Americans if it had been established.[69]

During the ARU's disastrous strike and boycott of Pullman cars in the summer of 1894, such a stance surely cut off white railroaders from potential black allies and weakened them in relation to their employers. "The colored have not lost any sleep over the [1894 Pullman] strike," one black editor explained, for "they had no interests directly at stake to be affected." Others argued that blacks should "let it alone," for the strike was "a white man's war; let him fight it out alone." More significant than editorial condemnation was the fact that black workers, barred from ARU affairs, played the role of strikebreaker assigned to them by their white working-class adversaries. In Chicago, one group of blacks formed an "Anti Strikers' Railroad Union" whose express purpose was to fight the ARU and replace its strikers. With black brakemen and firemen running their freight trains out of Birmingham, L&N officials could declare with confidence "the backbone of the strike . . . as practically broken" only shortly after it had begun. Decades later, Debs speculated that the admission of blacks into the ARU would have produced "a different story of the strike, for it would certainly have had a different result."[70] His revisionist perspective revealed more his political views and wishful thinking than a realistic reassessment of the balance of forces in the 1890s.

To be sure, white railroaders' views of nonwhites reflected many of the dominant culture's assumptions about African Americans and immigrants from Asia, Mexico, and southern and Eastern Europe. Yet it was the white workers' own distinctive experiences that shaped the contours of that thought. The origins of the brotherhoods owed much to their members' need for benevolent and insurance programs; accordingly, they not only provided sickness and death benefits for members and their families but also modeled themselves after older fraternal orders, drawing upon a long history and the rituals of Masonry (and other fraternal bodies) in the United States. From the era of slavery through the mid- to late twentieth century, few fraternal or benevolent associations were integrated, and white railroad brotherhoods were no exception. Indeed, the construction of fraternal solidarity, as Mary Ann Clawson has noted, "was based as much upon a process of exclusion as it was a ritual of unification," for neither women nor African Americans qualified for membership.[71] Labor economist Herbert Northrup concluded that the "social origins of the 'Big Four' made it almost inevitable" that they would exclude blacks, for most had been "founded as fraternal and beneficial societies" and they continued to place much emphasis on those "social features." "To admit Negroes, the Southern members declared, would be tantamount to admitting that the Negro is the 'social equal' of the white man," something "they refused to countenance."[72]

Yet the brotherhoods were more than exclusionary benevolent associations; they were trade unions whose attention quickly focused on issues of power. Railroad companies could be harsh employers, demanding long hours under poor conditions for low pay. Some of the most tumultuous labor conflicts of the late nineteenth century—in 1877, 1885–86, and 1894—centered on the railroads. In many instances, bitterly fought railroad strikes collapsed in the face of massive corporate, state, and federal repression, and failed strikers often found themselves effectively blacklisted out of the industry. Brotherhood leaders drew conservative lessons from these defeats, discouraging overt class conflict, decrying any sympathetic action on behalf of other aggrieved workers, and generally holding their organizations aloof from the affairs of other labor associations. In some cases, their caution paid off, for brotherhood members' skills, discipline, and organization, as well as their strategic position in a nationally vital industry, eventually enabled some to command impressive wages, impose elaborate work rules, and win adherence to strict seniority systems governing promotion and layoffs. By the early twentieth century, the brotherhoods had adopted a more confrontational stance toward railroad employers, although they retained their tendency to stand apart from the larger trade union movement.[73]

Throughout this period, members of the railroad brotherhoods perceived not just themselves but all white American workers, and even the nation, to be under continual threat from several related sources: capital, new immigrants, and African Americans. White male craft workers, maintaining a precarious hold on their political and economic autonomy, linked the changing composition of the labor force to the corporate assault on their prerogatives. In their eyes, new immigrants, blacks, and capital jointly challenged their entire way of life. At the beginning of the twentieth century, brotherhood men argued that they had entered a new era of economic concentration in which capital—alternatively described as "Big Business," the "Interests," the "Plutocracy," and the "aristocracy of wealth"—advocated unrestricted immigration and the use of blacks to lower whites' standard of living. "Between the cheap negro labor and the cheap foreign labor," one white firemen bitterly complained, "the intelligent American workingman is threatened in his desire to live and enjoy the benefits of our laws, to educate and raise up to some honorable calling the family about him without becoming virtually a slave himself, or permitting his family to sink into misery and squalor."[74]

From the brotherhoods' perspective, the new immigrants and African Americans constituted a deadly threat to the wages and working conditions of true American workers. From the 1880s through the 1920s, brotherhood members, like their skilled craft union counterparts in the American Federation of Labor, scorned new immigrants from southern and eastern Europe, Mexico, and especially China and Japan. Drawing on a powerful nativist tradition, they argued that the new immigrants were pauper laborers content to live in "misery and squalor," who transformed cities into congested wastelands, producing "death, disease, destitution"; they were the worst that Europe and Asia had to offer, exhibiting little independence or inherent capacity for virtue, representing a "lower grade of humanity" and the "scum of the earth" who were collectively turning America into "a dumping ground, a human scrap heap."[75] In this a period of rapid economic, demographic, and cultural transformation, the recycling and updating of these arguments proved useful both in focusing white railroad men's cultural disquietude and in rendering comprehensible the real and perceived erosion of their social and economic status.

Like new immigrants, black workers appeared to white brotherhood men as a serious threat to the white American working class and the civilization it had built. Portraying labor's struggle with business in life-and-death terms, brotherhood leaders saw black strikebreakers as a powerful weapon in the corporate war against trade unions. The degradation of white labor at the hands of capital and its willing pawn, black strikebreakers, was already a reality in midwestern coal fields and elsewhere; it was a problem, brotherhood men feared, that would only intensify over time. "It should be remembered that 'our colored brother' in the South is yet in his 'infancy' as a competitor in the labor market," a white firemen's official concluded. "This vast element . . . has lain semi-dormant in lazy lassitude beneath the warm Southern sun." But a "movement is gradually making itself felt that will produce havoc and consternation in localities where white labor and Eastern capital now feel secure."[76] There was little doubt that an industrial awakening by blacks would lead to harder times for whites.

Despite their low opinion of black intelligence and skill, southern white brotherhood men from the 1880s through the post–World War I era deeply feared and resented African-American participation in the labor market, holding it responsible for their own organizational weakness and for many of their other problems. Compared to their northern counterparts, southern white firemen and brakemen had considerable difficulty maintaining strong union locals. The "white firemen's organization has very little or no strength in the South, compared with the North," complained fireman C. S. Daniel in 1915.[77] With few union checks on corporate power, wages were lower and conditions worse than those that prevailed on northern railroads. Brotherhood members held that the presence of blacks in the labor force was responsible for harsh corporate practices, racially discriminatory hiring practices against whites on certain roads, comparatively lower wages, and the unions' regional weakness. Only on roads where white firemen were exclusively employed or where enough whites were employed to maintain a lodge did the union manage to negotiate wages and conditions comparable to those elsewhere in the nation.[78] The very presence of blacks on so many southern locomotives offended white firemen in one additional way. White men riding on an engine fired by a black, testified a firemen's brotherhood official in 1909, must "put his clothes in the same box as the negro when perspiring and smelling—in fact use all the utensils that the negro uses, and then be placed on the same equality."[79]

This physical proximity apparently did not bother the white engineer. "The truth of it is, a great many engineers like Negro firemen best," testified North Carolina's Commissioner of Labor in 1900. "They treat them differently—make them wait on them. The white man does not do that." Racial conventions affected just what work white and black firemen might reasonably be expected to carry out. The subservience demanded of blacks extended to the performance of after-hours favors. The black fireman was "a sort of servant for the engineer," a white member noted with resentment in 1914. They "will carry products home" for the engineer that "he buys out on the road, run errands and otherwise serve him in a personal capacity." For engineers, white supremacy manifested itself less in the elimination of blacks than in whites' absolute control over them, a control that made engineers' lives considerably easier. Black firemen had little choice but to comply, given the desirability of railroad work and their restricted options outside the industry. Their response changed abruptly during World War I, however, as they lodged angry complaints with the U.S. Railroad Administration, claiming that this tradition violated wartime regulations mandating equal treatment and pay for all workers, regardless of race, who were performing the same job.[80]

Engineers' preference for blacks not only undermined white firemen's ability to displace their black competition; it also constituted a direct challenge to their sense of themselves as skilled, dignified white workers. Blacks might submit before white authority, but white labor must not. It "is a hard matter to get a white fireman to crawl under one of these dirty old mills . . . to shine engineer's shoes and carry their grip home, and probably a watermelon or sack of potatoes, and at last cut some wood for 'de madam,'" a St. Augustine, Florida, fireman complained. And yet, where white firemen were few and the firemen's brotherhood was weak, managers often left their white employees little alternative but to perform the same range of tasks that blacks engaged in, at least on the job. According to a firemen's official, white workers were required to "clean engines, scour brass . . . and perform any service that may be required of them" on certain southern railroads.[81]

The issue of wages proved particularly troublesome for southern white brotherhood men. A white former L&N brakeman complained that the paltry salaries of his southern compatriots could be traced to the fact that on "every crew in the South you will find the 'coon,' a man who is perfectly contented with one dollar a day." W. S. Carter testified in a 1913 arbitration hearing that "the negro is the cause of wages being cheap in the south. There is no other cause."[82] If wage differentials were a badge of white superiority over blacks, they also ironically prevented whites from receiving a proper "white man's wage." As the firemen's journal explained in 1896, "Railway officials on Southern roads frankly give as a reason for not advancing the wage of white [union] firemen . . . that they can get the same work done for but little more than half the present scale by resorting to colored labor." The payment of "negro wages" is "making paupers of white people" in the South.[83]

Unlike some Gilded Age and Progressive Era southern longshoremen, coal miners, and timber workers who experimented with biracial unionism, the railroad brotherhoods dismissed any idea of making common cause with blacks or admitting them into their organizations. Some whites contended that blacks, as a group, were unorganizable. "They are too shiftless to leave any hope that they can ever be successfully organized," the firemen's editor concluded in 1898, "and therefore they are a menace to organized labor." Extending membership to blacks was "repulsive to any working man in the South," one respondent put it, a "direct insult to the members in the South," another insisted. A Denison, Texas, white fireman suggested that admitting blacks into the union might foster character traits that were incompatible with blacks' social position. Taking blacks under brotherhood care, he argued, would unleash dangerous forces, for equalizing wages would "urge the negro to ambition"; blacks would become "bold and hard to please." "We would rather be absolute slaves of capital," a Clarendon, Texas, fireman declared, "than to take the negro into our lodges as a *equal* and *brother*."[84] When it came to organizational efforts to build unions and extend working-class influence, the racial beliefs of white railroaders proved an insurmountable barrier separating white from black.

White workers went well beyond excluding blacks from their brotherhoods: they actively campaigned for restrictions on black employment and blacks' wholesale elimination from jobs in the railway operating crafts. The longstanding goal of the Big Four brotherhoods of firemen, trainmen, conductors, and engineers was to "have the railroad train and engine service tied up tight for a white monopoly, for a 'Nordic closed shop,'" civil rights attorney Charles Hamilton Houston reflected in 1949. But advocating such a goal proved much easier than accomplishing it in the decades before World War I. At a conference of the various brotherhoods in Norfolk in 1898, the Firemen's Grand Master, F. P. Sargent, looked forward to the day "when every locomotive in the country would be fired by a white man," and toward that end he promised an educational war, "a campaign in advocacy of white supremacy in the railway service."[85] But more than education was required to persuade or force railroad managers to relinquish cherished managerial prerogatives, increase their labor costs, and abandon their insurance against white union demands.

Before the 1890s, white railroaders' antiblack efforts did not involve coordinated or sustained campaigns of economic coercion or violence, but rather only sporadic efforts on the part of local unions. "I was . . . on the Southern Pacific Railway in 1884, when 295 colored firemen and an equal number of brakemen were discharged" through the influence of the white unions, a correspondent to the *New York Age,* a black weekly, recalled. "I could name five more roads where colored men have been relieved by the request of the white brotherhoods."[86] But the success of these white railroaders was the exception, not the rule. More often, employers possessed the power to resist white demands for black exclusion. As cheaper, nonunion workers, blacks served management strategies for meeting labor shortages and impeding unionism, and employers were loath to abandon them without a fight. In July 1909, a delegation of white Houston-based Southern Pacific railroad workers traveled to New York to petition the railroad's management to replace hundreds of blacks working on the Southern Pacific with white laborers. "Negro workmen were giving the railroad satisfaction," replied the managers, who flatly rejected the request. In that same month, Texas whites on the Harriman line similarly insisted on the discharge of black workers. While the president of the Houston and Texas Central railroad, a branch line, admitted sympathy for the white men, himself being a Texas native, he made clear that "some of the Negroes at work in the Houston yards have been loyal to . . . [the company's] interests for almost a generation" and that "they stood by the railroad when the whites deserted it and became strikers." Disposed to "appreciate loyalty of service, whether it comes from a black man or a white man," he ignored the whites' demands.[87]

When entreaties failed, white firemen, brakemen, and yard switchmen sometimes turned to more drastic methods. At one extreme were racial violence and terrorism. In 1891, for instance, the introduction of a small number of black brakemen into the previously all-white Mobile and Montgomery division of the L&N railroad provoked violent opposition. The new black trainmen found themselves dodging bullets along their routes, and local whites flogged a white brakeman "for consenting to make the run with the negro trainmen." Far more serious violence occurred during the economic depression of 1921 and continued into the following year on the Illinois Central's Yazoo division; during the early years of the Great Depression, white railroaders launched a similar round of physical assaults.[88] But racial terrorism was generally a tactic of last resort, a desperate ploy in desperate times, not a staple element of brotherhood tactics against black workers. Violence remained episodic, the product of local anger, racial beliefs and tensions, and fear of economic deprivation, receiving neither official sanction from brotherhood leaders nor general public approbation.

The strike, white railroad workers' most disruptive weapon, carried fewer risks; but, like terrorism, "race strikes" in the decades before 1910 engendered sharp employer opposition. In 1890, white railroad men on the Houston and Texas Central railroad walked off the job over the use of black switchmen in the company's yards. Three years before, a number of longtime black employees had become switchmen as replacements for whites who had walked out in sympathy with Southern Pacific strikers in the city. In 1890 union crew foremen for the Houston and Texas Central demanded the removal of those blacks. "There is little doubt about the real underlying cause of this movement," the *Houston Post* reported. "With negroes in any of the yards at Houston, which is the great distributing point of Texas, the united brotherhoods are not sole dictators of railway traffic. Transportation cannot be paralyzed by them at pleasure." The railroad held firm, dooming the Houston whites' campaign.[89]

The widely publicized Georgia "race strike" of 1909 demonstrated southern white railroaders' weakness. In an effort to reduce labor costs, the superintendent of the Atlanta Terminal yards removed ten white assistant hostlers from their regular positions, placed them on the "extra" list, and employed ten blacks at a lower cost to replace them. "We object to this policy . . . as men of the white race, on behalf of the white people throughout the world," union member F. S. Foster proclaimed. "Our cause is just and we know that we have behind us the almost countless millions of honest, liberty-loving members of the white race." White terminal workers struck and were immediately joined by eighty white firemen on the Georgia railroad, who nursed their own simmering grievances: over the previous four years, the numbers of black firemen had grown from zero to about thirty (out of a total force of roughly a hundred firemen), and white firemen's wage rates had slipped relative to that of engineers (dropping from 50 percent to 47 percent of the engineer's rate).[90]

The most important issue in the strike centered on seniority, a cardinal principle of white railroad workers since the early 1880s. Brotherhood members credited seniority rules with putting an end to autocratic managers' favoritism and discrimination. But the application of seniority in a racially stratified work force in a segregated society gave rise to ambiguities in interpretation and implementation. Could blacks exercise seniority rights to the detriment of whites? And if a company did not apply strict seniority—that is, if it maintained separate black and white seniority lists—which group would benefit? In 1909, Atlanta's black firemen exercised equal seniority rights with whites. This proved problematic for whites because the employment bar against black engineers, which prevented black occupational mobility, had the unintended consequence of allowing black firemen to acquire considerable seniority and enabled them to claim a large number of preferred runs on passenger and freight trains. Newer white workers were compelled, in the words of the firemen's brotherhood vice president G. A. Ball, "to take what is left by the negro." This state of affairs, white workers insisted, was unacceptable in a city and state that had disfranchised its black citizens and extended segregation statutes to public transportation and accommodations. As strike demands crystallized, white firemen insisted not only on the reinstatement of the displaced hostlers, but on the introduction of a dual seniority system that allowed the senior white fireman to "stand first for passenger engines or runs."[91]

Neither railroad managers nor federal officials mediating the strike looked favorably on whites' proposals for racial proscriptions that undermined fundamental corporate control. Whites' derogatory arguments about blacks' incompetence, their disgust at working side by side with them, and the need to uphold white supremacy failed to convince the mediation panel (convened under the terms of the Erdman Act, an 1898 federal law governing railway labor disputes) to grant preferential treatment for brotherhood members. The panel decisively ruled that the Georgia railroad could retain its black employees and preserve its existing seniority system. At the same time, it called for the elimination of the racial wage differential. Viewing the outcome as a temporary setback for their cause, the leaders of the firemen's brotherhood expressed hope that the equalization of wages would lead eventually to increased white employment, reasoning that the elimination of the cost advantage of black workers removed the incentive for railroads to employ them. They were wrong, for cost was only one of the reasons Georgia railroads relied on black workers.[92]

The strike was not only an offensive measure designed to extend whites' access to jobs, but also a defensive one aimed at countering management attacks. A year and a half after the failed Georgia race strike, white firemen again struck in response to fears that their employer was wielding the racial division of labor as a bludgeon against white workers' prerogatives. On January 3, 1911, the Cincinnati, New Orleans, and Texas Pacific railroad, also known as the Queen and Crescent (Q&C), deliberately provoked a conflict with the brotherhood when it assigned three black firemen, the most senior in the service, to preferred runs on passenger and freight trains on an eighty-four-mile section connecting Chattanooga and Oakdale, Tennessee, previously staffed only by whites. Outraged, white firemen declared war. Backed by a unanimous vote of the brotherhood local's members, roughly 250 white firemen and as many as 100 white engineers struck. For the next three weeks, passenger service was halted and freight service encountered numerous obstacles. The strikers' actions attracted considerable support from rural white mountain communities along the railroad's division in Tennessee and Kentucky. Along the route, sympathizers attacked trains staffed by black firemen; snipers and mountain marksmen fired at passing locomotive cabins; and crowds of masked supporters pulled white and black crew members off the trains and beat them.[93]

A great deal appeared to be at stake for strikers and sympathizers alike. The company's move, in the words of a white Cincinnati newspaper, was but the "entering wedge to place negro firemen on practically every railroad south of the Ohio River and east of the Mississippi." The firemen charged that managers had yielded "to their instincts of greed and avarice" in "subordinating white firemen to negro firemen." Company officials would increase the number of African Americans north of Oakdale until the Q&C railroad had "so many negro firemen that the white men would be practically helpless in wage matters, as they were on all other parts of the Queen and Crescent Route," union officials predicted.[94]

In the end, neither the company nor its union emerged wholly victorious. The final agreement produced by federal mediation prohibited black firemen north of Oakdale, as long as a sufficient number of competent whites were available (an extension of existing practice). But rail managers did accept two revisions dealing specifically with black seniority and advancement. The first legitimized contractual stipulations as a method for defining racial boundaries: in the future, the percentage of blacks in its service would not exceed their percentage in service as of January 1, 1911. Second, blacks, in order of seniority, would be assigned to no more than one half of passenger or preferred freight runs.[95] Rank-and-file white firemen expressed dissatisfaction with a settlement that did not secure their white supremacist agenda. As an editorial in the Jackson, Tennessee, *Daily Sun,* warned: "Americans have determined that neither the negro, the Chinaman nor the Japanese will 'run' either this country or its railroads. If the 'cause' of the strike had been removed much bloodshed, suffering and sin would have been avoided, and it is incumbent upon the railroad managers to REMOVE IT before more trouble results."[96]

More legitimate and less controversial than strikes and violence, lobbying state legislatures to pass laws mandating literacy tests for all members of their craft was a crucial element in the firemen's brotherhood's agenda to win restrictions on black employment. But winning restrictive legislation in the South would be as difficult as winning strikes, as white Georgia firemen learned in 1909. The firemen's brotherhood proposed the creation of a state-run board of examiners, to be composed of five former firemen, which would issue licenses to locomotive firemen who passed a written exam and won board approval. Their intent was obvious: it would be easy enough, a Georgia paper reported, "to provide such an examination that it would be impossible for a negro applicant to qualify . . . It would be, in effect, another case of negro disfranchisement." When a board of arbitration rejected the proposal, the firemen turned to the state legislature, without success.[97]

Northern brakemen were far more successful than their southern counterparts in seeking legislative relief for one of their priorities: restricting the employment of black porter brakemen. On some trains, the position of brakeman was always held by a white man, but the related position of porter brakeman (also known as a train porter) was the domain of the black worker. In addition to providing personal services for passengers and railroad officials, porter brakemen also performed the brakeman's job. Excluding black porter brakemen from their brotherhood because of race, white trainmen sought the elimination of porter brakemen altogether. The law proved to be one method through which they accomplished that task. In 1902, for instance, the trainmen's brotherhood lobbied the Ohio legislature to pass "an innocent-looking act," known as the full crew bill, that defined a train crew as an engineer, a firemen, and a specified number of brakemen. Left unenforced for many years, the state railway commission finally demanded in 1911 that an Ohio railroad replace its thirty black porters—who performed the work of brakemen but were not technically designated as such—with real, that is, white brakemen.[98] Two years earlier, in 1909, the Indianapolis legislature had passed a law on behalf of the white trainmen that, as William J. Gilbert of the Grand Rapids and Indiana railroad protested, aimed at "eliminating colored men from the train service" by requiring two brakemen on all passenger trains of five or more cars and barring brakemen from performing any porters' duties.[99] In 1913, the *New York Age* denounced a "well-engineered plan" to oust porter brakemen in the states of the West and Midwest through the passage of full crew bills; within two years, the legislatures of at least seven states—New Jersey, New York, Pennsylvania, Maryland, Ohio, Missouri, and Indiana—had enacted such laws. Black porter brakemen fiercely resisted legislative efforts to redefine their positions out of existence, forming their own short-lived Brotherhood of Railroad Train Porters and conducting their own lobbying campaigns against the restrictive legislation.[100]

Strikes, violence, and political activism failed to bring about the complete exclusion of blacks that white brotherhood men desired. But during the second decade of the twentieth century, as the brotherhoods grew in organizational strength, employers proved more receptive to less sweeping antiblack proposals. Utilizing the threat of strikes at the bargaining table (or, as in the case of Q&C firemen, the strike itself), the unions won formal, contractual restrictions on the numbers, percentages, and placement of black workers in the labor force as well as the creation of racially separate seniority lines. Ultimately white firemen and trainmen settled for percentage agreements as an attainable substitute for the elusive goal of outright exclusion. By 1918, the use of such contracts in limiting black employment was widespread.[101]

During their first century of operation, American railroads offered African Americans literally tens of thousands of jobs, providing a source of income that sustained more than a few black communities in the North and South

Yet from the start, race sharply defined the railroad industry's complex division of labor. Blacks found far more doors to employment shut to them than they found open. "Of the thousands of miles of railway in the North," one critic observed at the end of the century, "the only work, as a rule, that is open to negroes is that of porters on trains—the most menial and ill-paid" railroad occupation; in the South blacks found only low-paying positions as construction and maintenance-of-way laborers or as locomotive firemen and brakemen. Until the late 1960s and early 1970s, all of the industry's top positions requiring authority or involving supervision of other workers—such as conductors and engineers—remained completely closed to all blacks, regardless of their experience, skill, or seniority.[102]

The racial division of labor in railroading rested on, and reinforced, racist assumptions about African Americans' character and abilities. Few whites questioned the suitability of blacks, slaves or freedmen, for the backbreaking and often dangerous work of grading track and drilling tunnels, as much as they might bemoan those workers' propensity to migrate in search of other opportunities. Similarly, few whites questioned the slotting of black workers in railway service jobs, given prevailing beliefs about black subservience and inferiority. Whites disagreed, however, over the appropriateness of black labor in skilled positions: many railroad managers found blacks' performance more than satisfactory, while white workers denounced it as sloppy and inadequate. Informing their perspectives, of course, were their respective economic interests. Employers found black firemen and brakemen to be cheaper than white labor and an often effective deterrent against white unions; white workers found the presence of black labor a cause of their own low wages and poor working conditions, as well as unemployment. Neither side doubted the inferiority of blacks; they differed in their understanding of what white supremacy actually meant in practice and how it was to be achieved in the labor market.

With most skilled crafts and industrial jobs closed to them in the nineteenth and early twentieth centuries, African Americans had few alternatives to accepting either agricultural or common labor on plantations, mines, docks, sawmills, turpentine and lumber camps, and railroads; or service work in the homes of white people, in hotels, or on trains. Black railroaders carved out for themselves a number of solid occupational niches, taking what financial or other compensation those jobs had to offer. Those dissatisfied with their wages, working conditions, or lack of promotion opportunities might lodge a protest only at their own risk, for they received little sympathy from either the organized white labor movement or their white employers. Alternatively, they might vote with their feet, quitting their jobs in pursuit of real or elusive dignity and economic improvement elsewhere. As much as some black railroaders appreciated or even enjoyed their jobs, their grievances were real, as was their resentment of racial subordination. When opportunities to ameliorate their condition arose, black railroaders leaped at them. In an exceptional moment of dramatic social change in the years surrounding World War I, black railroaders would claim their place as legitimate railroad workers entitled to the legal and moral rights possessed by their white counterparts. Whether their employers, the government, or the larger white public would acknowledge that place, however, was a different matter.

2

Promise and Failure in the World War I Era

In 1919, the year of the most widespread labor upheavals in the nation's history, black laborers in Petersburg, Virginia, launched a union that quickly attracted virtually all black freight handlers employed locally by the Norfolk and Western (N&W), the Atlantic Coast Line (ACL), and the Seaboard Air Line railroads. The new freight handlers' association sought union recognition, the eight-hour day, "justice to all employees," and the retention of all former privileges. Soon it went farther, resolving to prohibit freight agents from laying off its members and insisting that in the event of a decrease in work, all remaining hours be divided equally among the handlers, "so all may live." Not surprisingly, rail officials rebuffed efforts at negotiation. The N&W, union secretary John Dailey reported, told its workers "that we are not recognized and that we are to him only common laborers and he will only recognize us as employees . . . and that we have got to work any way he say work or any number of hours he say work or any rule he so desires to change as he see fit to requirements." Black unionists complained that conditions in Petersburg's freight houses became even more intolerable, "as we are worst [*sic*] off than before organized." "We have put up fight after fight, petition for rights, grievances, sought time after time in conference by our committees with the agents . . . to reach some justice to our demands," a union committee informed its international union's president, "and must report the whole a miserable failure."[1]

When Dailey himself was discharged for insubordination in September, he insisted that the white Brotherhood of Railway and Steamship Clerks, the American Federation of Labor (AFL) international union to which his local, Freight Handlers Union 16700, had affiliated as an auxiliary lodge, intervene on his behalf. Directing his grievance to the official committeemen of the white brotherhood, he quickly discovered that "they seem more inclined to support the R.R. Agent in his theories against us instead of demanding the constitutional justice denied us." Indeed, white union officials concluded that the railroad was "not entirely at fault in this case," for Dailey was "insubordinate to a degree." The attitude of the white unionists rankled the black handlers, who were "tired of such men who seem to think we are ignorant," a union committee insisted. The N&W offered to re-employ Dailey, but only as a section laborer. Dailey declined the offer, preferring unemployment to demotion.[2] Opposed by rail managers and ignored by supposed white allies, the union of black freight handlers he had helped to found withered.

That a small local of black freight handlers should have failed to move large, powerful railroad companies is hardly surprising. That such a local would even try *is*. Surprising too is the audacity of the black laborers' demands, their anticipation of some degree of success, and their participation in the broader national upsurge of trade union organizing, working-class militancy, and black protest. It is difficult to imagine a John Dailey challenging the N&W or insisting on his international union's support in the late nineteenth or early twentieth century, given black railroaders' subordinate place in the hierarchy of railway labor and the levels of racial oppression and violence in the New South. By the end of the 1910s, however, Dailey was no anomaly in African-American communities in both the North and the South, for numerous black labor activists had emerged, and his freight handlers' association was only one of many black labor associations on the nation's railroads.

The American entry into World War I dramatically altered black workers' expectations and behavior. Growing labor shortages, the creation of federal agencies overseeing railway labor relations, and heightened black impatience with discrimination and exclusion contributed to a new spirit on the part of black railroaders. The wartime and postwar eras witnessed their widespread questioning of wage differentials based on race, their demanding of new and equal rights, their challenging of abusive treatment, and their insistence on recognition as patriotic American citizens. Through countless individual and collective acts, they impressed on the federal government and railroad companies that the prewar racial status quo would have to change. "I am a competent man in the Railroad service, an American citizen, and am due the same rights, and should receive the same pay, by the same rate, as any man, even if he is White," insisted New York Central employee George Segor of Cleveland.[3] While most black railroaders did not speak as bluntly or explicitly, they nonetheless seized the opportunities afforded by the war to seek equal pay for equal work and to receive a "square deal" on the job. The contrast with the prewar era could not have been more stark.

Even before the United States entered the military conflict in Europe, the world war had radically disrupted traditional sources of labor for northern industry. "The railway labor problem for 1916 presents more than ordinary difficulties to the intended employer," one observer of railroad maintenance concluded, for "the world's war has stimulated many manufactures and has created new fields of employment" while the "mandates of war have drawn many thousands of toilers away from the country to the trenches and to employment in war industries abroad. There is therefore a real shortage of labor in America at the present time." The Atlanta, Birmingham, and Atlantic railroad and the Frisco lines east of the Mississippi River traditionally employed all-black track crews in Georgia and Alabama, but the "considerable exodus of labor" had produced acute labor shortages for the companies. It has "reached the point," one general superintendent admitted in mid-1918, "that the labor is not there."[4]

Northern railroads were among the first industries to tap the southern black market in labor, dispatching labor agents throughout the region in search of black men interested in leaving the towns and plantations of the South for better-paying track building, repair, and yard work in the North. In early August 1916, the Union Station of Savannah, Georgia, was transformed into what one black weekly termed a "black paradise" when roughly 1,100 black laborers, supported by over twice that many friends and relatives, set off for Philadelphia on two specially designated trains to new jobs on the Pennsylvania railroad. This scene was repeated, though often on a smaller, less dramatic scale, in countless cities and towns throughout the South. Southern whites did what they could to prevent the growing exodus; in the words of historian James Grossman, "Anti-enticement laws dating back to 1865 were dusted off, reenacted, or tightened," while "scores of towns, cities, and counties" enacted laws restricting the recruiting abilities of labor agents. In August 1916, the Savannah city council unanimously passed a local ordinance requiring employment bureaus whose agents dispatched local workers to points outside the state to pay a $1,000 license fee. The Pennsylvania railroad's two labor agents immediately ran afoul of the new law, and police took them into custody. Released on bond, they were again arrested on the day of the train's departure. "All the slave catching machinery of the South is being put into motion to stop migration," claimed the *Crisis,* the journal of the National Association for the Advancement of Colored People (NAACP), later that year as hundreds of Savannah's blacks were rounded up at the city's Union Station and jailed. Across the South, white officials remained on watch for northern labor agents and harassed potential and actual black migrants in the hope of stemming the exodus. Try as they might, there was little they could do, given blacks' desire to escape the region's racial oppression and enjoy what they hoped would be the fruits of northern freedom.[5]

Although the railroad industry was hardly the only economic magnet attracting southern black migrants to the North, it offered thousands of jobs for men in railroad construction and track maintenance as well as positions as boiler washers, engine watchers, hostlers, and yard laborers. One upper South black weekly estimated that the Pennsylvania railroad hired between 3,000 and 5,000 black laborers in the last six months of 1916 alone, adding substantially to the size of the black community in South Philadelphia as well as to the "new colonies" of black section hands along the road's main line.[6] Unable to compete for alternative labor with a booming firearms and munitions industry in New England once their Austrian and Italian immigrant laborers enlisted to fight in their native national armies in Europe, the New York, New Haven, and Hartford railroad began what proved to be a successful experiment, importing initially 100 black laborers from Norfolk, Virginia, and eventually increasing that number to some 1,500. If the migration of black labor sparked by the call of northern railroads persisted, the *New York Age* predicted, "it will mark an economic epoch in the history of the race."[7]

If their numbers were smaller than in New England and the industrial Midwest, southern black laborers nonetheless also made inroads in the West during the war. By early 1917, the "largest invasions by members of the Race in the history of Wyoming" began when the Utah Construction Company received a contract from the Union Pacific for widening the Sherman Hill tunnel by 1,700 yards to accommodate a second track on its main line. As in the East, the Union Pacific had employed largely white workers until the war made it impossible to secure either native-born white Americans or the Greek and Italian workers it had relied on for the past several years. With insufficient numbers of Japanese or Chinese workers available, it contracted for the services of roughly 3,000 blacks from Alabama and Georgia. The "common labor situation" in roundhouses, shops, and track camps similarly troubled Ralph Budd of the Great Northern in the Pacific Northwest. Unable to persuade the federal government to allow the entry or reentry into the United States of thousands of Japanese workers to replace departing Italian, Greek, Bulgarian, Austrian, and Polish laborers, Budd was forced to draw on "petty criminals, blacks, and women," producing, in historian W. Thomas White's words, a rather "different and more heterogeneous workforce."[8]

Labor force heterogeneity included the substitution of women for men who were drafted or who left to secure more lucrative employment. At its height in October 1918, female railroad employment stood at just over 100,000, some two-and-a-half times the prewar level. The vast majority of women workers held clerical and semiclerical positions as stenographers, accountants, and clerks; most, if not quite all, of these women were white. Railroads offered a small number of African-American women jobs in two broad categories. The first was as car cleaners and linen clerks, positions closely related to domestic service. Car cleaners' work was "hard and dirty," involving "sweeping, mopping, washing woodwork and windows, and polishing metal fixtures," much of it performed out of doors. Linen clerks were responsible for counting and bundling soiled linen from Pullman cars, as well as counting and apportioning the clean linen.[9] Yet even car cleaning, with its resemblance to domestic service, was stratified by race and gender. In the Long Island railroad's Long Island yards, dining cars were off limits to black women, who were assigned only to coach cars. The Brotherhood of Railway Carmen, like the operating brotherhoods, barred African Americans and women from membership, depriving them of whatever protections its white members managed to win.[10]

Black women also found limited employment as common laborers in roundhouses, shops, and yards and on maintenance-of-way crews. By 1918, the Pennsylvania railroad had employed 500 women (one-third of them black) on its Baltimore division clearing tracks of rubbish, cutting grass, watching crossings, laboring in shops, and cleaning cars. The Wabash railroad employed several dozen black women that year as truckers and freight handlers; the Illinois Central used black women as section hands in its East St. Louis yards; and the Santa Fe employed them as roundhouse laborers in Emporia and Kansas City.[11]

The Women's Service Section of the U.S. Railroad Administration judged as "unsuitable" the use of women as section laborers alongside men "at a distance from any house or station" and discouraged "extraordinary physical exertion" on the part of female railroaders. That didn't stop some railroad supervisors from trying to employ them, however. It took one group of eighteen black women less than a day and a half to quit their new jobs on the Central of Georgia railroad in March 1918. Hired at a comparably impressive wage to pick up scrap along the tracks, the women spent their entire first day lifting heavy crossties. Their foreman found the women's work satisfactory and concluded that his railway section gang shortage problem was about to be solved. On their second day, after two hours of digging cinders, the women had had enough. Following an impromptu conference among themselves, they collectively resigned. If lifting and shoveling constituted their work so near the city, one woman stated, "there was no telling what they would be called upon to do if they were carried any distance from town with no means of getting back."[12] Like their male counterparts, these women did not hesitate to evaluate their jobs according to standards far stricter than prewar ones.

Employers' novel reliance on black female labor did not always go unquestioned. On at least one occasion, the gender of the labor force prompted black male protests. To meet a labor shortage in Little Rock, Arkansas, in

March 1918, the Missouri Pacific railroad advertised for twenty-five "ne-gresses," and the female job applicants expected to be "given a woman's job." What the company had in mind, however, was common labor, not cleri-cal work. Fifty black male employees immediately balked, dispatching a nego-tiating committee to inform managers of their refusal "to permit Negro women to do the drudgery and mean humiliating work" in the freight house or "in company with rough white men overseered and driven like cattle by them." It was not so much the class of labor the men objected to for the women, but the "humiliating and embarrassing attitude in which it placed them—For the race women to be cursed and abused, hated and despised, in a large measure to be unsexed and socially ignored in the very presence of the race men" by the "men of another race." While the women's responses to their initial job assignment and to the men's protest were not recorded, to one black religious paper the events signified "a new epoch . . . dawning in things racial," for the black freight house men had exhibited "a spirit of self pride and racial respect almost unheard of."[13]

Persistent labor shortages plagued railroad employers throughout the war and afforded black workers at least some alternatives to the lowest wages and harshest conditions. Southern employers in particular struggled to attract and retain common laborers. The Florida East Coast railroad began experi-encing war and migration-related problems in 1916, and over the next two years its labor supply constantly decreased. The road's Key West gang, for in-stance, had consisted of Cuban, Jamaican, and Central American laborers, but many returned to their countries of origin during the war while immigra-tion regulations scared off potential new foreign workers. Farming and agri-cultural processing, nearby shipyards and government air stations in Miami and Key West, and other industrial and construction facilities drew off the railroad's general supply of workers. Sawmills paid a daily rate of between $5.00 to $6.00 for common labor, while the Florida East Coast railroad paid only up to $3.50. Farther north, managers of the Potomac yards in Alexan-dria, Virginia, confronted an identical labor shortage. These yards, a gateway through which much freight of the Pennsylvania, the B&O, and various southern rail lines passed, experienced "a good deal of trouble in keeping our colored help," one yard official moaned. "They did not quit in a body, but they have been leaving us from time to time, until we only have about one-third of the force that we should have." The problem was that the nearby Al-exandria shipyards, the Washington Navy Yard, and various government con-tractors were paying as much as 35 cents an hour for common laborers, while the Potomac yards paid only 22¼ cents. With only 20 percent of his quota for common labor on hand, the Washington Division superintendent of Motive Equipment of the Richmond, Fredericksburg, and Potomac railroad admitted that he "had to do away with engine cleaning in a great measure and cleaning the shops and yards," adding that they "have been able to keep only the essential men needed."[14]

As great as the impact of wartime demand for unskilled railroad labor was on the economic fortunes of black workers, perhaps of greater significance for African Americans was the increased and unprecedented level of federal involvement in the administration of the railroad industry. For the duration of the war, the government acted to manage labor relations in an effort to attract and retain a sufficient number of workers in the transportation sector and to minimize disruptions caused by labor's dissatisfaction with wages and working conditions. As actual or potential sources of labor, African Americans drew the attention of government railway administrators. To the extent that blacks benefited during the war, it was less from a new federal commitment to civil rights than from fear of manpower shortages. But the very existence of a set of supposedly universal rules covering entire classes of railway labor, regardless of race, gave black workers yardsticks against which to measure their progress and to challenge discriminatory treatment. The creation of the U.S. Railroad Administration (USRA) to oversee the operation of the nation's rail system provided blacks with a set of bureaucratic procedures that they could follow in pursuit of their newfound rights. But although USRA rules gave black workers a mechanism for addressing racial and economic grievances, administration officials turned out to be fair-weather allies.

By late 1917, mounting problems—including shortages of boxcars and labor, equipment breakdowns, and substantial freight congestion—were interfering with the movement of critical military goods and personnel.[15] President Woodrow Wilson responded to the crisis by issuing an executive order on December 28, 1917, providing for government control of the railroad industry. Deriving his authority from the 1916 Army Appropriations Act, Wilson justified his action as a means of ensuring efficiency during wartime. Making the pill of quasi-nationalization easier for private rail operators to swallow were provisions guaranteeing profits based on 1916 rates and a promise to return the railroads to private control when the war ended. The President immediately appointed William G. McAdoo, his Secretary of Treasury and son-in-law, to serve as the first director general of the newly created USRA, established to oversee and operate the nation's railroad system.[16]

Government control of the railroads, which lasted from January 1918 to March 1920, ultimately proved a tremendous boon to the 1.7 million workers, men and women, unionized and nonunionized, white and black, in the railroad industry's employ. One of McAdoo's first items of business was labor stabilization. High rates of turnover reflected widespread worker dissatisfaction with wage rates. There was little doubt that with the military draft and enlistments, and other war industries offering higher wages, that something would have to be done to ensure adequate levels of manpower in the transportation sector. Early in 1918, McAdoo appointed a five-member Railroad Wage Commission, headed by Wilson's Interior Secretary, Franklin L. Lane. From January through April, the Commission conducted a thorough investigation of railroad wages, hearing extensive testimony from railroad managers, white brotherhood and other union officers, and leaders of black unions and informal labor committees.[17]

In May 1918 Director General McAdoo issued his momentous General Order no. 27, implementing many of the Lane Commission's recommendations. The order was a milestone in railroad labor improvements. Wage increases were made retroactive to January 1, 1918 (the beginning of federal control). In addition, the order and its supplements established eight hours as a basic day's work, with time-and-a-half pay for overtime. For workers at the low end of the industry's pay scale, the order was a godsend, increasing monthly wages of some unskilled railroaders up to 43 percent. Higher-paid workers, who received much smaller increases, remained dissatisfied, prompting McAdoo to establish a Board of Railroad Wages and Working Conditions and several Boards of Adjustment to which workers could bring their complaints during and shortly after the war.[18]

For African-American and women railroaders, the order contained an impressive equal pay for equal work clause. Black firemen and brakemen in the South had traditionally received wages lower than those of whites. Under McAdoo's orders, the wage differential was abolished. This provision "was not to be interpreted as a recognition of social equality," observed one contemporary shortly after the war. "Essentially it was a concession to the firemen's and trainmen's brotherhoods," which had recently come to advocate equal wages on the basis of their belief that eliminating lower wages would remove employers' chief incentive for hiring blacks.[19]

Whatever the reasons behind the equalization measure, black leaders and railroaders welcomed the change. "The recent increase of wages" issued by McAdoo "involves at least one advanced step, which under ordinary circumstances, would have taken a revolution to bring about," asserted the *Christian Advocate,* a black weekly. But "the most far-reaching and significant departure" was the equal pay provision, a "distinct forward step in practical democracy." With this provision McAdoo "wipes out a sore spot among the Negro laborers upon the railroads." Even more emphatic was S. A. Padgett, general chairman of the Colored Association of Railroad Employees from Knoxville: "June 1st. 1918, will go down upon the pages and annals of history in the railroad world as the greatest epoch . . . and will as well mark the revolution in the life of the Colored Railway Employees."[20]

As dramatic as the changes wrought by World War I were, they neither heralded a permanent revolution nor constituted a full and distinct break with the racial practices of the past. Southern black railroaders might have welcomed the unprecedented involvement of the federal government, but the heavy hand of Jim Crow, the pervasiveness of repression, and the absence of influential allies guaranteed heightened impatience and even anger. Predictably, blacks' grievances included the rising cost of living, their employers' failure to pay them their rightful increases or to improve working conditions, the persistence of unequal pay for equal work, white coworkers' hostility to black rights, and the federal government's inaction in documented cases of injustice. The war raised black expectations, but railroad labor and racial practices too often lagged behind the improvements promised by the USRA.

As a result, southern black railroaders' anger at times burst into the open. Even before the U.S. entry into the war, in October 1916, changes in company work rules had precipitated a short strike by black railroad brakemen engaged in through-freight service between Augusta and Atlanta, Georgia. The men objected to a management bulletin compelling brakemen to ride on the tops of trains between terminals—a dangerous practice. Their protests to the company having been ignored, the black brakemen walked off the job on October 1. In response, the company played the race card, calling on white flagmen to fill the black strikers' places. This time, however, exacerbating racial divisions failed to produce the intended result, for the Brotherhood of Railroad Trainmen, in an all-too-rare moment of support, advised the local whites to reject the company's offer. Within four days, the company surrendered, agreeing to a modification of the original bulletin and leaving the brakemen under the traditional supervision of the conductor.[21]

Small-scale protests by black workers became increasingly common. In the shops of the Texas and Pacific railway in Marshall, Texas, six hundred black helpers conducted a successful strike in 1916. The following year, one hundred black brakemen, unaffiliated with any union, struck the St. Louis, Brownsville, and Mexico railroad in Corpus Christi, Texas, for an increase in wages. In August 1917, seventy-five black Southern Pacific freight depot loaders and unloaders engaged in a peaceful walkout, demanding a 25-cent-per-day increase in their pay (their daily wages were $1.75 and $2.00). In May 1918, ten black laborers struck the Southern Railway yards at Hamburg, South Carolina, when their wages fell well below that of section hands. That same month, thirty-one black laborers on the Houston Belt and Terminal railroad collectively walked off the job when a white "special officer" cursed and struck an elderly black employee, and they refused to resume work under armed white supervisors. Over a year later, a strike lasting only several hours by black freight handlers at the Memphis, Tennessee, municipal terminal resulted in a wage increase to 40 cents an hour.[22]

To be sure, collective action often did not produce the results black workers desired. In Birmingham, Alabama, an area long familiar with traditions of black trade unionism and labor protest among coal miners and, more recently, iron, steel, and coke workers, some 250 black L&N freight house employees gathered at an "indignation meeting" and threatened to strike in the aftermath of the shooting of a black man caught allegedly breaking into a freight car in the fall of 1918. Demanding the discharge of the white railroad officer who fired the shots, they returned to work when a Justice Department official promised to investigate, after suggesting that they were "helping the Kaiser by going on strike." Their faith in the government representative was sorely misplaced. Not only did the company refuse to take any action, but freight handler leader Will Perry and several others were arrested and charged with interfering with the operation of the railroad. (They were eventually released for lack of evidence.) Joe Dennis, a black Texas and Pacific worker, was not so lucky. For his role in instigating a strike the following year, he was convicted of violating the Espionage Act.[23]

Government repression aside, labor shortages and black determination sometimes were not enough to tip the scales to African Americans' advantage. For example, some 500 black shop and yard laborers employed by the Atlantic Coast Line railroad in Rocky Mount, North Carolina, struck in September 1917 when they learned that the company had granted wage increases to all workers except blacks. Members of the newly formed Railroad Helpers and Laborers Union Local 15680, an AFL federal union, could not "understand why it is that the Swede, Pole, Jew, Italian and all save the Negro get the increase and the Negro must meet the advanced cost of living just like the others, give a harder day's work and yet must not be benefited by the increase of wages," as the black weekly *Norfolk Journal and Guide* put it. The workers' demands for "justice" and their "bold stand for better conditions for Negro laborers is a song that must be sung by the Negro race." ACL managers informally agreed to pay blacks the same rates as whites, but the company's refusal to put its promise in writing led the black strikers to reject the agreement. "Sinse there be a shortage of Labor on all the Railroads and still the A.C.L. officials are holding out [with] hundreds of skill Helpers and Labors who are willing to go to work Imedialy," wrote black union leaders C. J. Jones and W. H. Pack in June 1918, the USRA should intervene on behalf of the strikers. But the USRA declined, on the grounds that the strike had originated before the assumption of federal control of the railroads. Rather than sign a contract with its black workforce, the ACL offered previously black-held jobs to whites and put up with shortages. As for the AFL, the black helpers' membership offered them few concrete benefits, since whites, including unionized shop and yard workers, apparently filled many of the vacancies created by the walkout.[24] Staunch employer resistance and the indifference of white trade unionists could doom even the most steadfast determination on the part of black railroaders.

African Americans made clear their desire for economic security and dignity in a number of less confrontational and less dangerous ways. One was simply to quit. Wartime labor shortages provided African Americans with a range of employment options hitherto unavailable, allowing them to gain a significant foothold in packinghouses, steel mills, auto factories, shipbuilding plants, and cantonment construction sites. If southern railroads lost men to wartime industries and northern migration, northern railroad employers had a hard time keeping their southern black migrant labor force: black newcomers simply quit and moved on if conditions or wages proved disappointing. Early experiments with black labor by the Pennsylvania and Erie railroads, for example, proved frustrating to company officials. Black government official Emmett J. Scott estimated that fewer than 2,000 of the first 12,000 southern blacks brought into Pennsylvania for new jobs remained with that company. White employers may have attributed high turnover rates to the blacks' being footloose or lazy, but the workers knew perfectly well what they were doing. The *Railway Maintenance Engineer* explained their attitude: "When the men came to realize how sorely their services were needed," it concluded in 1919, "there were soon evidences of unrest characterized by unreasonable demands for increased wages, improved working conditions and a most unfortunate tendency to jump from job to job in an effort to seek the position that paid the greatest wages for the least amount of work."[25]

As important as labor shortages and turnover were in affecting African Americans' economic fortunes, it was black workers' new relationship to the federal government, and the USRA in particular, that shaped the contours of race and labor relations in the wartime transportation industry. For all of its flaws, the USRA represented a source of dramatic change for black railroaders. Its wage equalization ruling—issued as a wartime measure and not as a civil rights initiative—had the potential to wipe out racially based wage differentials, while its very existence offered blacks an outside agency toward which they could direct their questions, pleas, and demands. Not since the Freedman's Bureau during the turbulent Reconstruction era did southern African Americans have such a source of authority, rooted outside of the region, with the capacity to intervene and order improvements in their working lives. Yet transforming that capacity into reality required the active involvement of black railroaders themselves, who pressed the USRA to ensure that rail managers lived up to its rulings.

Before black railroaders could draw upon the USRA's resources or invoke its rulings, they had to know what those resources consisted of and what those rulings were. Even obtaining that information often proved a difficult task, for the lines of communication between the USRA headquarters in Washington, D.C. and the members of various black railroad communities in the South and the North were often weak or nonexistent. White members of the independent operating trades brotherhoods or the AFL-affiliated shop-craft unions could rely on their Washington-based lobbyists and legislative committees to provide detailed accounts of each and every directive and supplement affecting them, or read reprints of those directives in their monthly national journals. Black railroaders had no national organizations comparable to the white brotherhoods and could count on no reliable and steady source of information. The one institution that might have communicated such information—the black press—was uninterested in the administrative minutia of USRA rules; when it addressed workplace issues at all, it focused on blacks' access to new jobs, the persistence of racial barriers in employment, and conflicts between white and black laborers. Thus, many—perhaps even a majority—of black railroaders learned only the basic outlines of the Railroad Administration's rulings. "As to Order No. 27," H. S. Jeffery, the white officer of the Philadelphia Branch of the Federation of the Pennsylvania Railroad Employees (AFL) concluded, the black "rank and file know nothing of it. They have heard that it was issued, but have not seen a copy."[26]

With few sources of solid information to rely upon, black railroaders turned logically to the one authoritative source for answers to their questions—the USRA itself. Nine months after the war's end, black laborers of the Spencer, North Carolina, shops remained confused over a recent wage hike, unclear if their hourly increase was four cents, nine cents, or, as some of their supervisors told them, that they "will get nothing." Several months later, in October 1919, black employees of the Southern Railroad and allied lines around Selma, Alabama, heard about a government-ordered wage increase, but knew nothing of the details. Black employees of the Chicago Northwestern Railroad in Clinton, Texas, remained in the dark as to the USRA's rulings and various labor board decisions through the war's end. Led by the black men who worked at the Northwestern's coal chutes, the "colored people of Clinton have perfected a temporary labor union, including different classes of laborers, men and women," the union's secretary, George W. Slater, Jr., informed officials in Washington in early 1919. The new association sought to affiliate not only with "the colored labor organizations of the U.S." but with the AFL as well. The fledgling body, however, possessed neither significant contacts with the wider world of organized labor or politics nor had much knowledge of its members' rights under federal control of the railroads. Slater's job was to prompt the Department of Labor's chief black official, George Haynes, to provide him with copies of government decisions regarding hours and wage schedules. But even when such documentation was available, difficulties in interpretation could generate confusion. On behalf of black laborers of the Southern Railway shops in New Orleans, Louis J. Pierce informed McAdoo that "from announcements given out we are unable to determine accurately what our raise in salary will be under the new wage scale."[27]

Some southern black railroaders even doubted their right to organize at all. Seeking clarification, legitimacy, and a degree of protection, they turned to the USRA to refute their employers' claims that black unionization was illegal. When railroader H. G. Williams of Athens, Georgia, complained to the USRA of the "injustice of pay and working condition between us employees and the employers," administration officials advised him to present his complaints to some association of railroaders. Since there was no such organization in Athens, Williams helped found a local of the Railway Men's International Benevolent Industrial Association, an independent Chicago-based black labor federation. He quickly ran afoul of his employers, who suggested he would "get in trouble for an unlawful organization." Williams sought the agency's advice on whether or not "it is unlawful for us to organize." ACL porters, brakemen, and switchmen based in Richmond had the same question. They had begun to organize themselves "that we might have protection," the group's general secretary, Arthur B. Hill, noted. Just months later, in February 1919, black firemen in Columbia, South Carolina, posed a very different question; they sought confirmation of a rumor that the director general had *ordered* all firemen to organize. (There was no such order.)[28]

Southern employers often reacted unfavorably to the USRA's orders of wage increases or changes in work rules, especially when they affected African-American workers. Believing that they were "abused in a way most Damnatory," switchmen, firemen, and other black workers engaged in moving materials about the Birmingham-based Sloss, Sheffield Steel and Iron Company asked their superintendent why they had received no wage increase or retroactive pay, as they had expected. For their question they were roundly cursed: "if we do not like the D—— job," their superintendent declared, "get off of it . . . D—— negroes are getting too much money already." Northern employers too resisted treating their black employees with the same consideration as their white ones. Supervisors of the Erie railroad roundhouse in Kent, Ohio, persisted in paying blacks a lower wage than whites for identical work. When blacks "asked for their rights," a black car inspector recalled, "they was told they was to smart to be colored men and was told to get off company property." Managers at numerous shops, roundhouses, yards, and depots simply ignored directives from Washington ordering wage increases, overtime pay, or retroactive pay raises. In other cases, they implemented the changes for whites while denying them to blacks, or giving the black workers less.[29]

Individually and in groups, black railroaders scrutinized the details of the USRA director general's orders, compared the specifics to their own circumstances, and often found their situations wanting. Representatives of newly formed black railroaders' associations testified before the USRA's Board of Railroad Wages and Working Conditions, while delegates and rank and filers filed countless appeals with the agency, seeking an end to discriminatory treatment. They reminded USRA officials of their patriotism, dedication, and hard work and insisted that USRA officials enforce their agency's own rulings as a matter of right and principle. "We are colored Citizens of America," one group of L&N employees in Etowah, Tennessee, declared. "We have Friends that is Fighting in this war & are willing to Shoulder a Gun & go do the same But we do wont justice while we are working and we feel that we will get it from our Director General [whose General Order 27 states that] . . . all Employes shall be paid in proportion but we failed to get it."[30]

Wartime experiences provided African Americans with new arguments against their continued subordination as well as a new language of patriotism and Americanism that they could use when demanding their rights. Blacks' participation in the armed forces abroad and their home-front support for Liberty Loans, the Red Cross, and the like allowed them to invoke shared sacrifice and commitment to the nation to request, or demand, inclusion in the definition of citizenship and equal treatment with whites in the workplace. Prefacing their request for information about USRA-ordered wage increases, a group of four black St. Louis railroaders asserted, "We are good loyal citizens of America and patriotic to our country and we wants to help the boys in the trenches and on the battle field," assuming that their loyalty and support of the war effort entitled them to certain rights. While their dependence on the goodwill of rail managers muted their criticism of employers' practices—unlike some groups of workers, black railroaders did not depict their employers as homegrown Kaisers bent on autocratically denying workers' rights—they did complain vociferously when denied anticipated back pay or wage increases or when subjected to harsh or derogatory treatment. The language of patriotism and Americanism was common currency among all U.S. workers during the war years, but they assumed an even greater significance among African Americans, who had been excluded from otherwise shared notions of citizenship and definitions of proper American identity.[31]

Some blacks expressed gratitude to the railroad administration for its unprecedented support on many issues, but others sharply resented its failure to ensure that managers faithfully implement its directives and its refusal to tackle the thornier problem of employment discrimination. The variety of perspectives on the USRA and assessments of local conditions and maneuvering space informed the tone in which black railroaders cast their demands, which ranged from cautious to militant. "In this southland where prejudice and discrimination prevail we do not expect very much," William Spaulding of Atlanta wrote, prefacing his objection to racial differentials in wage scales. But "if the White employes are receiving the raise we cannot see why we are not receiving it also." Station porters and baggage, mail, and parcel handlers at the Dallas, Texas, Union Terminal Station couched their anger in terms designed to minimize southern white opposition: "We are not asking for Social Equality nor any Political rights or justice," they insisted in 1919, "but we do humbly ask that we be put on 8 consecitive [*sic*] hours base per day." While few blacks explicitly disavowed any interest in their broader rights, most preferred to frame their requests around the themes of equity and opportunity. "Now, the war is over, and all we ask for is fair play," one Selma worker stated. "We only ask for an opportunity to make a decent support for our families as men of other races, and we don't think that is too much to ask for." Some pushed that argument to its logical conclusion. "We seek no special favor, but do think we are entitled to a square deal in common with all other men to earn support for our families," concluded employees of the Union Pacific's Motive Power and Car Department in Salina, Missouri. A square deal was no simple matter, for it implied "no special favor" for whites.[32] As the Salina men would learn, wartime service meant little during the war and nothing after it.

Unable to count on the federal government, their employers, or white co-workers to banish the "evil" blocking their advancement, African-American railroaders organized to accomplish that goal themselves. The 1910s, and particularly the war years, witnessed an upsurge in African-American unionization the likes of which had not been seen since the rise of the interracial Knights of Labor in the 1880s. While the majority of African Americans, like their white counterparts, continued to stand outside of the ranks of organized labor, unionization appealed to a significant minority of black workers. And like their white counterparts, black railroaders pursued workplace organizing for logical economic reasons. The rising cost of living affected African-American railroaders as much as, and often more than, skilled white workers.[33] Blacks quickly learned that the new federal adjustment machinery responded far more to organized blocks of workers than to individuals. Representing their newly organized associations, wartime black activists Robert Mays, William Houston, S. A. Padgett, Rienzi Lemus, George Shannon, and numerous others testified before the wartime Board of Railroad Wages and

Working Conditions, seeking increased wages, fewer hours, overtime pay, equal pay for equal work, promotion possibilities, the establishment of equitable work rules and grievance procedures, and official recognition.

The second decade of the twentieth century, especially the war and immediate postwar years, witnessed unprecedented levels of working-class militancy in the United States. The syndicalist Industrial Workers of the World (IWW) captured national headlines and inspired passionate feelings for its organizing efforts among unskilled immigrant and even black workers, preaching the class struggle from the textile mills of New England to the timber towns of Louisiana and East Texas to the agricultural encampments of California. Although the AFL, which represented mostly skilled white craftsmen, was ideologically opposed to the radical IWW, its members too were swept up in the militancy of the decade, repeatedly striking for an eight-hour day, union recognition, higher wages, and an end to managerial abuses and scientific management. The outbreak of the war in Europe in 1914 and the American entry into the conflict in April 1917 only exacerbated an already tense situation, as sharply rising inflation and labor shortages produced an extremely volatile situation.

The intensification of black labor activism in the World War I era reflected more than a response to economic conditions or appreciation of patriotic language. The emergence of the "New Negro"—in part born out of disillusionment with fighting a war for democracy abroad while being denied democracy at home—reflected a new assertiveness on the part of African Americans that proved conducive to individual and organized protest. A "new era has come," observed the New York *Globe,* which has produced the "new Negro: a man who stands erect and looks the white man in the face; . . . a man who does not cringe or fawn . . . but demands his rights under the constitution—equal opportunities in the common affairs of life . . . in a word, justice." This new disposition, prominently manifested in the flowering of black literature and arts in the 1920s, also found expression in the dramatic expansion of black protest organizations, including Marcus Garvey's nationalist Universal Negro Improvement Association, the civil-rights-oriented NAACP, and a wide array of black labor groups.[34] Yet the "New Negro" in southern workplaces had to exercise extreme care, for overt expressions of racial militancy—on the job, in the streets, or anywhere, for that matter—provoked harsh white countermeasures. Racial violence, with lynching and rioting a not uncommon extreme, escalated during and after the war, as whites sought to restore the prewar racial order based on black social deference, political powerlessness, and economic subservience. Black strikers risked the wrath of white coworkers, their employers, and the state.

However much African Americans participated in the broad upheavals of the era or drew upon a common national discourse of Americanism and patriotism, the wartime black union experience was distinctive. Because black railroaders labored in an industry characterized by sharp racial divisions and racist practices, their unions could not be mere imitations of white unions. Black railroaders faced two distinct challenges to their employment security that whites did not: discriminatory job ladders, which barred them from key positions while reserving most subordinate positions exclusively for them; and a fiercely hostile white labor movement that sought to advance its members' interests at blacks' expense. Given widespread white hostility, black labor associations became vehicles for black railroaders to pursue their unique interests as *black* workers.

But blacks generated no single perspective or organizing approach in formulating effective responses to the challenges that faced them. Some black railroaders, particularly freight handlers, carmen, shop helpers, and laborers, reluctantly accepted a subordinate affiliation with the AFL and its constituent craft unions. Far more common and significant, however, was what the Tuskegee-based *Negro Year Book* called the tendency of black labor "to organize itself independent of white labor unions" based on blacks' belief that they were "not receiving a square deal at the hands of white labor."[35]

Among the autonomous labor associations constructed by black railroaders, at least four distinct union experiences can be discerned. The first involved the single largest group of railroad service workers, Pullman porters. Arguing that the Pullman Company had "become an essential and indispensable part of our transportation system" warranting government oversight, the USRA assumed operating control over Pullman cars in 1918. Porters wasted little time in utilizing the federal machinery to adjust grievances and increase wages, dispatching a variety of representatives to offer testimony on their behalf before the Board of Railroad Wages and Working Conditions. "For the first time in all their existence as Pullman porters," Frank Boyd, a Minneapolis-based former porter and member of the Brotherhood of Sleeping Car Porters later recalled, "they could speak their honest opinion on one of the most vital issues of life, security. For once their constitutional rights to this extent were not invaded. So Unionism became the topic of conversation among the porters."[36] New unionization efforts produced porters' locals across the country. In New York, the Pullman Employees League, formed in June 1918, insisted that porters "receive a living wage." The following year, in July 1919, some five thousand people assembled in a Harlem auditorium under the aegis of the Brotherhood Sleeping Car Porters Protective Union, which gathered to "lay a better foundation for future Colored Americans." "We are willing to work and at the same time be courteous," a porters' statement read, "but we are going to insist that we are men and as such entitled to a living wage . . . We are men and added to this WE ARE UNION MEN."[37]

Pullman porters had the unique disadvantage of working for a single, determined, and powerful corporation. During federal wartime control, the USRA, through its Board of Railroad Wages and Working Conditions, offered modest increases and improvements that fell far short of porters' demands. But even such limited progress did not outlast government control. Once the railroads reverted to private hands, the Pullman Company resumed its traditional anti-union stance. In the 1920s, it instituted an elaborate system of surveillance, fired union activists, and maintained its own employee representation plan—in essence a company union, the Pullman Porters Benefit Association, which effectively undermined porters' independent unions. Although a new Brotherhood of Sleeping Car Porters, headed by socialist journalist A. Philip Randolph, was formed in 1925, it would take another decade—one marked by repeated defeats, a severe economic depression, and a new political environment—for the union to achieve official recognition, and another two years to win its first contract.

Dining car cooks and waiters, who were employed by individual railroads, fared better organizationally than their Pullman counterparts. Pennsylvania railroad workers established the Cooks and Waiters Association in 1917, drawing in B&O and Lackawanna workers by the following year. In 1920, this group joined with the associations of waiters on the New York, New Haven, and Hartford line to form the Brotherhood of Dining Car Employees, while Atlantic Coast Line and Seaboard Coast Line food service workers maintained their own autonomous organizations. In that same year, a new National Brotherhood of Dining Car Employees, created by Robert Mays and his Railway Men's International Benevolent Industrial Association, united several independent locals based west of Chicago. The Brotherhood of Sleeping and Dining Car Employees Union was formed to represent workers on the Northern Pacific and the Chicago, Milwaukee, and St. Paul railroads. Working for diverse employers, some of these unions remained viable well into the 1920s and 1930s, winning union recognition and negotiating contracts that provided modest wage increases, grievance procedures, and other benefits.[38]

The experiences of black operating craft and yard workers illustrate a third approach to wartime and postwar unionization. Over the course of the 1910s, locomotive firemen, trainmen, and switchmen established numerous local and regional associations, including the Colored Trainmen of America (Texas and Louisiana), the Colored Association of Railroad Employees (Memphis), and numerous others. The two-thousand-member Interstate Association of Negro Trainmen of America maintained small chapters in over a dozen states. Aiming to perfect "a union of all unorganized colored employees of the railway lines of America, for their full protection in working conditions and wages," it sought to "maintain and insure standard working conditions and a uniform wage scale; to destroy caste and color prejudice that militate against justice as to these essentials; and to establish reciprocity between such other bodies of organized labor as shall be necessary for the promotion of the welfare of the Negro employees of the nation's railway."[39]

Lest there be any doubt where it stood vis-à-vis the labor upheavals of the era, association members declared that they were "not organizing nor combining themselves against industries but rather for them." Racial uplift, welfare, and protection, not class conflict, headed the agenda. In subsequent years, the association followed the advice of the black weekly, the *Atlanta Independent,* which editorialized that black railroaders should avoid "entangling alliances" with white unions prone to strikes, disorder, and Bolshevism. "The pathway of success for the Negro laborer is the pathway of peace, readiness and willingness to work and efficiency in its performance," while in contrast, white organized labor "seeks to master, control and command capital." The association followed that cautious and independent path, but as southern black railroaders would discover, it proved to be a dead end. As the independents would learn in the 1920s and 1930s, relying on railroad managers' generosity and sense of justice was not enough to prevent the serious erosion of blacks' job security.[40]

Finally, one group—the Railway Men's International Benevolent Industrial Association (RMIBIA)—sought to transcend craft divisions and construct a single federation of all black railroaders. Founded in 1915, the RMIBIA was led by dining car waiter Robert L. Mays during its decade-long existence. Unlike the strictly craft unions of porters, dining car waiters, firemen, and trainmen, the RMIBIA attempted to unify all black railroaders into a single federation. Its accomplishments did not initially match its aspirations, for its first three years were not impressive: with fewer than a hundred members at the start of 1918, Sterling Spero and Abram Harris reported, the RMIBIA "hardly functioned" at all. Yet Mays and other officials tirelessly testified before the USRA and its wage board, lobbied politicians for legislation prohibiting discriminatory contracts, and initiated a number of lawsuits over wages, job security, and working conditions. With largely supportive publicity from the *Chicago Defender* and the Associated Negro Press (ANP), Mays remained on good terms with *Defender* editor Robert Abbott and the ANP's founder Claude Barnett long after the RMIBIA had effectively folded. He personally assumed credit for the wartime improvements granted by the USRA, parlaying his press coverage into organizational growth. His association grew dramatically, claiming at its height in 1920 a membership of 15,000; Chicago alone boasted some seventeen chapters with about 1,200 members in 1922.[41]

Although it became the largest and most vocal of the independent associations of black railroaders, during the war the RMIBIA's relationship to the larger white labor movement was far from settled. Mays first sought the protection, strength, and legitimacy that affiliation with the powerful AFL could bring. Accepting segregation as a given, Mays requested an international charter for a huge industrial union of all black railroad workers at the federation's annual convention in 1918. With AFL sanction, the RMIBIA would embrace not just Pullman porters and dining car cooks and waiters but also black brakemen, train porters, firemen, switchmen, yard engine men, shop workers, boilermakers and assistants, machinists and helpers, coach cleaners, laundry workers, track laborers, and others. The AFL's Committee on Organization rejected his request on the grounds that Mays's proposed industrial union would violate craft unions' jurisdictional rights. Furthermore, the committee declared that the AFL did not grant charters along "racial lines." Some unions had "not yet opened their doors to colored workers," the committee admitted, but it anticipated "the day in the near future when these organizers will take a broader view of this matter"—wishful thinking at best, duplicity at worst. The most the AFL was willing to do was to issue federal charters to individual groups of black railroaders.[42]

Mays's grand overture spurned by the AFL, the RMIBIA leader next declared rhetorical war against the federation and the white railroad brotherhoods and preached the gospel of independent black organization. Black railroaders "must stand together," a RMIBIA bulletin declared in 1920, "in order first to prevent white unions from removing us completely from these jobs, second in order to get proper pay and working conditions from the Railroads." That same year, RMIBIA organizer Monroe James, a brakeman on the Gulf Coast lines in DeQuincy, Louisiana, conducted an organizing drive in the South. His work was made more difficult by the extensive publicity given to the AFL's recent but unenforceable policy pronouncement in favor of abolishing the color line in its ranks. "It was disgusting to me to see how many black men fell to such untrue propaganda," James reported. Aggressively pushing membership in the RMIBIA, he waged a "determined fight" to convince the men "to stay out of the white man's organization, and stick to the black man's that has the interest of the black man at heart."[43]

Mays publicly asserted that the racial practices of the AFL and the white railroad brotherhoods undercut any potential alliance between blacks and whites and set the agenda of the RMIBIA. "We agree with the policies and principles" of the AFL "so long as they are American and in the interests of the workmen," Mays announced in 1919, "but if their practices are against Negroes, then we are against the American Federation of Labor unflinchingly." AFL and railroad brotherhood practices were, simply put, "vicious, un-American and un-Christian." Mays personally vowed that "as long as there is one craft of colored railway men victimized by the evil practice of industrial segregation" he would "be out fighting for that craft." The day "will never come," he promised, when he would join the AFL.[44]

The RMIBIA parted company with the AFL in a number of crucial ways. Its espousal of the principle of the freedom to work on "any job" as a "paramount right of any American citizen" put the association at odds with the AFL and the white railroad brotherhoods. White craft unions on and off the railroads often erected barriers to black and other nonwhite participation in the union movement and labor market, using contracts, intimidation, and solidarity to guard white access to their jobs. Thus, in vowing to "fight industrial discrimination at its source," the RMIBIA theoretically sought to open the railroad labor market that white unions had artificially closed to blacks. In practice, however, like other independent black associations, it never demanded that blacks gain access to previously all-white positions like conducting or engineering, instead fighting only a defensive action to keep open those job classifications blacks still had access to, namely as firemen and porter-brakemen.[45] Tactically, the RMIBIA alerted its members to white brotherhood schemes to deprive blacks of jobs; appealed to company executives and stockholders; testified before government agencies; allied with Republican politicians such as white Chicago congressman Martin Madden, who was a regular at the RMIBIA gatherings; authored possible amendments to the 1920 Transportation Act giving black organizations equal representation before the new Railroad Labor Board; and promoted the appointment of black Boston attorney William H. Lewis to that board.[46]

Mays and other RMIBIA leaders counseled blacks "not to strike, but to fight for their inalienable rights" in less confrontational ways, preaching the "basic doctrine of 100 per cent efficiency in workmanship," presumably to convince white railroad employers of the indispensability of black labor. Their purpose, Mays instructed black firemen in Birmingham, was "to promote efficiency among colored men and keep them intact for continuous and helpful service both for themselves and for the Companies." In the event of a strike by white railroaders, RMIBIA members were advised to report immediately to their supervisors, remain at work as long as possible, and, if a shutdown occurred, declare their readiness to work as soon as conditions permitted. While the RMIBIA's conciliatory approach led observers to question its very character as a bona fide trade union, its advice reflected the outlook of many black railroaders. During the massive shopcraft strike of 1922, for instance, some blacks, organized into auxiliary locals of the white shopcrafts, participated in the bitter walkout, but many did not. Crossing union picket lines, they provided their employers with a welcome supply of strikebreakers and contributed to the white unions' ultimate defeat.[47]

By 1920, Mays began aggressively promoting black business enterprises to RMIBIA members. In what it described as a step of the "foremost rank," the association's annual convention authorized the incorporation of a "monster" Mutual Accident Insurance Company—distinct from the RMIBIA but administered by its officers—whose goals were to provide members with lower insurance rates and employment for children of black railroaders. Abandon the "beggar's 'Give' and use instead the emblem of real manhood, 'Make,'" Mays implored members in a plea for funds. Gendered appeals to racial pride proved inadequate to the task, for two years later the association was still trying to launch its economic endeavors. At an RMIBIA gathering in Birmingham in 1922, local black ministers, businessmen, and professionals joined railroaders at a conference to initiate a program of racial economic cooperation, "pyramiding into fuller Race support for business enterprises";[48] but this was equally unsuccessful. Mays's support for black business and the Republican party, advocacy of racial pride, and hostility toward white organized labor may account for the overwhelmingly positive support he received from leading black editors and journalists.

Mays's vision of one big, conservative union of black railroad workers ultimately foundered on the shoals of craft unionism and jurisdictional jealousies. The RMIBIA proved strongest in the service trade of dining car waiting and cooking, where it managed to enlist and retain some members. In 1920, it chartered the National Brotherhood of Dining Car Employees; it also briefly absorbed the Brotherhood of Sleeping Car Porters Protective Union, a group whose affiliation the AFL had sought.[49] But the RMIBIA and the porters soon went their separate ways, and Mays's subsequent efforts at organizing porters was little match for the Pullman Company's repression and sophisticated company unionism. The association's National Order of Railway Mechanics, Helpers and Laborers, formed in 1920, came to naught, and its Birmingham-based National Standard Brotherhood of Locomotive Firemen failed to attract members. Fanning the factional flame, RMIBIA leaders turned their rhetorical fire on dissenting or still independent firemen's leaders, denouncing them as outlaws and obstructionists, and accusing them of engaging in conspiracies at "clandestine proceedings" and "sowing the seed of craft prejudice" as well as "sectional prejudice"—the RMIBIA, after all, was based in Chicago.[50] Given the disparate interests and localistic loyalties of so many different crafts and organizations, it is hardly surprising that Mays's ambitions proved inadequate to the task of unification.

To a large extent, Mays based his appeals on delivering the goods. The problem was that he claimed exclusive credit for developments for which he was only partially responsible. *All* black railroaders' wartime advances were the results of Mays's personal campaigns, he insisted. Such assertions ignored labor market considerations, black rank-and-file pressure, and the appeals and testimony of numerous other black representatives before the Lane Wage Commission and the Board of Railroad Wages and Working Conditions. Yet Mays persisted in crediting himself with black labor's advance. "Every pay increase given Pullman porters . . . which the men now draw," he publicly declared in 1926, well after his organization had effectively disintegrated, "is the result directly or indirectly of the work of R. L. Mays." He claimed to have "personally negotiated or directed negotiations of a dozen working agreements," winning a "record of success unequaled by any person of our Race in the labor movement."[51]

Mays promised far more than he could deliver. Notwithstanding his scathing criticisms of the white railroad brotherhoods, Mays had little to offer black operating trades workers, failing to put even a dent into white brotherhood policies. Even the small wage increases Mays helped to win rendered him wholly dependent upon the U.S. Railroad Administration and subsequent Railroad Labor Boards. In the postwar era, the labor board had less reason to accommodate union wage demands; the favorable political and economic environment that had permitted him to deliver the goods—however meager—to his constituents had grown far more hostile to black labor. Since Mays had not actually built a grassroots movement but instead had constructed an organization around himself, he was in no position to back up his requests with a threat of force. His personalistic form of organizing left RMIBIA members with little reason to retain their membership when the chips were down.

The RMIBIA's disintegration left Mays profoundly bitter. In 1924, he was arrested in a police raid on a bootleggers' establishment in Chicago; police charged that Mays possessed three quarts of liquor and resisted arrest. Mays denounced the charge as a "malicious frameup," the "work of an unscrupulous enemy," and similarly denied accusations that he was a "constant frequenter of buffet flats where he spends the Pullman porters' funds on fast women and white lightning." The indefatigable Mays promised even greater activity, declaring that he was beginning a "vigorous campaign of organization of all classes of black railway workers."[52]

The following year, when A. Philip Randolph was selected to lead the new Brotherhood of Sleeping Car Porters, Mays found himself playing only a supporting role. Obviously uncomfortable in Randolph's shadow, Mays turned on the BSCP leader, blasting the upstart for "bungling" the BSCP's chance of success by failing to appear before the Labor Board and neglecting to participate in the Pullman Company's Employee Representation Plan election. Unmoved, the BSCP shot back, belittling Mays's accomplishments, rejecting his embrace of company unionism, and subjecting his failures to a blistering critique. The radical editors of the *Messenger,* the BSCP's official journal, now championed the superiority of narrow craft unionism, concluding that Mays was as wrong to believe that "he could organize anybody" or that he could "put all the different crafts of railroad workers into one organization" as a chef would be in trying to make "a half dozen or more soups in one pot."[53]

By the mid-1920s Mays's moment had decisively passed. On the eve of the Great Depression, all that remained of the RMIBIA was the Inter State Order of Colored Locomotive Firemen, Engine Helpers, Yard and Train Service Employees, a small, powerless body with Mays serving as labor counsel. Mays supported himself by working for the *Chicago Defender* and the Associate Negro Press's Claude Barnett, who was no fan of black unionization, authoring articles on the black fight for jobs in Chicago's traction industry and scouting out black Republican sentiment on Barnett's behalf.[54] Through Barnett, Mays attempted to influence the upsurge of black railroad unionism that arose in the mid-1930s. But he remained a marginal figure, excluded from the action by a new generation of black activists who came of political age during the 1920s and the early years of the Great Depression.[55]

The emergence of numerous black labor associations on the nation's railroads owed much to the determination of thousands of African-American workers to challenge their treatment and insist on their rights. But it was the unique conditions of wartime that enabled them to give voice to their aspirations. Black railroaders took advantage of growing labor shortages, the new federal regulatory agencies, and patriotic appeals to democracy to win real, if limited, improvements in their wages and working conditions. But the promises of the wartime era barely outlasted the cessation of military hostilities. With the rapid reassertion of the prewar racial status quo, the independent black railroaders' associations went into decline. The small number of forward steps they were able to take in the war years may have made the larger number of backward steps in the postwar years even more difficult for them to bear.

Shortly before noon on Saturday, January 11, 1919, a committee composed of four white switchmen of the Yazoo and Mississippi Valley (Y&MV) railroad's Nonconnah yards delivered an ultimatum to Edward Bodamer, their superintendent. Elected only the previous night by a mass meeting of individual yard workers—this was not official union business—the committee announced that as of that afternoon, no white switchman would work on a switching crew that contained an incompetent man, which it defined as any black crew member, regardless of his actual performance record. Unless the company immediately discharged its black switchmen and yardmen, the committeemen promised a walkout.[1]

Superintendent Bodamer was both unwilling and unable to comply with the committee's demand. Despite the signing of the armistice over a month and a half earlier, the railroads remained under federal control, and any decision of this magnitude would undoubtedly require formal approval from the U.S. Railroad Administration in Washington. Moreover, the union contract bound railroaders to follow their grievance procedures precisely and barred them from striking. Besides, Bodamer told the four workers' representatives, the company did "not have a contract with individuals, but with the brotherhood." Committeeman E. P. Tucker shot back that "the company had no contract with the negroes; yet the company saw fit to see and entertain a delegation of negroes who presented grievances" of their own. White rank-and-file resentment toward the company's employment, promotion, and layoff policies had reached the boiling point.[57]

Their demands rejected, dozens of white switchmen and yardmen refused to report to work. Within days the conflict had spread rapidly to the Illinois Central (IC), the St. Louis and San Francisco, the Union Belt Railway Company, and the Southern railroad. Ultimately, some 650 white switchmen from Memphis, all members of the Brotherhood of Railroad Trainmen (BRT), supported by hundreds of sympathetic firemen, engineers, flagmen, yardmasters, and conductors, participated in the five-day wildcat strike. At Mounds, Illinois; Jackson, Tennessee; Amory, Mississippi; and other towns along the Illinois Central route, hundreds of additional switchmen joined the walkout in sympathy.[58]

The Memphis hate strike in January 1919 was a spontaneous outburst of white racial anger, with strikers acting independently of the BRT, which officially represented them. Neither strike chairman Tucker nor the three other committee members were brotherhood officials, nor were they longtime employees of the Y&MV, each having been hired only in the previous year. Although BRT officials had long denounced the black workers who competed with their white members and had successfully fought for various restrictions on the jobs that blacks could perform and the percentage of blacks who could perform them, the strike apparently took the union's national officers by surprise. Still, in the months to come, top brotherhood officials would actively embrace the cause of the disgruntled Memphis yard workers, using their smoldering resentment and the likelihood of additional unsanctioned walkouts as a plausible threat with which to secure government concessions.[59]

In many ways only the latest chapter in a twenty-year campaign to restrict or eliminate black competition, the Memphis strike reflected acute anxiety among white railroaders, which the unstable wartime and postwar economic conditions had intensified. "Never in its history has the organized labor movement been confronted with greater peril than at the present time," asserted the journal of the white Brotherhood of Locomotive Firemen and Enginemen (BLFE) after the United States entered the European conflict. Those "interests that have accumulated fabulous wealth through the exploitation of the working class" would use the war as a "pretext" to destroy organized labor's greatest legislative achievements and "enslave wage earners generally." The BLFE maintained that large corporations were working to undermine workers' liberties and industrial rights, every sense of "propriety, justice and humanity," and specific political victories, including full crew laws, child labor laws, and the right to strike. Furthermore, employers were replacing men with women workers while formulating proposals to "suspend the Chinese exclusion laws and import hordes of Mongolians and Hindus to compete with American wage earners."[60]

With somewhat less hyperbole, white brotherhood leaders predicted that labor market disruptions would allow railroad companies or the federal government to use alleged labor shortages as a pretext for hiring large numbers of African Americans to weaken the white unions' power. W. S. Carter was convinced that "certain railway officials" would "take advantage of the present war situation to substitute negroes for white men" for the purpose of destroying "the influence of white men's labor organizations" in the North. Advising his locals to oppose any attempt to alter the racial composition of their craft, he vowed resistance to any effort "to exterminate the Brotherhood," for there could "be no greater grievance on any railroad than this attempt." There "are serious times ahead," predicted Carter. Remaining ever vigilant, the white firemen met the challenge. Upon hearing rumors that the Baltimore and Ohio (B&O) and the New York, New Haven, and Hartford railroads were planning to import southern blacks, the BLFE demanded the maintenance of the racial status quo, including the prohibition of black firemen on railroads that did not already employ them, the confinement of blacks to districts where they currently worked, and the freezing of their percentage on divisions where they were employed jointly with white firemen.[61]

Labor market shortages did lead to the employment of thousands of black migrants as construction and maintenance laborers on numerous northern lines. But the operating trades were never affected, even when labor shortages existed, given the opposition of the brotherhoods and federal officials. The brotherhoods feared, but did not actually encounter, increased black competition. On the local level, however, unease about the present and uncertainty about the future produced heightened levels of white racial anxiety that could easily spill out into the open, as it did in the Memphis switching yards.

Why did Memphis white yardmen engage in such precipitate action against their African American counterparts in early 1919? Blacks were by no means newcomers to the Memphis rail yards: they had worked there as trainmen and yard switchmen since 1872, and managers had increased their numbers in response to the 1894 Pullman boycott. Memphis was "not a Brotherhood town" because it was "a 'nigger' town as far as train and yard men are concerned," angrily complained white brakeman and BRT official S. J. Whitaker in the late nineteenth century.[62] For years white switchmen in the Memphis rail yards had complained, but had done little, about the allegedly debilitating effect that blacks in the yards had on brotherhood fortunes. Now, in early 1919, they finally resolved to end the almost half-century tradition of black labor force participation. Not only were blacks incompetents who endangered white workers' lives, but they had, strikers charged, "roundly cursed" whites and threatened them with violence; some blacks appeared "insolent, overbearing and vindictive, so that it is a menace to our lives to work with them"; they were "becoming rougher." Some were going around armed and "are more ready to use [their weapons] . . . than formerly." This was not a race question, a white union official insisted, but a question of "what is known as the 'bad' negro, the 'gun-toting' negro, whose word is worthless, who is overbearing."[63] Were these the paranoid fantasies of beleaguered white unionists? Not necessarily, for attorney R. R. Church, who sometimes represented black Memphis railroaders, observed that in the spring of 1919, "Negroes were arming" in Tennessee, as well as other southern and northern states, and were "prepared to defend themselves" if attacked. It is likely that black Memphis railroaders exhibited a new attitude toward their fellow workers even before the "red summer" of racial violence in 1919.[64] The "New Negro" who became an overnight phenomenon at this time was not just a product of black migration to the North. If perhaps less outspoken than their northern counterparts because the cost of violating Jim Crow was substantially higher below the Mason-Dixon line, at least some southern black workers took advantage of labor shortages and wartime rhetoric to defend themselves in interracial settings.

Whatever the actual behavior of black workers, the Memphis strike was less about their real or imagined disposition than about the racial distribution of available jobs. Before and during the war, the racial composition of the Memphis yard labor force fluctuated with little controversy. A regular yard crew customarily consisted of a white foreman, a white switchman, and a black helper. Although the BRT's contract stipulated that promotions and layoffs would be governed strictly by seniority, the uncontested quarter-century practice had been to use two separate seniority lists, one for blacks and one for whites. But at any given moment a shortage of whites or blacks might necessitate ignoring some racial traditions, filling crews temporarily with white or black switchmen depending on who was available. This flexibility worked to whites' advantage during the war. In 1917 and 1918, expanding opportunities in war-related industries and the military draft had reduced the number of available black railroaders. The Y&MV addressed the shortage of black labor by occasionally using white switchmen to fill in for absent black helpers.[65]

With the armistice, however, whites' temporary advantage vanished almost immediately. Growing numbers of blacks returned to the yards, expanding the black seniority list. Seeing whites occupying crew positions that had once gone to blacks, a black grievance committee urged the terminal yardmaster to restore the prewar racial division of labor. The receptive yardmaster then ordered that some eighteen white men be discharged and replaced by blacks. Predictably, white workers objected vehemently. The "seniority rights of the white men were disregarded while the negro was given preference," complained strike leader Tucker.[66] If developments in their immediate workplaces troubled whites, their concerns were greatly amplified by the uncertain economic prospects for the future. The year 1918 had been one of tight labor markets, continual labor shortages, and high turnover; but the outlook for 1919 was dramatically different. Early in the new year, a Labor Department official noted that there "never was a time when we could gauge the future of our labor supply less accurately than we can today," given a situation "so kaleidoscopic that changes in supply and demand reverse the market conditions over night."[67]

With immediate job losses and uncertain future prospects driving their anxiety, the white Memphis unionists focused their attack on the dual seniority system and the practice of reserving the helpers' position for blacks. If they could win the unification of seniority lines and keep certain positions off-limits to blacks, senior white switchmen would be able to bid for helpers' or other "black" jobs, thus bumping black workers off the crews completely, while junior whites could take the now-vacated positions barred to blacks. Managers, who had long depended on black workers and were satisfied with their performance, resisted whites' efforts to redraw the racial division of labor. General Manager A. E. Cliff maintained that white workers had no right to any work on the black seniority board; they were simply creating a "race question of giving the white man a position which he has not heretofore enjoyed." Federal manager C. M. Kittle felt that surrendering to the strikers' demands would throw the "whole matter into a RACE QUESTION" that would extend to every railroad and industry in the country. While opposed to the "Negro in politics, and to all his aspirations to 'social equality,'" Kittle firmly believed that "manual labor and the industrial pursuits makes his place in our civilization."[68] Fearing further disruption of freight traffic and the potential for racial violence, the USRA dispatched two federal mediators to Memphis within days of the strike's outbreak. The rank and file, pressured on all sides by government administrators, their union leaders, and a hostile press, soon voted to end their walkout and resume work, pending a full investigation of their grievances by the government mediators.[69]

Over the next year or more, a new chapter in the history of racial exclusion in railroad employment would be written in detail. Rank-and-file white switchmen bombarded the USRA with telegrams in which they listed their grievances against black coworkers, denouncing them as incompetent, unsafe to work with, prone to accidents, excitable, lacking good judgment, and being "unfitted mentally" for the job.[70] Drawing on their members' discontent, white brotherhood leaders pressed their case before federal officials and rail managers. "Our members are becoming very impatient," the president of the firemen's brotherhood, Timothy Shea, informed the USRA, because of delays and what he saw as the Memphis rail managers' prejudice against whites. Managers, he alleged, were laying off whites "on the pretense of no work, and the same day hiring negroes to maintain their percentage of the work." During the summer and fall of 1919, a special BRT wage committee met repeatedly with USRA officials and federal managers of southern railroads. The BRT's most important demand was its most far-reaching: No "nonpromotable men"—a euphemism for all blacks, who because of their race could not be promoted to the position of conductor, engineer, or foreman—should be "employed in road or yard service" at all. Federal officials rejected this sweeping demand, substituting a compromise proposal that was still favorable to whites, effectively settling the race question on the BRT's terms.[71]

"Nowhere in the long columns of fine print was the word Negro mentioned," novelist Lloyd L. Brown observed accurately of the postwar contracts in a fictional treatment of the era, "but to the black railroaders reading it every word was doom." The new rules eliminated the dual seniority system, raised entrance requirements to key positions (presumably putting less-educated African Americans at a competitive disadvantage), and reiterated the ban on hiring blacks for the positions of baggagemen, conductors, and flagmen. There was little doubt in the minds of both white and black workers that the single clause stipulating a unified seniority system would function to the detriment of black workers. The seniority change, complained the Colored Association of Railroad Employees (CARE),[72] which represented the black Memphis men, was "apparently fair on its face," but because certain positions were reserved for whites, "its enforcement unjustly and unfairly discriminates" against blacks. As CARE president John Henry Eiland explained, "at many points there are colored men who have been in the service of the railroads for years and who are forced to stand idly [sic] by without employment while young white men with only a few months' service record are given regular jobs." The application of what black railroaders termed the Jim

Crow seniority rule caused "hundreds of our men to be removed from those positions heretofore known as negro jobs"; it "would finally mean [blacks'] complete elimination."[73]

In the late summer and fall of 1919, brotherhood leaders and USRA officials met with the federal managers on numerous southern railroads, who agreed to approve the proposed rules. By the BRT's official estimate, a minimum of 150 whites who were on the "extra" or "out of service" lists gained jobs virtually overnight on the Central of Georgia railroad by displacing blacks. Similar increases in white employment were reported on the Charleston and Western Carolina railroad, the Georgia railroad, the Atlanta and West Point railroad, the Western railroad of Alabama, the Atlanta, Birmingham, and Atlantic (AB&A), and the Georgia Southern and Florida railroads. The following year, the Missouri Pacific accepted a similar racial provision, and in 1921 the AB&A agreed to a "nonpromotional" clause that barred the employment of any man as fireman who did "not stand for promotion"—effectively ending new black hires. On railroad after railroad, local committees of white brakemen aggressively enforced the new rules, raising numerous charges of schedule violations for adjustment by regional directors of the Railway Administration. Where managers proved hesitant to enforce new seniority provisions favorable to whites, as was the case on the Atlantic Coast Line in early 1920, a threat by white unionists to strike quickly brought them into line.[74]

The two railroads that aggressively resisted white labor's forward march were the roads on which the Memphis crisis had begun, the Y&MV and the IC. Given their size—they were vastly larger than any of the rail lines or systems that had capitulated to the BRT—and their role in triggering the current crisis, these companies were perhaps the most important target for the BRT's efforts. But Y&MV and IC managers did not take lightly restrictions on the right to choose their employees. For over a quarter-century, IC officials declared, "the officers of this railroad have employed negroes indiscriminately . . . and for economic purposes" (that is, until the promulgation of General Order no. 27 in 1918, the company had paid its black yardmen less than whites who did similar work). The Memphis hate strike did little to alter this company practice. After white strikers returned to work pending a governmental investigation, the railroad persisted in hiring blacks and placing discharged whites on the extra list. Compounding the insult to whites, in December 1919 the IC insisted on a new contract provision that would eliminate the dual seniority system on the condition that the contract apply "to all classes regardless of color." What this meant was that seniority would govern *all* promotions, opening up even the conductor's position to blacks. While most likely a negotiating ploy, the company's proposal raised the stakes dramatically. An angry BRT threatened to strike and forced the IC to back down. But when IC officials failed to attend a negotiating session in mid-January 1920 by conveniently leaving on a lengthy out-of-town trip, the BRT committee delivered its ultimatum: if there was no satisfactory settlement within five days, it would order a strike of all train- and yardmen in the two railroads' employ. Within days, the IC and the Y&MV had agreed to a final agreement similar to the one that prevailed on the other southern railroads. The BRT had won its battle.[75]

In its yearlong quest for racially exclusionary contract provisions, the BRT received considerable assistance from top USRA officials. Among the most sympathetic to the white unionists' cause were labor division head W. S. Carter—the Texas-born former president of the firemen's brotherhood who had long championed restrictions on black labor—and C. S. Lake, the assistant director of the USRA's Division of Operations. Lake had been general manager of the Seaboard Air Line and was a Virginian by birth—a "typical southerner," in the opinion the NAACP's Walter White. In a five-and-a-half-hour meeting between Lake and various black leaders in early January 1920 to discuss the new discriminatory contract provisions, White found it "exceedingly difficult to have Mr. Lake keep to a discussion of the matter which we came to discuss." When not professing his love for Negroes and recalling his "old black mammy," Lake denied that the rules were designed to discriminate against blacks. Lake concluded that "there was no power in Heaven and earth which would convince the Railroad Administration that such a rule was discriminatory" for it "made no difference to them what colored trainmen thought about the matter."[76]

More than racial sympathies lay behind the Railroad Administration's easy capitulation to the BRT's demands. Concerns over the brotherhood's repeated demonstrations of militancy, its advocacy of the permanent nationalization of the railroads, and labor unrest across the nation contributed to the government's decision. Facing radicalized unions on the rails and attempting to hold the line on wage increases, USRA officials sought to placate white railway labor unions through nonmonetary concessions; in essence, they traded the issue of white supremacy for others. B. L. Winchell, the USRA's southeastern regional director, confessed as much to CARE president Eiland in several meetings in Atlanta in early January 1920. Winchell's "attitude" was that he "had accepted the less of two evils,—that is, he had complied with the demands of the white trainmen rather than endure a strike. The crux of his opinion was that it was better to inconvenience a few men (colored) than to tie up the entire south for an indefinite length of time." Given the balance of power—large, strong, and potentially disruptive white unions on the one hand, and small, weak, and relatively powerless black workers on the other—and the absence of any federal commitment to African-American civil rights in the workplace or anywhere, Winchell's choice was logical and unsurprising. With these settlements, government administrators managed to avoid a potentially devastating strike over the race issue in the months before they would return the railroads to the private sector.[77]

Black yard workers and trainmen did not stand idle while white brakemen and switchmen negotiated them out of their jobs. Represented by the independent CARE, rank-and-file black workers formed yard committees, presented grievances to managers, submitted affidavits, and attended mass meetings, while their union leaders presented their complaints to company and government officials. These protests, however, were fundamentally cautious, aimed at persuading white elites to restore the earlier status quo, despite its racial inequities. Whatever the changes in disposition and expectation brought by the war, African Americans in Memphis and other southern railroad centers remained enmeshed in a system of racial subordination that made overt protest dangerous. The grievance committee of the Memphis branch of CARE, for example, asked the Y&MV to adhere to the long-standing tradition of maintaining separate seniority lists, which would offer some degree of protection to traditionally black jobs. But the committee did not—and could not—wage an aggressive public campaign. Nor could black workers bring economic pressure to bear on companies. Such action risked bringing down upon them the wrath of the Memphis police, who were all too eager to engage in antiblack and antilabor terror, and would have accomplished little. Gradually rising unemployment in the immediate postwar years, coupled with white labor's covetous interest in traditionally black jobs, virtually guaranteed their complete replacement in event of a walkout.

Black yard and train laborers lacked two advantages available to their white counterparts. While whites could stake a claim to black jobs, blacks could stake no claim to white jobs. And black workers could count on no extensive network of labor solidarity to bolster their claims. What made the threats of the Memphis hate strikers so compelling was the strong support provided by other white, skilled, and hard-to-replace railroaders. The USRA's receptivity to white demands derived from the power of organized white railroad labor; the BRT could cause disruption through a walkout of its own members allied with other white brotherhood men. Black workers possessed no such support. Despite the attempts of African-American firemen, trainmen, and service workers to form independent associations in the World War I era, their organizational reach remained limited by geography, their unity undermined by persistent craft divisions, their ideological outlook circumscribed by their belief in the need for caution, and their power weakened by their need to retain the support of white railroad managers. In their battle to preserve black jobs, African-American labor leaders were forced to appeal to rail managers, USRA officials, and judges. The arena of conflict was not the point of production—the yards or trains—but the conference room, boardroom, and courtroom.

Given the highly technical nature of the contract provisions and the bureaucratic procedures used to enact them, CARE logically turned for assistance to the NAACP. Robert R. Church, Jr., an attorney for CARE, requested the aid of James Weldon Johnson and the NAACP. Could NAACP officials "get in touch with the proper officials" and see that "these Colored men are given a square deal in the matter?" he asked.[78] The NAACP, of course, was no stranger to labor issues. In the pages of the *Crisis*, editor W. E. B. Du Bois repeatedly castigated white trade unionists—including white railroad men—for their racist attitudes and policies. During and after the war, NAACP officials challenged the AFL to force recalcitrant white unions to drop their long-standing color bars. They had even publicly denounced the USRA in November 1918 for an order limiting the hiring of blacks on the Northwestern railroad, which they succeeded in having rescinded.[79] Just months later, they wasted no time in attacking the Memphis strikers for depriving blacks of work. Over the next year, NAACP officials occasionally advised black labor leaders in their dealings with government officials, and Walter White attended sessions with USRA personnel. But labor remained a sideline issue for the NAACP, despite the influx of working-class blacks, railroaders included, into the organization after 1917. Other issues dominated its agenda. The association would take up the "question of discrimination shown towards Negro labor . . . as soon as it can possibly get to it," Walter White honestly admitted, warning that "our immediate fight at the present time is towards the abolishing of the lynching evil in America."[80]

It fell to black labor organizations alone to pursue the fight to its conclusion. During 1919 and 1920, Eiland and other CARE leaders lobbied railroad managers and federal officials, providing statistical information collected by local activists and personal evidence in the form of letters, petitions, and statements of fact about the impact of the white trainmen's discriminatory rules. Should the Railroad Administration comply with the BRT's request for the unification of racially separate seniority lines, Eiland declared, "it will indeed be a stab to my race," the "beginning of a move that will eventually mean the complete elimination of our race from the railroads . . . [which] will spread throughout the country into every industry where the Negro holds positions that amounts to anything financially." By virtue of their long service in the railroad industry, African Americans should be allowed to "retain these positions formerly held by us, and that our right to earn an honest living—

our constitutional rights—should be considered" regardless of brotherhood contracts.[81]

Access to traditionally all-black jobs may have been seen as a constitutional right, but access to all jobs apparently was not—or at least was not a realistic demand. Eiland believed, not without reason, that it would be impossible for any African American to assert such a right in the context of post–World War I American society. "No colored man in the employ of the railroad company in any department and particularly the operating department," he informed the Railroad Labor Board in 1920, "would ever dare to demand on account of seniority rights a place then filled and occupied by a white man. Both his life, liberty and property would be seriously endangered, in fact the law would simply invite him to commit suicide by doing what it apparently authorized."[82]

The caution that underlay Eiland's disclaimers of interest in traditionally white jobs led him further down the path of reinforcing black subordination in the job market. CARE went out of its way to reassure southern whites, rail managers, and federal officials of the essentially conservative and highly limited nature of its goals.[83] To the president of the Illinois Central, C. H. Markham, Eiland had earlier disavowed any broader challenge to segregated job lines and prohibitions on blacks in more skilled positions. "The negro in this department," he wrote in February 1920, "has never seeked [sic] promotion—furthermore, we have no special objections to the rule barring us from filling the position of flagman." Nor did they pursue "an equality of consideration of pay with the white man"—a surprising statement, given the popularity among black railroaders of the wartime General Order no. 27. Hoping to reassure the officials to whom he appealed, Eiland depicted his race as a loyal, hardworking people.[84] With bloody race riots less than a year in the past and with white brotherhood members in a particularly aggressive mood, Eiland navigated his association carefully between the shores of complete justice and the shoals of racial hatred. Pragmatic, and limited in what he could demand, he felt constrained to make a moral case on behalf of a racially unequal system that appeared preferable to the even more racially unequal system in the making.

Memphis switchmen and brakemen were by no means the only victims of the white brotherhoods' campaign; on virtually all southern railroads, black switchmen, brakemen, and firemen found themselves under contractual attack. Black train porters had been employed almost exclusively on the Missouri Pacific (MP) railroad's Valley Division for approximately forty years. By late 1919, black workers had formed their own organization, dispatching a grievance committee to approach the Missouri Pacific management with great care. By early 1920, they had affiliated as Local 20 of the RMIBIA and sought the railroad's formal recognition. The men "have not organized for the purpose of strife or injustice contentions," explained chairman Rufus Reed and secretary William A. Williams to the division superintendents of the road, "but for the purpose for better acquainting ourselves with the rules and regulations under which we work, and thereby better preparing ourselves for the performance of such duties as may be thrust upon us." Their goals were synonymous with those of the company: to "bring our efficiency up to the standard" by incorporating all unaffiliated black workers of their craft, by dealing with grievances in a systematic manner, "thereby relieving the office [of] much unnecessary annoyance." Underscoring their cooperative purpose, they directly insisted: "We want to help our Rail Road Officials with our men," plain and simple.[85]

The black workers of the MP approached their employer cautiously, invoking a paternalism that defined the rights and responsibilities of both employers and employees. Before the postwar employment crisis struck the MP, for example, Local 20 attempted to convince managers to provide older black workers with lighter work. On the Valley and Louisiana Division between Little Rock, Arkansas, and Alexandria, Louisiana, worked a number of aging black brakemen with long company service records. The increased freight traffic was now working "quite a hardship upon some of them." Their "years of constant servitude" were reason enough for giving them the lightest jobs available, "as a matter of right and appreciation for zealousness, and as a recognition of and in view of their approaching old age."[86] There is no record of the company's response, but workers' subsequent entreaties met with outright rejection. MP managers apparently neither needed nor wanted the help offered by their black employees.

A year later, the entreaties of black MP men—now affiliated with the Progressive Order of Railway Trainmen—turned sharper as its members' employment rights came under fierce attack. The cause of their concern was a set of new contract provisions governing seniority, promotions, and layoffs that the MP consented to in its negotiations with the BRT in October 1920. In contrast to most of the road's other divisions, the Valley and Louisiana Division—which had "always been known as the colored boys' division"— had long provided secure employment to black labor as brakemen, flagmen, switchmen, engine foremen, porter-brakemen, and as porters in most yards. On this largely black district, the MP manned its freight trains exclusively with blacks, save for the engineer's and conductor's positions. Under the new contract, the unification of seniority lines enabled senior whites to bump blacks out of their positions, as was the case on the IC and Y&MV. The October 1920 changes meant that "we cannot get a square deal [on] account of blended seniority," complained John Clark, the new president of Local 20 in

McGehee, Arkansas. White trainmen and yardmen "seem to take all and give us nothing," the union's committee complained. "Out of an old established custom," Reed explained, the porter's job "has been looked upon as being exclusively menial as such employment as belong to the race." Before the war, low salaries repelled white aspirants from "even considering the acceptance of such a position." But for Reed, two developments changed this situation: the increase in salaries during the war and the attaching of the word "brakeman" to the position have "so dignified the position" that the white brotherhood set its sights upon it. Under the new rule, Reed concluded, "the negro simply can't maintain himself. These rules create a compulsory process which absolutely drive him to the wall."[87]

MP black trainmen and yardmen pleaded for a restoration of the racial status quo. "We have never, during the period of our existence as employees," they implored, asked the MP "to extend our territory"; rather, they sought protection only of their divisions and branch lines. In a memorial to company officials, Reed asked that MP's black workers "be restored to our old Order, that we be put in a class by our selves, that the rules of seniority apply . . . to a group composed exclusively of Negro-porter-brakemen." Tradition, customer expectation, and loyalty demanded the repudiation of the single seniority line and the preservation of the largely all-black division. Perhaps most important, Reed concluded, was the black worker's allegiance to the company and the job: "He has persistently refused to engage in any movement, seeking to embarrass the company, but has endeavored at all times to so conduct his job as to bring pleasure to the passengers and superior officers; to increase thereby the revenues of the company." Now, in his time of need, he "feels that he deserves the further protection of the management."[88]

Loyalty, passenger expectations, and tradition notwithstanding, there was no restoration of the old order. MP managers ignored their black workers' requests for assistance, refusing to assume the part in the paternalistic drama that Reed had attempted to script for them. Not only did they stand by their new contracts and insist that company policy was "fixed," but they instructed their black employees to take up their complaints with their white working-class opponents; one of the consequences of the unification of seniority lines, at least in the minds of managers, was that all matters pertaining to black trainmen's work now had to be handled by the BRT.[89] The very group responsible for driving black workers from their jobs was now granted the responsibility for addressing black workers' complaints.

Two black organizations—CARE and the Protective Order of Railroad Trainmen (PORT), which apparently absorbed Local 20 of the RMIBIA—took the lead in the fight against the Jim Crow seniority, promotion, and lay-off rules. The first tack consisted of simply getting federal officials to pay attention to their complaint. In 1920, CARE attorney L. C. Going submitted numerous requests to the board for an investigation and hearings, only to be met with delay after delay. By September, his frustration was evident: his clients were "suffering greatly" from the enforcement of the seniority rule. With more than a hundred men displaced in just the past two months, "the future of the organization is imperiled on account of the fact that they cannot secure a hearing." Only in early December did the Board finally entertain Going's request and refer the complaint to Board of Adjustment no. 3. Yet when the Board finally handed down its decision in November 1921, there was no occasion for celebration on the part of black workers, for while it found some instances of whites bumping blacks, it declared the controversial seniority provision valid because it had been negotiated "by representatives of a majority of the class of employees interested in this dispute." The Board dismissed CARE's complaint.[90]

Over the next three years, the Memphis CARE local lodge continued its appeals to managers of the IC and the Y&MV and to railroad labor board members, protesting the effect of the Jim Crow seniority rule's application on black employment. The following year, the association—now renamed the Association of Colored Railway Trainmen (ACRT)—was back before the U.S. Railroad Labor Board no. 3. This time, Eiland insisted that IC and Y&MV officials apply seniority rules strictly, regardless of race, in the switching yards. The new practice of senior whites resigning their positions, allowing junior whites to replace them, and then bumping junior blacks was a "gross violation" of the seniority rule. An agreement that denies men on account of color full enjoyment of their seniority rights, Eiland concluded, "is subversive of the individual liberty . . . and out of harmony with the genius of our free institution." With no public explanation, the Labor Board accepted Eiland's logic. In its May 1925 decision, it concurred that the rules accorded black switchmen equal seniority rights on all yard crew positions (except for foremen's positions); technically, whites could not discriminate by bumping blacks out of their jobs, as that would violate their contract. After four years of black job loss, the Board weighed in on the side of the yardmen. The ruling's impact, however, was extremely limited, for it applied only to the switchyards of the two railroads in question. Elsewhere, the broader trend toward black exclusion continued unabated. Even in the Memphis yards, managers were slow to implement the decision. The case was "the worst move colored men ever had made," the IC vice president told Eiland. This and other black demands "would in effect run the colored me[n] off the property."[91] While that did not happen, black Memphis yardmen found that little changed over the next decade, and their grievances only accumulated.

The Protective Order of Railway Trainmen fared far worse in its challenge to the Missouri Pacific railroad. Following unsuccessful petitions to the company, PORT sought Railroad Labor Board support for its claim that black employees were discriminated against "in the matter of reduction of force and assignments." Dropping the earlier plaintive tones of Local 20's leadership, PORT president Lewis W. Fairchild, himself a Missouri Pacific train porter, and general chairman F. Aldrich insisted that these "colored men have devoted the greatest portion of their life's service to this particular class of work," having "made train service a life's occupation." Now, under the new rules, many of those men were out of work: only 180 black brakemen currently worked on the 700-mile district, down from 250 before the discriminatory contract took effect. Not only had no new black brakemen been hired since late 1920, but according to PORT's leaders, all of the new white hires—about 70—had less seniority than the black men they had replaced. PORT now asked the Board to order the company to reestablish segregated districts—"for the protection of life, company's property and the safety of the public"—and restore the conditions that prevailed as of September 30, 1920. At the same time, PORT asked that the black workers' own organization, and not the BRT, be allowed to represent blacks before management for purposes of negotiation and grievance resolution on the restored black districts.[92]

Lastly, PORT asked what right the white Brotherhood of Railroad Trainmen had to negotiate a contract that deprived blacks of work. The "right is not given" under law "to any organization of employes to force other employes out of the service." Yet this is precisely what had taken place. The BRT "arbitrarily takes jurisdiction over colored brakemen and switchmen," Fairchild complained two years later, "and at the same time will not admit them to membership. We can not meet with them in their lodge, we can not offer any suggestion relative to our wishes or desires to them, although they are at liberty to say just what we shall do, and what we shall not do. SUCH A CONDITION CURTAILS OUR CIVIL RIGHTS, and is out of harmony with our ideas of free Government." In the late 1930s and 1940s, black railroaders would reiterate these arguments, seeking federal court rulings on the unconstitutionality of federal railroad labor law that granted protected status to white unions that excluded blacks from membership and that negotiated away black jobs. But Fairchild and the MP men would have to wait another two decades for the courts to become sufficiently responsive to this line of reasoning and to issue landmark decisions overturning the legal basis for discriminatory unionism. In the 1920s, the Railroad Labor Board simply refused to entertain this argument. In its final disposition of the case in 1925, the Board dismissed PORT's complaint.[93] The long struggle to reestablish separate seniority lists for whites and blacks, to overturn discriminatory contract provisions, and to preserve (much less extend) black jobs ultimately proved unsuccessful.

However devastating the new rules were for black workers, many rank-

and-file white railroaders remained dissatisfied with the speed of racial displacement. In the months following the unauthorized Memphis strike, black resistance to contractual restrictions initially slowed the BRT's progress, and subsequent drawn-out challenges by black unions before the U.S. Railroad Labor Board kept unresolved the ultimate fate of black labor. "Because of the activity of negro lawyers, committeemen and others at Washington, protesting against the activity of committees of the Brotherhood, and endeavoring to prevent the organization from securing settlement of these questions," the BRT president informed his members, "sufficient pressure has been brought to bear on the Railroad Administration." At the very least, blacks' appeals prompted the white trainmen to even greater efforts. Eiland worried that his association's appeals to the Labor Board created "more hostility toward us from the men of the other race." In the meantime, the continued (if reduced) employment of black switchmen and brakemen indicated to some whites that they had not yet finished the job of ridding the railroads of black competition. With that goal in mind, they sought to accelerate their takeover of black jobs by invoking their most deadly weapon: racial terrorism.[94]

White-on-black violence was nothing new on the railroad. A year before the United States entered World War I, white brakemen on the Y&MV in Mississippi "terrorized" black brakemen, ordered them to quit their jobs, and shot at them from ambush. The period of violence was brief in duration, however, and paled in intensity with that of the post–World War I era. The first postwar blow, in March 1920 in Nettleton, Mississippi, was apparently a spontaneous act of racial violence. Declaring that "he would get all of the colored brakemen off the Frisco System," white brakeman Fred Lewis provoked an argument with black brakeman James Henderson. In "true Southern Barbaric style," the militant *Chicago Whip* reported, Lewis first mauled Henderson with his fists, then shot him in cold blood and "beat the brains out of the unfortunate Henderson with a club."[95]

The undeclared war against black trainmen began in earnest the following year. Y&MV brakeman Horace Hurd—married, age twenty-seven, a resident of Lake Cormorant, Mississippi, and a five-year veteran of the railroad—was the first victim in early 1921. While performing his duties on board train no. 59, he was shot with buckshot and "literally torn to pieces by the terrific discharge of the weapon." Pinned to the coat of the murdered man was a note that read: "Let this be a lesson to all nigger brakemen." Next to die was brakeman Arthur Tyler, employed by the railroad for eleven years, who was shot on April 9, just five miles south of where Hurd had been killed. According to the *Chicago Defender*'s investigation, white applications "flooded the railroad offices" after Hurd and Tyler's deaths, which the black weekly viewed as a "test to determine the stand of the railroad officials in this matter." Twenty-three-year-old Henry Hager met an identical fate on May 6, when whites ambushed him after his train stopped for water at Raines, Tennessee, just south of Memphis.[96]

Survivors of white attacks told their stories in detail in an effort to secure outside intervention on their behalf. Three white men approached brakeman Bob Grant while his train was stopped at Lambert, Mississippi. They "halted me demanding that I throw up my hands at the point of pistols," he recalled. "They snatched my lantern and threw it away, and had me to march across the field about a mile." Didn't Grant know that "they didn't want any negroes braking on the head end of those trains," the whites asked. One of the attackers wanted to beat up Grant, but the "other two insisted that he not do it, 'because he is a good old negro, I know him' is what one of them said." Bob Grant was lucky that night. His attackers merely warned him "not to come through there any more and to tell all the other negroes not to come through there." After being questioned carefully and threatened with violence, Grant concluded, "they finally turned me loose." By then, his train had left.[97]

Jesse Ficklin, a brakeman for the Gulf and Ship Island Railroad and a member of CARE Lodge no. 30 based in Hattiesburg, Mississippi, was not as lucky as Grant, but he too escaped with his life and a warning. His train, en route from Laurel to Saratoraga, Mississippi, on May 14, 1921, was stopped after being flagged by white men. Two armed assailants boarded the train, beat Ficklin, and "threatened to kill him if he ever came to Laurel again on that train." Reluctantly, Ficklin heeded their advice. Black brakemen, he later complained, were "being shot, beaten and white-capped off the railroads with threats of death, stating in their words, that the job is a white man's job, and they must not be caught on it again."[98]

By the summer of 1921, the black press was complaining of an organized conspiracy to intimidate black workers into relinquishing their positions. African-American railroaders, it appeared, were the targets of what Eiland called a "well laid plan" by "midnight assassins" to strike "terror to the hearts of the black men," thereby enabling whites to "come into possession of those positions which [the black brakeman] has been successfully filling for 50 years." The arrest of a young white man, J. M. Baker, for the shooting of white conductor A. S. McDowell (Baker had apparently missed his intended black victim, a "tall yellow nigger"), and of a former white IC fireman, John Phillips, and a former Y&MV firemen for the murder of Henry Hager, lent credence to the charges. Baker confessed that he had been hired by a group of whites to kill black brakemen, flagmen, and firemen in exchange for a $300 bounty for every assassination. The arrests and confession did little to halt the "carnival of blood," as the *Defender* put it.[99]

Far more than discriminatory contracts, racial violence seized the imagination and heightened the indignation of NAACP officials. At Eiland's request, NAACP Assistant Secretary Walter White pursued a legalistic strategy designed to provoke federal intervention to stop the killings, hoping that the Interstate Commerce Commission would agree with his interpretation of a wartime law that made it a crime against the federal government "for any person to interfere with the passage of interstate freight." Since peace had not yet officially been declared with Germany, White argued, the federal government had the jurisdiction and responsibility to investigate the intimidation and murder of southern blacks. But the Interstate Commerce Commission and the Justice Department rejected White's interpretation of law. Government officials argued that the Joint Resolution of Congress, approved on March 3, 1921, provided that acts of Congress enacted for the war's duration "shall be construed . . . as if the war . . . had terminated on March 3, 1921." Moreover, an assistant attorney general informed White that the U.S. Constitution gave no power to the federal government in matters of this kind. As in the case of lynching, the Fourteenth and Fifteenth Amendments "do not vest jurisdiction in the Federal Government to punish wrongs committed by individuals on persons of African descent on account of that descent." Hence, it followed that the government would undertake no investigation or prosecution of the killings; labor-related terrorism remained a matter for the individual states and communities, not the federal government, to handle. In the end, only the appointment of special agents by managers to guard train employees began to turn the tide. While sporadic terrorist attacks continued into the spring of 1922, they eventually came to an end.[100]

The upsurge of black labor organizing on the nation's rail systems had run its course by the mid-1920s. CARE's campaign to overturn discriminatory contracts failed, its calls for justice largely rejected by employers and an indifferent Railroad Labor Board. The RMIBIA lay in shambles, its appeals ignored by black workers who were more interested in results than ideology, in craft organization than one big union. Pullman porters' locals too collapsed in the face of hostile employer opposition. It would take the Brotherhood of Sleeping Car Porters, formed in 1925, more than a decade to establish itself as an institution capable of transforming labor and race relations. The numerous independent craft locals of trainmen and firemen were unable to transform themselves into bona fide unions capable of taking on discriminatory employers or brotherhoods. At a "loss as to what to do," Spero and Harris concluded, their conciliatory program "shows that they are well aware of the weakness of their position. They know that they are doomed but they hope that there may still be a chance to save themselves by acquainting the public with the injustice of their fate." Appealing "to press, to prominent citizens, to leading politicians, and, above all, to the stockholders . . . [t]hey still rely upon the rich white man's sense of justice as their best protection"—which was, in the postwar era, little protection at all.[101]

The wartime transformations that promised dramatic improvements in black railroaders' position proved fleeting. By the early 1920s, the larger political, social, and economic environment had turned increasingly inhospitable to black demands, shifting the balance of power toward employers and white labor. Unable to strike because of their vulnerable position, some black workers sought to promote amicable relations with employers in the hope of securing a more solid place for blacks in the industry. But their success remained dependent on the receptivity of the wartime Railroad Administration and the postwar Railroad Labor Boards. The imperative of reducing labor turnover vanished with the war's end, as did the government's need to meet basic black demands. Government benevolence toward black railroaders, which had fostered important gains in 1918 and 1919, was based on expediency, not principle, and when it no longer needed them, the government quickly sacrificed blacks' hard-earned rights and achievements. In the postwar era, government and corporate officials took far more seriously threats from white labor, leading them to grant fewer black requests as time went on.

The rise and fall of the World War I–era black labor movement must be seen in the context of the rise and fall of a more general popular insurgency in which workers, black and white, sought not merely to advance their own interests but also to reshape American society.[102] These were years of intensified social, class, and racial conflict, as different groups clashed over fundamental values and visions. Ultimately, the sense of new possibilities for the labor movement and for many working-class African Americans had been crushed. The charting of an independent course in the railroad industry provided only weak protection to black workers in the years following World War I. Appeals to employers, to white labor leaders, and to the black community proved insufficient to combat employer anti-unionism and white union racism in the railroad industry. Substantive breakthroughs would have to await the dramatic political and economic upheavals of the Great Depression of the 1930s.

3

The Black Wedge of Civil Rights Unionism

When Asa Philip Randolph walked up to the pulpit of the African-American First Baptist Church in Memphis in March 1944, he openly challenged the city's white political boss, Edward H. Crump, and the system of harsh racial and labor control that Crump upheld. The virulently anti-union and anti-black Crump operates a "dictatorship with a vengeance," declared the president of the Brotherhood of Sleeping Car Porters (BSCP), and "out-Hitlers Hitler" in his domination of the region's politics. Flanked by a group of eighteen black and white union leaders, Randolph addressed an interracial crowd numbering between 1,100 and 2,000 at a meeting sponsored by a coalition of black Memphis unions, including the local BSCP. The fact that he was able to deliver his speech at all in Boss Crump's city was a victory for free speech and the Constitution, Randolph argued. Throwing down the gauntlet to Crump, the Pullman porters' leader recounted tales of violence against Memphis blacks, sharply denounced police terrorism, advocated the teaching of black history in every public school, and called on southern black and white workers to organize and join unions. Virtually everything Randolph said was guaranteed to raise the ire of the antiblack, antilabor, and antidemocratic ruling strata of the city.[1]

Randolph's speech was the culmination of a four-month controversy over his right to address African Americans and trade unionists in Memphis. In November 1943, his scheduled appearance was canceled abruptly when the Crump machine denounced the BSCP president and cracked down on local black leaders. City officials insisted that an appearance by Randolph—an "upstart, vicious, demagogic type, out to create trouble," in Crump's words—would result in a race riot and bloodshed. After summoning over a dozen local black leaders to the courthouse, the city's sheriff locked them in a cell before lecturing them against permitting Randolph to speak. The conservative, all-white Memphis Trades and Labor Council endorsed the city's action, calling Randolph an "insincere, rabble rousing demagog, who devotes his time and efforts to advocating social equality for the people of his race." With the backing of American Federation of Labor (AFL) president William Green, southern AFL organizer George L. Googe, and an independent black Memphis pastor, Reverend G. A. Long, a coalition of black Memphis unions reissued an invitation to Randolph to "invade" what the *Chicago Defender* called "the South's worst lily white center."[2]

The "invasion" that occurred in April 1944 did not topple Boss Crump's regime or lead to the downfall of Jim Crow in the South, but it did enable Randolph, even in the face of fierce opposition, to articulate an agenda that fused civil rights and labor issues and demonstrated how black trade unions could serve as a vehicle for promoting black rights in the workplace, in the community, and in the political arena.[3] Indeed, since its founding almost two decades before, the BSCP had earned a reputation not only as the most prominent black trade union in the United States but as a leading civil rights organization as well. Nor was the porters' brotherhood alone in its championing of African Americans' economic, social, and political rights. The rise of the Joint Council of Dining Car Employees in the late 1930s also symbolized a new black activism that spread far beyond the workplace. By World War II, the porters' and dining car employees' unions were engaged in a wide range of civil rights initiatives, including campaigns for fair employment practices, challenges to racial barriers to occupational advancement, protests against racist violence and disfranchisement, and organizational assaults on the racial practices of the American labor movement.

The emergence of the BSCP and the Joint Council as prominent advocates of racial and working-class advancement was related to three fundamental developments in the 1930s. The first was the increasing political ferment in northern and even some southern African-American communities. As a result of the New Deal's economic benefits (albeit limited, and enjoyed only by some blacks) and the receptivity of some policy makers to civil rights concerns, the Democratic Party, and President Franklin Roosevelt in particular, earned the political allegiance of a growing bloc of black voters. Yet black activism increased far beyond the voting booth. Anger against the persistent denial of blacks' civil rights found expression in such bodies as the National Negro Congress, the Communist party, revitalized chapters of the NAACP, and in some labor unions. On the local level, aggressive "Don't Buy Where You Can't Work" campaigns, antilynching and anti–poll-tax committees, and numerous organizations established to fight discriminatory municipal and state legislation and practices rapidly spread from Seattle to Boston, touching even some areas in the urban South.[4]

The second critical development was the rise of industrial unionism in mass production industries and the forging of a new and often positive relationship between some segments of organized labor and African-American workers.

"Sweeping irresistibly over America today," the black weekly, the Houston *Informer and Texas Freeman* observed in 1937, was an "upsurge of labor." This was no exaggeration: By 1941, some 27 percent of industrial workers were union members, compared to only 12 percent in 1930. Proponents of industrial unionism had successfully broken away from the AFL's orbit in 1935, repudiating its narrow, business unionism, to create the Congress of Industrial Organizations (CIO). The CIO had committed itself to organizing regardless of race. The successful unionization of certain industries, such as automobile manufacturing, packinghouses, and steel, required the inclusion of black workers. But beyond pragmatism was something more; as social scientists Horace Cayton and St. Clair Drake put it, the CIO was a "crusading movement" that incorporated a "belief in racial equality" into its ideology. To be sure, not all, or even most, CIO internationals deserved this complimentary description, but many did. And while many of the AFL's affiliates retained their color bars against blacks or actively worked against black interests, the Federation also sheltered a number of black unions, such as the BSCP and the Joint Council, offering them organizational, moral, and occasionally financial support. By 1943, over 400,000 blacks had become members of trade unions, and growing numbers of black elites—who had long been opposed to organized white labor—threw their weight and prestige behind the black workers' organizing efforts.[5]

For all of their leaders' dedication, the rank and file's energy, and the broad support of their allies, the BSCP and the Joint Council succeeded largely because the federal government adopted policies that proved neutral or even favorable toward organized labor. In particular, the railroad workers' victories rested upon a single piece of labor legislation, the Amended Railway Labor Act of 1934. Like the National Labor Relations Act (Wagner Act) of 1935, which covered workers in other sectors of the economy, the 1934 act guaranteed railroaders the legal right of collective bargaining and bestowed a political legitimacy on their efforts to do so. Coverage under the act meant that Pullman porters and dining car workers could invoke the services of the newly created National Mediation Board (NMB) to conduct impartial elections for union representation and use the services of the National Railroad Adjustment Board (NRAB) to adjudicate disputes in contract interpretation or grievance resolution. With the passage of the 1934 act, the BSCP rose from the organizational ashes to deliver a decisive defeat to Pullman's company union, while dining car workers were victorious in representation elections on numerous railroads across the country. But the legislation and labor relations machinery that worked to the advantage of the BSCP and the Joint Council also actively deprived other black workers, particularly those in the southern operating crafts, of their workplace and collective bargaining rights.

The civil rights crusades that Pullman porters and dining car employees engaged in over the course of the 1930s and 1940s would highlight the discriminatory consequences of the very legislation that sustained them.

By most objective measures, the Pullman Company was an unlikely target for successful unionization in the 1920s. Whatever the legitimate grievances of its workforce of black porters, the company retained widespread support among many sectors of the African-American community. It was, its supporters never hesitated to point out, the single largest employer of black labor in the United States, with roughly 12,000 black men (and a small number of black women) on its payroll by the end of World War I, most working as porters but with roughly 1,700 employed in Pullman shops in Chicago, St. Louis, Buffalo, and Wilmington. If that alone was insufficient to secure it unqualified black gratitude, the company's generous program of "good works" should have accomplished the task. In the 1890s, the Pullman Company began funneling charitable contributions to Chicago's South Side black institutions, such as Provident Hospital; in the early twentieth century, it contributed generously to the Wabash Avenue YMCA and the Chicago Urban League. Company officials also fully cooperated with the Pullman Porters Benefit Association (PPBA), an ostensibly independent body formed in 1915 to provide sickness and death benefits and to promote good citizenship and Christian character, by assisting in the collection of PPBA funds and participating in its annual conventions. The Pullman Company "is the greatest benefactor of our race," one observer effused.[6]

Following public protests by porters during and immediately after World War I, the Pullman Company focused on managing its employees' discontent. In 1922, it hired Major N. Clark Smith, the former musical director of the Tuskegee Institute and for eight years the leader of the Eighth Illinois Regimental Band, to train Pullman porters and dining car waiters as entertainers. Not only would the porters' singing "furnish amusement" and "relieve the tedium and monotony of long railroad journeys" for passengers, it also would "be a good thing for our men," according to a Pullman official. "They are a singing race," he concluded, and "music adds to their cheerfulness." Pullman also expanded its welfare programs, publishing an in-house employee magazine, the *Pullman News,* promoting a limited stock ownership plan, and sponsoring a Pullman Porters Athletic and Field Day Association. "What ever short comings the Pullman Company was guilty of in the past regarding their porters," concluded porter and *New York Age* columnist James H. Hogans, "they are certainly making amends by taking a wholesome interest in their welfare today."[7]

Pullman's most significant innovation was its Employee Representation

Plan (ERP). Often a centerpiece of American business's welfare capitalism programs in the 1920s, ERPs were, in historian David Brody's words, "the most celebrated labor experiment of the decade," intended to hold trade unionists and political radicals at bay, to stabilize labor relations by addressing workplace complaints, and to offer workers a form of "industrial democracy" that in no substantive way disturbed capital's control. In an effort to comply nominally with the provisions of the Transportation Act passed in 1920, Pullman inaugurated its own ERP to handle employee suggestions and complaints, hear grievances, discuss (but not determine) wage levels, and work with company officials to increase efficiency. Although Pullman rarely fired an employee for a first offense, by the time a discharged porter or maid presented their case to the ERP, "it is always a hopeless one." The company's careful and detailed record of employee wrongdoing left ERP members with little choice but to vote to sustain management's decisions. The ERP was "little more than a smoke screen—a contrivance to pacify and fool the porters," declared Thomas Dabney a few years later. It "does not mean that porters get justice . . . Practically all cases are lost before the local grievance committee."[8]

By 1925, several ERP delegates had concluded that company-dominated employee representation was no substitute for an independent union. The ERP did little to address the fundamental issue of low wages and tips, although it did grant an 8 percent wage increase in 1924. Such workplace issues as promotions to conductor, the abolition of tipping, abuses by supervisors, and absence of what many porters considered to be a genuine and equitable grievance procedure were not on the agenda. "Far worse than the low wages paid were the harsh working conditions," a former ERP member turned BSCP organizer recalled years later. "Fear of the haughty superintendent and other officials was a recognized fact. The porter was expected to pay special homage when the superintendent yelled, raved and ranted at him. In no case was the porter right and the complaint of a passenger or railroad official was always accepted as true regardless of how ridiculous it sounded."[9]

The immediate origins of the BSCP lay in the defection of three participants in Pullman's welfare program. Roy Lancaster, Ashley Totten, and William Des Verney were veteran Pullman porters who served as ERP representatives in New York. In early 1925, the three quietly approached A. Philip Randolph, a thirty-six-year-old socialist orator, writer, and magazine publisher who had recently addressed the New York Pullman Athletic Club at Des Verney's invitation, with an offer to lead a new porters' union. By the summer, Randolph's monthly journal, the *Messenger,* was highlighting the porters' plight, and in mid-August, he formally announced that he would undertake the organizing of Pullman porters into a trade union. With five hundred people in his audience, Randolph convened the first meeting of the new BSCP in the auditorium of the Imperial Lodge of Elks' in Harlem on August 25, 1925. The BSCP had gone public, and the battle for the allegiance of Pullman porters had begun.[10]

Randolph's status as an outsider to Pullman and the industry—he had never been a porter or even worked in the railroad industry—both made him attractive to the BSCP's organizers and rendered him a convenient target of attack by the union's opponents. For the BSCP, Randolph's independence meant that he would be immune to Pullman's retaliation or pressure, while for Pullman, it meant that he was a meddler whose political radicalism dictated his program. Although Randolph was never a tool of the American Communist party or of Moscow, as Pullman officials charged, there was no question that his radical politics drew him to the workers' cause. Born in 1889 the youngest son of James Randolph, an African Methodist minister, and his wife, Elizabeth Robinson Randolph, Asa Philip Randolph grew up in Jacksonville, Florida, in a family that inculcated a deep appreciation of education and racial pride. After his graduation from high school, Asa moved permanently to New York, where he hoped to pursue an acting career. Instead, he became caught up in the world of radical politics, taking courses at the City College of New York and the socialist Rand School of Economics and joining the Socialist party. In 1917, Randolph launched a monthly magazine, the *Messenger*, with co-editor Chandler Owen. From its pages and from lecterns across the country, Randolph denounced American participation in World War I; castigated the AFL for its racist policies; condemned the United States for its segregation, racial violence, colonialism, and capitalist oppression; advocated armed self-defense for blacks; and championed the idea of interracial working-class solidarity. For his efforts he earned the title "most dangerous Negro in America" by Attorney General A. Mitchell Palmer. But by 1925, Randolph's dream of working-class unity remained unrealized, and the *Messenger* was on the brink of insolvency. The offer to lead the nascent BSCP gave Randolph a rare opportunity to put his considerable oratorical and literary talents to good use and to accomplish something concrete.[11]

The Brotherhood's strategy combined a savage critique of the Pullman Company's practices with concrete demands for substantial improvements in working conditions. The plight of the porter was "miserable and tragic," Randolph charged, for the company treated him "like a slave." "In very truth, the Pullman porter has no rights which the Pullman Company is bound to respect," he declared. "So far as his manhood is concerned, in the eyes of the Company, the porter is not supposed to have any." BSCP secretary-treasurer Roy Lancaster added that the men did "not want to be treated as children," and resented the company's welfare workers, who both investigated the workers' family life and habits and organized field days, baseball teams, picnics, quartets, and choruses "to keep them contented." Indeed, Pullman's encouragement of singing made porters the "*monkeys* of the service," Randolph claimed, a "disgrace to the porters . . . [and] an insult to the race." Finally, he argued that both the PPBA and the ERP served porters poorly.[12]

An independent union, BSCP officials declared, would increase porters' wages, reduce their working hours, improve working conditions, and ultimately dignify porters' jobs. First, the union called for an increase in porters' monthly wages—from their current $67.50 to $155 minimum—along with the abolition of tipping. Second, it demanded a reduction of work hours to 240 a month. Under the existing system, a porter often had to put in 400 hours a month to make the 11,000 miles of travel required for the $67.50 salary. Such hours, the BSCP argued, were onerous and deprived the porter of time with his family or for recreation. Additionally, the union demanded that all unpaid preparatory time be fully compensated; that provision be made to allow on-duty porters some sleep; that the company, not the porter, supply shoe polish; and that porters-in-charge, who performed conductors' duties, be paid a conductor's wage. Dispensing with the "gratitude complex" toward Pullman, the BSCP substituted a new slogan—"Not servitude, but service"—and heralded the birth of a new Pullman porter, one with a "new vision" whose "creed is independence without insolence; courtesy without fawning; service without servility . . . [and] [o]pportunity not alms." The new porter was a "rebel against all that the Uncle Tom idea suggests" and was "not amenable to the old slave-driving methods" of the company.[13]

No sooner had the BSCP announced its existence to the world than the Pullman Company responded with a full-blown counteroffensive. The first to be discharged from service were declared supporters of the BSCP, while undercover Pullman agents ferreted out clandestine members for similar treatment. Complementing the internal crackdown was a public relations campaign to discredit the fledgling union. "When the movement to organize the porters was launched," black socialist and BSCP backer Frank R. Crosswaith recalled, "a chorus of Negro voices especially was raised everywhere advising the porters not to organize; 'to let well enough alone,' that 'the Pullman Company was the Negroes' best friend,' . . . and, that to organize would be an indication of ingratitude." To a white supporter, it appeared that "for subtle slander and devious corruption it is difficult to match its [the Pullman Company's] tactics in the annals of industrial struggle."[14]

But what appeared to the BSCP and its allies as falsehoods and character assassination was only common sense, solid business practice, and good racial strategy to Pullman's defenders. To communicate its views, the company relied on the broad network within the African-American community that it had carefully cultivated over the years. The PPBA loudly sang its company's praises, undercutting the Brotherhood's critique of wages and working conditions, while PPBA president Perry Parker insisted that the existence of the PPBA and the ERP meant that there was no need for an additional organization. While the PPBA took out half-page advertisements in black newspapers denouncing the BSCP, the editors of the *Chicago Defender,* the *Chicago Whip,* the *St. Louis Argus,* and other black weeklies leapt to the corporation's defense. During the 1910s, the *Defender*'s editor, Robert Abbott, had been a proponent of the porters and a critic of the company. By the early 1920s, however, he had climbed aboard the Pullman bandwagon and now, in the company's moment of need, wasted no time in aiming his journalistic guns against the BSCP. Whether from ideological conviction or from Pullman's financial patronage, the pro-company editors unleashed a barrage of anti-BSCP and anti-Randolph charges.[15]

The company next retained as special counsel Perry Howard, a former Pullman porter, a lawyer, and a Justice Department employee, who charged that the BSCP was "inspired, directed, and fostered by Communists," a charge echoed by former Pullman employee J. Finley Wilson, the Grand Exalted Ruler of Black Elks. Black Chicago politician and anti-union propagandist Melvin J. Chisum reminded porters of the recent campaign of terror waged by southern white firemen and brakemen against their black counterparts, an object lesson in the foolhardiness of any relationship with organized labor.[16]

While the Pullman Company took nothing for granted by orchestrating its anti-Brotherhood campaign, it could take some comfort in the historically rooted antipathy toward organized labor held by a considerable number of African Americans. Black editors, politicians, and religious leaders had long advised black workers to cast their lot with capital in the labor conflicts that often wracked the industrializing nation. Capital, unlike unions, had something to offer loyal, hardworking blacks: jobs. Cautioning black workers against the evils of the white labor movement, black leaders condemned trade unions for their exclusion of minorities, their propensity toward engaging in violent strikes, and their deleterious effect upon the American economy. With their ideological opposition to organized labor and their appreciation of Pullman's generous financial contributions, leaders of many religious and fraternal organizations initially rallied to the company's side in its battle with the BSCP. In Chicago, for instance, most African-American churches in the mid-1920s closed their doors to Randolph and his union and urged their parishioners to demonstrate loyalty to the company that they said was loyal to the race.[17]

Even porters themselves were not of one mind regarding the BSCP. Without polling data or election results, it is impossible to gauge fully porters' support for or opposition to the BSCP, for both Pullman and the union claimed the allegiance of the company's workforce. Throughout the late 1920s and 1930s, the PPBA remained in existence with a membership numbering in the thousands. It is not unlikely that support for the BSCP split somewhat along generational lines, with older porters who had considerable seniority preferring the cautious path of sticking with the company. The Pullman Company "offers greater and more desirable opportunities to the colored workers than any other company in the United States," declared longtime employee George Louis Ford; it provides good pay and the opportunity to travel and meet the "very best element of the citizenry." An anonymous porter working in the South feared that the union threatened blacks' monopoly of porters' positions. "Let us not jeopardize our inheritance to that position," he declared in opposition to the BSCP. "Let us not betray our best friends, or change the long existing friendly relations for those of antagonism." Even if the company and its supporters exaggerated porters' opposition to the BSCP, the union itself acknowledged bitterly that veteran porters counseled younger men against joining the BSCP.[18]

The BSCP's fundamental task, then, was to neutralize Pullman's hold on the broader African-American community and to win over a majority of the porters themselves. By the late 1920s, the BSCP had earned the endorsement of a small but growing segment of the black middle class. Individual ministers, the NAACP, the Chicago Woman's Forum, the Ida B. Wells Club, and the Chicago and Northern District Association of Colored Women broke ranks with other, more conservative black elites to offer the BSCP staunch support. White liberal organizations, such as the Women's Trade Union League and the Garland Fund, provided organizational and financial assistance, as did the AFL. The BSCP promoted the shift in black public opinion by organizing boycotts against pro-Pullman newspapers like the *Defender,* by sponsoring numerous mass meetings and conferences on black labor, and by creating a Citizen's Committee of prominent African-American leaders to promote black unionization. By the time it won its 1935 representation election, the BSCP had few public opponents among major African-American organizations. Although the rise of the CIO in the late 1930s and early 1940s was needed to cement the programmatic alliance between black organizations and portions of organized labor, the BSCP prepared the way by its decade-long campaign against black antilabor arguments and by its careful courting of black elites.[19]

Permanently winning over porters to the union banner, ironically, proved to be a tougher job. Indeed, attracting and retaining members required evidence of success, which was in short supply. Pullman repression took its toll, as did the onset of the Great Depression in 1929. It was, however, the BSCP's own highly public, but ultimately unsuccessful, strategy to force the company to negotiate that soured many on the union's judgment and prospects. With the Pullman Company adamantly opposed to recognizing the union, the BSCP turned to the federal government for results. Its 1927–1928 campaign to convince the Interstate Commerce Commission to abolish tipping—itself a controversial measure among porters—failed, as did its attempt to utilize the provisions of the 1926 Watson-Parker Act, which established a multitiered system of voluntary mediation and arbitration leading to the creation of a presidential emergency board if a conflict threatened interstate commerce. When the new railroad mediation board determined that the BSCP did, in fact, represent a majority of porters, the stage was set for arbitration. Throughout, the BSCP eagerly embraced federal intervention; throughout, the Pullman Company rejected it. The matter would end there unless the BSCP could threaten to disrupt interstate commerce. Raising the stakes, the union's members voted to strike and prepared to do battle.[20]

Randolph had grossly miscalculated. His faith in the Watson-Parker Act's voluntary arbitration provisions was misplaced, for the Pullman Company had no incentive to arbitrate anything. Had he listened to rivals Robert L. Mays and dining car union leader Rienzi Lemus, staunch opponents of the act's abolition of the old Railroad Labor Board, he might have understood the disadvantage that the new law placed on a weak, black union.[21] In addition, he overestimated the BSCP's ability to disrupt interstate commerce—or at least his own ability to convince the mediation board of its ability to do so. Although some BSCP leaders strongly advocated a strike, others, including Randolph, viewed the vote as a threat. The mediation board called Randolph's bluff, ruling in June 1928 that no emergency existed and no presidential emergency board would be created. With the Pullman Company hiring potential strikebreakers and readying itself for a fight, Randolph backed down. Taking rhetorical cover behind a request from AFL president William Green to postpone strike action, the BSCP leader canceled the walkout hours before it was to begin.[22]

The BSCP descended into a period of sustained crisis. Although it continued to build popular support among African Americans for the idea of black unionization generally, its actual accomplishments were few and its organizational fortunes declined. The black press condemned Randolph and the union for cowardice; internal factionalism among BSCP organizers increased; the *Messenger* went out of business; financial contributions dried up; and membership dropped off precipitously. Unable to raise rent money, the BSCP was evicted from its New York headquarters in 1928. Deeply unconvince legal maneuvering from 1932 through 1934 to obtain a court injunction against Pullman's ERP, the BSCP's efforts came to naught. By 1930 no more than 2,000 porters retained their membership in the Brotherhood (down from approximately 7,300 in the fall of 1927), estimated Sterling D. Spero and Abram L. Harris, who held Randolph largely responsible for the BSCP's near collapse. But the "great pity of the virtual collapse of the porter's union lies not merely in its effect upon the porters who have grievances which sorely need correction but in its effect upon Negro labor generally," they argued in their 1931 study, *The Black Worker*. The "hope that this movement would become the center and rallying point of Negro labor as a whole is now dead." While acknowledging that a "substantial nucleus of the Brotherhood" remained intact, they believed it would be a long time before it could grow into an important movement.[23]

As it turned out, the BSCP's fortunes revived only a few years later, placing it in a position of becoming the "center and rallying point of Negro labor" that Spero and Harris had hoped it would. Its recovery derived from a broader shift in the fortunes of railway labor unions occasioned by the inauguration of the New Deal. The pro-union 1933 Emergency Railroad Transportation Act dealt not only with the growing problem of railroad bankruptcies but with labor relations as well, ostensibly outlawing both the "yellow dog contract" (which required workers to remain nonunion as a condition of employment) and company financial support for company unions on the railroads. Drafted in part by Donald Richberg, general counsel for the white railroad brotherhoods, Section 7 granted workers the "right to organize and bargain collectively through representatives of their own choosing . . . free from the interference, restraint, or coercion of employers of labor, or their agents." Randolph invoked the Emergency Act again to call on the Pullman Company to negotiate. When the company refused, Randolph appealed to the new Coordinator of Federal Transportation, Joseph Eastman, only to discover that the Pullman Company, because it was not technically a rail carrier, was not subject to the terms of the 1933 act. Without the law's coverage, the BSCP could neither dislodge the Pullman Company union nor call upon the government for support in its efforts to win recognition.[24]

Everything changed the following year. With the support of the all-white Railway Labor Executives Association and transportation coordinator Eastman, the BSCP, along with AFL locals of dining car workers, successfully lobbied for the inclusion of Pullman porters and dining car cooks and waiters in the 1934 amendments to the Railway Labor Act. In addition to extending coverage to on-board service workers, the amendments retained the ban on company unions and created two new institutions: a new National Mediation Board would oversee union representation elections at either managers' or unions' request and assist in mediating disputes in contract negotiations, and the National Railroad Adjustment Board would issue binding interpretations of disputed contract provisions and rulings on irresolvable grievances. With the amendments providing a huge boost to the BSCP's fortunes, the *Crisis* observed, the BSCP took on "new life." The final battle for recognition had begun.[25]

The showdown came in June 1935, when the BSCP was pitted against a new rival, the Pullman Porters and Maids Protective Association (PPMPA). Shortly after the 1934 amendments to the Railway Labor Act made the Pullman Company's ERP illegal, the PPMPA emerged as an ostensibly independent association composed largely of older porters who had supported the ERP and were now desirous of maintaining friendly relations with the company. Hostile to outside agitators, the PPMPA was adamantly opposed to any affiliation with the AFL, which the PPMPA president described as "the most bitter enemy of Negro labor in this country." With a clear-cut choice before them in June 1935, Pullman porters voted in a NMB-administered representation election overwhelmingly in favor of the BSCP by a vote of 5,931 to 1,422. The BSCP's decade-long crusade for union recognition as the legal bargaining agent for porters had finally borne fruit.[26]

Legal recognition was one thing, a contract another. It took another two years before the Pullman Company signed its first contract with the BSCP. The company did not accede graciously to the union's election. Following a series of hostile conferences with the company, the BSCP enlisted the NMB's services to force the company to negotiate. But although the NMB could bring opposing parties to the bargaining table, it could not make them agree on substantive issues. It was only after a constitutional challenge to the Railway Labor Act was rejected by the Supreme Court that the company relented, signing its first contract with the BSCP on August 25, 1937.[27]

The union, its allies, and the black press hailed the agreement as a signal victory for the BSCP. The contract raised wages by $12.00 a month to a minimum of $89.50, provided time and a half for overtime, set the work month at 240 hours with time and a half for hours exceeding 260, and established a new grievance procedure. The victory had implications not just for porters, but for the entire black population. "As important as is this lucrative contract as a labor victory," the *Crisis* noted, "it is even more important to the Negro race as a whole, from the point of view of the Negro's up-hill climb for respect, recognition and influence," as well as economic advancement. The black union's persisting over a decade of obstacles, its winning legal recognition, and its securing a contract with a major American corporation were bound to set a powerful example to other black workers. Indeed, the *Chicago Defender* applauded the BSCP for the "inspiration it will give other black workers of hand and brain and the Race generally to organize and fight for our rights." Riding the wave of labor unrest and unionization that the CIO had inspired, the Brotherhood served as a "black wedge, or rather an ebony catapult, driving the problem of the Negro worker realistically home to the American Federation of Labor." Cognizant of the Brotherhood's precedent-setting accomplishment and its singular, pioneer status as the largest and most prominent black union, Randolph and his compatriots wasted little time in spreading the gospel of unionism among African Americans and taking the struggle against racial discrimination into the heart of the AFL, of which they were now members.[28]

Like their Pullman counterparts, dining car cooks and waiters also challenged their managers' unilateral authority by attempting to build trade unions during the 1920s. The experiences of the two groups, however, differed sharply. A huge labor force of Pullman porters confronted a single, powerful company with deep, historic ties to the black community. In contrast, vastly smaller units of dining car employees had to deal with a multitude of separate railroads. While the organizing drives of dining car workers attracted neither public attention nor fired the imagination like the BSCP did, their efforts met with far less corporate resistance. In some cases, railroad companies offered them recognition and small improvements, incorporating dining car locals into their broader structure of labor relations. With few financial and organizational resources, these locals struggled to retain their employers' approval and win what benefits they could.

The independent Brotherhood of Dining Car Cooks and Waiters (BDCCW) dominated the field in the eastern states during the 1920s. Formed in a merger of two World War I–era unions in 1920 with the assistance of the National Urban League in New York, the BDCCW eventually won recognition on the New York, New Haven, and Hartford, the Boston and Albany, the Boston and Maine, the New York Central, the Pennsylvania (eastern division), the Atlantic Coast Line, and the Southern railroads. Claiming roughly 3,000 members in nine locals in 1926, the BDCCW's president, waiter Rienzi B. Lemus, appeared before the Railroad Labor Board and negotiated contracts with individual railroads to produce modest wage increases and other improvements. Lemus also organized railroad men for the "colored section" of the Republican National Committee, directing his locals to eschew La Follette's third-party candidacy and remain loyal to Calvin Coolidge in the 1924 presidential election. Initially supportive of the BSCP's efforts, Lemus distanced himself from any form of radicalism, insisting that blacks had little interest in either socialism or communism, or any "isms as panaceas" for blacks' many problems.[29]

Lemus shared none of Randolph's enthusiasm for joining the AFL and kept his association at some distance from organized white labor. But Lemus applauded the National Urban League's engagement with the AFL, endorsing the idea that all blacks who desired membership in AFL unions be admitted to their respective craft internationals on terms of equality with whites. That, of course, was the catch: its proclamations against discrimination notwithstanding, the AFL was hardly committed to ensuring blacks equality with whites within its affiliates' ranks. In March 1926, Lemus participated with the Urban League's T. Arnold Hill in a conference with the AFL Executive Council, but subsequently turned down AFL president William Green's invitation to affiliate with the Hotel and Restaurant Employees International Alliance (HRE), to which the AFL had granted jurisdiction over dining car employees. Lemus objected strongly to joining the HRE, insisting that dining car cooks and waiters belonged in the AFL's Railway Employees Department, whose constituent unions barred African Americans from membership. Well into the 1930s Lemus would fend off the jurisdictional encroachments of AFL/HRE-affiliated dining car locals. Following his ouster in 1941, his union would eventually affiliate with the CIO.[30]

Lemus's anti-AFL stance placed his independent union at odds with a growing number of dining car workers who were unimpressed with the BDCCW's achievements. Various dining car locals accepted HRE's offer of affiliation in the late 1920s and early 1930s. In Los Angeles, railway chef Clarence R. Johnson and a number of coworkers capitalized on a "seething unrest" among the Southern Pacific's cooks and waiters over being forced to work 285 hours a month to be guaranteed 240 hours' pay. Founding the Dining Car Cooks and Waiters Union in May 1926, they joined the HRE as Local 582 and, in cooperation with their Oakland counterpart, succeeded in signing a contract with the company in 1928 that included a 5.5 percent wage increase. The Los Angeles local quickly developed into a broader community institution. By 1931, its 150 members had purchased and equipped their own clubhouse, established a credit union, and sponsored fund-raisers for the unemployed. By the mid-1930s, numerous locals from St. Louis, Fort Worth, Omaha, Oakland, Chicago, and New York had formed a Dining Car Employees' Division within the AFL-affiliated HRE.[31]

Through the mid- and late 1930s, the AFL locals battled the nonaffiliated independent unions for the support of dining car workers nationwide. With the passage of the 1934 amendments to the Railway Labor Act, the locals availed themselves regularly of the NMB's services to conduct representation elections, attracting previously unorganized recruits into their associational fold. But they also trained their organizational sights on both Lemus's BDCCW and the remnants of Robert L. Mays's Railway Men's International

Benevolent Industrial Association (RMIBIA). With the occasional assistance of the BSCP, the AFL dining car men attacked Lemus as a weakling "with a big bark, but lacking the courage, will and conviction to honestly fight" and his BDCCW as little more than a company union.[32]

Lemus and other independent activists responded by waving the red flag of race, charging the HRE locals with affiliating with a racist organization. AFL organizing efforts, particularly those on the railroad, constituted a menace to black workers, Lemus declared in 1935. The white Brotherhood of Railway Carmen's attempts to absorb black car cleaners put the latter at a disadvantage, he correctly noted, for the union's officers were white. Blacks were segregated into separate locals, and the black auxiliaries could be represented only by white officers. Moreover, the very HRE to which his opponents belonged had a long record of racial discrimination in the hotel industry. Even the increasingly popular BSCP came in for withering attack: the porters could show little for their decade of agitation, while their AFL charter had done nothing to compel recognition by the Pullman Company. "A union not recognized by the employer of its members is worse than no union at all," he concluded. The all-white Order of Sleeping Car Conductors, and their (ultimately unsuccessful) efforts to assume jurisdiction over the BSCP, also made an easy target. "It was colored men who started the organized labor movement among the colored men of the railroads," insisted Joel Miles of the RMIBIA's National Brotherhood of Dining Car Employees and the Association of Rock Island Railway Dining Car Employees. "Every experience which we have had with the A.F. of L. has been to our detriment. We warn waiters against this invasion."[33] These warnings were to no avail. The HRE locals' jurisdictional raids against their rivals were largely successful. In NMB-supervised elections in the mid-1930s, the AFL unions defeated the RMIBIA on the Rock Island railroad and the BDCCW on the Pennsylvania, the New York Central, the New Haven, and the Boston and Albany. Only on the Atlantic Coast Line and the Boston and Maine did the BDCCW narrowly hang on. The explanation for the passing of Lemus's union was "quite simple," veteran porter and columnist James Hogans reflected: "younger men with younger ideas, and the current trend of all classes of workers toward the new labor movement."[34]

Despite their losses to the AFL, Lemus and the other independent unionists had touched a raw nerve. While engaged in bitter jurisdictional battles with Lemus, HRE activists had downplayed the race issue. Lemus's most "effective weapon" for "poisoning the minds of the colored race" was the "propaganda that the A.F. of L. does not cater to colored people," fulminated Percival A. Moore of Local 370. But once the electioneering was over, many black HRE activists would admit that the charges of racism were true, and they bristled at the persistent discrimination within the HRE and the inability, or reluctance, of HRE officers to do much about it. Moreover, the perception that the international knew little about dining car problems—Lemus's original objection in the 1920s—was widespread. Despite their shared membership in the AFL's HRE, dining car workers remained fragmented, working for many companies marked by "sharp variations in wages, hours, and working conditions." Individual dining car locals struggled to organize on their own, despite the existence of a dining car department within the international union. Stopping short of issuing a declaration of black independence from the AFL, two union officials and Communist party members—Local 456 business agent Ishmael Flory of Oakland and Local 465 president Solon Bell of Omaha—proposed the creation of a distinct dining car group, or what Bell called "a movement that will serve to better the entire political, social and economic life of this class of employees through pooling our strength for collective action on a national scale."[35]

The Joint Council of Dining Car Employees was thus born in October 1937 when delegates representing eleven HRE locals and one independent union, along with A. Philip Randolph, gathered in Bell's hometown of Omaha. The "main and central problem," Randolph declared, "is the existence of many isolated organized groups of dining car workers that are too weak to protect and advance the basic interests of dining car employees"; the solution was simply "integration and coordination" into a common body, as the Joint Council's organizers had proposed. Conference co-convenor Flory focused on the relationship of black dining car workers to the HRE. "We are living under a tyrannical situation," he declared, with HRE leaders winking at the racism prevalent in the union. Most important, the new body insisted that it, and not international officers, direct the affairs of dining car workers within the HRE. With that autonomy, it would coordinate the efforts and programs of the numerous dining car locals, promote a uniform wage contract covering all rail lines, and represent its collective members before the NRAB. Elected chair and secretary-treasurer respectively, Bell and Flory used the conference to make larger political points as well. Before dining car delegates dispersed to their home cities, the new Joint Council passed resolutions condemning the Supreme Court for refusing to review the Scottsboro case, urging the AFL and CIO to resolve their differences amicably, calling on Congress to pass an antilynching bill, and advocating affiliation of dining car workers with the National Negro Congress and the League against War and Fascism. Despite the initial objections of HRE officers, the international eventually recognized the Joint Council, which established its headquarters in Chicago under Flory's direction.[36]

A driving force behind the formation of the Joint Council, Ishmael Flory found that his activist background trained him well to be the council's spokesmen in its first three years. Born in 1907 in Lake Charles, Louisiana, Flory was the youngest of seven children; his father was a gang foreman in a sawmill and his mother worked as a washerwoman. After migrating with his parents to Los Angeles at age eleven, Flory worked odd jobs as a repairman and as a golf caddy before finishing high school in 1926. Subsequently, he attended the University of California at Berkeley, earning money for fees and textbooks by working as a janitor, an insurance salesman, and a railroad service worker. His wife's uncle, a Pullman employee in Los Angeles, secured for him a porter's job in 1928; subsequent summers he worked as a dining car cook and dishwasher. In 1931, Flory graduated with a bachelor's degree, having majored in political science and economics.[37]

Flory's radicalization began at Berkeley and continued after graduation. He joined the International Labor Defense to participate in the struggle to save the Scottsboro Nine, dedicated himself to the labor movement, and became a member of the Communist party. Attending Fisk University on a fellowship in 1933, he found that his political commitments interfered with his educational goals. As a co-organizer of the Denmark Vesey Forum at Fisk, Flory angered university administrators with his vocal condemnation of the Jim Crow treatment of the Fisk Jubilee Singers, who performed before an all-black audience at a local theater. His resulting expulsion from Fisk attracted significant coverage in the national black press, which praised him for his courage. A hero in the pages of the *Chicago Defender*, Flory returned to California.[38]

In the world of radical politics in Oakland and Berkeley, Flory's activism intensified. Working first as a relief case worker, then as a Federal Writers Project supervisor, he found his organizational niche with Dining Car Local 456, which was affiliated with the HRE in 1936. Drawing on his prior experience as a summer dining car waiter and as an organizer, Flory became the local's business agent and successfully completed the recruitment of some 450 to 500 workers into the union. From his base in Local 456, Flory was a founder, along with BSCP leader C. L. Dellums, of the East Bay Council of the National Negro Congress and a delegate to the Central Labor Council of Alameda County. Once in Chicago in 1937, he threw himself into local labor and civil rights struggles, representing the Joint Council and pursuing the Communist party's goal of supporting the New Deal and allying with a wide range of liberal groups.

From the late 1930s through the mid-1940s, the Joint Council consolidated its position and attended to the nuts-and-bolts aspects of union building, dramatically transforming labor-management relations on the trains. Before the Joint Council, union member Edward H. Himes recalled, waiters were often "required to perform extra service, such as changing cars, doubling trains, protecting runs, and deadheading, for which they received no extra pay." Their seniority and grievance rights were denied, while the superintendent was "invested with unlimited and unrestricted powers to 'hire and fire,' which he often grossly and unjustly abused. In cases of discipline, his word was final, the right of a hearing or an appeal being denied . . . In the surveillance of keeping these workers in hand, every petty official on the entire road acted as a detective over them." The Joint Council put an end to at least some of these abuses. It won contracts with many railroads that respected the principle of seniority, provided an effective grievance procedure, and offered gradual wage increases, reductions in the hourly workweek, and a paid vacation. It also managed to end the long-disliked practice of workers' having to sleep on tables by requiring railroads to provide adequate sleeping accommodations en route and during layovers. By 1942, the Joint Council had grown from nine local unions to fifteen, with over 9,000 members and contracts with forty-seven railroad systems covering roughly 120 railroad lines.[39]

For all of their emphasis on the labor dimension of the experiences of Pullman porters and dining car workers, socialist A. Philip Randolph and communists Ishmael Flory and Solon Bell forged a unionism that was as much, if not more, about race and civil rights than it was about class. Appeals to racial pride, challenges to racial discrimination, and advocacy of an aggressive civil rights unionism characterized the BSCP and the Joint Council from their formation. While their leaders' political commitments and ideological outlooks would have unquestionably propelled the organizations in this direction, the railroad industry's century-long legacy of occupational segmentation by race and persistent racial stereotypes was also a determining factor: porters' and dining car workers' positions could not be advanced without confronting the intertwined realities of class and race. The BSCP and the Joint Council were ultimately *racial* unions that turned the disadvantages of race into organizational assets and transformed trade unions into civil rights associations.[40]

From the outset, Randolph and the BSCP made race a centerpiece of their analysis of the porters' plight and of their strategy to unionize porters. Always framing their crusade against the backdrop of African-American history, they repeatedly characterized the company-porter relationship as one of master and slave and likened their unionization campaign to emancipation. Journalist George Schuyler contended in his typical acerbic style that the Pullman Company never thought of its porters "except as 'good old faithful niggers' destined to forever get most of the inadequate remuneration for their toil, by ̄ping and clowning for the entertainment of passengers, who were expected to flip them a dime when they grinned." To Randolph, the "company's mind is incrusted and warped with the fallacious and unscientific dogma and superstition that Negroes are inferior beings" who should keep their place. It is hardly surprising that the union would denounce black porter instructors and welfare workers as of the "old decrepit, antiquated, fossilized Uncle Tom, hat-in-hand, me-too-boss type." But Randolph also attributed the porters' plight in part to the existence of "too many Uncle Toms in the service," who, possessing a "slave psychology," would "bow and lick the boots of the company officials, who either pity or despise them." In imaginary encounters between older, pro-Pullman porters and new, pro-BSCP porters in the pages of the *Messenger*, the former appeared as accommodationist, dull-witted, and fearful, speaking in crude black dialect, the latter as intelligent, articulate, and proud. The porters who made up the BSCP membership were representatives of the "New Negro," insisted union officials, who struggled not only for economic justice and social equality, but for dignity and a sense of manhood as well.[41]

To accomplish these ends, the BSCP and the Joint Council simultaneously pursued a trade union agenda along with a broader program that addressed the political, social, and economic concerns of African Americans. Beginning in 1928, the BSCP hosted an annual National Negro Labor Conference in Chicago, drawing together BSCP activists, other black workers, middle-class reformers, the clergy, white union officials, and black politicians. The promotion of trade unionism among blacks shared the spotlight with analyses of racism in the AFL, unemployment, juvenile delinquency, overcrowding in housing, disease, economic cooperatives, the denial of civil liberties, and women's work. These annual educational events, as well as the Brotherhood's larger organizing program, popularized the idea of black participation in the American labor movement, forged crucial ties between the BSCP and middle-class leaders, and promoted a new style of black protest politics. In the upsurge of African-American grassroots activism during the depression decade, the BSCP and later the Joint Council figured prominently. Randolph, Milton Webster, Halena Wilson, and other BSCP activists were members of a "New Crowd," whose collective demands and organizing tactics based on mass action successfully challenged the "Old Guard" in more staid, gradualist organizations such as the NAACP.[42]

One "New Crowd" organization that bore the particular stamp of the BSCP and the Joint Council in the 1930s and 1940s was the National Negro Congress (NNC). Founded in 1936 by Randolph, dissident NAACP members, Communists, and others impatient with the NAACP's cautious, legalistic approach to civil rights, the NNC brought together unions, civic and religious groups, and political organizations to promote militant, grassroots action. It formally opposed trade union discrimination, police brutality and lynching, fascism, and the Italian invasion of Ethiopia; supported the labor movement, the right of blacks to obtain jobs at decent wages, and political equality; and advocated unemployment insurance, relief, and social security for needy families regardless of race.[43]

On the local level, AFL railway service union officials assumed some NNC leadership positions. In the San Francisco Bay area, BSCP vice-president C. L. Dellums served as president of the region's NNC, while BSCP women's auxiliary president Halena Wilson assisted the Chicago branch in organizing the Inland Steel Company in Indiana Harbor. Meanwhile, Joint Council secretary-treasurer Ishmael Flory promoted the enlistment of black workers into the ranks of the trade union movement, especially the CIO. Randolph's tenure as president of the NNC, as well as most of his BSCPs involvement, ended in 1940 when he resigned over the issue of growing Communist influence in the organization. But party member Flory, ousted from the Joint Council by HRE's top official in late 1939, remained active with the NNC as a field organizer, forming a Tenant's League to fight high rents and force landlords to follow building codes, participating in a variety of job campaigns to break down barriers to black employment on street cars, buses, and elevators, and in phone companies, and directing mass protest campaigns against segregated public housing and restrictive covenants in Chicago.[44]

The NNC was but one vehicle for promoting black activism in the 1930s. Individual locals of railway service unions, particularly those outside the deep South, often launched civil rights campaigns in their cities or participated aggressively in local civil rights coalitions. In Seattle, for instance, dining car Local 516, the BSCP, and their respective women's auxiliaries spearheaded a "Spend Your Money Where You Work" campaign in 1939 designed to open up jobs in all-white business to blacks. In 1944, the Seattle BSCP joined with the local NAACP, the Urban League, the YMCA, the Anti-Defamation League, and the AFL to push for a statewide fair employment practices law, which was finally enacted in 1949. Under the chairmanship of BSCP leader Kelly Foster, a Colored Citizens Taxpayers League was founded in 1945 to protest the growing number of "We Cater to White Trade Only" signs in restaurants and stores in Seattle. Immediately before and during World War II, black railroad unions in Minneapolis and St. Paul were the driving force behind a variety of political movements. Unions of porters, dining car waiters, and red caps joined with packinghouse workers to form a Joint Negro Labor Council in 1940 and participated actively in the Minnesota Negro Defense Committee, the Twin City Council for a Permanent Fair Employment Practice Committee, the NNC, and a variety of other black and interracial organizations to advocate antilynching legislation and fair employment on the state and federal levels and to condemn the poor treatment of African Americans in the military.[45]

Union political programs received further reinforcement from the women's auxiliaries sponsored by railway service unions. The oldest, largest, and most active was the BSCP's Ladies' Auxiliary. Initially the Colored Women's Economic Councils, founded in 1925 in New York with chapters established in other cities shortly thereafter, the Auxiliary raised funds, encouraged male porters to join the BSCP, convinced porters' female family members to support the union, and sponsored social events at BSCP meetings and conventions. The Auxiliary was at all times subordinate to the BSCP's male leadership: it took direction from Randolph, submitted its program to BSCP officers for approval, and by definition was required to carry out the union's agenda. Popularizing a pro-union female domesticity that aimed to neutralize the potential opposition of porters' wives to trade unions, the Auxiliary also sought to enlist them in the labor movement cause. Unions were the "means through which a husband or a father can be assured protection for his family and his home," Auxiliary president Halena Wilson insisted, with the union struggle "built around the home, wife and child." Wives needed to understand their husband's working conditions and strengthen their resolve in order to "raise our children and to build strong, sound institutions for the future of our race."[46]

Subordinate status and the domestic ideal did not prevent the Auxiliary from carving out a more substantive role for itself over time. In the BSCP's first and most difficult decade, the *Chicago Defender* observed in 1938, the Auxiliary was the "lone Negro women's organization connected with labor to walk picket lines, to join mass demonstrations . . . to advocate with other groups meatless days in an effort to force prices down . . . to attend labor and legislative conferences as well as to take an active part in the Consumers movement." From the 1930s through the 1950s, the Auxiliary promoted classes in labor history, sponsored black history week celebrations, and ran small labor libraries in various cities. Through its fund-raising activities, it provided scholarships to black working women to attend trade union leadership training institutes. During World War II, the BSCP impressed Auxiliary chapters across the nation into service to raise money and organize locally for the March on Washington Movement. Later, in addition to advocating consumer cooperatives, the Auxiliary donated clothing to black schools in West Virginia, supported antilynching and anti–poll tax legislation, and contributed financially to the Montgomery Improvement Association's bus boycott in 1955–1956. Auxiliary chapters should be "vigilant and alert" to the "civil, social, and religious problems" of the black community, Halena Wilson insisted in 1954. The "Auxiliary fight[s] prejudice and discrimination wherever it is found." The Joint Council's auxiliary played a comparable role: its members participated in the NAACP, the NNC, and the New York Consolidated Tenants League.[47]

While black service unions and auxiliaries pursued a multifaceted civil rights agenda, they also nurtured heightened racial activism on the job. Rank-and-file dining car workers and porters had long chafed at racial insults and abusive treatment from white supervisors and passengers, and the number of racial incidents rose dramatically during World War II. "As the tempo and fury of war increases, so does the number of soldiers, sailors and marines using the railroads grow," a member of New York Local 370 of the Joint Council observed in 1943. Coming from all sections of the country, some did "not always exemplify the conduct we expect from members of our Armed Forces." Indeed, military police assisted white stewards in enforcing segregation, ousting black patrons from dining cars, and disciplining black dining car waiters, even to the extent of forcing crews off trains for alleged insubordination. While advising dining car waiters to offer speedy and polite service, Local 370's leaders also insisted they did "not expect our members to suffer abuse and humiliation at the hands of these men while serving them." Waiters were told to report any incidents of abuse or insult to their steward and request him to "silence the individual or have him removed from the car." In the event the steward refused to comply, waiters should under "no conditions" argue with their abusive patrons; instead, *all* waiters should refuse to serve the offending parties.[48]

With their union's encouragement, individual dining car workers took matters directly into their own hands. When military police ejected black Chicagoan Edward J. McCoo, who was accompanying the body of his son for military burial, from a Southern Pacific dining car in Utah, the dining crew was so angered that it refused to serve anyone until McCoo was readmitted. Missouri Pacific waiters and porters provided the South with a "real lesson in democracy" when they too refused to serve passengers after the steward and conductor barred two black servicemen from eating, instead telling them to "go back where you belong." When a steward on the Birmingham Limited repeatedly announced, "No N——s are going to eat on this train until all white passengers are served," waiter Oscar L. Myrick and his fellow crew members simply retired to the pantry, refusing to work; for that behavior, the steward ordered them off the train. Harry L. Thomas, a World War II veteran working as an Atlantic Coast Line waiter, was discharged for refusing to draw the Jim Crow curtain around a black female diner on a trip from Washington to Florida, but his entire crew stood by him, refusing to go out on their next run unless Thomas went with them. The existence of union contracts meant that whatever the immediate punishment, waiters and cooks had recourse to their company's grievance procedures and the protection of their union. In at least some cases, the discharged protesters were reinstated.[49]

The civil rights issues that absorbed most of the BSCP and the Joint Council's energy centered on the labor market in which their rank and file worked and on the labor movement with which they affiliated. Even when white workers were not erecting obstacles to black advancement, white railroad managers blocked their promotion through racial restrictions on certain occupations. A black porter remained a porter, a black dining car waiter a waiter; the positions of sleeping car conductor and dining car steward were reserved explicitly for whites. The occupational designation of "running in charge" allowed railroad companies the flexibility of utilizing black "porters-in-charge" or "waiters-in-charge" on shorter or other specified runs in lieu of white conductors or stewards. But although it paid more than portering or waiting (though considerably less than conducting or stewarding), running in charge brought with it no permanent change in status or pay and constituted a racially discriminatory occupational dead end. White supervisory personnel, fearing displacement by lower-paid blacks bearing an inferior occupational designation, opposed the practice. Unable to win satisfactory restrictions on the practice at the bargaining table, the Order of Sleeping Car Conductors (OSCC) turned to Congress in 1940 for legislation outlawing "in charge" porters and mandating the assignment of bona fide white conductors on interstate sleeping cars as a job preservation and safety measure. Oddly, the BSCP remained silent during the Senate hearings. "No porter appeared against the Bill, or sent even a letter or postcard in opposition," Senator Sherman Minton, the bill's sponsor, claimed. It was the Pullman Company, not the BSCP, that "stirred up the porters in opposition to this Bill by a representation that it was an attack upon their race." Although porters' representatives belatedly recommended that the bill be defeated, the chief opposition came from black religious and civic groups. In the end, unwilling to permit the legislation to "be used to stir up a race fight," Minton withdrew the bill from consideration. Although Randolph was on record as opposing the existence of "in charge" positions, the BSCP never pressed the promotion issue. He might have been hesitant to provoke the AFL-affiliated OSCC or endorse an encroachment on its occupational niche. Not until the 1960s did the BSCP address the issue of promotions to conductor, and did so only reluctantly when forced by a disaffected member's legal action.[50]

The Joint Council, unlike the BSCP, made the racial barrier to occupational advancement a prime target, linking the elimination of the waiter-in-charge position to the promotion of qualified dining car waiters to stewards. With the creation of the Fair Employment Practice Committee (FEPC) during World War II, it got its chance to press its case. FEPC officials readily accepted the Joint Council's arguments that the railroad companies' policy of barring blacks from becoming stewards constituted discrimination and called on managers to begin promoting African Americans. In 1944, the Chicago and Northwestern, the Milwaukee, and the Pennsylvania railroads took the unprecedented step of hiring African-American waiters-in-charge as stewards. The Joint Council's victory, however, was hardly clear-cut. A major sticking point was seniority: unlike the Chicago and Northwestern, the Pennsylvania railroad refused to extend retroactive seniority to its new black stewards. That meant that waiters-in-charge received no credit for the time they had worked in that position; in essence, they gave up what seniority they acquired both as waiters and as waiters-in-charge in accepting a promotion. Moreover, in the postwar era the industry continued to use waiters-in-charge, and the Brotherhood of Railroad Trainmen—which represented white stewards but barred black ones—attempted to squeeze black stewards out of their jobs. During the late 1940s and 1950s, some black waiters concluded that the trade-off was not worth it; they preferred to retain their seniority than have to both start over at the bottom of the stewards' seniority roster and face the hostility of the white BRT.[51]

The BSCP and Joint Council both devoted considerable attention to addressing racial inequality within the labor movement. While the AFL had admitted black service workers into its fold, it did not do so on terms of equality. Many of its constituent unions refused blacks membership by constitutional decree or ritual, segregated black members in inferior, auxiliary locals, subjected black unionists to racist derision, or simply ignored black concerns. Long a bastion of skilled, white workers, the AFL was not a welcoming institution for minority workers, even after it lowered some bars to their participation.[52]

Neither union was under any illusion as to the nature of their relationship with the AFL. Although the Hotel and Restaurant Employees International Alliance (HRE) eliminated its policy of restricting blacks to distinct locals in 1934, black dining car workers' dissatisfaction with white control of the HRE remained sufficiently strong to prompt the creation of the Joint Council three years later. Only in 1929 did the BSCP and the AFL work out a compromise that admitted to AFL membership the Brotherhood's thirteen locals as individual federal unions. With far fewer votes and less clout than organizations chartered as international unions, the BSCP occupied an inferior place within the house of labor. And federal status did not protect the black union from the predatory tendencies of the all-white Order of Sleeping Car Conductors. In 1934, the OSCC declared its intent to make the BSCP a subsidiary unit in an effort to stop the Pullman Company's use of porters-in-charge. The AFL acquiesced, granting the white conductors' union complete jurisdiction over black porters. In response, the BSCP publicly rejected the ruling; it would "prefer functioning as an independent organization, outside the A.F. of L., rather than put its fortunes under the Order of Sleeping Car Conductors," declared BSCP organizer Ashley Totten. Only after the Brotherhood decisively won its certification election in 1935 did the AFL back down and agree to grant the first international charter to a black union.[53]

Insisting on an equal place among other railroad unions, the BSCP and the Joint Council found the doors of solidarity sealed shut. When the AFL's Railroad Employees Department held its annual convention in Chicago in 1938, Ishmael Flory and other dining car delegates found themselves barred from admission, their application for membership rejected. The following year, the Joint Council publicly appealed to the brotherhoods of white trainmen and clerks to drop their discriminatory clauses. Predictably, they had no success. Black railroaders also targeted their exclusion from the Railroad Labor Executives Association (RLEA), an organization that formulated joint wage demands, constituted a united front representing white railroad labor's interests before the government and industry, and selected labor's representatives to the National Railroad Adjustment Board, which adjudicated grievance and contract disputes. The board regularly heard cases involving charges of racial discrimination and almost universally ruled against black workers. The Joint Council won admission to the RLEA in 1943. Its official representative to the association, however, was not a black dining car official but a high-ranking white officer of the HRE. Randolph, too, sought admission for his organization. "I wrote the association, I suppose, twenty-five different letters" requesting the BSCP's admission, he recalled in 1952. "They seldom answered . . . and when they did they dismissed it with some noncommittal statement." Only the threat of legal action forced the RLEA to open its doors to the porters in 1949.[54]

Even the annual gatherings of the AFL often proved humiliating or offensive to black trade unionists, prompting spontaneous or organized protests by black delegates. At the meeting of the State Federation of Labor in Tillamook, Oregon, in 1938, a hotel clerk canceled the reservation of Oceloa Henry on discovering that he was black. Henry's union, the Protective Order of Dining Car Workers, Local 465, anticipated the clerk's response and put it to good use. Housed in a "very poor room," Henry proceeded to bring to the convention floor his local's resolution, calling on the state federation to endorse a state civil rights bill. Although it had failed the previous year, the resolution "went over big" following Henry's recounting of his recent experience. Only months later, representatives to the HRE's national convention in San Francisco went farther, voting overwhelmingly to move to other hotels when the Whitcomb Hotel, the convention's headquarters, denied rooms to Joint Council officer Flory and another black delegate. The California State Federation of Labor took similar action in 1939 when a hundred or so delegates marched through Sacramento hotels forcing them to honor the reservations of black delegates. In the Midwest, a BSCP protest closed down a private restaurant housed in the AFL Labor Temple in Detroit when it refused to serve black delegates at the BSCP's biennial meeting in 1948.[55]

The sporadic discrimination encountered in the North and West was nothing compared to the enforced Jim Crow at meetings in the southern states. While such gatherings allowed black delegates from around the country to meet southern black workers and solidify ties with local black groups, they also exposed delegates to racist rituals to which many were unaccustomed. For some northern BSCP organizers, the South was dangerous and inhospitable territory. "Anyplace below Washington should be left out as being uninhabitable," BSCP Eastern Zone supervisor Thomas Patterson concluded in 1942, while Oakland-based BSCP vice-president C. L. Dellums simply referred to the South as the "Fascist fourth of this country." A. Philip Randolph, Milton P. Webster, and other black delegates often tried to spotlight southern segregation, transforming their members' second-class treatment into negative publicity for the region. Blacks attending AFL conventions in the South were subject to "various forms of humiliation and insult," Randolph told his fellow delegates. It is "not easy to convince" white hotel functionaries "that a colored gentleman has even a right to make use of the front entrance to the hotel, to say nothing about entering upon the sacred precincts of the passenger elevators." Randolph implored the federation to select convention sites above the Mason-Dixon line.[56]

Over the years, Randolph raised the issue of race at every opportunity, though the force of his criticism varied with his political strength. In its early years in the late 1920s, the porters' union desperately needed the institutional support the AFL had to offer; by the mid- to late 1930s, the BSCP was an established trade union committed to a broad civil rights agenda whose targets included the racial policies of the AFL and its members. Randolph's tone changed dramatically as his union gained stature. In 1929, when the BSCP was small, weak, and barely functioning, Randolph called on the AFL to endorse an educational and organizing program to enlist blacks into "the trades and callings represented" by the AFL. As the issue of union racial discrimination intensified, the AFL created a special committee of five white union officers to investigate the conditions of black workers in 1934. Stressing the autonomy of the federation's affiliated internationals, the resulting report merely called for a campaign of education to convince white workers of the need for greater unity among all workers. At the federation's 1935 gathering, Randolph blasted the watered-down recommendation as wholly inadequate, and a year later he condemned the federation for failing to create any sort of educational program, much less undertake any systematic and coordinated effort to eliminate union discrimination.[57]

Randolph's annual challenges to the AFL's racial practices came to assume ritualistic form. At virtually every convention, he would call on the AFL to appoint black organizers, establish an interracial committee to investigate charges of union racism, ban discrimination in its member internationals, and endorse the abolition of all forms of racial discrimination. He pressed the federation to condemn the assignment of black workers to federal unions or auxiliary locals of white internationals. When appeals to morality and democracy failed, Randolph invoked the potential costs of black alienation. Persistent union discrimination could push a million and a half black workers leftward into the arms of radical unions, Randolph warned in 1935, though the likelihood of that happening was slim. More convincing was the threat of the CIO's appeal to African Americans. "Beyond reasonable doubt," Richard Smith, secretary-treasurer of the Joint Council informed the AFL in 1944, "the average Negro worker is pro-C.I.O. in his sentiments." In National Labor Relations Board elections, the discrimination issue led significant numbers of blacks to vote for the CIO, causing the AFL locals numerous losses in plants around the country. Only when the AFL took the affirmative step of requiring affiliates to eliminate discriminatory clauses or face expulsion could the AFL compete successfully for workers' allegiance in the postwar era.[58]

Smith was not exaggerating when he complained about the CIO's competitive racial advantage, for the AFL's racial record often made the job of organizing difficult. Randolph became "all hot and bothered" when a dining car unit of the BSCP shifted its allegiance to the CIO in 1945. "Don't know why he should worry about the A.F. of L.," organizer C. L. Dellums remarked. "It wouldn't make any difference with me if all of the Negroes voted to get out including us." The San Francisco Bay area BSCP was involved in a wide range of wartime political movements—for a permanent national FEPC, for state and city FEPCs, and for the appointment of blacks to various policy-making boards in city, county, and state governments. "We get wholehearted support from the CIO but absolutely none from the A.F. of L.," Dellums complained. Black workers knew it and asked why. To this and other questions about the AFL's racial restrictions, Dellums admitted he could offer no adequate explanation. Eastern Zone supervisor Thomas Patterson concurred that "for progress and idealism the CIO is blazing the trail," although the AFL had the "best of the CIO" from the standpoint of "material stability." But the Brotherhood's "strategic position to fight against discrimination from within" cautioned against any BSCP defection from the AFL. Whatever hostility black workers felt toward the AFL or affinity for the CIO was irrelevant to the BSCP, and the question of affiliation moot. As unquestioned leader of the nation's most visible and respected African-American union, Randolph alone determined the organization's path, and continued affiliation in the AFL was simply not a subject for debate. While acknowledging that certain conditions in the AFL were "repulsive and unfair to the colored worker," dining car leader George E. Brown of the Joint Council also insisted that these conditions could be fought only from within. "The trouble with some of our colored labor leaders," Brown argued in 1942, "is that they will not face and fight these problems; they try to solve them by running away."[59]

Still, nothing the BSCP or Joint Council did seemed to have any effect on the AFL, except to earn their leaders a reputation as professional agitators and disrupters. At best they were ignored and at worst vilified from the AFL convention floor by labor's top white leaders. "We gave them hell every year," Randolph recalled to biographer Jervis Anderson near the end of his life. "They didn't pass our resolutions, but we brought them religion." While many black leaders and editors applauded Randolph's lonely crusade against AFL racism, others questioned his judgment. Randolph "had the faith to believe that if he got on the inside, he could do more to destroy these practices than he could on the outside," black journalist P. L. Prattis concluded in 1943. But the BSCP leader had nothing to show for over a decade of prodigious effort. "Year after year, he has made his eloquent plea and, year after year, the convention and the offending internationals have ignored him."[60]

With AFL recognition and numerous successes at the bargaining table behind them, organizers for the BSCP and the Joint Council had considerable cause for optimism over their wartime and postwar prospects, notwithstanding the glacial pace of change in the AFL. Both organizations commanded the wide respect of African Americans; both had played a major role in shifting black support toward organized labor; both used their institutional position to initiate and sustain a militant civil rights campaign. On many fronts, the two black service unions continued down the path they forged, winning further improvements in their members' working conditions and pay and spearheading the wartime crusade for fair employment in the 1940s. Yet the emergence of sharp conflicts within the Joint Council over the issue of communism and between the various black service unions over jurisdiction undercut their moral authority in the struggle for black freedom as well as their organizational strength in the labor movement. Racially egalitarian gadflies in the AFL, the BSCP and the Joint Council were also craft unions that proved no more immune to organized labor's debilitating divisions than their white counterparts.

The American labor movement exhibited no monolithic attitude toward communists during the 1930s. While the new CIO relied on talented communist organizers to build industrial unions, the AFL's longstanding antipathy toward communism showed little sign of abating. HRE officers may have been unaware of the political affiliation of the Joint Council's top leaders for most of the 1930s, but by the late 1930s the stance of at least one such leader came to their attention. Ishmael Flory, the young, energetic secretary-treasurer of the Joint Council, increasingly worried his HRE superiors, less for his on-the-job performance than for his political loyalties. While neither he nor Solon Bell had advertised their Communist party membership—it "wasn't something they wore on their sleeves," recalled Molly West, Flory's former secretary—Flory's organizing agenda reflected the Popular Front strategy of the party more than it did the craft unionism of the HRE. Over the course of 1939, he disregarded AFL policy, offering support to striking Hearst newspaper workers and cooperating with CIO activists in a variety of projects. Ignoring instructions from HRE officials to confine his activities to those appropriate to the office of union secretary-treasurer, Flory helped to found, and became chairman of, the short-lived South Side Labor Council of Chicago. An ambitious body composed of AFL, CIO, and independent unions, the council was committed to organizing every South Side worker and breaking down discriminatory barriers in existing white unions. Even more problematic for the HRE was Flory's alleged recruitment of party members. At a special meeting of the railroad worker's branch of the South Side section of the Communist party, an unnamed informant told HRE officials, Flory laid out plans for recruiting enough new members to allow the party to take control of the railroad industry, enabling it to paralyze the country in the event of a general strike. Although highly implausible, the story contributed to the AFL's crackdown on the Joint Council. Seizing upon Flory's refusal to retract a public statement in which he implied that a certain railroad was responsible for a recent train crash, HRE president Edward Flore fired him.[61]

Thereafter, the HRE maintained a closer watch on the Joint Council, assigning HRE vice-president Richard W. Smith to replace Flory as secretary-treasurer. But Flory's ouster did not yet presage a purge of the left. Solon Bell, who maintained a lower profile, remained the council's chairman, and numerous communists or communist supporters continued to hold positions of influence. During and after World War II, Joint Council organizers and activists, particularly those centered in Local 351, participated in coalitions supporting not just the war effort but fair employment, particularly on the railroads, the integration of Chicago public housing, and the hiring of blacks on municipal buses, streetcars, and rapid transit trains. By the war's end, however, the leftward shift of American communism prompted communists in the Joint Council to renew party recruitment and consolidate power blocs within specific locals. To their critics, the communists' efforts were a blatant effort to take over local unions through the election of party-supported officials. The formation of a left-led Committee for a Democratic Union in 1944 placed the communists on an eventual collision course with the HRE.[62]

In the play for power within the union, the communists lost decisively. In Local 351 in Chicago, according to its president, Bert Jones, members of the Committee for a Democratic Union attended every union meeting, voted as a bloc, and constantly volunteered for tasks. But when Jones refused to accept the committee's repeated invitations to join the Communist party, the committee assumed an oppositional stance, vowing to oppose the incumbent "Uncle Toms" and to replace Jones with a communist in the next union election in 1946. With the international HRE officers overseeing the local's election, the progressive slate was defeated. The leftists' response was to seek a court injunction overturning the election on the grounds of voter fraud. When that move failed, the HRE officer suspended the progressives from membership. Tensions between communists and noncommunists intensified, coming to a head at the HRE's 1947 convention. There, the left's efforts to elect Solon Bell to the position of international vice-president at large for dining car employees and one of his noncommunist allies as secretary-treasurer were easily rebuffed. Amending the union's constitution to bar those suspected of Communist party association from holding office, the HRE ousted Bell from his chairmanship of the Joint Council for "subversive activities" and placed the council under the international's direct trusteeship.[63]

Expelled from the council he had cofounded, Bell immediately turned to the task of building a new union. In the summer of 1947, Bell and some 250 delegates established the independent Dining Car and Railroad Food Workers Union (DCRFWU) in Chicago. For "too long, Negroes in the Joint Council were the forgotten, maltreated stepchildren of a dictatorial gang that cares nothing for the job security of its darker members," declared Bell. A party newspaper, the *Railroad Workers' Link,* weighed in with fierce denunciation of the HRE for its "conspiracy to seize despotic and dictatorial control" of the Joint Council, likening the HRE's trusteeship to a "Hitler-like 'purge' of those who have bucked the iron-fist control by the international officers." With a leadership drawn from or close to the Communist party and its railroad workers' division, the DCRFWU promised aggressive action on workplace and civil rights issues. Its one organizing success was on the Pennsylvania railroad. Ignoring A. Philip Randolph's staunch defense of the HRE, workers voted heavily for the new DCRFWU over the Joint Council's Local 370 in a representation election in 1948. Surviving periodic raids by the AFL and senate hearings into "communist subversion" in the new union, the DCRFWU's Pennsylvania local remained an organizational and ideological thorn in the AFL's side into the 1960s.[64]

Far more common than conflicts between communists and anticommu-
nists were jurisdictional disputes endemic to the trade union movement. In
the early 1940s, some unionists advocated a movement for the unification of
red caps, dining car waiters, and porters in an independent federation under
one leadership, while others floated the idea of a more informal alliance
to coordinate strategy. Rather than presenting a common front and collabo-
rating as genuine allies, the BSCP, the Joint Council, and the United Transport Service Employees of America (UTSEA)—the CIO-affiliated red caps'
union—were competitors for the allegiance of black railroaders. The three
unions had been mutually supportive of the others' efforts to organize and
achieve union recognition in the mid-1930s, but by the war years, the larger
ambitions of the AFL's BSCP and the CIO's UTSEA, in particular, brought
them into conflict. During the 1940s, the porters' and red caps' unions
launched campaigns to recruit other black workers, particularly those in
other railroad occupations. The BSCP and the UTSEA competed unsuccessfully in NMB-sponsored elections, along with the white carmen and clerks'
brotherhoods, to represent Pullman yard workers and car cleaners. The
UTSEA's interest in Pullman laundry workers, despite the BSCP's disin-
terest, was not appreciated by the porters. After the BSCP protested, the
UTSEA withdrew from organizing black locomotive firemen on the Florida
East Coast railroad, leaving the porters' union to battle a variety of independent black firemen's associations. The UTSEA's forays into the dining car
sector involved not just absorbing the remnants of Rienzi Lemus's BDCCW
but occasionally contesting the Joint Council in representation elections as
well. Castigating the HRE and promising greater bargaining-table success,
the UTSEA charged that the "Joint Council has never been self-sustaining
and exists only through the subsidies granted by the International Union."
To the Joint Council, UTSEA president Willard Townsend was nothing
more than a "Labor Fifth Columnist" and his followers "a bunch of rank op-
portunists," for the red caps' union had committed "an indefensible crime"
by "invading its territory." Enmity between union leaders of the porters and
the red caps intensified, with Milton Webster publicly referring to UTSEA's
chief Willard Townsend as "the joker" and the two associations engaging in
occasional court fights over libel.[65]

Part of the conflict stemmed from the grand ambitions of the unions' leaders, Randolph and Townsend, each of whom sought the title of undisputed
leader of black labor. As early as 1941, Horace Cayton bemoaned the existence of "two rival union groups"—the BSCP and UTSEA—"who are attempting to deal with the problems of the Negro" in the railroad industry.
For Cayton, a scholar of black labor, it was "imperative . . . that there be developed at the earliest possible moment some overall vertical organization
which would represent this group of Negroes." But neither Randolph nor

Townsend appeared willing to put their claims to leadership aside to "get together on a plan of organization to bind them into a federation to enable them to, to some extent, protect themselves." Personalities aside, the conflict also stemmed from broader organizational rivalries. Black labor journalist George McCray viewed the "broadening struggle" between the CIO and the AFL as placing a "dangerous strain upon interracial labor relations." The "rivalry poisons the relations between various Negro CIO and AFL labor leaders," he argued in 1945, forcing them to demonstrate their loyalty to their respective federations and to spend "thousands of dollars annually from AFL and CIO sources to fight each other for workers already organized."[66]

Trade union affiliation was ironically both a source of strength and a source of division for black railroad service workers. As solid labor unions, their associations attracted resources, allies, and publicity. These unions provided black railroad leaders with effective platforms from which to launch unprecedented challenges to racial discrimination in employment and in the labor movement. Cloaked with the legitimacy afforded by membership in organized labor, black railroad activists aspired to build, and at times actually became, an unprecedented social movement. Trade union affiliations and craft union structures, however, rendered black organizations susceptible to the jurisdictional conflicts endemic to the AFL and even the CIO. Their affiliations within the fractured House of Labor exacted a measure of loyalty that undercut their independence and strategic maneuverability. As they pursued their goals of economic improvement and racial equality, neither the Joint Council nor the BSCP overcame the organizational parochialism fostered by their craft structures and the limits imposed by their union allegiances.

While conflicting personal ambitions and organizational rivalries prevented black railroaders from creating a united front in the 1940s, they did not prevent individual unions from winning a significant degree of dignity for their members, as well as substantial improvements in working conditions. "Unless one has been actively engaged in dining car service for some time," waiter Edward H. Himes concluded in 1938, "it is almost impossible to comprehend the vast changes that are taking place." Both the Joint Council and the BSCP were effective trade unions that served most of their members well. Not only did they do much to win approval for the labor movement within African-American communities across the country, but they also brought an activist, rank-and-file–oriented approach to black and interracial organizations on the local, state, and national level. Laying a foundation for future civil rights struggles, they forged a new kind of civil rights unionism that trained a generation of activists and lodged protests and effected changes that chipped away at the edifice of Jim Crow during the Great Depression and World War II years.[67]

4

Independent Black Unionism in Depression and War

"The railway industry today presents itself as a great battle ground for Negro employment opportunities," black labor activist Ernest Calloway contended in 1939. "Once the aristocrat of Negro labor, the railroad worker, is being fast pushed out of the industry by various and sundry forces." In the years following World War I, it was evident that many black railroaders were losing ground, and by the Great Depression blacks' status in the industry had reached a crisis point. The "story of the Negro in the railroad and transportation industry is most pathetic," St. Louis Urban League executive secretary John T. Clark observed privately in 1934. Even in the "fields in which he has been given a complete monopoly as in porter work and dining car waiter work," he concluded, "he has been mistreated miserably."[1]

For the tens of thousands of black workers in the railroad industry's operating and service trades, the "great battle ground" for employment opportunities involved the related issues of law, civil rights, employment discrimination, and union affiliation. The 1930s and 1940s were years of new opportunities as well as deepening crisis for blacks laboring on the nation's vast railroad systems. For one group of black railroaders—service employees, including Pullman porters, dining car waiters, and red caps—the politics of the New Deal and World War II years worked somewhat to their advantage, and they pressed their demands with considerable success. Many other railroaders, however, notably southern black firemen and brakemen, discovered that the promises of the New Deal were hollow. Unlike most groups of industrial workers, they found no salvation in New Deal labor legislation, which for them represented not labor's Magna Carta but rather a major setback to their organizational aspirations and even their livelihoods.

Unlike many African Americans in basic industries such as meatpacking, auto, and steel, black railroaders were neither invited to participate in, nor could they initiate, interracial unions. Those who were swept up into labor's organizational crusade and affiliated with both the AFL and the new CIO joined not interracial but largely all-black locals. Unlike many all-black auxiliaries of staunchly racist unions in shipbuilding or the building trades, these locals proved independent, aggressive, and protective of their members' on-the-job civil rights. Much of their success might be attributed to the lack of job competition they faced from whites.

Black operating craft workers also formed all-black locals, but in contrast to service employees, they eschewed any affiliation with the larger organized labor movement, partly because that larger movement, building upon long-standing traditions of racial exclusion, wanted nothing to do with them. An unintended consequence of that exclusion was the fostering of a fierce racial solidarity and pride among black craft workers. Instead of seeking affiliation with the AFL or the CIO, they followed the path forged by their World War I era predecessors and formed all-black associations that prized and defended their institutional independence. Over the course of the Depression and World War II, the black independents fought an uphill battle against their employers, their white union counterparts, and even such established black AFL leaders as A. Philip Randolph. In their struggle to maintain their independence, they articulated a vision of a road to black economic security that differed sharply from that of Randolph and forged a strategy that would ultimately lead to significant, but limited, success.

The crisis of the black railroader in the 1930s was partially rooted in the broader crisis of the railroad industry in that decade. Even before the Great Depression wreaked havoc on American business and labor, the railroad industry's long monopoly of freight and passenger traffic confronted a growing challenge from alternative forms of transportation. The automobile, the airplane, and especially the intercity bus began drawing small but growing numbers of travelers away from railroad coaches. Railroads commanded 75 percent of all forms of inland transportation revenue in 1926, but brought in just over 52 percent by 1937, with intercity buses capturing much of the railroads' loss in market share. Despite lower rates, improved service and scheduling, new comforts, and faster speeds by the late 1930s, railroads failed to stem the loss of passenger traffic. Freight too was being diverted to the growing army of trucks, albeit at a slower rate than passengers, with railroads' receipt of 75 percent of inland ton-miles of freight revenue in 1926 dropping to 65 percent by 1937. "Supreme for sixty years," one journalist observed in 1936, "now the railroad is being assaulted on all dimensions, above, below, and on both sides; or by airplane, pipeline, boat, and motor vehicle."[2]

Competition from alternative forms of transportation combined with the Great Depression to produce a dramatic reduction in the size of the railroad labor force. The year 1920 proved to be the historic high point for railroad employment, with roughly two million people at work in the industry's many job classifications. The post–World War I recession—and the predicted post-war reduction in the labor force—eliminated some 400,000 jobs, leaving a more or less stable number—1.6 million people—on company payrolls until the Great Depression. By 1930, however, the railroad industry provided employment to less than a million people. And railroads in 1940, observed industrial relations specialist Harry D. Wolf, "had only half the employees of two decades ago." Their industry in crisis, black railroaders suffered considerably. Census figures in 1930 placed the number of African Americans in the industry at roughly 143,000; by the end of the decade, the number had fallen to 75,000.[3]

While railway employment in general unquestionably fell sharply from the early 1920s to the late 1930s, black railroaders, particularly those in the operating trades, bore a disproportionate brunt of the reduction in employment. In 1917, roughly half of the locomotive firemen in the Yazoo and Mississippi Valley railroad's Memphis terminal were black; by 1943, they constituted only 30 percent. The decline on the entire railroad was even sharper: by 1943, blacks' share of firemen's jobs had dropped to 30 percent from a high of 75 percent in 1917.[4] Overall, labor economist Herbert Northrup found that in ten states with the overwhelming number of black operating trades workers, blacks composed 41.3 percent of the firemen and 29.8 percent of the trainmen in 1910; twenty years later, their percentages had dropped to 33.1 and 16.3 percent respectively.[5]

What accounted for the disproportionate decline in employment suffered by black operating trades workers by the 1930s? The reduction in rail traffic during the Depression years and the introduction of technological innovations can account for some of the lower levels of employment generally, but not for blacks' proportionately greater losses. The forces eroding black workers' job security and even access to employment were neither impersonal nor passive; they wore a human face. They were the white railroad brotherhoods, railroad company managers, and government officials who debated, negotiated, and implemented strategies designed to advance the interests of whites at blacks' expense. From 1919 onward, the white firemen's and trainmen's brotherhoods, either officially or through unwritten "gentlemen's" or "vest-pocket" agreements, won numerous antiblack rules, including provisions that prohibited the further promotion of blacks, that eliminated them from designated job classifications, and that reduced their percentages in the labor force. On the Atlantic Coast Line, leaders of the 548-member Progressive Order of Colored Locomotive Firemen complained that management had "turned its back on the colored employees." Harrison Bruce, the organization's general secretary, recalled that during the pre–World War I era, the "firemen had to get down and get under the engine, at that time the white firemen would not have the job; these were classified as Negro's jobs" with low rates of pay and high levels of danger. But once the federal government took over the railroads and equalized black and white pay levels during World War I, "Negro firemen have had a hard time trying to hold these jobs since." Bruce believed that it was "the policy of the brotherhood [of locomotive firemen] to rob Negro firemen of their jobs."[6]

The Memphis-based switchmen and brakemen of the Illinois Central (IC) and Yazoo and Mississippi Valley railroad (Y&MV) would have agreed with this general indictment. In 1933, members of the Memphis branch of the Association of Colored Railway Trainmen and Firemen (ACRT) lodged formal protests against their managers and the white trainmen's brotherhood for unexplained violations of blacks' seniority. "Sinister and evil influence has been at work not only to prevent Negroes from securing jobs, but to take from hundreds of other jobs that they already possessed," the black weekly, the *Memphis World*, asserted. While in 1927 some 100 black brakemen worked for the Memphis division of the IC and the Y&MV and 150 in their Memphis terminals, by 1933 those numbers had dropped to 27 and 70 respectively. Black IC and Y&MV workers insisted that the company was recalling laid-off whites to displace more senior blacks and otherwise giving whites with less seniority preference over blacks. While the company denied the charge, top officials privately admitted that they did "not have sufficient detailed information . . . to determine definitely just what the facts are in each employee's case, or whether there has been discrimination against any of our colored employees at Memphis." Black workers were also unaware of a new rule, adopted in 1932, that allowed the company to remove from the seniority roster the names of any workers who had not worked on the extra board for the past six months (previous practice put the duration at one year). The rule had been negotiated between the company and the white union without blacks' input, consent, or notification. While ostensibly applied to blacks and whites alike, the rule "was resorted to only to close the records" of black workers. Subsequent complaints to other company and white union officials, as well as an ACRT legal suit against them, brought no satisfaction. "There seems to have developed a hatred for the colored employees by the officials of the company in this division," concluded J. C. Strickland, Jr., the attorney for the aggrieved men, "in that they are resorting to every method available to prevent the colored employees from working and exercising their seniority rights."[7]

The destruction of black railroaders' seniority and other job rights offered advantages to the white brotherhoods and rail managers alike. White firemen gained access to employment and better job assignments that otherwise would have gone to blacks. In a decade in which employment rates were dropping, the industry's economic distress generated chronic employment insecurity. Rail carriers, for their part, could use "the Negro as a pawn for trading purposes with white labor," in the words of attorneys Charles Hamilton Houston and Joseph Waddy. In some cases, management "has sacrificed the interests of its Negro workers to obtain concessions in demands by white workers. In others it has used the Negro as a threat to white workers in an effort to lower wages and depress working conditions." Agreeing to give white workers preference in employment, to limit further blacks' percentage in the workforce, and to adopt secret rules that deprived blacks of jobs cost the railroads virtually nothing and strengthened their bargaining position in negotiations with white railroaders. While the Gulf, Mobile, and Northern railroad refused to sign the Chicago Agreement of March 15, 1937 (stipulating that white firemen would be placed in the cab of all locomotives, even those with diesel engines, where they were not needed), it placated irate white firemen by secretly agreeing with the Brotherhood of Locomotive Firemen and Enginemen (BLFE) to grant white firemen preference on stoker-fired engines, despite the fact that black firemen possessing considerable seniority had contractual rights to those jobs. The carriers' acquiescence to the white railroaders' campaign against blacks represented nothing less than a "Betrayal by Management in Conspiracy with the Brotherhood," in Houston and Waddy's words.[8]

By the late 1930s and early 1940s, the fate of black firemen appeared sealed. Most southern railroads had agreed that they would no longer hire nonpromotable men, a euphemism for black firemen. The Interstate Commerce Commission had ordered a program of dieselization in late 1937 that would require that by July 1, 1938, all new passenger locomotives weighing 160,000 pounds or more and by July 1, 1943, all existing coal-burning freight locomotives weighing over 175,000 pounds be equipped with mechanical stokers.[9] The government-mandated dieselization of the industry meant that the black fireman, one sympathizer predicted, would become "as much an economic anachronism as the Confederate dollar."[10]

During the Great Depression, black firemen and brakemen were not yet anachronisms, but that moment could not come soon enough for white operating craft workers. There "had been an uneasy peace for the beleaguered black railroaders" during the 1920s, novelist Lloyd Brown wrote accurately of Mississippi black firemen. With the onset of the Depression, "now it would be worse. For again there were Negroes working while white men were jobless." What ensued was a "shooting war. A strange war, secret and implacable, that raged in Mississippi" from 1931 to 1934. The shooting began in the summer and fall of 1931 with the wounding of four African-American brakemen and firemen. Frank Kincaid was the first victim in August, when unknown assailants shot him on the job. He managed to recover and return to work, only to die in a second assassination attempt while going to work at the IC shops from his home in Canton, Mississippi, on November 10, 1931. As he climbed into the cab of his train, the Creole, during a crew change, "against the lighted window he made a perfect target for a gunman in the darkness outside," in journalist Hilton Butler's account. As buckshot hit his head, he fell "back into the coal tender to die." The Creole departed for New Orleans with a replacement fireman, who just happened to be white. His assailants, or someone putting his death to use, reminded black railroaders of Kincaid's death: "You know what happened to Old Frank at Canton," one "blackhand letter" sent to a fireman read. "Now if you don't watch your step and keep off of that local you are going to have the same trouble, maybe worse."[11]

Next to die was brakeman Ed Cole, while stepping down from his train as it entered the IC shop yards at Water Valley, Mississippi, on February 4, 1932. On March 13, Turner Sims was seriously wounded in his engine cab by a shooter from an overhead bridge in McComb. Days later, on March 19, Aaron Williams, the oldest black fireman on the IC's Vicksburg division, was gunned down in his cab. A masked assailant murdered fireman Wilbur Anderson on March 23 when Anderson's freight train stopped to investigate a red flare by the side of the tracks some three miles south of Vicksburg. In Natchez, a gunman firing a shotgun from a car killed fireman Will Harvey on March 31. The following week, Clarence Booker was killed as his freight train passed through Shady, four miles from Bolivar, Tennessee. The forty-two-year-old Booker was a member of the Locomotive Firemen's division of the National Federation of Railway Workers (NFRW) who, along with the federation's president, L. R. Moloy of Jackson, Tennessee, had first notified the NAACP of the wave of killings and requested its speedy intervention.[12]

Two more black railroaders died violent deaths that year. On July 17, Southern railroad brakeman Edgar Scott was found dead in a coal car in Macon, Georgia, his head crushed by a lead pipe. The year ended with the assassination of Grant Johnson, a long-term railroad veteran from New Orleans. In October 1932, Johnson was wounded in the neck when an unidentified gunman fired into his cab. Recovering from his injuries, he resumed work. But on December 24, his body was riddled with bullets from an ambush as his train was coaling near the Y&MV roundhouse outside of Baton Rouge, Louisiana. Just half a year earlier, his father, fifty-five-year-old Frank Johnson, a fireman on the Gulf Coast line, had been found dead in the Baton Rouge Y&MV roundhouse, a probable murder victim. In 1930, as standing representatives of IC and Y&MV black firemen, the Johnsons had contacted company officials to protest what they had heard was a proposal of white firemen for 75 percent of all work. "[We] are not agitators," they claimed, reminding the IC's general manager that "the colored firemen [had] stuck by the company loyal and faithful without a word," even when firemen's wages were low and conditions poor in the past. By 1932, the younger Johnson was president of his union local. Both Johnsons, father and son, paid with their lives for their refusal to relinquish their jobs and their leadership of fellow black railroaders.[13] But Grant Johnson was the last fatality in the Mississippi whites' war against black railroaders. Episodic violence persisted, resulting in one wounding and several misses over the next year and a half. But negative publicity, heightened company and police vigilance, and a lack of results brought the killings to an end. The final death toll included a minimum of ten firemen and brakemen out of a total of twenty-one attacks.[14]

To black railroaders and their supporters, there was nothing mysterious about the murder wave. White "Mississippi, in its own primitive way, had begun to deal with the unemployment problem," one journalist concluded. Before the shootings began, white firemen requested and were granted an alteration in the percentage agreement that allocated 50 percent of all available positions to blacks and 50 percent to whites, winning for themselves a 55 percent share, despite protests by President L. R. Moloy and the NFRW. But given the severity of unemployment in the region and the extent of the layoffs, whites found that negotiating "discriminating working contracts" was a "very slow" method to attain their goals. The "quickest and surest manner in which to dispose of the negro workmen," Moloy suggested, "would be to frighten them away." To that end, they simply "resorted to murdering and wounding the negro."[15]

As they had during the earlier wave of terrorist attacks a decade before, southern black railroaders turned to the NAACP for help. Following Ed Cole's murder in February 1932, Moloy and local NFRW leader Clarence Booker informed NAACP secretary Walter White of their plight. Their earlier appeals to the Illinois Central for greater protection had gone unheeded, for the company refused to augment its force of special agents, which, Moloy believed, offered hardly "any protection at all." (The IC later offered a $5,000 reward for information leading to the arrest and prosecution of the attackers.) Given the unwillingness of local law enforcement officials to conduct a proper investigation, Moloy implored the NAACP to dispatch someone to Mississippi who could "cope with this condition." That person, he cautioned, "should necessarily be white because what ever information or clues that is obtained must come principally from whites."[16]

Although the NAACP assigned no investigator to the case, Walter White took up the black railroaders' cause, characteristically assuming a legalistic stance and pursuing it behind the scenes. His first overtures to the IC for greater protection for the aggrieved railroaders produced only bland reassurances and a disavowal of ultimate authority. Only the government could "successfully investigate, prosecute and properly punish," IC Chief Special Agent T. T. Keliher told White, promising that the IC would assist the proper authorities when it could.[17] White next placed his hopes on prompting federal involvement in the case by finding "some peg on which to hang justification for investigation by the Department of Justice." When White met with Justice Department officials in April, he learned that there was no federal criminal statute under which prosecution against the assailants might be instituted; the case of presumably private individuals acting independently of a state or government in attacking African Americans was governed only by the laws of the state in which the crimes took place.[18]

White's attempt to work through southern white community leaders produced more ambiguous results. He appealed to Will W. Alexander, the executive director of the Atlanta-based Commission on Interracial Cooperation, about the possibility of arousing sentiment and action in Mississippi against the "mobbists." The commission, founded in 1919 by moderate whites to promote dialogue across racial lines, promoted greater fairness toward African Americans while accepting the basic tenets of Jim Crow. The organization's opposition to lynching and its desire "to educate the [white] public to an awareness of conditions which result in injustice" made it receptive to the NAACP's appeal for involvement against the racial violence on the southern railroads. A sympathetic Will Alexander put White in touch with prominent local men, who he believed might influence local law enforcement and other officials. One of these men, Alexander Fitzhugh, head of Vicksburg's largest wholesale concern and a "high-grade" man of "courage and influence," spoke out at public assemblies in Vicksburg against the "intimidates and outrages" on the IC. But his highly positive assessment of police and company efforts to stop the shootings differed sharply with those of Moloy; the authorities, he believed, had "spared no effort to apprehend the guilty parties and bring them to justice."[19]

The efforts of men like Fitzhugh likely contributed to the Mississippi white elite's growing condemnation of the assassination campaign. By April 1932, Vicksburg's newspapers and Chamber of Commerce had condemned the shootings, and with the killing of Grant Johnson in December, Louisiana editorial opinion similarly turned harsh. "Baton Rouge rankles today beneath the strain of dishonor, left by the lurking killer of a vicious clique," the *Morning Advocate* inveighed. The city was faced with a "warped gang, who scorning decency, justice, and the forces of the law, indicates it will murder ruthlessly when it chooses, and for whatever depraved justification it can find in the deed."[20] Grant's killer was never found, and few Mississippi like to would believe that justice was ever served. The arrests and prosecutions that did take place during 1932 only served to remind blacks that the law was not their ally.

In late May, police charged Y&MV white fireman Charles B. Coon with the killing of Will Harvey, and a week later arrested three other white Mississippians suspected of involvement in the violence—seventeen-year-old Lee Edward Middletown of Meadville, Mississippi; his thirty-two-year-old stepfather, Vernon Campbell of Vicksburg; and M. Bailey of Brookhaven. In August, another five whites—J. Matt Lewis, M. F. Varnado, Emmett Smith, Reatie Lee, and Charles J. Miller, all McComb, Mississippi, residents—were taken into custody.[21] While the full story behind the assassinations and other shootings will probably never be known, enough fragments exist to offer a detailed if incomplete portrait of the perpetrators of some of the violence. On the night of their arrest, Emmett Smith and Reatie Lee were planning yet another attack. Both were firemen—Smith with six or seven years of experience and Lee with about thirteen years—who had been laid off. The two men drove to Jackson on the night of August 16, 1932, to "look the situation over and figure out how to make a get-away." In their car was a pistol belonging to Lee and a shotgun borrowed from his neighbor. Their goal was to shoot black fireman Ross Smith on the switch engine as it started out of the yard. At midnight, the black fireman went to work, but although the worker was alone, Lee got cold feet. Smith told police that Lee repeatedly urged him to shoot the black fireman, but that he too refused. In the end, the men went back to their car and fell asleep, only to be awakened by plainclothes policemen at two-thirty in the morning. Their attempts at bribing the police got them nowhere, and the two were placed into custody.[22]

Although Lee and Smith were unable to carry out the killing on the night of August 16, there was little question that they, along with Lewis, Miller, and especially Varnado, were involved in planning and executing many other attacks in the Vicksburg area. On the basis of their confessions, it seems likely that Varnado—a twenty-four-year-old with a previous conviction for automobile theft and the only nonrailroader among the assailants—did many of the shootings. He shot Pete Lewis on Christmas night 1931, and Sam Barnes in February 1932, both with the assistance of Lee and Miller; Varnado shot another black fireman with Matt Lewis in August 1932, in an attack arranged by Lewis, who promised Varnado $50. The "purpose of making the trip" that night was to shoot black firemen "regardless of what negro it might be," Varnado admitted to police. With Lee and Miller, he also shot Sam Barnes and Turner Sims.[23]

Their admissions notwithstanding, justice did not prevail. J. Matt Lewis was tried in Brookhaven, Mississippi, in September 1932. Pleading guilty to the lesser charge of assault in the wounding of a black fireman, he was sentenced to only a year in the state penitentiary, six months of which were suspended when he agreed to testify against others involved in the killings. Varnado also pleaded guilty to assault (but not murder) and received a five-year sentence. The rest of their accomplices fared even better. When Charles Miller's case came to trial in October 1932, justice suffered a "particular bad break," for on October 1, an African-American man allegedly raped a white woman a few miles east of the county seat where the IC case was tried. With a mob threatening violence, the accused black rapist was moved to another jail before being secretly brought into court. Pleading guilty, he received a life sentence and was hastily transported to the state penitentiary. "Feeling was running very high in Pike County," an IC special agent reported, "and a large number of the citizens thought this negro should have been hung." It was in this context that Charles Miller pleaded not guilty and was quickly acquitted of all wrongdoing. Reatie Lee and Emmett Smith also were never convicted for their role in the killings. It took the all-white Mississippi jury a mere thirty-five minutes to free Reatie. Despite his possession of a firemen's seniority list with checks next to those men killed, Charles B. Coon, the first white to be arrested, was similarly acquitted, as was B. G. Gunner, a white fireman who was charged with killing activist Clarence Booker.[24]

"It must be understood that these murders are not committed by one person but [by] an organized band of men, either sponsored by the white trade unions or members of the unions," insisted NFRW president Moloy. That most of those involved in the violence were, or had been, railroad firemen and brotherhood members was revealed in the police investigation, as was the fact that most had been laid off from railroad service and sought to create vacancies for whites through the murder of blacks. Whether their actions were sponsored by the white union they belonged to, however, remains undetermined. It is highly unlikely that the BLFE organized or even secretly co-operated with the killers. Brotherhood leaders may well have recalled the widespread condemnation that union violence had provoked in 1909, 1911, and 1921–22; union sponsorship of further violence would only undermine the brotherhood's legitimacy as a national player in the larger arena of politics and of labor and industrial relations. Given the extremely limited extent of the terrorism—it was restricted almost entirely to the IC railroad in and near Mississippi—it is probable that the violence was carried out by a band of white union members acting on their own.

If the BLFE did not participate or organize the violence, it certainly sympathized with and supported those who carried it out. After the attacks ended, the Jackson BLFE lodge threw its weight behind the efforts of Reatie Lee and Emmett Smith to get their jobs back. At the time of the killings, Lee and Smith had been cut off the IC's extra board, but by May 1933, they stood next in line to be recalled to work. IC superintendent J. F. Walker conducted his own hearing on their eligibility, and on the basis of their statements to police after their arrest the previous year, he dismissed both of them from service. In early 1934, Lee and Smith each sued the IC for slander (Walker had reportedly fired them because they had "shot the negroes"). They dropped their cases, they claimed, only when several engineers promised to help them win reinstatement. This Superintendent Walker refused to do. C. A. Tweedy, chair of the BLFE's General Grievance Committee in Chicago, intervened on Lee's and Smith's behalf, charging the company with "postponment [sic], deception and subterfuge" for failing to reinstate his members. The IC did not relent, and the case dragged on for years. In 1937, the BLFE renewed its efforts on Lee and Smith's behalf, threatening to take the case to the National Railroad Adjustment Board unless the company finally reinstated the men, with their full seniority. The union failed to win them reinstatement.[25]

Violence never provided a permanent or effective means for white railroaders to further their cause. After World War I they discovered that contractual agreements were a more acceptable and efficient, if sometimes slower, means of reducing black competition. With the coming of the New Deal in 1933, the white brotherhoods quickly found that the transformations in federal labor law could be put to uses somewhat different than what their framers had originally intended. Indeed, revisions in railway labor law in the mid-1930s placed new and powerful weapons in the hands of white workers who were determined to eliminate their black competitors, and these legislative changes continued to exert a largely negative influence on the fortunes of African-American railroaders through the early 1960s.

Sanctioning racial discrimination was not one of the purposes of the 1934 amendments to the Railway Labor Act; ensuring labor stability in the industry was. "It shall be the duty of all carriers, their officers, agents, and employees to exert every reasonable effort to make and maintain agreements," the amendments declared, "in order to avoid any interruption of any carrier growing out of any dispute." The amendments also strengthened considerably the hand of organized white labor. In a critical victory for the white brotherhoods, the amendments outlawed company unions and company domination of or interference with workers' associations. They also created a National Mediation Board (NMB), which was empowered to mediate contract disputes, to oversee secret-ballot elections for union representation if requested by either labor or management, and to certify the election results. (Under the 1926 Act, the Board of Mediation could step in only if both labor and management requested its services.) The amendments also established a National Railroad Adjustment Board (NRAB), composed of equal numbers of management and brotherhood representatives, to resolve grievances and conflicts over differing interpretations of existing contracts. Unquestionably, this piece of New Deal labor legislation was a tremendous victory for many American railroad workers, as it enabled hundreds of thousands in the operating and shop crafts and on Pullman and dining cars to make substantial gains.[26]

But not all railroaders benefited from the 1934 Amended Railway Labor Act. African-American firemen, brakemen, and porter-brakemen found the rules governing union elections devastating. Under the 1934 amendments, a single union elected by a majority of workers in a given craft or class possessed the right to bargain on behalf of all workers in that craft or class. This prevented employers from pitting one union against another, or undermining a larger union by favoring a smaller one. The NMB clarified voting eligibility in 1936, ruling that a craft or class of employees "may not be divided into two or more on the basis of race or color for the purpose of choosing representatives. All those employed in the craft or class, regardless of race, creed or color must be given the opportunity to vote for the representatives of the whole craft or class." In practice, the right to vote meant little to black operating trades workers, for by the mid-1930s, whites constituted a majority of employees in virtually every job category in the operating trades on virtually all roads. In election after election, white workers voted for all-white brotherhoods. Winning a majority of votes, these all-white railroad brotherhoods were then recognized by government and management alike as the legitimate bargaining agents. As long as they were in the minority, black workers found it impossible to vote in their own associations, even if 100 percent of them voted for one.[27]

As a result, black operating craft workers almost universally found themselves without effective representation. While the elected white brotherhoods had the mandate to bargain on behalf of all workers, in practice blacks found that representation by the exclusionary white brotherhoods was worse than no representation at all. The white unions legally negotiated contracts and secret agreements that reduced the percentage of blacks in the labor force, excluded them from key job assignments, disregarded their seniority, and ensured that few if any African Americans would be hired in the future. Also under the law, black railroaders had to accept the contracts negotiated on their behalf by whites, even if those contracts disregarded their hard-earned seniority or deprived them of promotions or even their jobs. As one sympathizer put it in 1942, "Imagine the wolf setting himself up as guardian of the vital interests of Little Red Riding Hood, and you will have an exact analogy with the current employment practices of the Southern roads as dictated by the Brotherhoods."[28]

The newly created National Railroad Adjustment Board, created to resolve grievances and conflicts over different interpretations of existing contracts, proved to be another vehicle for discrimination. Only legally recognized unions could bring grievances before the board. Under its procedures, therefore, an individual black firemen had to present his grievance first to the white union that denied him membership but still legally represented him. That white union could pursue the black worker's grievance or ignore it altogether. The individual worker could not bypass his union and appeal directly to the NRAB. In cases where the grievance was against the white union or against racially discriminatory company practices, the union simply took no action. But should black workers actually succeed in bringing before the board a grievance against the white unions, they could expect no sympathy, for the NRAB, much to black workers' dismay, was composed equally of representatives of management and the white railroad brotherhoods; that is, the men who sat in judgment were the representatives of the very unions against which black workers were complaining. The efforts of black firemen and brakemen to bring their complaints to the board's attention in the late 1930s got them nowhere. The NRAB was, one critic charged in 1950, "the greatest single stumbling block in the fight for equality in the railroad industry."[29]

The New Deal revolution in labor legislation, then, not only offered black operating craft workers no benefits, but it provided whites with powerful weapons against them. Willard Townsend, the leader of the national red caps' union and the highest ranking African-American official in the CIO, identified railroad labor law as a chief reason for black firemen's plight in the early 1940s: with a powerless Fair Employment Practice Committee on the one hand and the Supreme Court "granting dictatorial powers to the National Mediation board" on the other, "the Negro railroad worker finds himself much in the same position as Dred Scot, the runaway slave, who had entered a free state and was ordered back to slavery by the United States Supreme court." The "maintenance of this brotherhood-management-government axis," Townsend argued in 1944, "converts racial discrimination into a profitable flourishing big business, where craft unionism declares dividends each year to their own compact membership at the expense of the lower paid unskilled Negro and other race minorities." "The Negro railroad worker today," he concluded, "actually becomes an industrial fugitive in an industry of opportunity."[30] If the railroad had once provided a source of employment in its yards and on its trains for tens of thousands of black southerners, by the Great Depression the industry offered work to only a small and shrinking number. In what had been an industry of opportunity that had become an industry of decline, black workers struggled to retain the few positions they still held.

* * *

The independent associations of southern black firemen, brakemen, and yard workers did what they could to maintain their small membership and survive in an overwhelmingly hostile environment. In some ways, they continued to resemble fraternal orders as much as trade unions, offering life insurance to members, infusing their meetings with religious music, prayer, and biblical readings, and engaging in secret rituals. The Texas- and Louisiana-based Colored Trainmen of America (CTA), the only independent association for which extensive archival records survive, is a case in point. Prospective members of the CTA were escorted through an elaborate initiation designed to transform a "stranger" into a member. Prior to admission to the lodge meeting, the candidate's head was hooded and he divested himself of all "medals and jewels." The rites required that he disavow any benefits of membership for himself, instead stating that he sought them for his "children and the coming generation" alone. Once vouched for by a "worthy brother" of the lodge, the candidate was brought to an altar, where he knelt and swore the obligation of the CTA on the Bible. Once unhooded, he further swore to keep the order's secrets, to do nothing to bring disgrace upon the CTA, and to do everything in his power to assist a traveling brother of the order. Upon completion of the oath, the order's president announced that the stranger had "disappeared from our midst and substituted a brother in his place."[31]

Possessing no legally enforceable bargaining rights, the CTA nonetheless functioned as an advocate of black railroaders' interests on the Gulf Coast line, the one railroad on which its members worked, politely calling to management's attention its members' particular grievances or pleading for special consideration on their behalf. From World War I through the 1940s, CTA officers routinely asked company officials to reinstate discharged workers, and they represented blacks before formal disciplinary or investigative hearings. Association leaders pleaded with managers, offering facts and appeals to managers' paternalism. The CTA's chairman of brakemen in Kingsville, Texas, for instance, implored the company's superintendent to reinstate a number of discharged black men in a time of labor shortage. These "men are good men" and they "have been well punished" for their acts, he argued, "beleaving [sic] that they have a good record with the company and will be of great benifite [sic] to the company and the men to allow them to return back to work." The entreaty was successful: the company gave the discharged men a second chance by reinstating them for a six-month probationary period. "I will be the sole judge of your fitness," Assistant Superintendent T. P. Mock informed brakeman Jordan Jefferson. If "your services are not satisfactory to me, I will remove you from the service without the formality of an investigation." Given its lack of power vis-à-vis the railroad, the CTA's appeal among black workers must have rested on its ability to intervene successfully on behalf of its members.[32]

The Gulf Coast line, for its part, used the CTA as a means of communicating with its black employees, urging the association to foster acceptable behavior by its members.[33] Resolving a conflict between a white conductor and a black brakeman, for example, became the occasion for a company superintendent to solicit the broader assistance of the CTA local chairman in Kingsville. In October 1937, conductor Nosler apparently struck brakeman Willie Greene with a lantern when Green directed language at his boss "too bad to put into writing." "Where you can get in some mighty good work among the brakemen," a manager informed the CTA chairman, "is to prevail on them to stop directing vile language at their conductors, take whatever comes up and if they feel that they are being abused, there is a way out of it and we want them to pursue the right way"—that is, by informing their superior officers in the railroad office of the abuse. The incident reveals that even within the strict occupational and racial hierarchies that always placed whites in positions of superiority over blacks on the trains, African-American railroaders frequently refused to play the part of docile subordinates assigned to them, verbally and, in other cases, even physically lashing out against their abusers. It also suggests that to ensure the smooth functioning of the labor system, rail managers had to rely on more than the stick. Securing black workers' consent and socializing them to follow rules that required them to suffer abuse silently forced managers to enlist the aid of the black workers' leaders. If the CTA depended heavily on the fairness of company officials, or at least their willingness to listen to blacks' requests, those same company officials depended, albeit to a much lesser extent, on the CTA's ability to inculcate proper behavior among its men.[34]

A lack of legal standing, an inability to invoke the services of government railway labor bodies, the hostile encroachment of the white brotherhoods, and extreme dependence on their employers promoted a conservative, conciliatory, and sometimes accomodationist attitude on the part of the independent black unions well into the 1930s. "We are being warned daily by the press, Negro and White, of the Negro Worker's precarious condition," observed J. A. Brown, Grand Secretary of the ACRT at its 1929 convention in Knoxville. "We must awaken, marshal all our forces and fight for a chance to survive." Brown's program for tackling railroaders' problems consisted of devising some means of "establishing closer contact with those who hire," ascertaining "what R.R. require and deliver the goods," offering strict performance of duty ("Be on the job at all times and do our bit") and, finally, selecting "wide awake intelligent leaders."[35] Such a program strongly echoed Booker T. Washington's philosophy of promoting bootstrap economic advancement of the race through demonstrating its indispensability and loyalty to the nation's captains of industry. Even as they repeatedly attempted to call discriminatory practices to their companies' attention and to convince federal agencies to intervene on their behalf, the black independents during the 1920s and early 1930s pursued a largely cautious path that involved appeals, not challenges, to the companies that employed them.

Their already precarious position, coupled with job losses during the early years of the Great Depression, prompted some southern black railroaders to adopt an even more submissive, accomodationist stance. One group of Shreveport, Louisiana, firemen, members of NFRW Local no. 36, appealed plaintively to the Y&MV railroad, an IC subsidiary. "We . . . humbly and submissively appeal to you in behalf of our jobs," they wrote in 1931. Members of the group were being displaced, "in spite of the fact that we have always been loyal in the discharge of our duty, and have always been content with our wages." In asking for the company's assistance, the Shreveport firemen insisted that they had "never been implicated [in] nor caused a 'strike'; nor do we intend to. We have always believed that the company would allow us a sufficient salary to take care of our families and prepair [sic] for our older days." Finally, these firemen stressed that they were not challenging the industry's broader divisions of labor based on race: they did not ask "nor expect to be ranked or classed as any other group" than as firemen, "but we simply ask that such steps be taken as will enable you to take care of our jobs for us." Like so many other appeals, this entreaty, couched in terms company managers could hardly construe as threatening in any way, was ignored. The percentage of black firemen on the Y&MV continued to decline, and the shooting war against black firemen that erupted within two years provoked only a slow and initially ineffective response on the part of company managers.[36]

The experiences of black operating trades workers during the Great Depression gradually caused them to question their conciliatory approach. While they never disappeared completely, appeals to managers' goodwill and sense of fair play lost ground to a more confrontational stance. A decade and a half of polite but futile protests had demonstrated—at least to some—that black railroaders simply could not count on railroad managers to respect their seniority or even their jobs. By the mid-1930s, Thomas Redd, a Louisville-based brakeman on the Illinois Central, had become a chief architect of the new, more aggressive approach. The roots of Redd's activist vision extended back to the World War I era, and he too initially framed his appeals according to the dominant framework of conservative reliance on managerial benevolence. But Redd's growing frustration with his employers' indifference to black railroaders' fate contributed to the dramatic evolution of the independent associations' outlooks and strategies.

Born shortly after the Civil War, Thomas Redd entered the service of the

IC's Louisville district in 1895. Since the World War I years, Redd brought to the attention of his employer not only his personal grievances but also those of his fellow black workers. Over the years, he earned a reputation, in the eyes of company officials, as a "smart negro," a "persistent letter writer" and complainer, and a troublemaker whose never-ending stream of letters and protests were "ill advised" and had produced a "great deal of ill feeling" toward Redd and his fellow black workers. He never got very far with his protests. Yet company officials' repeated efforts at "straightening him out" proved unsuccessful, for Redd remained committed to seeing that "the colored men got their rights."[37]

Redd did not protest alone, for he had joined the Louisville chapter of the Association of Colored Railway Trainmen and Locomotive Firemen, which had been founded in 1912. In 1920, he was elected chairman of the Louisville general grievance committee, rising to the position of president of the Louisville chapter in the late 1920s. But IC managers never recognized the legitimacy of Redd's group, agreeing only to deal with Redd as an "individual," never as a representative of Local 10 of the ACRT. Indeed, the IC managers expressly refused to meet with committees of black workers on the grounds that the company recognized only the white railroad brotherhoods.[38]

As a local leader of black railroaders, Redd pursued an aggressive and unsuccessful campaign for black rights during the 1920s and early 1930s. For over a decade he directed a steady stream of queries, requests, and petitions to IC managers on behalf of individuals and groups of black workers about promotion possibilities, the provision of washroom and toilet facilities for black workers, blacks' access to particular seniority districts, the discriminatory application of seniority rules, and rates of pay. In 1924, a time when other leaders of black independent associations had reluctantly accepted a racial division of labor in train and yard service, Redd denounced as unfair the application of the seniority rule that permitted senior white trainmen to displace junior black trainmen on the front end of a train while forbidding senior black trainmen to displace junior white trainmen on the rear end. The rule simply "serves to pacify the whims and wishes of a selfish and narrow minded organization of white employees." In private, IC managers sometimes acknowledged the validity of Redd's charges; in 1922, the IC general superintendent offered his frank assessment that black train and engine men did indeed suffer discrimination that would result in their "gradual elimination." But never in public did managers deviate from the line that discrimination did not exist and that all the rules were applied fairly and reasonably.[39]

The pursuit of black railroaders' rights by the "self-appointed" leader of black Kentucky division trainmen did not automatically lead to the advocacy of full equality or to a direct challenge to the company. At least three times—in 1921, in 1924, and again in 1932—Redd proposed the re-establishment of wage differentials between blacks and whites, presumably as a means of making black employment more attractive to the company and to guaranteeing a set number of positions for blacks, just as ACRT president John Henry Eiland had proposed in 1920. The reduction in black employment led Redd to reconsider his opposition to the racial division of labor as well. The BRT's "negro elimination program" and the existing seniority rule, with its "freeze-out and eliminating effects," suggested to Redd that blacks' best occupational hopes lay in a return to wartime and prewar customs. In a 1928 petition to the IC, Redd and his fellow Louisville workers requested a "restoration of the former agreement, 100 percent of all head end and swing jobs in the freight service on the entire Kentucky Division, which is ours by right, justice and inheritance." With whites assigned to one set of jobs and blacks to another, the "white trainmen have no fear of invasion from the colored trainmen and the colored trainmen should not be made to fear invasion from the white trainmen."[40]

Redd also pleaded with company officials on the basis of long-standing and "boundless" black "loyalty" to the Illinois Central. When white workers had demonstrated their antagonism to the company during the labor troubles of 1894, blacks had remained the "most faithful servants in the service"; in the systemwide strike of 1911 they "responded cheerfully to the company's call for loyal employees"; and during the 1922 national shop yardmen's strike, their "loyality [sic] and faithfulness toward the Company cannot be questioned." By retaining their efficient and dedicated black workforce, the IC had a "safeguard against future trouble" by strike-prone whites. By hiring only whites, some IC managers were serving the "insiduous [sic] purpose" of the Brotherhood of Railroad Trainmen by "enlarging their membership and strengthening their ranks, thereby enabling them to come back at us with greater force, this organization for many years past have been endeavoring to eliminate all colored men from train and yard service." When the BRT had accomplished this task, "God help the railroads."[41]

A decade and a half of requests, petitions, complaints, and protest had gotten Thomas Redd and his allies virtually nowhere. If anything, circumstances had deteriorated since the end of the war. Redd and his fellow black firemen and brakemen confronted higher unemployment during the economic depression of the 1930s, a new round of white violence, and intensified efforts by white workers to squeeze them through the manipulation of contract provisions. Not only did their legal representatives, the white brotherhoods, turn a cold shoulder to their requests for redress, but company officials refused to play the part of benevolent paternalists that at least some black railroaders had assigned them. On its own, Redd likely reasoned, the ACRT was simply too weak to effect change. It was in this context that Redd sought new allies, launching a movement that would link up his beleaguered associates with black railroaders across the nation in the hopes that in numbers and unity would come at least some strength. The result was the formation of the International Association of Railway Employees.

Acting on the basis of his correspondence with Redd, ACRT attorney Nelson Willis approached Claude Barnett, head of the Associated Negro Press in Chicago, for assistance in early 1934. "The new federation . . . actually had its impetus, if not its inception, in our office," Barnett recalled. Willis had "nothing more than the germ of an idea," but Barnett was in a strong position to help. For several years he had employed former RMIBIA president Robert L. Mays, who Barnett admitted had been "down on his luck." But Barnett believed that Mays knew "more about organizing railway men and people of that strata than anyone else in the country," and he introduced Mays to Willis. The result was a publicity campaign conducted by Mays on behalf of Redd's proposed federation.[42]

Redd's fiery call to arms reflected his years of frustration and represented an abandonment of appeals to managers' paternalism on the basis of black loyalty. "The Negro Train and Yard Service Employees throughout the entire South are rapidly losing their jobs and white men are taking their places," he asserted. "This transition has gone on so rapidly during the last few years, that if it keeps up at the present pace, it will only be a matter of a very short time, when there will not be a single colored train or yardman working on any of our American railroads." Black workers had resisted the decline, but to no avail. ACRT Louisville Lodge no. 10, as well as a few other groups, had tried "to do something really worthwhile . . . by fighting the jim crow seniority and other unfair methods of the treatment." But, Redd concluded, "none of us have gotten very far with our efforts." Their failure had a simple cause: "we have been fighting as an individual unit, instead of an organization of units." Redd called on the numerous local and regional associations of black service, yard, and operating workers to form a single national body and invited them to send delegates to Chicago for a conference in September 1934. All black railroad employees regardless of craft "must get together, organize and fight our battles as one. We must do this immediately, and if not done the death of our railroad life is just around the corner."[43]

The International Association of Railway Employees (IARE) was thus born in the fall of 1934. The September gathering brought together dozens of delegates from numerous organizations in the South, East, and Midwest, who used the occasion to lay out their stories of abuse and discrimination in a pubic forum. The agenda for discussion consisted of a long list of black grievances: the lack of "proper representation at contract meetings; . . . discriminatory contracts . . . ; misapplications of such contracts to the detriment of Negro workers; the gradual and in some cases drastic reduction from the service of Negro rail workers"; the assassinations of black firemen and brakemen and the need for legal means to prevent further killings; delegates also called for "congressional protest against the use of Filipinos to displace Negro Pullman and dining car employes." Organizers made clear that they would "boost no particular organization or its program" and promised to impinge on no group's autonomy. Instead, it sought to consolidate all groups into a single body of "protest and action" by appealing to the broadest possible constituency around the goal of organizing all railway labor groups "of the Race behind the fight for justice" on behalf of those affected by "prejudicial contracts." No formal organization emerged from the "Get Together" gathering, for the Urban League representative, John Clark, effectively forestalled Robert Mays's efforts by arguing that delegates possessed no authority to so organize. When the delegates met again in Washington, D.C., in early November, however, they did possess such authority, and they formed the IARE as an umbrella organization dedicated to protesting discriminatory contracts, white terrorism, and seniority inequality. With Redd as president and Mays as secretary, the IARE was composed of twenty-eight member organizations from at least sixteen states, and claimed to represent 15,000 black railroaders.[44]

If the fall 1934 conferences repudiated a strategy of appeals to company benevolence and offers of racial wage differentials, they also represented something of a return to the strategies of the World War I–era Railway Men's International Benevolent Industrial Association (RMIBIA). From the start, Robert Mays played a prominent role in the IARE's formation. Not only did he handle the group's publicity through his position with the Associated Negro Press (featuring himself prominently in his write-ups); he also served as the new organization's secretary. But Mays's tenure with the IARE proved to be brief. After positioning himself so centrally, he soon found himself expelled from the new organization. "He is absolutely undependable," his employer, Claude Barnett, privately confessed, and Mays's fellow officers charged him with failing to "report money properly," among other unspecified charges. At some point in 1935, the association ousted Mays, replacing him with Leyton Weston, an official of the dining car workers' local in St. Louis.[45]

With or without Mays, the IARE bore some resemblance to its predecessor, the RMIBIA. Although little of the burning, quasi-nationalist rhetoric of the older association infused the new body, it did share the RMIBIA's fundamental orientation of relying on federal officials and agencies for its success.

In some ways, the black independents substituted a reliance on the federal government for their earlier reliance on their employers. Present at the September and November 1934 meetings was Labor Department official Lawrence Oxley, who, as chief of the Division of Negro Labor, was to play his customary role of representing black workers' views to the Secretary of Labor. The outcome of the September conference was an understanding that the black railroaders' delegates would win an audience with Joseph P. Eastman, federal coordinator of railroads, and members of the National Mediation Board in Washington. That meeting took place in November when the white government officials courteously listened to a small IARE delegation lay out their tales of white terrorism and discriminatory treatment.[46]

Courteous treatment was one thing, results another. The November meeting was a onetime event that led to nothing. When some 1,500 white railroad labor officials and general chairmen of the twenty-one standard railway organizations met in Chicago in January 1935 to hear Eastman address proposed transportation legislation, no IARE delegates were invited to attend. In order to get into the assembly, Robert Mays and Nelson Willis had to crash the gate.[47]

Like the RMIBIA, the IARE initially saw few options beyond a legalistic appeal to federal agencies. Unlike the RMIBIA, however, it met with no favorable response from established labor regulatory bodies. In March 1935, attorney Nelson Willis and his co-counsel, Ben L. Gaskins of Washington, D.C., filed a complaint with the NMB, formally requesting that the board take jurisdiction of cases brought by black workers and "not shut the door of opportunity to work in their faces on the grounds of a flimsy technicality." The NMB quickly put an end to any illusion that it would take up black railroaders' cause. Black complainants should first raise their concerns with the carriers that employed them; if that failed, they could file a request for the services of either the NMB or the NRAB.[48] Black railroaders did just that two months later, when Redd's ACRT Lodge no. 10 petitioned the NRAB to take jurisdiction in a dispute with the IC and the BRT. It would not. The IARE quickly learned that neither federal agency was inclined to ignore its own procedures, which required it to deal only with legally recognized labor organizations. In all cases involving black operating trades workers, this meant the white brotherhoods and not the black independent associations.

How, then, were black railroaders to compel the NMB or the NRAB to take jurisdiction of their complaints? One approach was to seek changes in the law itself. In late December 1934, the IARE announced two legislative goals: the passage of a law by Congress aimed at making the killing of black railroaders a federal, as opposed to a state, offense—in essence, a kind of antilynching law adapted to their industry—and an amendment to the Railway Labor Act making discriminatory contracts adopted by the white majority illegal.[49] Neither proposal gained any congressional support, and the IARE's legislative program died quickly. By 1936, the association appealed publicly to President Franklin Roosevelt, imploring him to help them in their struggle to save their jobs. The "very boards set up by the government" to handle railroad labor disputes such as the ones black workers were involved in were the issue, for they denied black workers the right to officially protest. Again, the IARE received no response.[50]

Unable to change the law that barred their representation before federal labor agencies, the IARE turned to the courts, adopting a strategy of litigation that would dominate its agenda for the next several decades. Redd's base, Louisville ACRT Lodge no. 10, set the initial case in motion even before the IARE's formation. For Lodge no. 10, the specific issue was a reinterpretation of existing contractual provisions that deprived black trainmen of their positions; the larger issue was the hostility of white unionists and managers toward blacks and the role of the law in upholding discrimination. In June 1933, Redd accused the Brotherhood of Railroad Trainmen (BRT) and the IC management of not "living up to" contract provisions that stipulated equal treatment of black and white employees and the maintenance of a single seniority line. The white brotherhood officials, who themselves had engineered and benefited from the reinterpretation of the rule Redd complained of, predictably denied Redd's request. Claiming "no violations" of any rules, General Chairman T. S. Jackson informed Redd, "You are evidently dumb or to say the least, very persistent." Redd's appeals to the company over the course of the next year were similarly to no avail.[51]

In June 1935, the ACRT requested that the National Railroad Adjustment Board hear its complaint. The board flatly denied any jurisdiction on the grounds that the white brotherhood, as the duly elected representative of the majority of the class or craft, was the only body that had the right to petition the board.[52] In 1936, the ACRT filed suit in federal court, seeking to compel the NRAB to take jurisdiction, arguing that portions of the Railway Labor Act were unconstitutional. The sections of the act that granted the BRT, a racially discriminatory union, exclusive rights of representation had the effect of denying black trainmen their "liberty and property rights without due process of law" and deprived them of the law's equal protection.[53] In early 1937, the U.S. Justice Department filed a motion to dismiss the case on behalf of the NRAB; in February, the court concurred with the NRAB's attorney that the board lacked jurisdiction and dismissed the challengers' petition. The independent black association's first legal challenge had utterly failed.[54]

This setback did not discourage Redd or other railroad activists in independent black associations from investing their hopes in the legal process. From however, was the activists' faith (expressed in 1934 and 1935) in the benevolence of government officials, who, it had been assumed, on hearing the story of black suffering and rampant discrimination, would intervene on the side of aggrieved black workers. The departure of Robert Mays from the scene in 1935 removed the chief proponent of the RMIBIA strategy of reliance on government and political officials; the indifferent response of the NMB and the NRAB to their complaints convinced the leaders of the IARE, the ACRT, and other groups that such a strategy simply would not work. Railroad labor law, the black independents reasoned, was itself the key institutional roadblock to black participation in the system of labor representation; that same law, they believed, unconstitutionally deprived them of their rights. Redd and his supporters had followed the rules of the game to the letter and had gotten literally nowhere; the rules of the game had to be changed.

"The time has come for concerted action on our part," Redd declared in 1938. That "concerted action" would not assume the form of labor militancy at the point of production. Rather, he argued, the "only effective course for us to pursue is by way of the courthouse." But pursuing such a strategy was not cheap. To accomplish their desired ends, Redd and his fellow black unionists launched a legal defense fund to defray the costs of litigation. They also turned to the one national civil rights organization that specialized in the courthouse route, the NAACP. While the NAACP had assisted the black independents twice before—during the wave of violence in 1920–21 and again in 1931–34—the NAACP now saw the black independents' overtures as an important opportunity to widen its social base. As Roy Wilkins reported, "I vote for our taking an interest in this thing. If we can turn one of these tricks, the laboring groups over the country will be for us 100%. Now they think we are all right, but not able to help them much." The first task for the NAACP was to consult with IARE representatives in an effort to understand the multiple "complicated and intricate methods of easing the brother off the railroads." After all, "each occupation has its own problems and very often the problems differ even in the same occupation on different roads." Then the NAACP would have to determine what course of action might have a chance of success. "It will be a big job and will involve declaring war on the railway brotherhoods," Wilkins observed to Thurgood Marshall, the association's young attorney, but it "will be a tremendously popular campaign." The NAACP dispatched Marshall to the IARE's annual convention in Atlanta in May 1939, where he promised his organization's support, provided that the black railroaders helped to finance the legal struggle. The IARE unanimously accepted the offer.[55]

As it turned out, the NAACP did not spearhead the campaign against trade union and employment discrimination in the railroad industry. But the closer contacts between the independent associations and the nation's leading civil rights organization did bear fruit in the late 1930s and 1940s. Returning to private practice in 1938, the NAACP's chief lawyer, Charles Hamilton Houston, developed a keen interest in the plight of southern black firemen and brakemen, and the ACRT and the IARE (and later the CTA) decided to retain Houston and his partner, Joseph Waddy, to represent them in court and in negotiations with railroad management. Ultimately, as Thomas Redd predicted, it would be the courts, not collective bargaining, that would outlaw discriminatory contract provisions. Despite years of legal setbacks, Houston and Waddy would eventually make civil rights and labor law history on behalf of their clients.

Independent black unionism was a pragmatic response to white union exclusion. Even when offered the option of affiliation with national bodies associated with the AFL or the CIO, including all-black unions like the BSCP, many black railroaders preferred their own associations and valued their institutional independence. "No group of colored workers who are in the majority . . . should join a white labor organization," insisted George Keys, the general chairman of the CTA's Texas and New Orleans Train Porters, in the late 1930s. Those unions had "caused the loss of more jobs for Negroes than any other factor in the south." A. Philip Randolph, Milton P. Webster, and others were simply wrong in telling blacks to join white organizations "at every chance they had." The fact that neither Randolph nor Webster had asked black railroaders to join white organizations—they invited them to affiliate only with the BSCP, *not* with the AFL—mattered little. Damon McCrary, chairman of the DeQuincy, Louisiana, CTA lodge, put the matter even more bluntly. It "would be unsafe for us to affilate [*sic*] with any thing that the white race have any thing to do with," he insisted.[56]

If southern black railroaders had practical reasons for avoiding entanglements with the AFL and the CIO, they also defended their independent associations forcefully on ideological grounds. Perhaps the strongest advocate of independent black unionism in the 1930s and 1940s was C. W. Rice, publisher of the Houston-based weekly *Negro Labor News*, president of the Texas Negro Business and Labor Men's Association, and special organizer for the National Federation of Railway Workers. Born in 1897 in Haywood County, Tennessee, Rice completed three years of high school at Lane College in Jackson, Tennessee, before moving to Corsicana, Texas, in 1914, where his aunt lived. While studying at Samuel Houston College in Austin in 1916, he supported himself by working as a domestic for local whites, just as he had done in high school. Rice's role model and source of philosophical inspiration was Booker T. Washington. As a boy in Tennessee, Rice read the two books that constituted his family's library—the Bible and Washington's *Up from Slavery*. The Wizard of Tuskegee's autobiography "filled me with an idea of the dignity of labor and influenced tremendously my selection of a career," he recalled in a 1939 interview. His affinity for Washington's outlook represented a conscious choice, for numerous alternatives were in the air in the wartime South. Rice was not among those seeking to "convert the war to make the world safe for democracy into a fight for citizenship at home."[57] To the contrary, he staunchly advocated black support for the war and, in the postwar era, launched a career based on firm Washingtonian principles of allying with white businessmen to promote black advancement.

The organization that Rice would ride to prominence was the Texas Negro Business and Working Man's Association (TNBWMA), initially called the Beaumont Negro Business League. Rice was one of the organization's founders in 1921 and served as its business manager before becoming its vice-president and general manager in 1925 (the year it incorporated) and eventually its president. The TNBWMA's goals were twofold: "to promote the industrial, commercial, financial and agricultural development of the Negro race" on the one hand and "to cooperate with recognized educational agencies and commercial bodies" such as boards of trade and chambers of commerce "with the idea in view of helping Negroes in the rural communities and cities of Texas" on the other.[58]

By the mid-1930s, Rice was openly and loudly preaching against white trade unions. In the pages of his newspaper, the *Negro Labor News,* which he began publishing in 1931, Rice filled column after column, issue after issue, with outspoken condemnation of the national labor movement and its local affiliates. He repeatedly counseled his readers in the sharpest of terms to reject any overtures from either the AFL or the CIO, for both were harmful to black interests. The AFL's long racist record spoke for itself. As for the CIO, despite its overtures to African Americans, its program "calling for equality for white and colored workers" was simply "not practical in the South and is calculated to do the Negro race more harm than good." And wherever organized white labor, regardless of federation affiliation, got the upper hand, blacks lost jobs.[59]

But if white labor organizers were bad, white labor organizers who were communists were even worse. A staunch anticommunist, Rice did not hesitate to exploit the issue of the communist presence in the CIO, arguing that radicals were simply using the labor movement as their "Trojan horse." The "situation is a grave threat to the Negro race as well as the industries hiring them," Rice asserted in the early 1940s. "I am afraid that unless the American people wake up . . . when this world war is over . . . some radical labor organization will lead a revolt that will place this nation definitely under Communist or some other foreign ism domination."[60]

Eschewing organized labor, Rice offered black workers three pieces of advice. First, he strongly cautioned against black participation in strikes and against affiliation with either CIO or AFL locals in the numerous union organizing drives and representation elections in Houston and Port Arthur. Second, in the spirit of the late Wizard of Tuskegee, he insisted that black workers aim for "getting and holding more jobs." If the race was to "continue to make progress, the masses must be employed." That, however, was something that organized white labor could not or would not accomplish. Nowhere had blacks "gained new employment or regained lost jobs by the union movement."[61] Third, Rice offered black workers an alternative both to membership in the AFL or CIO and to no organization at all. From at least the mid-1930s, he aggressively promoted an independent black unionism that stood outside of, and in opposition to, the established white trade union movement. Independent black unions ostensibly offered numerous advantages over their white or integrated counterparts. Without whites dominating their organizations, black associations would foster black leadership, give black members complete control over their own institutions, and allow blacks to "learn the technique of organization" and become "organization conscious through their own efforts." To some extent, this is precisely how many members of all-black locals of longshoremen viewed the biracial unionism that placed them in one body and whites in another. But Rice's vision of the relationship of black independent unions to management differed sharply from that of longshoremen's locals on the waterfronts of the Gulf coast. In contrast to what he saw as the antibusiness orientation of AFL and CIO unions, the independents would work in concert with employers, fostering cooperation and goodwill, not class conflict, between labor and capital. In practice, Rice threw his weight behind company and other "independent" unions as bulwarks against the AFL and the CIO. His own TNBWMA, ostensibly an independent union, was but a "one man organization," in the opinion of a young student sympathetic to Rice, with its "members little more than pawns in the great labor game played by Mr. Rice with the employers."[62]

Rice had more than his share of critics within Houston's African-American community. His ideological enemies included local NAACP officers and the editors of the rival *Informer and Texas Freeman*, who saw Rice as little more than an apologist for company unions and a front for corporate interests. Indeed, by the late 1920s, contributions from whites—employers interested in the "stabilization of Negro employment"—covered between 60 and 75 percent of the TNBWMA's operating expenses; Rice's semiannual Domestic and Industrial Workers Institutes were wholly funded by a group of about sixty local employers; and a large part of the funding for his *Negro Labor News* came from advertisements, many of which came from white employers.[63]

For all of the fury he directed at discriminatory union practices, Rice remained not only silent about employers' discriminatory practices, but upbeat in his assertions of blacks' economic security and prospects for social mobility in the South. "Probably in no other country can a worker start at the bottom of an industry and rise, step by step, through the merit system, to the head of that same industry," he believed. His local critics were unimpressed. The "arguments in favor of trusting capital do not seem natural in the columns of a paper presumably dedicated to the advancement of the Negro worker of the south," editorialized the *Informer* in 1937. "Everybody knows that Negro workers are restricted to unskilled labor and are paid the lowest possible wages by southern employers." Although Rice undoubtedly would have taken exception to the charge that he was a member of a group of "black, rascally leaders" and "shallow-brained Uncle Toms" for his opposition to the AFL and the CIO, Rice wore the label of apologist for company unions proudly, insisting that such bodies were more effective for African Americans than their AFL or CIO counterparts.[64]

His fierce opposition to organized white labor, staunch advocacy of independent black unions, and editorship of a fiery weekly newspaper recommended Rice as a logical and valuable ally to one group of African-American workers: car coach cleaners employed by the Texas and Pacific railroad (T&P). Between 1935 and 1937, Houston's black coach cleaners—who composed roughly 90 percent of that job category—were represented by the independent National Federation of Railway Workers (NFRW). Founded twenty years earlier, the NFRW enrolled most of its members in Texas, Missouri, and Louisiana. By 1937, it counted at least several hundred train porters, brakemen, mechanics, coach cleaners, and track laborers in its ranks. But its hold on Houston's car coach cleaners came under challenge by the AFL's Brotherhood of Railway Carmen (BRC), which claimed jurisdiction over them, even though it barred blacks from participating in union governance. Following a hearing, the National Mediation Board called an immediate election. But the board's mediator, Robert F. Cole, rejected Rice as an election observer, although he was the NFRW's designee, appointing instead F. W. Washington, general chair of the coach cleaners' division of the NFRW. Black workers should "go along with white organizations until they could learn more about the technique of the organized labor movement," Rice reported Cole as telling him. When the ballots were counted, the Carmen emerged victorious by a seven-vote margin; the NMB certified the BRC as the legal bargaining agent in December 1937.[65]

Rice and the NFRW cried foul. But their demands for a new hearing and another certification election were ignored by the NMB. The black union then retained the black Washington, D.C., law firm of Cobb, Howard, and Hayes, secured a temporary injunction in a Washington district court blocking the certification of the BRC, and set about collecting evidence of voting irregularity. More important than biased officials and the likelihood of voting irregularities, however, was the issue of the law's sanctioning of discriminatory unionism. Rice and the NFRW asked the same question posed by the International Brotherhood of Red Caps: Could the National Mediation Board certify a union as a legal bargaining agent for all workers in a craft or class when that union discriminated against members or barred them from membership altogether because of race? Rice believed not, and brought suit against the NMB in order to test the constitutionality of the Railway Labor Act.[66]

The courts, much to Rice's dismay, proved no more receptive to the NFRW than they had been to the ACRT, the IARE, and the red caps, and ultimately rejected his arguments. A Washington, D.C., appeals court upheld the NMB's ruling in 1940, and the U.S. Supreme Court declined to review the decision the following year. The appellate court's decision struck a sharp blow at Rice's strategy: to "hold that colored employees could be represented only by colored persons for bargaining purposes," it read, "would be to introduce into the administration of the act the very discrimination which the federation seeks to avoid." White discrimination against blacks was legitimate, but black demands for black representation were not. Further, the court had concluded that the "Brotherhood, a private association, acting on its own initiative and expressing its own will, may limit the rights of its colored members without thereby offending the guarantees of the Constitution."[67]

The legal battle not only pitted the BRC against the NFRW but revealed divisions within Houston's African-American community between advocates and opponents of independent unionism. "All fair-minded people will be glad to have any injustices done to the Coach Cleaners union corrected," the *Informer* admitted. "But the big query behind the surface issues is: Even if injustices are found and the case is remitted for another hearing, will the colored union be able to muster a majority?"[68] The T&P coach cleaners never got the opportunity to resolve that question, but other groups of black Texas railroaders did. The results were inconclusive. In a 1938 union election, Southern Pacific shopmen rejected CIO overtures, retaining their interracial Association of Shop Craft Employees, which critics called a company union and supporters called an independent one. Negative memories of the 1922 shop craft strike apparently remained alive among some of the company's 300 black railroaders. "I have talked with scores of employees," Rice reported, "and they bitterly denounced the AFL recalling the dirty deal that workers received in the shops" under the AFL before the 1922 strike. The Association won 608 votes to the BRC's 597. BRC supporters claimed that company intimidation and a fear of reprisals kept blacks from joining. But while the BRC had promised to treat blacks fairly and respect their seniority, the white union had failed to establish any distinct body for potential black members, who could not participate in the BRC's regular affairs.[69]

To black participants and observers, however, the matter of which union to support was not clear-cut. The following year, South Pacific coach cleaners from New Orleans to El Paso voted to be represented by the BRC. Rice inveighed against the white union, declaring that every black worker "who has a spark of race pride" should investigate the BRC thoroughly and then reject it. Black workers may have followed the first order, but they ignored the second, for the AFL union won the representation election. Was this a matter of blacks turning their backs on race pride? The African-American labor leaders of the Houston Amalgamated Union Council disagreed, believing that the men had joined a bona fide union. "Let us not accept the false doctrine that is being preached by the self-styled labor leaders" like Rice, the League's publicity committee announced. On the Houston Belt and Terminal Railway, black coach cleaners similarly divided into pro-Rice NFRW and pro-AFL factions. "We do not contend that everything of the A.F. of L. is all roses," explained C. E. January, a member of the Coach Cleaners' Association that invited the BRC to represent them. But "as compared with the so-called independent union sponsored by C. W. Rice . . . we choose rather to bear the afflictions with whatever shortcomings we have found in the A.F. of L. as against a lot of baffling disappointments we have found in our dealings" with Rice.[70]

If Rice and other opponents of the AFL and the CIO could point to countless examples of labor movement discrimination, black supporters of the organized labor movement could themselves invoke numerous positive examples in making their case. During Labor Day celebrations in 1937, shortly before the NFRW lost to the BRC on the T&P, over 1,500 black workers marched in the AFL parade, while several hundred black CIO workers took part in that federation's program. The most prominent and successful of Houston's black AFL unions were the all-black locals of the International Longshoremen's Association (ILA). During the 1930s, ILA members were deeply involved in the city's black community, donating to YMCA, YWCA, NAACP, and Community Chest drives, paying their poll taxes, and providing aid to other black unions; in addition, as affiliates of the Central Dock and Marine Council of the South Atlantic and Gulf Coast and Sabine District of the ILA, they jointly formulated and administered union policy with their white counterparts. Houston's black longshoremen "are the strongest labor organization and one of the most potential groups in this area," the *Informer* concluded. Even Rice had to agree. But biracial unionism and black influence on the waterfront had a long history in the region, and it was unlikely that other groups of black workers could replicate the waterfront workers' experience without considerable difficulty. Ultimately, if investing one's hopes in independent unionism meant settling for less, investing one's hopes in the AFL or the CIO meant taking a gamble, a leap into the unknown that could produce either beneficial or harmful results. Proponents of both approaches would continue to appeal for support from black Texans well into the 1950s.[71]

In 1939–40, Rice carried his crusade against organized white labor into the national arena. His target was federal labor law, which stood as a central pillar upholding union discriminatory and exclusionary practices. As his ultimately unsuccessful lawsuit against the National Mediation Board and the Railway Labor Act wound its way through the courts, he articulated a distinct vision of labor law reform that he believed would go a long way toward solving black workers' problems. At the hearings to amend the National Labor Relations Act, Rice proposed amendments that would penalize discriminatory unions and would allow excluded workers to represent themselves. First, any union that, through ritual, custom, or constitution barred members on account of race, he suggested, should be denied certification as the sole bargaining agent in its craft. Second, evidence of discriminatory behavior by a certified union would be sufficient grounds for voiding its certification. Third, where unions are found discriminating against "otherwise eligible members because of race," those who are discriminated against "shall have the power to form an independent unit" with the right to bargain with employers on behalf of its members. Defending this final principle of "minority representation," Rice insisted that the "colored people are asking under the law, that they be given the same privileges and rights that other people have—no more, no less."[72] In the pages of his weekly newspaper, in his personal involvement in numerous labor conflicts, and in his testimony before Congress, Rice's vision was forceful and unambiguous: there was absolutely no common ground between black workers and the larger labor movement. With the exception of a very few of their locals, the AFL and the CIO were enemies of black America.

C. W. Rice's stance of attacking trade union discrimination from outside the larger labor movement's ranks contrasted sharply with the approach of attacking discrimination from within its ranks pursued by black activists like A. Philip Randolph of the BSCP, Ishmael Flory of the Joint Council of Dining Car Employees, and Willard Townsend of the International Brotherhood of Red Caps. Affiliated black unionists, of course, were hardly blind to the prejudice and racist practices of fellow white trade unionists, but they sought to wage a "vigorous fight" from within to "break down this discrimination in unions." There is "one thing Negroes must understand," the BSCP journal *Black Worker* proclaimed in 1944, "and that is that there is no organization in America composed of white people which does not have some racial discrimination in it, but if the Negro is going to take the position that he should come out of every organization [that] racial discrimination is in he will come out of both the A.F. of L. and the CIO. He will also come out of the Church and the schools of America. He will refuse to go to Congress. In fact, this ridiculous position will lead him to the conclusion where he will be compelled to get out of America and eventually off the earth, for racial discrimination is everywhere." Communist Solon Bell of the Joint Council of Dining Car Employees would have agreed with the anticommunist Randolph: "In the cities and states and in national government itself," Bell told a group of Los Angeles dining car unionists in 1939, "prejudice exists, but we do not move away from these places nor do we shun our responsibility in fighting for our rights. We should, therefore, join labor unions and do likewise from within."[73]

Neither strategy, to be sure, was "pure" on the issue of racial equality. Rice's anti–organized labor and pro-business positions gained him the appreciation of employers, yet his ideological commitments and his dependence on the goodwill of capitalists prompted him to ignore their racist practices. Black leaders in AFL and CIO unions found that membership in interracial labor federations offered African Americans a degree of legitimacy and protection and provided a platform from which to wage attacks on racial inequality. At the same time, such membership also limited the tactics and proposals they could reasonably advocate. If Rice could demand the revocation of union certification on the grounds of discrimination, black AFL or CIO trade unionists and black radicals like John P. Davis of the National Negro Congress could not. Nor could they accept the concept of minority representation, which would allow black workers separate recognition and bargaining rights. Opening the door to minority representation, in Randolph's view, would spell the "death knell of the principle of democracy" in the union movement, "stimulate the growth of Company Unionism and institute widespread chaos and confusion"; it would bring about the "eventual disruption of every unionized trade in the railroad industry," as management would resort to spies and agent provocateurs to create further divisions in labor's ranks. Black workers' only alternative was "self-organization," not for the purpose of amending labor law but to "win entrance into the standard railroad unions." Ultimately, then, if membership in larger, interracial labor federations provided concrete advantages to Randolph's Brotherhood and other affiliated black unions, it also carried a steep price.[74]

Randolph was convinced that it was a price worth paying, for the alternative offered by the independents had proved to be a dead end. In contrast to his own BSCP and the AFL-affiliated dining car workers' union, the southern independents appeared weak and pathetic. There was no question that few independent black unions exercised much influence in labor-management affairs. With virtually nothing to show for their efforts by the late 1930s, the independents appeared to represent desperate men with few allies outside of a small number of black lawyers and, importantly, the NAACP. In Randolph's view, their chapters were "isolated, distinct and unrelated," their organizations "small, weak and helpless," lacking in "both number and money of any consequence." Well meaning but ineffective, they resembled "company unions" that went along with management more than bona fide unions. Randolph, of course, was no objective observer, for he was setting his sights on the operating crafts as fruitful areas for expanding his organizational influence. Still, his assessment was correct. By the end of the Great Depression, the independents had accomplished nothing and struggled to retain what few members they had. In 1942, two of the most important of the independents, the ACRT and the IARE, consisted of a mere 400 and 900 official members, respectively.[75]

At the end of the decade, Randolph tentatively moved to assume at least symbolic leadership of not just Pullman porters but all black railroaders. The National Conference of Negro Railroad Workers, which Randolph and the BSCP convened in Washington, D.C., in 1939, attracted delegates from black unions of red caps, dining car waiters, locomotive firemen, brakemen, and train porters. Primarily a forum for exchanging information and urging cooperation, the gathering also endorsed an extensive wish list, including proposals for a black railroad labor lobby and greater coordination among black unions, and demands for federal health insurance for railroad workers, elimination of the color bar in the white brotherhoods, and the appointment of a black member to the National Mediation Board. Despite the appointment of a continuing committee made up of leaders from the black service unions, little resulted from the conference.[76]

Within a year and a half, Randolph and the BSCP had intensified their efforts in reaching out to southern train porters and firemen. In March 1941, the BSCP formally launched its Provisional Committee to Organize Colored Locomotive Firemen, attracting some fifty delegates, largely from the South Atlantic states, to its inaugural meeting. "The colored locomotive fireman . . . is at a crisis," Randolph declared. If the process of displacement continued, "it will be only a matter of time when there will not be a black face in the Cabin of an engine in America." The BSCP president praised the IARE and attorney Charles Hamilton Houston for their efforts on behalf of black railroader Ed Teague in legally challenging the Gulf, Mobile, and Northern railroad and the BLFE for destroying black firemen's seniority rights. A victory for Teague would be "the most important legal victory for Negro labor in the history of the race." It would have "favorable repercussions" by giving the black railroader "a new sense of importance, value and power" and stimulating "his will to fight for his rights." But such a legal victory would have limits as well, for it could not change the "existing numerical relationship" between black and white firemen, compel railroads to hire blacks, prevent railroads and the white brotherhood from "making secret and collusive contracts," or nullify the power of the BLFE. A victory by Teague would mean little "unless the colored firemen organize into a bona fide labor union, which embraces the majority of the colored firemen." Their power, Randolph concluded, "does not inhere in the law, but in their own self-organization."[77]

To achieve such self-organization, unity was absolutely necessary. But standing in the way of that unity was the existence of multiple organizations, themselves a "source of weakness and an invitation to exploitation by the employer," argued Randolph. What was needed was "one, big, strong, all-embracing organization." "The existing organizations of the colored firemen have served a splendid purpose," Milton Webster disingenuously declared, "but it is no injustice to them to state that they are not adequately gauged and geared to master and grapple with the problems of organization, propaganda and negotiation, to measure up to the challenge that faces them." The veteran BSCP organizers offered the Provisional Committee as an alternative to the independents. A single, unified organization of black firemen under the BSCP's jurisdiction (it would not be affiliated with the AFL in any way), Randolph promised, could bargain with the BLFE over questions of representation and grievances; fight more effectively for black membership in the white union; mobilize public opinion against rail carriers (something the "little organizations" could not do); provide moral and financial support for legal battles; and sponsor legislation against union discrimination. Many of the delegates enthusiastically endorsed Randolph's analysis and agenda. "We have had so many organizations, so many diversified objects, without any program as to how to attain these objectives," a supportive delegate, James Page of Richmond, agreed; "there is little wonder about the confusion." Some delegates were ecstatic: The "Lord has sent us Moses to bring the children to the Promised Land," exclaimed Lloyd Lawson, president of a black independent union of Atlantic Coast Line firemen from Portsmouth, Virginia. Delegates to the conference overwhelmingly elected Randolph as chair of the Provisional Committee, accepted without modification the structure proposed by BSCP organizers, and formally affiliated with the BSCP.[78]

Not every voice sang the praises of Randolph, the BSCP, and the Provisional Committee, however. Three leaders of the independents—ACRT president Samuel H. Clark of Roanoke, Virginia, and IARE leaders F. C. Caldwell and Arthur Lewis of Memphis—attended the conference and engaged in sharp debate with Randolph and Webster. Clark, Caldwell, and Lewis defended their record and rejected the idea of merging their associations with the Provisional Committee. More than organizational jealousies separated these rival bodies, for the leaders of the independents expressed little interest in the Provisional Committee's goal of eventually joining the all-white firemen's brotherhood and instead advocated "minority representation" before federal railroad labor agencies, in which workers excluded from white unions could be legally represented by their own distinct organizations. In contrast, Randolph believed that the committee's ultimate goal was to eliminate all forms of Jim Crow in the firemen's craft, which meant the eventual destruction of the BLFE's ban on black membership and the integration of the union. The Provisional Committee also rejected minority representation as opening the door to the wholesale fragmentation of labor representation and the weakening or even destruction of railroad unions. Rather than accept racial exclusion through the advocacy of "minority representation," Randolph insisted that the Provisional Committee had to become strong enough to bargain with the BLFE, force its integration, and win for blacks equal rights in the union.

Although Randolph had at his disposal several weapons that the independents lacked—namely, a pre-existing, experienced organization with connections to the larger world of political and labor reform—he failed to win a majority of southern firemen to his banner. Loyal to their own associations, suspicious of outside labor leaders, and hostile toward the AFL, black firemen were reluctant to embrace fully the alternative that Randolph offered. During World War II, the independents happily worked with and placed considerable faith in the Fair Employment Practice Committee that Randolph and his March on Washington Movement had helped bring into existence, while Randolph and the Provisional Committee focused much organizational energy on pursuing legal remedies to railroad employment discrimination first pioneered by the independents.

The imperviousness of railroad brotherhoods and managers to any pressure black railroaders could bring to bear demonstrated that only external forces—political and legal—could have any chance of effecting change. By the 1940s and 1950s, even black railroaders in the AFL and the CIO agreed that the tactics and strategies first adopted by the independents were the only effective means to cracking employment discrimination. As early as 1935, Virginia Blanton of black Chicago hotel union Local 444 admitted to an Independent Railway Employees Convention in Louisville, "Neither diplomacy, stratagem nor threat is likely to have any effect . . . on the anti-Negro policy of the four railroad brotherhoods." Against the brotherhoods "there is a weapon of defense which Negro labor has not used enough in the past—legal action."[79] That was precisely the conclusion that the independents had arrived at. Randolph and the Provisional Committee too would ultimately find the argument persuasive; in the end, for all of their differences, the Provisional Committee would follow the same path as the independents it criticized. But both groups would find that legal action alone would chip away only slowly at the armor of the white brotherhoods and their managerial allies.

African Americans have worked on the railroads since the industry's inception in the early nineteenth century. As common laborers in the American South, they dominated construction and maintenance-of-way crews, performing the physically arduous, unpleasant, and poorly paid work of laying and repairing tracks, as in this Civil War photograph. (Courtesy of the Library of Congress, Prints and Photographs Division)

Above: These men, members of the U.S. Military Railroad's Construction Corps, are using levers to loosen rails in northern Virginia during the Civil War. Union forces relied on such men to construct emergency rail lines, repair tracks, and destroy rail lines used by the Confederate Army. (Courtesy of the Library of Congress, Prints and Photographs Division)

Facing page, top: In the decades after the Civil War, southern railroads remained dependent on African Americans for common labor. White section foreman Tom Massey, at right, is featured with his black crew on the Georgia, Florida, and Alabama Railroad, circa 1900. (Courtesy of the Florida State Archives)

Facing page, bottom: Southern train work crews, like these of the Seaboard Air Line in the late nineteenth century, were often composed of both whites and blacks, with blacks always subordinate to whites and whites monopolizing supervisory positions. (Courtesy of the DeGolyer Library, Southern Methodist University)

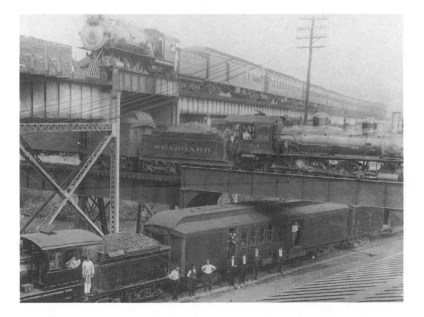

A racial division of labor barred African-American firemen, like this employee of the Central of Georgia railroad in the late nineteenth century, from work outside the South. (Courtesy of the DeGolyer Library, Southern Methodist University)

In the nineteenth and twentieth centuries, engineering was among the most highly skilled and best-paid railroad occupations. The engineers' craft remained all white until the late 1960s and early 1970s. (Courtesy of the Chicago, Burlington & Quincy Railroad Company and the Chicago Historical Society)

While African Americans were barred from most highly skilled mechanics' jobs, they constituted significant portions of the unskilled and semiskilled workforce of many southern roundhouses and repair shops, as in this Georgia repair shop force in the early twentieth century. (Courtesy of the DeGolyer Library, Southern Methodist University)

During the twentieth century, railroad car cleaners across the nation tended to be African Americans. These cleaners labor in Southern Pacific rail yards in Nevada. (Courtesy of the California State Railroad Museum)

During World War I and World War II, black women found employment in railroad freight yards as loaders, car cleaners, engine oilers, and sweepers. In this 1943 photograph, Hortense W. Thompson works as a freight handler in Kansas City, Missouri. (Photograph by Jack Delano; courtesy of the Library of Congress, Prints and Photographs Division)

In most of the country, African Americans dominated the railroads' service sector as dining car cooks and waiters, Pullman porters, and station red caps. Before formal dining car service in the 1860s, they sold food to arriving passengers, as in this stereotyped image from Virginia. (Drawing by J. Wells Champney, in Edward King, *The Great South,* vol. 2; New York: Burt Franklin, 1875)

As the dining car became a standard feature on trains, many railroads relied on accomplished black chefs. As shown in this 1957 photograph, these men often worked in hot and extremely cramped spaces. (Photograph by Philip R. Hastings, M.D.; courtesy of the California State Railroad Museum)

Waiters might take considerable pride in their work, as this promotional photograph for the Union Pacific railroad in the mid-twentieth century implies. But waiters also endured white diners' slights and abuses while working in confined quarters. (Courtesy of the Union Pacific Museum Collection, Image Number SO1967)

Another Black and Tan Problem

"Say, Porter, how come? I've one black shoe and one tan!"

"Well, dat sure am funny, suh! Dat's the second time dat happened dis mawnin'."

—Drawn by Night Agent G. A. Bowler, Chicago Eastern.

Despite his respected status in African-American communities, the Pullman porter was often the butt of white racial humor, as in this cartoon from the Pullman Company's monthly journal. The founding of the Brotherhood of Sleeping Car Porters in 1925 prompted the company to drop such racist cartoons. (*Pullman News,* December 1924; courtesy of the University of Illinois at Urbana-Champaign Library)

By the beginning of the twentieth century, the Pullman porter not only was familiar to a traveling white public but also was an established stereotype in American popular culture. Here he figures prominently in a poster for Primrose and West's minstrel show in 1896. (Courtesy of the Library of Congress, Prints and Photographs Division)

Pullman sleeping cars, portrayed as "hotels on wheels," promised comfort and personal service for their white passengers. Blacks made up the overwhelming majority of Pullman porters, while Pullman conductors remained all white. (*Pullman News,* January 1946; courtesy of the University of Illinois at Urbana-Champaign Library)

In contrast to the image promoted by the Pullman Company's advertisements, portering subjected black men to long working hours with little rest and to condescending and abusive treatment by white passengers. This porter, photographed in January 1943, worked out of Chicago's Union Station. (Photograph by Jack Delano; courtesy of the Library of Congress, Prints and Photographs Division)

The New York division of the BSCP celebrates its eleventh anniversary in 1936. One year later, the black union signed its first contract with the Pullman Company, a major victory for African-American railroaders, who had been striving since the early twentieth century for recognition and respect from their employers. (Photograph by Brown Brothers; courtesy of Brown Brothers and the Library of Congress)

Redcapping, which involved carrying passengers' baggage to and from trains within railroad stations, began in New York in the 1890s. In this drawing, black red caps carry the heavy bags of prosperous white passengers in New York's Grand Central Station. (Drawing by Wallace Morgan, in Julian Street, *Abroad at Home: American Ramblings, Observations, and Adventures of Julian Street;* New York: The Century Co., 1914)

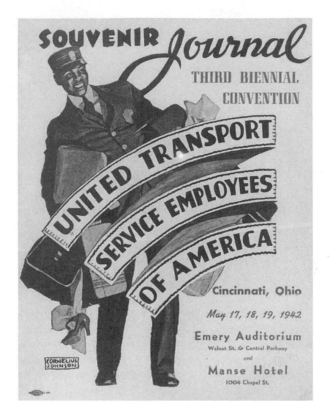

Like Pullman porters and dining car workers, many African-American red caps
unionized in the late 1930s. After winning legal recognition as railroad employees,
they negotiated wage increases and grievance procedures with railroad stations.
(Courtesy of Transportation Communications International Union)

A. Philip Randolph stands (center front) with a group of African-American firemen, circa 1939, at a YMCA in Washington, D.C. Randolph tried aggressively to unify all southern black railroaders into a single organization to protest racial exclusion and discrimination. (Photograph by the Scurlock Studio; Library of Congress, courtesy of the Archives Center, National Museum of American History, Smithsonian Institution)

Despite Randolph's efforts, many southern black firemen and brakemen remained loyal to independent, unaffiliated associations. Black associations like the International Association of Railway Employees, to which this group of Seaboard train porters affiliated, remained small and exercised little power, but they pursued legal challenges to employment and union discrimination in the 1940s and 1950s that eventually bore fruit. (*Quarterly Bulletin of the International Association of Railway Employees,* January–April 1957; courtesy of the Department of Labor Library)

By the early 1950s, cars, buses, and planes captured a growing proportion of travelers' business. The dramatic decrease in passenger service affected all sectors of railroad workers—porters, dining car waiters, and red caps as well as firemen and brakemen. In this photograph, Chester A. Wilkins carries bags in Chicago's Central Station in November 1951. (Courtesy of the Chicago Historical Society)

By the late 1950s and early 1960s, black railroaders like this Carolina Southern switchman stood on the precipice of major legal, economic, and institutional changes, which would allow them to achieve unprecedented occupational mobility and finally join all-white railroad brotherhoods. As the levels of railroad employment declined in the decades following World War II, black railroaders overcame color bars in the American labor market and the labor movement. (Courtesy of the California State Railroad Museum)

5

The Rise of the Red Caps

Red cap Benjamin Ransaw, an employee of New York's Penn Station, was assisting an elderly, ill African-American passenger into a taxi in July 1940 when two white men—"probably Southerners"—approached him from behind. As he was bending over to load the luggage, the men struck him, called him a "damned nigger," and demanded that they, not the ill passenger ahead of them in line, get the cab. While defending the black passenger's right to the cab, Ransaw raised his arms and pushed one of his assailants. What happened next perhaps took Ransaw even more by surprise than the initial assault. His now indignant white attackers refused the next cab, summoned a station policeman, and demanded that the red cap be fired. An assistant stationmaster immediately dismissed Ransaw from service.[1]

"Just 40 months ago," the red caps' union journal, *Bags & Baggage,* declared, "Benjamin Ransaw would have gone the way of thousands of red caps who have had similar experiences with inconsiderate passengers and station-loafers during the past 40 years." Now, however, because the United Transport Service Employees of America (UTSEA) possessed legal standing as a bona fide railroad union, members like Ransaw had access to the complex machinery governing alleged contract violations and grievances. When efforts to secure an impartial hearing with the Pennsylvania railroad failed, UTSEA officials filed a complaint of "unwarranted discharge" with the National Railway Adjustment Board, the federal agency that oversaw disputes between rail companies and unions. The company immediately requested a meeting with the union, settling the case by reinstating Ransaw and providing him with almost $300 in back pay in exchange for the union's withdrawing its complaint.[2]

"More than all the legal fights we have before the courts of the nation, this case symbolizes the passing of the old antiquated 'hat-in-hand' order among red caps and the introduction of the new era of group responsibility, job investment and freedom from self-intimidation, coercion and fear," *Bags & Baggage* editorialized.[3] The successful resolution of Ransaw's complaint was by no means unique. One of the more significant results of unionization was the establishment of genuine grievance procedures that allowed red caps to challenge, often effectively, their employers' exercise of arbitrary power. In 1940, Grand Central Station dismissed twenty-three red caps—some with ten to twenty years of service—for alleged rule violations. At the same time, Penn Station fired roughly twenty-seven red caps for allegedly not giving passengers precise change and receipts and for other "flimsy excuses." In both instances, union grievance committees responded quickly, generating negative publicity for the companies. The stations relented, reinstating the men.[4]

The experiences of Benjamin Ransaw and his fellow red caps at Penn and Grand Central Station illustrated the transformation in perception, demeanor, and even balance of power in railroad terminals' labor relations. More than anything else, it was unionization that made the difference. The emergence of the International Brotherhood of Red Caps (IBRC), which changed its name to the UTSEA in 1940, was no isolated occurrence in black America. The fate of red caps as an occupational group and as a union was inextricably linked to the broader development of labor and black protest during the Great Depression. "The very same trends and developments which have swept the basic and mass production industries," the red caps' journal editor explained in September 1937, "have had their corresponding effects upon workers hitherto untouched by the trade union movement."[5] The rise of the CIO, the industrial union federation committed formally to organizing blacks as well as whites in basic industry, and the AFL's Brotherhood of Sleeping Car Porters (BSCP) sparked a wave of labor organizing among numerous groups of black workers. African-American tobacco workers, freight handlers, store clerks, and even domestic laborers took advantage of the limited political and organizational openings afforded by the New Deal and the CIO respectively to establish trade unions among groups of workers previously thought unorganizable. In the railroad industry's service sector, station red caps joined the Pullman porters and dining car waiters as the latest to embrace organized labor's new crusade.

But red caps' experiences, in the workplace and in their union, differed from those of other black railroad service workers. They occupied a far weaker labor-market position; even more than porters or waiters, redcapping required no particular skills, leaving workers with virtually no leverage vis-à-vis railroad station management. Even the "craft or class" status of redcapping was less clearly defined than that of portering and waiting, rendering it vulnerable to the jurisdictional designs of the predatory, and prejudiced, white clerks' union. Although the BSCP fought its share of jurisdictional battles with white unions, the red caps' association faced a much stronger and determined threat from its white competitors. During the crucial period of union formation and recognition, red caps spent significant energy combating not only their employers but fellow white workers as well. Thus, the red caps were wholly dependent on labor law and its administrative agencies. Their early successes in the late 1930s depended on winning government recognition of their very status as railroad employees. To make matters even more difficult, during the 1930s and 1940s, the heyday of service unionism, red caps' distinctive brand of civil rights unionism put them increasingly at odds with the AFL service unions that had initially inspired them.

Before the creation of redcapping at the end of the nineteenth century, railroad and express companies, particularly in New York and some other major cities, assumed responsibility for the care and transport of major pieces of passenger baggage during the trip and especially after arrival. From the 1850s onward, customers could "express" their luggage by delivering it to a counter in a railway station or to a train's baggage car, where a clerk or baggage master would attach a numbered brass check with a leather strap to each bag. Before arriving at the destination, the baggage master or agent from the express company circulated through the train inquiring where customers wanted their bags delivered. For a fee, luggage was carted directly to a passenger's hotel.[6]

Travelers' assessments of this system of "expressed," or "checked," luggage was mixed. Some found the system efficient and comfortable; others complained of the "tyranny of the check," the late arrival of luggage, and the considerable damage often inflicted upon it. Porters who unloaded railway vans were "baggage smashers," one irritated traveler complained. Rail passengers often had to fend for themselves in boarding and disembarking from trains, either carrying their own bags or asking a porter or janitor (who in many parts of the country was black) to put aside his broom and other cleaning supplies and assist them in exchange for a small tip. American railroad stations, unlike English ones, had yet to employ station platform porters in significant numbers, much to passengers' dismay.[7]

Station employees' indifference to the inconvenience of passengers led to the emergence of the redcapping system. The red cap's origins, according to popular lore, could be traced to the efforts of one individual, James H. Williams, a black New York teenager. On a busy Labor Day in 1892, the enterprising Williams fastened a piece of red flannel to his hat as a means of identifying his availability to carry luggage to the passengers of Grand Central Station. "It worked—he had a big day," the story went, and the "Red Cap came into being." The idea slowly caught on. Williams proposed to the Grand Central management that it employ blacks exclusively as red caps when white station employees were promoted or resigned. Soon, numerous railroad stations formally adopted the red cap system, placing on their pay-rolls specific men whose principal job was the greeting of passengers at station entrances and at Pullman cars. Within two years, the Pennsylvania Station in Washington, D.C., employed its first red cap; by 1896 "red-capped porters" had made their official appearance at the Pennsylvania Station's Cortlandt street terminus as well as at the Chicago and Northwestern Station in Chicago, which promoted a "corps of uniformed attendants" to assist passengers at no charge; the New Haven Station hired its first red cap in 1911.[8] Williams himself prospered from the occupation he helped establish. As Grand Central's chief of red caps—a position he held until his death in 1948—he oversaw a staff of roughly five hundred black red caps by the mid-1930s.[9]

But if Grand Central employed a veritable army devoted to carrying passenger baggage, smaller stations sometimes imposed additional labor requirements on their smaller forces of red caps for the "privilege" of working. As late as 1942, the Illinois Central terminal at Jackson, Mississippi, employed no janitors, insisting that red caps wash windows, clean waiting rooms, lavatories, and halls, and sweep the station's exterior. Smaller stations usually provided work for only a handful of men. The Jackson station employed eighteen red caps in the 1930s, while the New York, New Haven, and Hartford railroad station in New Haven employed a mere twelve, and the Dayton Union Railway Company ten, with three or four extras. Some six hundred or so red caps worked in Chicago's six stations, one hundred seventy in Philadelphia's three stations, and one hundred sixty-nine in Washington, D.C.'s Union Station by the Depression.[10] The Department of Labor estimated that there were 110 railroad stations in the country that employed only one red cap each. While the large number of individual employers and the often informal character of employment relations made comprehensive figures impossible to come by, Labor Department researchers put the number of red caps by the end of the Great Depression at 3,787, with an additional 316 "non-redcaps" who sometimes carried baggage and 161 supervisors.[11]

From its earliest days, redcapping was dominated, but not monopolized, by African Americans. Roughly one third of Chicago red caps in the early 1940s were white, while red caps in Salt Lake City's Union Depot were all white. In Seattle, Japanese workers, who outnumbered blacks in that city through the 1930s, held all of the station porter positions at the Northern Pacific and Great Northern's King Street Station and Union Pacific's Union Station. Only the increased black migration to Seattle during World War II and, more importantly, the wartime internment of the Japanese by the federal government made it possible for African Americans to secure these jobs in significant numbers. Racial conflict between blacks and whites did not break out often at the terminal level, for stations hired strictly from one group or the other.[12]

Employers, not workers, determined the specific racial composition of the labor force. Prior to World War I, station managers could, and sometimes did, dramatically alter the racial composition of their workforce. Chicago's Northwestern depot before 1911, for example, employed only white ushers. In that year, however, managers abandoned that "time-honored custom" by hiring blacks for the first time. Black ushers were simply "easier to obtain," railroad officials asserted, and "inasmuch as the Pullman porters are now all of that race it is thought advisable to make the system uniform throughout." In 1915, Utah's Ogden Union Station dismissed its four white red caps and replaced them with African Americans.[13] Such changes, however, were rare. Once the racial composition of a particular labor force was set, it proved remarkably durable over time.

The position of red cap, like that of Pullman porter and dining car waiter, attracted a wide variety of men. Those with little formal education, as well as highly educated but out-of-work professionals, might be joined during seasonal rushes by an influx of African-American college students seeking to earn extra cash between semesters. In the early 1920s, perhaps as many as a third of Grand Central's three hundred red caps during the summer were college students seeking to earn money to pay their fall and spring semester expenses. Penn Station too employed a large number of young black men enrolled at Howard, Lincoln, Columbia, and New York University, Amherst College, and other schools. Not only college students but also college graduates filled the red caps' ranks. Many black station porters were highly educated and, in some cases, possessed professional skills. A union official informed social scientists St. Clair Drake and Horace Cayton in the early 1940s that seventy-two of the ninety black red caps in his Chicago station were college graduates. Because of the limited job opportunities available to African Americans, Cayton believed, redcapping had long been a "stop-gap form of employment for ambitious doctors of philosophy and medicine." Indeed, among the African-American red caps' ranks during the Great Depression were "doctors, dentists, lawyers, preachers, social service workers, musicians, artists, [and] chemists," a pro-union journalist observed in 1938. "M.A.'s are common; men studying for doctor's degrees are no rarity." She estimated that 40 percent of the Northwestern Station's red caps were "college men."[14]

Whether an opportunity for aspiring students or a stopgap for professionals temporarily down on their luck, the job also attracted many long-term workers. "The average Negro Red Cap," the president of a black IBRC local noted in 1937, "stays in the service a lifetime, because it is fairly lucrative and a fairly steady occupation, and somehow it 'gets' you." Surveys conducted by Wage and Hour Division investigators in the Department of Labor substantiated his claim. In 1941, for instance, just over 60 percent of Grand Central red caps in New York had worked in their positions for a decade or more, with twelve years being the average term of employment for those on the seniority roster. It is unlikely, however, that these workers possessed the same educational level as professionals, who tended to move on.[15]

In contrast with blacks who were drawn to redcapping, contemporaries suggested that whites with few skills and relatively low levels of education were attracted to the job. Those whites who possessed skills or education could more often find work more appropriate to their level of training, both in railroading and in industry in general, than their black counterparts. At least half of the white red caps, one black union official believed, had never attended high school. The "white man doesn't usually make for an educated man becoming a Red Cap. The educational status of the whites in the union is lower than that of the Negroes."[16] Whatever their respective backgrounds, race—not quality—determined workers' future employment opportunities. Department of Labor researchers concluded in the early 1940s that redcapping was "only a stepping stone to other railroad positions" for whites; after putting in their time, they could expect to "rise to clerical, supervisory, or even executive positions" in their terminals or for their railroads. Even if their new jobs initially paid them less than what they might receive from tips as red caps, the "prestige of white collar work and the chances which it held for eventual promotion" motivated whites to seek promotion. In contrast, redcapping was "a permanent job" for blacks and the small number of Japanese who were red caps.[17]

While the job of red cap called for a strong back and a friendly demeanor, African-American workers also invested it with a degree of pride and professionalism. A station porter had to be "more than a mere carrier of baggage"; he had to be a "walking information bureau," according to Penn Station's black chief, W. H. Robinson. "He must have at his finger tips the time of arrival and departure of all trains in this station and the platforms where they leave and come in. He must know where the piers of the transatlantic liners are situated."[18] This "corps of front-line veterans" were "public relations men of the first order," in the words of a conservative black journal. The red cap "has built himself up from casual hanger-on to an intelligent, informative terminal employee who has become a necessary indispensable fixture," concluded Penn Station union activist E. C. Robinson.[19]

Early twentieth-century railroad and terminal companies paid their ushers a basic wage and "the tips that they received were so much 'gravy.' They lived well, bought homes, and sent their children to college," noted the Urban

League's monthly in 1939. Wage rates before 1930 could vary sharply. The small number of Utah's red caps received an exceptionally high monthly salary of $60 shortly before World War I; for the much larger force of ushers at Penn Station it was only when the federal government assumed control over the railroad industry in 1918 that wages were institutionalized, first at $25 per month, then rising to $45. By August 1919, however, wages had dropped to $19.75 plus tips for 30 fortunate attendants, while some 160 extras received only a dollar a month. Shortly thereafter, Penn Station discontinued paying its red caps any wages at all. By 1923, tips were their only compensation.[20]

Allan S. A. Titley, a sixteen-year red cap who quit in 1926, recounted the trade's transformation in the pages of the *Messenger*, A. Philip Randolph's monthly magazine. The early twentieth-century Grand Central red caps, numbering under a hundred, enjoyed favorable working conditions, possessed seniority rights, and received a salary. Despite hardships, the men "considered Red Cap work as the best unskilled job in those days." That, however, did not last very long, for the "time came when the officials observing that there were more applicants for Red Cap work than they cared to pay, decided that something had to be done so that a large force of men could be available with little expense to the company." The result was a two-tiered system: a small number of men were placed on the company's payroll, while a larger number were taken on as unsalaried "extra" men who would substitute for the regulars in their absence. The "work of an extra man was very tedious," Titley recalled, and he was "greatly imposed upon. He was made to sweep the platforms in the summer, and in the winter he shoveled snow and threw sand on the platforms." Only in 1913 was a regular cleaning force hired. When the federal government ordered the payment of wages during World War I, managers responded by reducing the number of employees to about one hundred men. By the late 1920s, Grand Central had restored a two-tiered system, employing forty daytime and three evening regulars, who were responsible for suburban trains at a monthly salary of $18, and hundreds of extra, or freelance, red caps. A nine-hour day was standard, but forced overtime was not uncommon; the extras dominated the labor force, and the rules that had once governed on-the-job conditions had become obsolete.[21]

The onset of the Great Depression exacerbated problems experienced by red caps during the more prosperous 1920s. Most stations that had continued to pay monthly salaries ceased to do so. Illinois Central's Jackson, Mississippi, station ended its $45 a month salary in 1930, while Washington, D.C.'s Terminal (Union) Station abandoned red caps' $35 monthly salary in July 1932. Left to work for gratuities alone, red caps quickly learned that the economic crisis of the 1930s directly affected the ability, or willingness, of the traveling public to tip. In 1929, Willard Townsend testified, "In the station where I was employed the tips had dwindled down to a very, very small amount. There were days when we actually made just about enough to pay our car fare and buy lunch." Looking back on the "deplorable" conditions of the 1930s, Penn Station red cap E. C. Robinson recalled that the "continued depression, and strict supervisory regulations have cut heavily into the income of Red Caps," forcing many to "lower their standard of living" or "go on relief or seek aid from outside agencies."[22]

Deprived of a salary, depending on unreliable tips, and lacking seniority rights and other on-the-job protections, by the early years of the Great Depression red caps tentatively sought to organize themselves to address their occupational problems. Unlike the Pullman porters, who occupied so prominent a place in the national imagination and who had over fifteen years of off-and-on organizational experience by the mid-1930s, red caps had few traditions of labor militancy of their own to draw on. Following an announcement of salary cuts immediately after World War I, Penn Station red caps formed a short-lived Brotherhood of Railway Station Attendants, which affiliated with the AFL as a federal union. In nearby Philadelphia an all-black Red Cap and Railroad Employes Association formed in April 1921 fared only a little better: by 1928, it reported "fair success" but acknowledged trouble retaining its 150 members because of their lack of interest and fear of losing their jobs. In Baltimore, too, several unionizing efforts at the city's three stations collapsed by the mid-1920s.[23]

The reasons for the failure of red caps' trade unionism were complex. For some, the job's flexibility and tips during the 1920s proved disincentive enough. "It's a great life in the station and highly interesting," a Baltimore red cap reported in 1926. The following year, Grand Central's Allan Titley put forth a completely different explanation for the lack of union activity. Notwithstanding the low morale and the spirit of "unrest and dissatisfaction," the red caps of Grand Central took no action toward unionization because they understood that if "every Red Cap in the Grand Central Station resigned, they could be replaced by double the amount of men within 24 hours." Iconoclastic black journalist George Schuyler considered neither satisfaction nor fear in his explanation of red caps' failure to organize before the late 1930s; for him, the problem rested in both the job and the men it attracted. Ignoring the heterogeneous makeup of the red cap labor force, he asserted in 1942 that it "was once believed that you could only organize red caps for a crap game, a gin session or perhaps a picnic, on the assumption that they had nothing under their caps except hair." Redcapping "was regarded as a filling station on a dirt road to the future, and the road was a dead end. A red cap was regarded as a man who thought twice before acting, and then rested from the exertion. To unionize a man without a wage was considered akin to making an omelet without eggs or a honeymoon without a bride."[24]

Schulyer's pessimistic assessment contained more than a grain of truth, but it was in part belied by red caps' collective efforts of a rather different sort. Station porters formed weak trade unions only occasionally, but they often established fraternal and benefit societies. New York's Grand Central men formed the Red Caps Beneficial Association in 1911 to provide for "sickness, death and charity." The station boasted a number of additional "clubs," which saved and distributed money. Employees of three Chicago railroad stations met at the city's Appomattox Club in 1914 to "unite fraternally all men of sound health and good moral character" to provide help for the sick and disabled and to provide burial assistance for its members; by 1930, the group, then called the Northwestern Red Caps Benevolent Association, boasted nearly 100 percent membership among the red caps and had become a "liberal contributor to the charitable agencies of the community." In 1917, the Pennsylvania railroad terminal red caps formed a "Moore Red Cap Etheopic Propaganda" organization to support foreign missionary work and to help solve "the many complex and intricate problems now confronting and impeding the progress of the Negro." Its goal was to provide scholarship money to allow one or two missionaries to work in Africa and through the study of the "laws, customs, institutions, languages and traditions of our mother country" to research the "ancient principles of life that gave such illustrious and magnificent history of achievement to the black race."[25]

However attentive to their members' security or to broader African-American concerns, these associations posed no threat to managerial authority. Perhaps the most important and influential of company-dominated associations was the Illinois Central Red Caps Club of Chicago. Founded in December 1923, the Red Caps Club initially included in its membership Illinois Central, Dearborn Street, and Northwestern Station ushers. During the 1920s, the organization sponsored a glee club, a literary society, minstrel shows, and numerous speakers at its monthly meetings. By the early 1930s, the Dearborn and Northwestern men had lost interest, leaving the organization to the IC men. Now known as the Illinois Central Colored Service Boosters Club, it retained close ties to the company, sponsoring efficiency classes and dispatching its officials to IC-sponsored meetings.[26]

The IC underwrote numerous boosters clubs for its employees, enrolling red caps, black yard workers, white conductors and engineers, and managers—indeed, members of the entire IC labor force and their families. These clubs maintained strict segregation between white and black locals in many of the cities in which they operated, and racial segregation was observed at booster events. Segregation notwithstanding, the overall purpose of the many clubs was the same: to drum up business and generate positive publicity for the Illinois Central. The various clubs have "devoted themselves to the solicitation of business" through the personalizing of service, IC president L. A. Downs reflected in 1938. "If we can create that atmosphere in respect to every customer, it will not take us long to make our service so famous that everybody will want to use it."[27]

The chief figure behind the Red Caps Club in the 1920s and the IC Boosters in the 1930s was Sandy W. Trice, the Illinois Central Station's chief usher. Born to ex-slave parents in New Providence, Tennessee, in 1868, Trice moved to Chicago in 1884 in search of employment. In the early twentieth century, he founded and published the weekly *Chicago Conservative,* and by the 1930s he headed the Third Ward Republican Club. In addition to serving as a high officer in several fraternal orders, Trice was also president of the Pyramid Building and Loan Association and chair of the Metropolitan Community Church's board of trustees. As a prominent member of Chicago's black middle class, Trice used his position as IC's chief usher to encourage the further education of the young red caps in his charge and to cultivate the profession's image of respectability. Until his retirement in 1940, he kept the IC's financial and managerial interests close to heart, delivering speeches on such topics as "how we can best cooperate to promote the welfare of the company." His response to the efforts of the newly formed International Brotherhood of Red Caps to secure representation rights for IC terminal workers in 1937 and 1938 was predictable. Under Trice's leadership, the Boosters Club assumed the full-fledged function of a company union and quickly signed a contract with IC officials to thwart the IBRC. Under Trice, the IBRC charged, Illinois Central station had become "a bedlam of wrongs, coercion, intimidation and special privilege," while Trice himself was a "petty stooge" who played a "bootlicking role" for the company, selling his red caps "down the river."[28]

By the mid-1930s, red caps were no longer resistant to labor organization. Prompted by a further deterioration of working conditions during the Depression on the one hand, and inspired by the revival of the American labor movement on the other, small and largely powerless locals began to spring up across the country. In 1933, red caps organized the Brotherhood of Washington Terminal Station Porters in the nation's capital. The following year, station porters in Detroit and Cleveland followed suit. The Cleveland Red Caps Association, which transformed itself into Station Porters' Union no. 19673, an AFL federal local, in 1934, mistakenly believed that it could take advantage of provisions in the amended Railway Labor Act to secure collective bargaining rights.[29] Red caps, "citizens of the United States, many of them with families to support," labored "under deplorable working conditions." In many cases, they were required to purchase their own uniforms, "work regular hours under strict discipline and supervision," and receive "no compensation at all from their employer," complained Kenyon Burke, chairman of the Cleveland local. At first Burke's association turned to the National Urban League for assistance in linking up with similar groups. The league put it in contact with socialist labor organizer Frank Crosswaith, who promised his cooperation, but nothing came from this overture. By 1937, however, AFL-affiliated locals of red caps had sprung up in the Midwest and on the West Coast, while a variety of groups—the New York Central Brotherhood of Red Caps, the Pennsylvania's Brotherhood of Railroad Station Porters, the Washington Terminal Brotherhood of Station Porters, and the Boston Red Caps Association—maintained their institutional independence.[30]

A group of Chicago-based activists initiated a campaign to unify red cap locals in 1937. In late January, 200 workers from six Chicago railroad stations and two bus terminals formed the Brotherhood of Railroad Depot, Bus Terminal, Airport and Dock Red Caps, Attendants and Porters, becoming AFL federal local 20342. Reflecting the interracial character of the city's station porter labor force, it divided its leadership positions between blacks and whites, with Boland L. Hosie, a white red cap who worked at the LaSalle Street station, as president and Willard S. Townsend, a black red cap at the Northwestern station, as vice-president. Immediately, officers issued an invitation to scattered red cap locals elsewhere to discuss unification; they were assisted by Pullman porters, who dropped off bundles of leaflets in stations across the country.[31]

In late May 1937, over a hundred delegates, representing over a thousand red caps, gathered in the Windy City. The interracial character of the gathering impressed observers, for the membership was divided almost equally between black and white, and, the Associated Negro Press reported, they "work harmoniously together for the common cause." Union officials carefully promoted a vision of interracial solidarity: the Brotherhood was marked by a "lack of prejudicial feeling," declared newly elected vice-president John Yancey, Jr., of Memphis, and accepted "all men on equal basis." A white journalist observed that the convention had reflected a degree of "race equality in a labor organization never before attained in this country." The result was unprecedented, for the "color line in labor relations was smashed." A black union official proudly celebrated the alliance of whites and blacks, informing black researchers St. Clair Drake and Horace Cayton, "This is a mixed union. There is no discernible difference between the white and the Negro Red Caps. There is no advantage in separate locals."[32]

The celebration proved premature, however; the "honeymoon period of Negro-white relations," in Drake and Cayton's words, "was short." The new International Brotherhood of Red Caps remained an interracial union, but its formation was hardly free of racial tensions. African Americans numerically dominated the gathering and accordingly helped to elect Willard Townsend to the presidency of the new organization. The promotion of the Chicago AFL federal local's black vice-president, and the eclipse of its white president, Boland Hosie, proved too much for some white delegates. Hosie, who was elected general organizer, had apparently expected to be the leader of the new organization and bristled at the prospect of serving under a black president. Following the convention, a group of dissident whites approached the National Mediation Board (NMB), requesting assistance only on behalf of whites. Shortly thereafter a white faction quit the new union. "The trouble with colored men is that they want to run things," a white secessionist asserted. Another argued that it "doesn't do for white and black to be in the same organization. The whites have no respect for the Negroes and the Negroes have no respect for the whites." The secession of these whites rendered the IBRC "for all practical purposes a Negro organization," Cayton and Drake concluded. White red caps turned to the Brotherhood of Railway and Steamship Clerks, who were only too happy to grant them membership. Yet not all whites withdrew; white red cap Matthew King was elected as a national vice-president of the IBRC and a white attorney, Leon Despres, served as the union's chief legal council for the next several decades.[33]

Committed to interracialism but overwhelmingly African-American in membership, the new IBRC immediately took a fateful step that redefined its strategic course and organizational identity: it withdrew from the American Federation of Labor and established itself as a wholly independent body. Leaders disavowed any fundamental challenge to the AFL's organizational structure or any involvement with the newly organized CIO. But as members of federal locals within the AFL, they found themselves "unable to carry on an effective fight . . . due to the isolation of each local and the lack of assistance from the parent body." That body, the AFL, proved uninterested in providing funds for the IBRC to pursue a legal battle for inclusion under the provisions of the Railway Labor Act, and federal union status within the AFL offered red caps few advantages. Leaving the AFL was a "foregone conclusion," attorney Leon Despres recalled. "You couldn't operate as a federal union in the A.F. of L. The people who the A.F. of L. assigned to monitor the federal unions were stuffy people. They had no conception of civil rights. They looked down on black workers . . . [s]o that there was absolutely no point in staying on as a federal union."[34]

Equally significant, red caps' status as subordinate members of organized labor rendered them vulnerable to the "unusual and amazing jurisdictional claims" of the Brotherhood of Railway and Steamship Clerks (BRSC), the largest of the principal railroad labor unions. Initially representing just white white-collar railroad employees, the brotherhood grew to embrace numerous groups of station workers, including freight handlers, janitors, and even red caps. While a significant number of these unskilled station men were black, the BRSC officially maintained a "color clause" barring them from full membership; until 1934, the brotherhood simply ignored them altogether. That changed somewhat in the mid-1930s when the Clerks agreed to organize black station workers into federal unions under the direct control of the AFL. As many as 6,000 black station workers had been so organized by 1939, because, according to Herbert Northrup, "of the realization that the wages of white workers could not be substantially increased so long as those of the Negroes remained depressed." The Clerks also benefited financially, with its local system committees receiving the per capita tax from the all-black federal locals. Some blacks in these federal locals did benefit from wage increases negotiated by the BRSC on behalf of the entire station labor force, but none received the same representation that their white counterparts did. Barred by the BRSC from voting for BRSC officers, serving on negotiating or grievance committees, or participating more generally in union affairs, black members of the BRSC were voiceless. The solution, they argued, lay in "temporary withdrawal from the parent body," the AFL. This, they felt, would end the overshadowing jurisdictional claims of the BRSC and ensure black independence and proper representation.[35]

From May 1937 to the unification conference in January 1938, the IBRC's organizers laid the groundwork for the building of a national union. That fall, Willard Townsend toured the East and the South, inviting numerous locals to affiliate with the IBRC, and, in the case of the South, to help establish new locals.[36] They also received needed assistance from the older, more experienced Brotherhood of Sleeping Car Porters, whose recent, unprecedented successes demonstrated the feasibility of service workers' unionization. What appeared to be a natural alliance, however, required careful construction and the suspension of organizational rivalry. "Randolph would have liked very much to organize the red caps," an early union supporter believed, "but he couldn't because jurisdiction under the A.F. of L. charters over red caps was given to the Brotherhood of Railway Clerks." Since Randolph had based his standing "in the labor movement on support by the A.F. of L. . . . he could not go against them and raid the jurisdiction of an A.F. of L. union . . . That was why the field was open for the International Brotherhood of Red Caps and Townsend to go ahead." Yet when the question of affiliation with the BSCP came up in May 1937, the new IBRC flatly rejected the prospect.[37]

Relations between the BSCP and the red cap union activists were tense, although Pullman porters publicized the red caps' cause by distributing leaflets to station employees across the nation, urging them to attend the May 1937 Chicago union meeting. Well into 1937 Randolph had been "most unfriendly to the Chicago organization of red caps," the younger union's officials later recounted, while BSCP vice-president Milton Webster "spent much of his time in the East castigating and defiling Townsend—thus, adding to the disunity." In March 1937, the BSCP discussed plans in Philadelphia for the formation a "strong organization" of red caps while apparently offering no support to the Chicago plan for the formation of the IBRC. When this effort went nowhere, the BSCP quietly and unsuccessfully advanced for president of the IBRC the candidacy of Alfred J. McGhee, president of the Penn Station red caps' local, not Townsend. Red caps insisted on institutional autonomy and rejected the BSCP's efforts to subsume them. Over the next decade, the IBRC's own story of its organizational rise afforded no significant role to the BSCP: "As far as Red Caps are concerned," the IBRC president declared, "they pulled themselves up by their own boot straps."[38]

Compounding these initial tensions were the conflicting ambitions of the two men who led these organizations. There "has never been any usual warmth between us," Townsend later remarked on his relationship with Randolph. Observers readily concurred: "Each one of them thought that he was or ought to be the leading black trade unionist," a friend of Townsend's recalled. "There was never really any serious disagreement . . . Both of them had a great deal of ego and both of them thought they were going to be the savior of the black worker," Ike Golden, the UTSEA comptroller in the 1940s and early 1950s, concluded.[39]

By the end of 1937, a public alliance between the two groups made sense for both sides. The IBRC needed Randolph for his extensive influence, and Randolph's reputation as the nation's premier black labor leader could only be served by his support for the new union. At the IBRC's request, Randolph agreed to lend his name and prestige to the drive for unification. Following a meeting at the Harlem Labor Center attended by Randolph, Townsend, Frank Crosswaith (Socialist party activist, former BSCP organizer, and then-organizer for the International Ladies Garment Workers Union,) and several New York red cap leaders, the IBRC issued a call for a national unification conference to be held the following month at Poro College in Chicago.[40] The affiliation of the huge, independent Grand Central local was particularly important. "The time is long past when the Negro shall forever be a mendicant at the table of the employer class for such crumbs as may fall to our churches, schools and charitable organizations," declared John R. Lee, the president of Local 1 of the Brotherhood of Red Caps, New York Central, on behalf of unification. "We must take our place in the front ranks of the upstanding workers of this country. We as a race have long clamored for social and economic freedom. To acquire this, we must assume our obligations as men and workers . . . organize thoroughly, pool our resources and use the same methods as other exploited groups because we have indeed been the forgotten man." Almost 60 delegates representing as many as 4,000 workers—overwhelmingly black but including some whites and Japanese—attended the January 1938 unification conference, affiliated with the International Brotherhood of Red Caps, and elected Townsend as its president.[41]

From the outset, the IBRC attracted a dynamic group of organizers who embodied, in many ways, the ambitions of the men they were organizing. Relatively young and well educated, many of these activists had encountered racial barriers to their occupational or career advancement in other spheres. Committed to civil rights and social justice, they found in the labor movement a vehicle to advance their goals and to channel their ambitions. They arrived at their positions, however, by a variety of very different routes and brought to their organizing a range of ideological and religious perspectives.

The union's most important organizer and public presence was Willard S. Townsend, who would lead the IBRC/UTSEA for two decades. Although Townsend would become a leading black railroad unionist like Randolph, their coming of age in the early twentieth century led them down different developmental paths. Randolph, born in Florida in 1889, migrated to New York in 1911, where he became active in socialist politics and made a name for himself as a radical journalist, an advocate of interracial industrial unionism, and a fierce critic of Du Bois, Garvey, the U.S. government, and the capitalist system. For Townsend, the route to trade unionism leadership was neither politics nor ideology, but work.

Born in Cincinnati in 1895, Townsend was the great-grandson of Hiram W. Revels, the only African-American senator from Mississippi, the grand-nephew of Samuel J. Mitchel, a former president of Wilberforce University, and the son of William Townsend, a building contractor. When Europe plunged into war in 1914, the 19-year-old Townsend was working as a red cap in Cincinnati's Union Depot. While Randolph was condemning American participation in the Great War, Townsend served as a first lieutenant with the 372nd Infantry in France. Following his discharge from the service, from 1921 to 1925 he was a dining car waiter on the Canadian National Railroad, working weekends and the summer months while attending school during the winter. He matriculated at the University of Toronto to prepare for a career in medicine before entering the Royal Academy of Science, where he earned a chemistry degree. Townsend also served as secretary of a local of the

Canadian Brotherhood of Railway Employees until the Canadian National Railroad replaced many of its black waiters with whites in 1926 when the blacks pressed for equal wages.[42]

Moving to Chicago, Townsend held jobs at the Adler Psychological Laboratory and as a special messenger to a bank president. By 1930, he was working as a red cap at Chicago's Northwestern Railway Terminal. At the time of his first election to union office in 1937, he was supplementing his income from tips as a red cap by regularly serving lunch across the street from the terminal to executives at the Northern Trust Company. But when Townsend's union activity came to light, "they terminated him for that reason. They [just] couldn't have him there."[43]

The labor movement quickly became Townsend's consuming interest. Over the next two decades, he devoted himself to building the red caps' union, eventually expanding its organizational base to embrace Pullman laundry workers, shop workers, and even locomotive firemen. Having brought the UTSEA into the CIO in 1942, Townsend instantly gained national recognition as the CIO's highest-ranking black official when he was appointed to the industrial union federation's executive board. Townsend vied with Randolph for the spotlight as the nation's leading black unionist. Like Randolph, Townsend used his union office to promote civil rights in a broader arena. Over the years, he served on the executive boards of the Urban League and the Hampton Institute, whose teachers he urged to join a union; ran unsuccessfully for the Democratic nomination to Congress in Chicago; testified regularly before Congress against discrimination in housing and labor law; blasted the Fair Employment Practice Committee for its failure to confront racism in the railroad industry; and lambasted white railroad and AFL unions for discriminatory policies. In the late 1940s through the mid-1950s, Townsend traveled abroad extensively on behalf of the CIO and the U.S. State Department, carrying a message of anticommunist unionism to workers in Japan, China, France, Mexico, and Cuba. At the time of his death in 1957, Townsend had joined Randolph as a vice-president of the newly unified AFL-CIO.[44]

Townsend was assisted in the task of building and sustaining the IBRC by other motivated unionists. John Yancey was born in 1904 in Memphis to "poor parents, but not in poverty." He had aspired to become an architect but found that financial pressures dictated an alternative course. Completing two years of college course work in business administration at Wilberforce University's School of Commerce, Yancey worked as a stenographer before being promoted to bookkeeper, teller, and assistant cashier at the Solvent Savings Bank. But the Great Depression put an end to both his seven-year stint in banking and the institution which employed him. Having worked earlier as an Illinois Central red cap to earn money to pay for his schooling, Yancey returned to redcapping and was "subjected to all the oppression and indignities to which the job, at that time, was heir." When Yancey picked up a bulletin distributed by a Pullman porter inviting red caps to attend an organizing conference in Chicago in 1937, he was immediately interested and traveled to Chicago that April to discuss unionization plans with Townsend. He signed on and became the IBRC's first southern regional director and its third vice-president; the following year, he became its secretary-treasurer. Like other red cap leaders, Yancey found the IBRC/UTSEA to be an effective launching point for his activist career.[45]

Yancey's union activism was not only a response to the indignities he and his fellow station porters suffered; it was also deeply rooted in his Catholic faith. Yancey remembered, "I could not understand why I was permitted only certain seats when I attended Catholic Churches in the South outside of my neighborhood; or why certain Catholic educational institutions excluded Negro students; or why some Catholics were just as prejudiced and more vicious in their practices than were some non-Catholics; or why some priests were outspoken in favor of discrimination and segregation." Believing that God created all in "His own image and likeness," Yancey argued that the "cause of interracial justice is the cause of every Catholic." He quickly emerged as a prominent black Catholic unionist, becoming an active participant in Catholic organizations and representing black workers' views before Catholic audiences.[46]

Ernest Hays Calloway was cut from a dramatically different cloth than fellow officer Yancey. Born in Heberton, West Virginia, in 1909, he moved with his family five years later to eastern Kentucky, where his father helped found a United Mine Workers' local, based in Letcher County. After dropping out of school and running away from home, Calloway worked as a dishwasher in Harlem and a miner for the Consolidated Coal Company. In the early years of the Depression, he traveled extensively across the United States as a drifter before resuming his mining labors back in Kentucky.[47]

By 1934, Calloway's life had taken a turn toward labor and radical politics. His firsthand experiences in the mines and his familiarity with organized labor had made him a sharp critic of the mining companies, the subcontracting system, southern industrialists, and even organized labor. Southern employers profited handsomely from their "economic exploitation," he wrote in the pages of the Urban League's journal, *Opportunity*. Although he cautiously praised the United Mine Workers in Kentucky for winning modest benefits for its members, he excoriated the AFL for its exclusivity and incompetence in organizing America's unskilled workers. Black leaders also came in for withering criticism for their indifference or acquiescence to the plight of the southern black poor. Some would "stoop to anything," he argued, "even betraying themselves and others for temporary security, making the really industrious southern Negro hemmed in by a vast legion of 'Stepin Fechits' and a corps of 'Uncle Toms.'"[48] Calloway eventually received a scholarship to attend Brookwood Labor College in Katonah, New York; next he moved south, where he helped organized Works Progress Administration workers into the Virginia Workers' Alliance.

Arriving in Chicago in 1937, Calloway was a man in search of a cause and a job. "It was while getting better acquainted with the Chicago labor movement (and job hunting in many plants) that some one told me that there was a fellow by the name of Townsend who had been successful in organizing the Chicago red caps into a federal local of the American Federation of Labor," he later recalled. Finding Townsend in the Chicago and Northwestern Station locker room in July 1937, Calloway soon signed on as the editor of the red caps' new journal, *Bags & Baggage,* and as its educational director, a position he held through the 1940s. His new position allowed him to be "part revolutionary, part civil rights activist, and part union organizer." In subsequent years, Calloway remained dedicated to pacifist, labor, and civil rights causes, cofounding Conscientious Objectors against Jim Crow during World War II, participating in the CIO's southern organizing drive in the late 1940s, establishing a research department for St. Louis teamsters, and serving as president of the St. Louis NAACP in the 1950s.[49]

Under this diverse group of leaders, the newly formed IBRC recognized that outside intervention was required to shift the balance of power in their favor. Toward that end, they enlisted the support of the broader trade union and left-liberal community, establishing an advisory council that attracted the participation of then University of Chicago economics professor Paul H. Douglas and a variety of progressive white labor leaders.[50] More important, the IBRC sought government recognition of its members' right to organize. From the short-lived National Industrial Recovery Act of 1933 to the more enduring National Labor Relations Act (also known as the Wagner Act) of 1935, union activists repeatedly invoked the legal recognition of the right to organize collectively as a spur to generating support. Although the National Industrial Recovery Act was ultimately declared unconstitutional in 1935 and the National Labor Relations Act was not upheld by the Supreme Court until 1937, American workers did not wait patiently for the courts to approve their right to organize. Moreover, once the Court had upheld the Wagner Act, American workers had access to the machinery of adjudication. If the law in some ways circumscribed the range of tactics and the scope of vision of many trade unions, it also bestowed legitimacy on workers' struggles and inspired many to take personal and organizational risks to achieve their goals.

The National Railroad Adjustment Board and the National Mediation Board (NMB) afforded railroad workers a structured forum to protest conditions, present their case for wage increases, and insist on elections for representation. But the law applied only to those who worked on board trains; it did not cover red caps. As a result, the benefits of New Deal labor legislation bypassed red caps altogether; while railroad workers were governed by the Railroad Labor Act, red caps had "an inferior employee status compared to that of other workers in the industry," in Calloway's words. Red caps, the IBRC repeatedly insisted, were treated as "privileged trespassers" on railroad property; they were "beggars permitted to solicit alms from the traveling public." Falling outside of the definition of "employee," they possessed no legal access to the complex labor relations machinery of the National Mediation Board. Nor were they covered under the new Railroad Retirement Act, which provided for voluntary retirement at age sixty-five.[51] The first step, then, was for red caps to win recognition as employees of the railroad.

Gaining access to the governmental machinery that oversaw union elections and the resolution of conflicts became the centerpiece of the IBRC's strategic efforts. During the summer of 1937, the union's leaders met repeatedly with Paul H. Douglas, a specialist on social insurance. Douglas had introduced Townsend to Leon M. Despres, a white former NLRB staff attorney, member of the Socialist Party, and instructor of labor law at the University of Chicago Law School and at the Chicago Labor College, who became the brotherhood's chief legal counsel and remained its legal strategist for the next several decades. Despres formulated a "March Forward to Job Legality" campaign, which aimed at prompting the Interstate Commerce Commission (ICC) to define red caps as bona fide railroad employees, which would entitle them to coverage under the Railway Labor Act. In late 1937 and 1938, the ICC conducted surveys and hearings on the subject of red caps' duties, responsibilities, wages, conditions, and overall status.[52]

Finally, in late September 1938, the ICC handed down its decision, concluding that the red caps' "'independent' status was wholly fictitious" (as a Wage and Hour Division report later put it). Red caps were "subject to the supervision and control of railroad or station officials," were required to wear uniforms, and were subject to reprimand or dismissal for infractions of official rules. In sum, they qualified as railroad employees (at least in cities of over 100,000) and as such were entitled to the protections and services of the Railroad Labor Act. The African-American press, with more than a touch of exaggeration, described the ruling as "one of the most momentous decisions . . . in the annals of American labor law." Yet this victory immediately transformed the rules of the game, allowing the IBRC to call upon the National Mediation Board to conduct representation elections in stations across the nation. The ruling, Calloway concluded, bestowed a "recognized legal status" on the job of redcapping, which was now "ready to take its place as an equal craft or class representative with other labor organizations" in the railroad industry.[53]

In the immediate aftermath of the ICC's ruling, the IBRC capitalized upon its newfound status by invoking the services of the National Mediation Board. Earlier, in 1937, two railroads, the Chicago and Northwestern and the Chicago and Western Indiana, had decided not to fight and agreed to recognize the IBRC as the red caps' representative and to enter into collective bargaining with the union.[54] On the West Coast, the Southern Pacific's Red Cap Station Porters Federal Local 18329, which remained outside of the IBRC until 1941, concluded a five-year campaign by signing the first contract in the nation between an all-black red cap union and a railroad company. The agreement provided union recognition, created twenty-eight new jobs, and protected seniority rights. Until the ICC ruling, few other railroads followed suit. After that ruling, however, companies had little choice but to accept NMB oversight of union elections. Immediately, the IBRC filed roughly twenty applications for certification with the NMB. Road after road fell in line, with station porters overwhelmingly voting for the IBRC.[55] Within two years, the union boasted over 3,500 members.

Only on the Illinois Central did the union encounter significant opposition. Shortly after the formation of the red caps' federal local in early 1937, the IC turned to its ace in the hole, the Colored Service Boosters Club, which was composed of IC red caps. Thirty-three club members voted to authorize club president Sandy Trice to bargain for them with the company, and on June 1 the company signed an agreement with the Booster Club chief on behalf of the club's members. The IBRC cried foul: the Boosters Club was nothing less than a company union. "All Red Caps in Chicago are aware of the unscrupulous acts, coercive methods, intimidation, special privileges, petty favoritism and many other evils of the Trice regime," the IBRC declared. IBRC members faced layoffs for attending union meetings or for failing to attend company union meetings; conditions at IC had become "so terrible" that the union "was compelled to operate in an under-ground fashion."[56]

Anticipating an unfavorable ruling from the Interstate Commerce Commission on the employee status question, IC managers again turned to their Colored Service Boosters Club the following year. In late February 1938, only a month after the IBRC unification conference, the IC publicized its signed agreement with Sandy Trice, which recognized the IC Boosters Club as an independent organization and sole bargaining representative. The agreement guaranteed Trice, as chief usher, a monthly salary of $85, with a select group of workers receiving $15 a month. Yet the IC's tradition of culti-vating employee loyalty and its sponsorship of club activity paid few divi-dends. In a NMB-supervised election, the IBRC defeated the club by a vote of 106 to 36. Trice "might have had a base in Central Station," attorney Despres believed. But once "the bargaining unit was the whole Illinois Cen-tral"—beyond the scope of his influence—he "didn't have a chance."[57]

Once certified by the NMB as the legitimate union representative, the IBRC began the hard job of negotiating contracts with their employers. While company managers relented on the issues of signed contracts and grievance committees, they dug in their heels on financial matters, and there was absolutely nothing that the NMB or the National Railroad Adjustment Board could do. Wages in the railroad industry were traditionally a matter settled by collective bargaining, not government intervention. Collective bargaining, however, initially produced no wage gains for red caps. Thus, from 1938 through the mid-1940s, the IBRC sought leverage outside the collective bargaining process, relying on favorable publicity, the assistance of friendly black organizations and sympathetic politicians, and especially the courts to bolster its rather weak position.

Since railroad labor law offered them no advantage on the wage front, red caps turned to the final labor reform measure of the New Deal: the Fair La-bor Standards Act (FLSA) of 1938. The FLSA specified a maximum work-week of forty-four hours (dropping to forty-two after a year and to forty by 1940) and a minimum hourly wage of 25 cents the first year, rising by five cents an hour for the next three years, for workers engaged in interstate com-merce. It also created within the Department of Labor an investigative and enforcement mechanism, the Wage and Hour (W&H) Division.[58] During congressional hearings on the FLSA, national labor leaders had been divided about its provisions; the CIO was generally supportive, its president John L. Lewis was "ambivalent," and the AFL was wary of minimum wage laws for men and feared for the sanctity of its collective bargaining contracts. The IBRC, however, had no doubts. Supportive of the bill's backers, it wasted lit-tle time in citing the act for economic protection. The FLSA promised to do for red cap wages what collective bargaining had yet to accomplish: raise them significantly. For the roughly 70 percent of the nation's station porters who worked strictly for tips, the FLSA would virtually guarantee them a base salary of 25 cents an hour—or $2.50 for a ten-hour day—in addition to the tips they received from appreciative passengers.

Such a legislatively induced wage increase met with stiff and immediate re-sistance. On October 22, 1938, just two days before the FLSA was to go into effect, the railroad industry unveiled its "Accounting and Guarantee" system. If the ICC had redefined red caps as employees, the industry's plan redefined tips as wages to be counted toward the minimum wage required by the new FLSA. Only if a red cap failed to make an amount equal to the day's minimum required by law would the company make up the difference. Station supervisors informed individual red caps by memorandum that they now were required to fill out daily report slips on the tips they had received; as a condition of employment, station porters would have to sign the memorandum. By the end of October, 180 stations had adopted the plan; by the end of the year, that number had risen to 226. In one swift move, the industry hoped to negate most, perhaps all, of the FLSA's economic impact.[59]

Over the next five years, the red caps' union waged a highly public and ultimately unsuccessful campaign against the railroad industry's inclusion of tips in the determination of wages. Upon notification of the plan's unilateral implementation, Townsend sought an administrative ruling against the industry's plan and immediately contacted Elmer Andrews, administrator of the Wage and Hour Division of the Department of Labor, who summoned a red cap delegation to Washington for discussions. According to the IBRC, the accounting and guarantee plan evaded the law; terminal or railroad companies should be required to pay bona fide wages—a minimum weekly wage of $11 for forty-four hours of work. Next, the union dispatched letters to various railroads calling for discussions of the wage-tip issue, but the companies uniformly ignored the request. The controversy again shifted to Washington. In June 1939, the Wage and Hour Division conducted public hearings on the matter.[60]

Were tips wages? The question sharply divided red caps from terminal managers. It was a question on which the Fair Labor Standards Act was silent. The companies felt that since the FLSA required the payment of wages, tips belonged not to the individual red cap but to the railroad or terminal company. The matter was that simple. The union, of course, cried foul: the accounting and guarantee plan was inherently coercive, was designed to evade the law, and in practice resulted in falsification of records as well as overt and covert harassment. Eugene F. Shepard, a Chicago and Western Indiana red cap, testified that he initially submitted accurate information on his tip slip—he had received 95 cents on one day, $1.15 on another. For his honesty, Shepard was reprimanded by his station manager, who insisted that he put down $2.00 a day on his slip. When he declined, the manager himself erased Shepard's figure and wrote in $2.00. Shepard learned his lesson. Subsequently, he obediently put down 25 cents an hour on his slip, regardless of the actual amount he earned, fearing "discipline or discharge" for any failure to comply with the company's wishes.[61]

Such coercion was limited neither to the Chicago and Western Indiana nor to large stations. The Illinois Central's Jackson, Mississippi, station dismissed eleven of its twenty-one local red caps and offered the remaining men a mere three hours of employment a day. That was changed to six hours a day a few weeks later, but when the men failed to report $2.00 a day, managers told them to "go up on your slips" or face dismissal. Workers at New York's Grand Central Station who failed to report the minimum were issued "short slips" on their time cards, which specified just how far short the amount was. The station's threat was underscored by the dismissal of about thirty-six red caps.[62]

The IBRC's arguments carried the day with the officials of the Wage and Hour Division, who agreed that the stations sought to evade the law and had resorted to outright coercion. The W&H Division ordered the maintenance of separate records of tips so that if and when a legal ruling against the industry plan was issued, a proper financial settlement could be easily reached. It also went to court, filing a test case to seek an injunction against the Cincinnati Union Terminal Company's treatment of tips as wages. No injunction was forthcoming, but the W&H Division remained supportive of the IBRC's contention that the stations' use of tips constituted "an evasion . . . of their absolute obligations to pay the Red Caps the minimum wage and to keep accurate records."[63]

Unable to wrest voluntary concessions from the industry through collective bargaining, the IBRC resorted to a strategy of litigation, filing civil suits to force companies to follow the requirements of the FLSA. The IBRC's legal team, led by white attorney Leon Despres of Chicago and black attorney George E. C. Hayes of Washington, D.C., sought the recovery of the wages red caps would have been paid had railroad and terminal companies paid the legal minimum wage. They failed.[64] Several similar lawsuits filed by the Brotherhood of Railway and Steamship Clerks on behalf of its small red cap membership made their way through the court system more quickly. In the most significant, *Pickett v. Union Terminal Company,* a Dallas judge ruled in favor of the Clerks' forty-four red caps at the Dallas Union Terminal, declaring tips to be tips, not wages. The Fifth Circuit Court of Appeals, however, came to the opposite conclusion. "Every passenger paid for service unless he or she was very stingy or financially unable, or else ignorant that pay was expected," the appeals judges found. "The acceptance of service carried an expectation of reward on both sides. What the Red Cap received was not gifts but earnings." In March 1942, the U.S. Supreme Court, in a 5–3 decision, concurred, ruling that tips were wages and that the wage recovery suit be dismissed.[65]

By then, red caps had other compensation problems to worry about. In February 1940, the Cincinnati Union Terminal Company introduced a new ten-cents-a-bag plan. All customers utilizing red cap service would henceforth be charged a dime per bag or parcel carried. Under the terms of the plan, which quickly spread to numerous stations across the nation, as a further evasion of the spirit of the minimum wage law. Cincinnati station porters protested the system for transforming them into simple revenue collectors for the company and for the "enslaving of the red cap porters." The tagging of bags and the collection of fees was time consuming and had "destroyed the pleasant relationship which formerly existed between red cap and passenger." Failure to collect fees equal to the minimum wage, they feared, would bring company charges of inefficiency and disciplinary action against them, producing in effect a "speed-up" that was particularly hard on older and physically less able porters. Perhaps most important, the plan threatened to reduce substantially their take-home pay, cutting into and in some cases eliminating their tips, which the men still viewed as just, if unofficial, compensation.[66]

By 1942, the ten-cents-a-bag plan had the red caps of the Pennsylvania railroad system "seething with discontent." "The whole procedure makes for bad service to the public," charged UTSEA local 602 chair E. C. Adams. "We have no incentive to work because old-fashioned tipping is practically non-existent." Their frustration proved so great that 110 Penn Station red caps signed an order instructing their paymaster to terminate payroll deductions for war bond purchases and requesting an immediate refund of all money previously withdrawn. "We felt we just couldn't support our families and buy war bonds too," explained F. A. McFeeters, a fifteen-year veteran red cap. Following a raging debate in the Penn Station locker room in which the "whole question of the colored man's place in the war effort was threshed out," the Penn Station men rescinded their war-bond cancellation plan.[67]

In the fight over the bag fee, the railway station managers came out ahead. At the union's insistence, the ICC conducted extensive hearings into the plan and concluded that while red cap charges were subject to ICC approval—requiring companies to file official tariffs for approval—the actual ten-cent fee was "not unreasonable, unjustly discriminatory, or unduly prejudicial."[68] Subsequent union efforts to block fee increases in the late 1940s similarly failed; by 1950, terminals were regularly charging twenty-five cents per bag. Red cap wages and benefits did rise over the course of the decade. As a result of a ruling of the Wage and Hour Division, red caps' minimum hourly wage rose to 36 cents in 1941 and 40 cents in 1942; subsequent negotiations with various carriers and terminal companies raised hourly wages to 57 cents by 1945, 91 cents in 1947, $1.28 in 1951, and $1.39 in 1952. A significant improvement over their 1930s remuneration, red cap wages in the 1940s were hardly impressive by many unions' standards. But the UTSEA's fear that higher bag fees would result in declining demand for red cap services was not unjustified. While increased fees did not "mean the extinction of red cap employment" predicted by Townsend in 1949, they contributed to the long-term decline of the trade.[69]

Indeed, travelers arriving at rail terminals found "the search for the familiar red cap of a porter a desperate one" by 1955, one observer noted. With air travel skimming off "the cream of the luxury travelers" and buses and cars competing with trains for passengers, stations were substantially reducing their red cap labor forces; Grand Central employed a mere 140 and Penn Station only 192. For the railroads, this writer argued, "the Red Cap operation is a losing proposition"; the need to economize had led to a reduction in forces. By the mid-1950s, two-wheeled baggage carts were appearing in stations. Under the "do-it-yourself plan," passengers essentially became their own red caps. By the early 1960s, railroad folklorist Freeman Hubbard counted a mere forty-two red caps in Grand Central.[70]

The UTSEA's reliance on federal involvement and the law was a double-edged sword. Sympathetic government officials in the Department of Labor and the Interstate Commerce Commission issued directives that enabled members of the small union to break out of their occupational limbo and define themselves as bona fide railroad workers. The law governing labor relations on the nation's railroads rewarded larger and stronger unions; the very rules of the game made it difficult for smaller unions to compete when established union interests were at stake. Nowhere was this truer than in the red caps' jurisdictional conflicts with the Brotherhood of Railway and Steamship Clerks, where the issues of race and democratic rights infused organizational competition between the two.

In the late 1930s and early 1940s St. Paul's Union Terminal became a battleground between the two organizations and their respective visions of organized labor. The question at issue was simple: did the IBRC/UTSEA have the right to represent station porters at the terminal? In 1938, forty-five St. Paul red caps joined the IBRC and approached the terminal's general superintendent the following year to negotiate a contract. The superintendent refused to meet with them, first claiming that red caps were not employees, then (after the ICC ruling) claiming that red caps were covered by an existing contract, a "scope" agreement, with the Brotherhood of Railway and Steamship Clerks. That agreement, signed in 1921, granted the Clerks jurisdiction over not only clerks but also "other office and station employees" and "baggage, mail and parcel room employees." During the life of the contract the Clerks had never sought to enroll red caps as members or even bargained on their behalf. Now the mere existence of this agreement allowed management to ignore the IBRC. The Brotherhood of Railway and Steamship Clerks was only too happy to play along with the company; it was eager to block the IBRC's advance.[71]

As it did in all cases where terminals refused to recognize it as the legitimate bargaining agent for red caps, the union invoked the services of the National Mediation Board, with the expectation that the IBRC would win a union representation election. This time, however, the NMB rejected the IBRC's petition. Following formal hearings in May 1940—over a year after the IBRC's initial petition—the NMB held that the St. Paul red caps were "part of the craft or class of clerical, office, station and storehouse employees and not a separate craft or class for the purposes of the Railway Labor Act" and certified the Clerks as the union for the red caps without the holding of an election. A clear minority in the larger union, the St. Paul red caps could not dislodge the Clerks or compel a change in its policies. The NMB decision in effect saddled black red caps with the same burden as black workers in the operating trades—firemen and brakemen in particular. As a minority, they were continually at the mercy of a majority of white workers whose unions excluded blacks, failed to bargain for them, and even worked to harm blacks' employment interests.[72] Red caps were engaged in a "life and death legal struggle," the Negro Labor Committee's Alfred Baker Lewis believed, predicting that if the decision stood, it would "wipe out" the UTSEA.[73]

The IBRC, like the BSCP's Provisional Committee and the independent associations of southern black firemen and brakemen, challenged the NMB decision through the courts, filing suit to overturn it. To the UTSEA, the ruling "amounts to a denial to the individuals in question of a voice in collective bargaining, making them, against their will and desire, a part of a craft or class in which they must of necessity always be a hopeless and voiceless minority." To be represented against their will by the Clerks would effectively leave them "without representation of any kind or character." In contrast, the Clerks portrayed the UTSEA's challenge of the NMB as a threat to organized labor: "[T]o transfer authority to designate collective bargaining agencies from the National Mediation Board to the federal courts would be a highly dangerous proceeding. It would mean stripping the Board of its most valuable function. It would mean numerous and indeterminable [*sic*] delays in the federal courts . . . That a labor union should seek to destroy the authority of a great mediating body in its own industry for the obviously trifling advantage gained by establishing a craft union of negligible proportions is beyond understanding."[74]

Both a U.S. District Court and a Circuit Court of Appeals sustained the UTSEA's charge, ordering the NMB to set aside its ruling conferring bargaining authority for the St. Paul red caps and ordering the certification of the UTSEA. The NMB's ruling would "force this particular group of employees to accept representation by an organization in which it has no right to membership, nor right to speak or be heard in its own behalf," wrote Circuit Court Chief Justice Groner in his decision. "This obviously is wrong and, if assented to, would create an intolerable situation." The decision, black labor journalist George McCray declared, "struck the shackles of jim crow unionism from the legs of the Negro railroad worker and sounded the death knell for discriminatory practices which have enthroned prejudice in the railroad industry."[75]

As was so often the case with legal victories, the pronouncement of the demise of racist labor and employment practices proved premature. In early December 1943, the Supreme Court without comment reversed the Circuit Court, upholding the Clerks' right to control the St. Paul red caps, simply citing its earlier rulings opposing court interference with the administrative determination of bargaining units. In one sharp blow, the Court handed the St. Paul red caps back to the Clerks. The Court's decision, however, proved less sweeping than its critics feared, for "scope" agreements were hardly widespread; the decision largely affected the St. Paul men alone.[76] It was also one of the final rulings that blatantly upheld railroad labor law's built-in support for racial discrimination. And, despite the Court's ruling against the UTSEA, the black red cap union continued to rely on the NMB's services to oversee free and fair elections to determine a bargaining agent. As the Brotherhood of Railway and Steamship Clerks moved to assert greater jurisdiction over workers in the occupational category of red cap, the board oversaw more and more such elections. In an overwhelming number of cases, the UTSEA was able to defeat the BRSC.

Faced with serious competition from the new independent union, the Clerks in 1939 authorized its executive council to arrange better representation and more contact with black workers. Consequently the Clerks, which excluded blacks from membership, announced the creation of Negro auxiliaries for black red caps. In contrast to biracial unions, which were organized along strict racial lines but whose constituent black and white locals claimed equal power, auxiliaries were unquestionably separate and unequal. In exchange for the payment of dues, black members received no voting rights or meaningful leadership posts; instead, they received white representation, nothing more. Once content to ignore many red cap unions that remained federal locals directly under the AFL's jurisdiction, the Clerks now insisted that those federal locals surrender their federal charters by March 1, 1941, and become full-fledged auxiliaries. Failure to comply would result in the full revocation of the local's federal charter—in essence, their expulsion from the AFL. As Clerks' Grand President George M. Harrison informed John R. Hoskins, a black red cap union leader in Oakland, California, in 1940, "We are not [sic] longer agreeable to continuing these arrangement for the reason that we now offer membership to these workers, in Auxiliary local Lodges." Lest Hoskins have any illusions about the relationship between the auxiliaries and the Clerks, Harrison dismissed the black leaders' concerns. "Frankly, the thing for you to do is to get into this organization and discontinue arguing about what has passed or what your status may be. We have no intention of revising our Constitution and Laws to meet the views of any groups of people who are not in affiliation."[77]

The Clerks' threats backfired. African-American freight handlers and express and station workers were the first to fight back. Refusing to be "shunted into a powerless, jim-crow organization," spokesmen informed the AFL president that they would not abide by the order to affiliate with the Clerks' new auxiliary. An auxiliary charter was a "poor substitute for a Union," they declared. The 1940 AFL convention witnessed black protests against the Clerks' move, but to no avail—the AFL revoked the federal union charter and the freight handlers "got the stab in the back, just another victim of A.F. of L. duplicity and its discrimination against the negro," in black union leader Jerry Orr's words.[78] Some fifty federal locals—including those in Birmingham, Philadelphia, Chicago, Roanoke, New Orleans, Cincinnati, and Louisville—formed a National Council of Freight Handlers, Express, and Station Employees. The freight handlers' "venture was doomed from the start," Herbert Northrup later concluded. To win independence or recognition required the NMB to classify them as a separate class of freight handlers or station employees. But just as the board had rejected the red caps' contention that they constituted a distinct "craft or class" in the St. Paul case, the mediation board also refused to separate freight handlers from the larger classification of clerks and station employees. By 1942, the National Council had disbanded. Some of its members joined the UTSEA; most joined the CIO's Utility Workers' Organizing Committee.[79]

The red caps had far greater success, for despite the NMB ruling in the St. Paul case, the UTSEA had already achieved widespread recognition and success where "scope" agreements were not in effect. When workers had a choice, they rejected racist auxiliaries and voted for the UTSEA. "As everyone knows, this union [the Clerks] has a color-bar in its constitution and has manifested no interest in the welfare of the Red Caps," the NAACP's executive secretary, Walter White, informed C. M. Dickson of Penn Station. "Now that the Red Caps are attempting to organize," George Harrison "arrogantly demands" that the UTSEA "disband and come into his union and accept its jurisdiction without any voice or vote." Calling on red caps to reject Harrison and "his Negro-hating clique," the UTSEA advanced the argument that the "best and only way red caps can protect themselves is by their own organization and their own collective strength."[80]

Most station porters apparently agreed. Workers at the New Orleans terminal, for instance, voted 100 percent for the UTSEA over the Clerks in a NMB election. More important was the revolt of West Coast federal locals. By early

1941 California, Utah, and Arizona locals had refused the Clerks' ultimatum, severed their ties with the AFL, and joined the UTSEA. This "tidal wave of organized protest against the formation of 'jim-crow' auxiliary locals," as the UTSEA put it, involved the defection of federal locals in Phoenix, Ogden (Utah), the San Francisco bay area, Los Angeles, Santa Barbara, and elsewhere. "Our membership will never submit to the dictatorial policies outlined by the Executive Council of the A.F. of L. in conformity with a jim-crow conspiracy fomented by George M. Harrison," declared John R. Hoskins of San Francisco and James A. Gray of Los Angeles, leaders of the West Coast federal locals.[81] In the subsequent NMB election, the UTSEA swept the race, winning the votes of most Southern Pacific railroad and Ogden Railway Depot station porters; only months later, it similarly carried the Los Angeles Union Terminal by a huge majority. To Ernest Calloway, it was a "great day for the step children of American democracy, and it was Jim-Crow's 'Last Union Stand'" among red caps. With the election, California had become the "grave-yard for the malignant and diseased body of jim crowed unionism."[82] Despite the judicial setback in the St. Paul case, the UTSEA emerged as the clear victor in head-to-head contests with the Clerks.

By the end of the 1940s, red caps could look back with a sense of accomplishment at how far they had come since the Great Depression. As early as 1941, the Wage and Hour Division of the Department of Labor could report significant improvements in the red caps' overall condition: "Union negotiation won seniority rights, decreases in working hours, the elimination of the 7-day week, adjustment procedures, and other changes," including coverage under New Deal era unemployment compensation and retirement laws.[83]

In the larger arenas of race, politics, and the labor movement, the union could point to a number of developments with considerable satisfaction. In 1942, the UTSEA finally ended its five-year experiment as an independent union and affiliated with the CIO, providing its leaders with a much firmer and larger organizational platform from which to attack racism in the railroad industry, the labor movement, and in American society generally. Along with formal affiliation came the appointment of Townsend to the CIO's executive board, making him the first black appointment to the board and the highest-ranking African American within the CIO. In 1946, the UTSEA for the first time negotiated contracts with the Savannah Union Station and the Memphis Union Station that afforded black and white station employees equal protection and equal opportunity for promotion.[84] That same year, the union completed a nine-year campaign to make long-term red caps eligible for railroad retirement benefits. Excluded by the old Railroad Retirement Act because they had worked strictly for tips and had paid nothing into the retirement fund before 1938, red caps now won the same benefits as those received by other railroad workers.[85] And in 1947, the UTSEA finally faced down the opposition of the Railway Clerks, winning official designation as one of twenty-three "standard" railroad labor organizations, with the right to participate in the selection of labor representatives to the National Railroad Adjustment Board and the National Mediation Board.[86]

In the late 1930s and early 1940s, red cap unionists were swept forward by the same tide that lifted the Brotherhood of Sleeping Car Porters and black workers in numerous CIO unions to an unprecedented place in the American labor movement. The IBRC/UTSEA carved out a legitimate place for itself in face of tremendous employer opposition and won for its members conditions and rights undreamed of in the pre-union era. But much remained to be done. On the economic front, union members failed to secure satisfactory compensation, and the railroads dramatically reduced the size of the red cap labor force. On the racial front, they continued to spar with the hostile white Clerks, to operate under a set of labor laws that often discriminated against them, and to deal with unsympathetic officials on railway labor agencies. And in the 1940s, the UTSEA's attempts to broaden the occupational base of its membership met with only modest success, as its efforts brought it into sharp jurisdictional conflict with both the BSCP and the dining car workers. Despite these limitations, the UTSEA provided a solid platform for Willard Townsend and his fellow union leaders to launch their own campaigns against discrimination in the labor movement and American society.

6

The Politics of Fair Employment

When they opened on September 15, 1943, the hearings of the Fair Employment Practice Committee (FEPC) into racial discrimination in the railroad industry promised "to be the biggest show ever scheduled" by that federal wartime agency. The four days of testimony did not disappoint the committee's supporters. A dedicated FEPC staff carefully choreographed the entire event, scheduling strong testimony from the victims of discrimination, coordinating testimony to avoid repetition, and placing the revelations of contemporary injustices in a larger context of the railroad industry's long history of racial discrimination. The staff even consulted a public relations firm, whose director, Winthrop Martin, assisted in crafting the opening statement. Martin advised "that moral indignation has a deserving spot in this whole deal, and that the plight of the victims of discrimination must be dramatized at the same time that it is factually presented." This was advice FEPC personnel needed little encouragement to follow, given their commitment to black economic equality and their distaste for the record of discrimination they uncovered.[1]

Among the roughly five hundred people who gathered in the auditorium of the Department of Labor in Washington, D.C., were the principal leaders of the black trade union movement in the railroad industry—A. Philip Randolph of the Brotherhood of Sleeping Car Porters (BSCP) and the Provisional Committee to Organize Colored Locomotive Firemen, Richard Smith of the Joint Council of Dining Car Employees, Samuel Clark of the Association of Colored Railway Trainmen (ACRT), and others. Dozens of rank-and-file black railroaders had also made their way to Washington to observe the proceedings or testify to the persistent discrimination against dining car waiters, car cleaners, switchmen, locomotive firemen, brakemen, and train porters. Black activists Ed Teague, Bester Steele, and Zelner Clay, current or future litigants in employment discrimination lawsuits against railroads and white brotherhoods, also participated in the hearings.[2]

Targeting twenty-two railroad companies and fourteen white labor unions, chief FEPC counsel Bartley Crum minced no words in his lengthy introductory statement. Crum laid out a detailed case against railroad companies and white unions based on the FEPC's two-year investigation into the railroad industry. The parade of fifty witnesses that followed provided the evidence to illustrate Crum's case. The black workers' tales of individual and collective exclusion from white unions, demotion to lower-paying jobs, bars on their promotion, and countless stories of personal slights and systematic racism they experienced were powerful and compelling.[3] No white trade unionists testified in defense of their brotherhoods, for the large white railroad unions simply stayed away.

"In a certain sense, these hearings are ritualistic," the *Washington Post* suggested. The "evidence of discrimination against Negroes is apparent to the naked eye of anyone who has ever traveled on the railroads of the United States," and even the railroad companies openly "acknowledge that discriminatory practices are written into their agreements with railway labor organizations."[4] Yet the ritual was important, for what was supposedly apparent to the naked eye had rarely found its way into the broader public consciousness. By the end of the fourth and final day of the hearings, black railroaders had successfully made their case, FEPC members had vindicated themselves, and the expectations of civil rights activists and supporters were high. Two months later, the FEPC issued "Findings and Directives" to twenty railroads and seven unions. The FEPC ordered the immediate elimination of numerous discriminatory practices and contract provisions and insisted that employment and promotion policies disregard race and that all workers be accorded equal seniority rights and equal work opportunities.[5] Never before had a government agency targeted such widespread, systematic, and deeply entrenched employment discrimination.

The World War II years offered black operating craft workers unprecedented opportunities to showcase their plight and to enlist new allies in their war against discrimination. Even as the white railroad brotherhoods and railroad companies conspired to reduce further their numbers and otherwise block their advances, African Americans on the nation's railroads had good reason to be guardedly optimistic. With the American economy shifting into high gear after more than a decade of depression, they could point to the irrationality of a system that barred them from vital railroad positions that went begging for white labor. They could also point to the immorality of racial exclusion during a war ostensibly fought on behalf of democratic nations in Europe against an expansionist and racist Germany. At last it seemed possible not only to publicize their industry's racism widely, but also to undermine or even overturn it. Backed by a growing chorus of African-American associations, liberal and radical white organizations, and the FEPC, black railroaders allowed themselves a moment of hope as they intensified their struggle for equality.

For all the innovative changes it brought about in American society, the New Deal failed to accomplish its intended task: the ending of the Great Depression. But what political programs failed to produce, preparing for and fighting a major global war did. Filling war orders for the Allies and for its own military pulled the American economy out of the depression by 1940–41. By the early 1940s, production levels had skyrocketed and overall unemployment was negligible. World War II proved to be a tremendous boon to the American economy, as rapidly expanding military production absorbed industrial and human resources. By the time the war ended in 1945, the United States had emerged as the world's foremost military and economic power.

African Americans were slow to reap the benefits of economic recovery. Indeed, it took almost three years of the defense buildup before black workers benefited from the war-induced economic expansion. At the outset of the country's mobilization for war, many defense industries refused to hire black workers, and those they did hire were concentrated disproportionately at the bottom of the job ladder. In contrast to the World War I experience, when the economy of the industrial North experienced significant labor shortages, mobilization for World War II began with labor surpluses. Large numbers of unemployed whites could be absorbed into the economy, and employers were free, at least at the outset, to indulge their racial preferences without serious consequences. Over the course of the war, the military draft caused the labor supply to contract. With the resulting competition for labor, black workers were again drawn upon in large numbers. But certain sectors of American industry and the trade union movement continued to discriminate, preventing the full utilization of black labor for the war's duration.

The war in Asia and Europe placed severe pressures on the American railroad industry. Researchers have estimated that the industry moved some "91 percent of all military freight within the country and 98 percent of all military personnel," while freight traffic, "measured in ton miles, soared from 373 billion in 1940 to 737 billion in 1944" and passenger traffic reached a historic high in 1944 that "would never again be equaled."[6] Accordingly, the railroads' wartime appetite for labor was voracious. Yet the industry resisted hiring and promoting blacks to skilled positions.

The strains involved in recruiting and maintaining an expanding railroad labor force were evident early in the war. By 1943, for instance, the Union Pacific "was losing employees as fast as it hired them," as the draft and especially competition from other industries drained away its workers.[7] To address its labor problems, the Southern Pacific (SP) railroad arranged to re cruit workers from other parts of the country. One study suggested that as many as 3,100 men, most of whom were black southerners, were recruited and transported to California, at Southern Pacific's expense, to work as laborers. Contrary to the SP's promises, the railroad recruited minors, ignored requirements to conduct medical exams, and provided inadequate transportation facilities. A lack of coordination meant that at times between 300 and 400 men would arrive in Los Angles in a single day, without adequate arrangements in place for their reception or effective deployment. The program failed to retain many of its black laborers. Only around half of those recruited actually went to work for the SP; 15 percent deserted en route to California, 15 percent refused to work once they arrived, and another 20 percent quit after a short stint on the job. The "unusual severity" of working conditions, particularly along the SP's desert sections, and the availability of better-paying wartime jobs prompted significant turnover. The Southern Pacific's negative experiences convinced Pennsylvania railroad executives to recommend against the employment of imported southern blacks. But even among northern blacks, the allure of higher wages and better jobs caused high turnover. The Pennsylvania railroad's black section hands employed in its Maryland division camp car outfits and its loaders and truckers in Chicago were "floaters" who would quit work after they were paid, while section men in New York would "quit without giving any reason."[8]

Confronted with serious shortages of brakemen and freight handlers that threatened to slow war-related freight traffic, the Baltimore and Ohio railroad (B&O) collaborated with the War Manpower Commission (WMC) and the Brotherhood of Railway Trainmen to procure workers. "Are you working in essential industry?" a B&O advertisement read. "If not—get a job as railroad brakeman—help move troops and war material to battle fronts." The company maintained its lily-white employment policy, however, launching a recruiting campaign to attract "white men only." Such explicit racial preferences extended even to the ranks of unskilled freight handlers. While the doors of the Railroad Employment Board, established by the WMC to "stabilize and recruit railroad labor," were open to anyone regardless of race, the board exercised no influence over the railroads to which it referred its recruits. "As to whether the men are hired or not," observed Lawrence E. Fenneman, Maryland WMC director, "that is beyond the limits of the commission." A member of the B&O employment office staff admitted that the company "was not even considering the hiring of colored men for fireman and brakeman jobs." Rather, the only vacancies open for black men and women were rail yard labor jobs. With little response from local white men in Baltimore, the WMC appealed to out-of-state whites to fill empty jobs and resorted to hiring white women to work not only as clerks in its offices but as telegraphers, ticket sellers, yard and shop workers, guards, maintenance-of-way crew members, and, in a small number of cases, as brakemen.[9]

From virtually every part of the country, black workers testified to the persistent exclusion they encountered despite labor shortages. Cornelius C. Hill, president of Local 339 of the International Brotherhood of Firemen and Oilers for the B&O in Dayton, insisted in 1942 that the company "would do without before hireing [sic] Negro workers." Only when jobs were "too dirty" or paid too little for whites were blacks employed.[10] In Memphis, black activists claimed that the Illinois Central had hired some five hundred brakemen, firemen, and switchmen between 1941 and September 1942—all of them white. A large number of young black men, "all high school graduates," found their applications for work rejected "because of racial identification." "We have consistently been requesting that some of our boys be hired," an anonymous black writer complained, "but we are always turned down." When twenty-four-year-old Wade Lee Jackson applied for a fireman's position on the IC's Memphis Terminal Division in August 1943, he was informed that although he possessed sufficient experience, the IC "was not hiring any Colored Firemen at present," for the traveling engineer had "six white boys coming out of school and would have to place them" before he could consider Jackson's application.[11]

Black workers already in the employ of railroads sought better-paying jobs with little success. The Chesapeake and Ohio Railway locomotive shops at Huntington, West Virginia, were promoting white laborers with little experience to machinist and other helper positions during the war. When Charles Wilson, a shop laborer with seniority dating to 1923 and a member of the black Firemen, Oilers, Helpers, Roundhouse and Railway Shop Laborers' Local no. 637, became the first African American in almost fifteen years to be promoted to machinist's helper in October 1942, a shop committee of the white International Association of Machinists immediately filed a complaint with the company. After a mere three days on the job, the C&O removed Wilson from his helper's position and reassigned him to his old laborer's job.[12] Employment bars extended to the West as well. In Cheyenne, Wyoming, sixty firemen and oilers on the Union Pacific were promoted to become helpers of various mechanical crafts, but blacks and men of Mexican descent were turned down "without a satisfactory excuse." These men, union official Jesse Gonzalez predicted, "are doomed to remain laborers as long as they are employed by this railroad."[13]

Black women became an increasingly important source of railway labor during the war. By 1943, when the military draft had depleted the ranks of its train porters, a job classification held exclusively by black men, B&O managers temporarily replaced them with black women. At its Orangeville shop in

East Baltimore, the Pennsylvania railroad put at least fifty women to work as water and fire watchers, engine oilers, cleaners, tool gatherers, and sweepers. More commonly, black women secured work as common laborers. The Pennsylvania railroad as early as 1942 put them to work as section hands on maintenance track crews, having the women perform "light tasks," such as cleaning and trimming ballast between Philadelphia and Harrisburg, reserving heavier work for men. In the Missouri Pacific's Kingsville, Texas, division shops, black women washed and steamed engines, swept, moved freight, and cleaned boxcars; office work was reserved for whites.[14]

Like black men, black women encountered significant resistance to their attempts to enter fields of work previously closed to them. When Mildred Johnson answered a Pennsylvania railroad advertisement for shop workers in Pittsburgh in 1942, she was told that the road "would not hire colored women because they had no rest rooms for colored women." Johnson observed twenty-five to thirty women applying for the shop jobs that morning, of whom only two were black. "Two Colored women as clean and neat as any women there. Without work, no support, turned away because they have no rest rooms for colored women." In the end, "ten women was hired while I stood there." "I am discouraged enough to die," she reported to the War Manpower Commission. "Where do we fit in? Our men are fighting—for what? So women like me . . . are driven to the highest point of desperation?"[15]

"Women and Negroes now hold many transportation jobs in which they have not previously been employed," an Office of War Information report concluded in 1943, "but, war or no war, unwillingness to employ Negroes in many types of railroad jobs persists in many places." That unwillingness extended from the ranks of organized white labor and management to federal officials. In 1944, the Office of Defense Transportation (ODT) formed a Railroad Manpower Mobilization Committee—composed of representatives of the ODT, the WMC, the Railroad Retirement Board, white unions, and the Association of American Railroads (AAR)—to conduct another labor recruitment drive in the hopes of filling an estimated 100,000 existing and predicted job vacancies among the ranks of trackmen, brakemen, firemen, clerks, telegraphers, signalmen, towermen, and freight handlers.[16] But African Americans were largely bypassed in the near desperate search for new labor. By the following year, the Children's Department of the Department of Labor was cooperating with the AAR, various brotherhoods, and government agencies in establishing advisory standards for employing sixteen- and seventeen-year-olds. "With the shortage of labor what it is and with 'railroading' as glamorous as it is to the average American boy," the Bureau noted, "some direction is needed."[17]

To the director of the ODT, veteran railroad administrator Joseph East-man, procuring labor was an issue of manpower, not "a question of social re-form." The ODT would not follow the FEPC's confrontational approach, which, Eastman believed, generated too much unnecessary heat and too little light with its "inflammatory publicity, mass meetings, et cetera." The FEPC might have accomplished more if it had adopted "quieter, less emotion-rous-ing tactics." In practice, Eastman's approach required "a certain tolerance even of intolerance," but under his authority the ODT tolerated more than a little intolerance and solved neither the manpower shortage nor racial con-flicts in the transportation industry. Just weeks before the FEPC railroad hearings in September 1943, the ODT unveiled a thirteen-point manpower program urging intensified recruitment of women, Mexicans, and even pris-oners of war; just months after the FEPC issued its "Findings and Directives" ordering an end to discrimination in railroad hiring, the southeastern rail-roads—which retained their antiblack employment policies—issued an SOS for 7,000 new workers, calling on a receptive ODT for assistance in their re-cruitment drive. Severe and persistent labor shortages of track labor eventu-ally led the WMC to authorize a railroad bracero program, recruiting over 100,000 Mexicans for work on some thirty-six railroads from 1943 until the war's end.[18]

Even when it possessed unquestioned authority, the federal government refused to move decisively to uphold its stated goal of nondiscrimination. To prevent a threatened general strike by white nonoperating workers in late 1943, the federal government briefly took control over the nation's railroad system. Any walkout would constitute not a strike against a private company but against the government. Would the Army, which had effected the take-over, use its power to implement the FEPC's antidiscrimination directives? The FEPC had just certified its case and had turned it over to the president for action; the federal seizure of the railroads to ensure continuous produc-tion offered a unique opportunity to strike a blow against discrimination. Army officials quickly put a stop to any such wishful thinking. "We are not going into this job to adjudicate labor disputes, wage arguments, and things of that kind," announced General Brehon Somervell. Instead, the Army would maintain the status quo and would not involve itself in any way with matters of discrimination.[19]

Railroad labor demand remained high through 1944 and 1945, and short-ages contributed to slowdowns of hospital and troop trains. By late 1944, the shortage of workers in certain occupations in the Minneapolis–St. Paul area—including refrigeration laborers, tarmen, and shop and roundhouse la-borers was acute. By mid-1945, nothing had improved. The "present criti-cal shortage can be laid in a great measure to the failure of certain of the railroad unions . . . to upgrade qualified Negro workers, and to the outright, violent opposition of others to even hiring them," concluded the *Minneapolis Spokesman*. To meet the desperate demand for labor, the Army proposed releasing 4,000 white railroaders from its ranks while continuing recruitment campaigns. "Now, when the railroads should be able to dip into a huge reservoir of Negro labor," the *Spokesman* argued angrily, "they cannot do so because of the discriminatory customs which have grown up practically unchallenged." By systematically excluding blacks from "integration into all branches of railroad employment, except in the lowest paid brackets," the railroads were forced to address their manpower shortages by depending "on restricted 'barrel scrappings' of white labor."[20] Shortly before the end of World War II, Elmer W. Henderson, the Chicago regional director of the FEPC, was "amazed to learn that the railroads had informed the War Department that no other alternative to the use of soldiers was available." There was an alternative, he suggested: "remove the racial bars in these jobs."[21] By the end of the war, however, the moment for reform had passed. If the railroads proved resistant to the use of African Americans when they were desperate for labor, they were hardly about to reverse their policies in the postwar era, when the demand for labor would undoubtedly fall.

Against the backdrop of extensive discrimination, African Americans debated the proper strategies for effectively breaking into war-related jobs as soon as it became evident that military-induced prosperity was going to leave them behind. The NAACP, in characteristic fashion, worked behind the scenes in 1940 and 1941, seeking meetings with midlevel government officials to complain about persistent employment discrimination in defense industries. A. Philip Randolph raised the stakes considerably. Growing increasingly dissatisfied with President Roosevelt's refusal to take a forthright stand against defense discrimination, Randolph conceived an idea of a march on Washington to pressure the administration into taking action. In mid-January 1941, he publicly announced his plan; by March, he had formed a March on Washington Movement (MOWM) to carry it out. "Only power can effect the enforcement and adoption of a given policy," he declared. "Power and pressure are at the foundation of the march of social justice and reform. I suggest that TEN THOUSAND Negroes march on Washington, D.C . . . with the slogan: WE LOYAL NEGRO AMERICAN CITIZENS DEMAND THE RIGHT TO WORK AND FIGHT FOR OUR COUNTRY."[22] Promising at first to bring ten thousand African Americans to Washington, he soon raised that number by a factor of ten. With the financial and organizational backing of the BSCP and the NAACP, the MOWM established chapters across the country devoted to organizing support for the march and getting out the marchers. Whether the MOWM could have brought out 100,000 black protesters remains a matter of debate, as does the question of whether it really intended to try. But unquestionably the march proposal struck a nerve in black American communities. Thousands "will invade Washington, D.C., the nation's capital and the fountain head of racial prejudice, in a mammoth mass demonstration," the *Michigan Chronicle* enthusiastically predicted.[23]

Randolph's gambit both tapped into and helped shape the mood of black Americans. Black support for World War II was not, as it largely had been in World War I, uncritical. W. E. B. Du Bois's 1918 call to African Americans to "close ranks" behind the war effort found few echoes among national black leaders two and a half decades later. The *Pittsburgh Courier* promoted a Double V campaign, calling for "victory over our enemies from without . . . [and] victory over our enemies from within," that is, against fascism abroad and against racism at home. Less a grand campaign per se, Double V was more an idea, one that was picked up by national and local groups who used it to justify their protests during a period of national emergency. At the grassroots level, many blacks expressed an ambivalence toward the war that deeply worried military and political officials. "I wouldn't mind fighting for a country that gave me a chance to make a living," Charles Johnson reported one black Georgia janitor as saying. "I don't feel like fighting for a country that gives everybody a chance but me."[24]

The 1940s witnessed an organizational upsurge in black America that was unprecedented in its scale, involving not only urban African Americans in the North but black southerners as well. Nationally, the NAACP alone grew from 50,000 in some 355 branches in 1940 to 450,000 in over 1,000 branches in 1946. For all of the persistent discrimination in the trade union movement, African-American membership in the new Congress of Industrial Organizations (CIO) reached at least half a million.[25] The growth in protest and activist organizations reflected a dispositional change on the part of growing numbers of black Americans. "Traditional patterns of behavior between Negroes and whites are being suddenly disturbed by the war," Charles Johnson noted in his 1943 assessment. "Negro masses are becoming more articulate and their methods of protest more varied and intense, including . . . petitions and picketings, protest parades, mass meetings, and mob violence." Building on these observations, historians of African-American protest in recent years have pushed back the origins of the modern civil rights movement from the 1950s into the 1940s and even the 1930s. World War II "was the seedtime of the racial and legal metamorphosis that was to sweep over the South," argues historian Steven Lawson. "The war propelled a growth of racial consciousness and a burst of militancy that foreshadowed the assault on Jim Crow."[26] Randolph's confrontational challenge was among the first large-scale expressions of this new mood and the willingness to act on it.

Randolph's threat caught the government's attention and raised the issue of discrimination as virtually nothing else had. Over the next several months, Randolph and the NAACP's Walter White engaged in high-level negotiations with administration officials and their allies. As early as September 1940, Randolph, White, and the Urban League's T. Arnold Hill demanded that the government mandate integration in the defense industries and the armed forces. Their demands at first ignored, the threat of the march now commanded the administration's attention, if not agreement. But nothing the New Dealers could say would satisfy the march supporters. Eleanor Roosevelt, considered a better friend of civil rights than her husband, warned that the march would generate tremendous bitterness in Congress; others cautioned that it would embarrass the president, weaken national defense, and encourage America's foreign enemies. All proved unable to dissuade Randolph from carrying out his threat. Even President Roosevelt's personal commitment to support better treatment for African-American war workers left Randolph and his allies unmoved.[27]

In the end, the president blinked first. The result was an executive order, written by a young white lawyer in the Office for Emergency Management, Joseph Rauh (who would, after the war, become one of the BSCP's leading attorneys), in close consultation with Randolph. There "shall be no discrimination in the employment of workers in defense industries or government because of race, creed, color, or national origin," declared the president in his Executive Order 8802 issued on June 25, 1941. Both defense industries and unions should allow all workers to participate fairly in defense work. To implement the order, the president established a Fair Employment Practice Committee to investigate and resolve charges of discrimination. Having achieved much of his aim, Randolph called off the march days before it was to have taken place.[28]

For black workers, the executive order resoundingly validated their antidiscrimination campaign on the moral and political level but offered imperfect tools to accomplish their goals. To some, the order was the "most significant move on the part of the government since the Emancipation Proclamation," for it placed the government boldly on record as opposed to employment discrimination, at least in defense industries. But others, including a number of MOWM local chapters, denounced the order as inadequate. The order addressed only part of Randolph's agenda—employment discrimination—and said nothing about segregation and discrimination in the military; moreover, the organization it created, the FEPC, lacked enforcement powers. Calling off the march was premature, claimed black labor journalist George McCray. "We definitely lost an excellent opportunity to clarify or crystallize our thinking on the woefully neglectful problem of building the internal economic solidarity of the Negro community." Defending his actions, Randolph vowed to keep the MOWM alive as a watchdog over the FEPC. Over the next four years, the MOWM would sponsor numerous rallies to maintain political pressure on the Roosevelt administration. The pursuit of equality continued to require black protest.[29]

From the administration's perspective, the creation of the FEPC at least temporarily addressed two competing goals. "Certainly we have accomplished what the President wanted," FEPC head Mark Ethridge privately confessed to the White House on the eve of his resignation in late 1941. "We paralyzed any idea of a march on Washington and we have worked honestly for a better measure of justice for the Negroes." However, in subsequent months, the tension between the twin goals of neutralizing black protest and ensuring black equality would resurface sharply. Continued black protest and the emergence of a white backlash guaranteed that the politics of fair employment would remain anything but settled.[30]

During the course of its brief wartime life, the FEPC was not an independent agency; initially situated within the Office of Production Management, it was transferred, without warning, in July 1942 to the new War Manpower Commission, which simply overruled FEPC policy when it clashed with its own priorities. That transfer, committee secretary Lawrence Cramer believed, "indicated a lack of confidence in and disapproval of the Committee's activities . . . [and] was intended to strangle the Committee with or without sound." Many FEPC supporters agreed, fearing that the annexation revealed the hand of "Machiavellian Southerners anxious to hamstring the committee."[31] Lodging an appeal to have the FEPC's independent status restored, the NAACP found it "fantastic to have two agencies under one director, one of which permits and almost invites discrimination, while the other is charged with the duty of opposing discrimination." Even the National Negro Business League, a group not known for its radicalism, recommended a restoration of the committee's independent authority.[32]

The FEPC's problems extended well beyond its lack of institutional autonomy. Its powers remained weak. It had no authority, for example, to subpoena witnesses or documents; it could only make formal requests, which witnesses could refuse. Its orders carried only moral weight, for the committee had no means to actually enforce them. From the start, the committee's staffing and funding levels were inadequate to the magnitude of its task; recalcitrant trade unions and businesses thumbed their noses at FEPC investigators; and hostile congressmen and senators erected numerous roadblocks in its path. The new policy of antidiscrimination clashed with the more dominant policy of uninterrupted war production. Where addressing racial discrimination promised to disrupt production, more powerful government agencies either looked the other way or simply ignored the FEPC altogether

Even within the FEPC, appointees had varying degrees of enthusiasm. Its first chairman, Louisville editor Mark Ethridge, a white southern liberal who supported segregation, described Executive Order 8802 as "a war order and not a social document."[33] What the FEPC could—and did—do was shine a spotlight on the racist practices of unions and employers, pushing them to change their ways. In some cases, the committee was successful; in too many others—that of the railroad industry in particular—it met with repeated failure.[34]

Despite its weaknesses, the FEPC became the focus of black railroaders' efforts to document and protest the pervasive and worsening employment discrimination they confronted. Because of inadequate staffing and funding levels, the FEPC had to rely on the initiative and cooperation of individual black workers and their organizations. "We have got to have specific instances of actual discrimination and alleged violations of the Order since the Order was put into effect," committee member and BSCP official Milton P. Webster insisted. "We want facts, figures, names, dates, and places."[35] Complaints from individual black locomotive firemen, porter brakemen, firemen and oilers, coach cleaners, dining car waiters, mechanics, and others began flooding the FEPC office by the fall of 1941. Many of these men sought the FEPC's help, offered to provide detailed information on specific instances or patterns of discrimination, and volunteered their services.[36]

Indeed, local organizations of black workers carried out much of the actual legwork for the committee, at least initially. These local groups supplied a steady stream of damning evidence: Provisional Committee members in Selma, Alabama, for instance, forwarded the names of black men who had unsuccessfully applied for work as firemen, while officers of the ACRT and the International Association of Railway Employees (IARE) provided lengthy reports on the conditions facing their members.[37] Committee member Milton P. Webster appealed to Thomas Redd of the IARE to draw upon his "wide contact" with black railroad organizations, urging them to get together and collect the relevant information. The left-led Chicago Committee on Railroad Employment circulated questionnaires to black workers in that city, assembled data for the FEPC's use, and sponsored mass meetings in support of black railroaders. In 1943, it submitted a lengthy brief outlining discriminatory practices against black railroad labor.[38]

FEPC field representatives were themselves actively gathering information in the South by the fall of 1942. Maceo Hubbard, who was overseeing the preparations for the railroad hearing, began interviewing complainants in Virginia, the Carolinas, Alabama, and Georgia, while two white field representatives directed their efforts toward white unions and company officials. The committee appointed Harry Epstein, a former solicitor general from

New York, as the FEPC's special counsel in preparing the railroad case and two African-American attorneys, Charles Hamilton Houston and Harold Stevens, as assistant counsel. With its investigators in place, the FEPC finally announced its plan for three days of hearings in early December, soon postponed until late January 1943.[39]

However weak the FEPC appeared to some supporters, to its detractors it seemed far too powerful. Following the November 1942 election, in which New Dealers fared poorly, southern Democratic senators intensified the pressure against the FEPC. Dispatching a delegation to the White House, they "laid down an ultimatum that unless the hearings were canceled, the administration could not enact any of its legislation." Moreover, presidential aide Marvin McIntyre, no friend of the committee, fueled opposition to the scheduled hearing into industry and union abuses by leaking an internal FEPC report to the president of the Brotherhood of Railway and Steamship Clerks, George Harrison, who then lobbied the White House. "Certain ambitious negroes" were using the FEPC "to promote negro labor unions," Harrison complained. The "agitation [of the] Negro question . . . was unfortunate and . . . creating dissension among the people."[40] The FEPC's opponents got their way. In mid-January, Roosevelt pulled the plug on the railroad hearings scheduled for January 25. Without consulting or even warning FEPC members, he ordered WMC director Paul McNutt to postpone them indefinitely.[41]

The cancellation of the railroad hearings struck black railroaders and their supporters like lightning.[42] Condemnation of the cancellation was swift and far more harsh than the protests half a year earlier when Roosevelt had suddenly transferred the FEPC to the War Manpower Commission. Special counsels Harry Epstein, Charles Hamilton Houston, and Harold A. Stevens immediately resigned from the FEPC in disgust. "Mr. McNutt's action followed the traditional pattern of sacrificing the Negro whenever an attempt to do him justice antagonizes powerful reactionary forces in industry and labor," Houston wrote. "But if the Government thinks it has purchased domestic peace and has satisfied the reactionaries by this surrender of principle, it has forgotten the lessons of history, including Chamberlain at Munich . . . Mr. McNutt has not merely repudiated the Negro; far worse for the future of this country he has made a mockery of the nation's war aims."[43]

Across the nation, grassroots and established African-American organizations sprang into action. "Negroes," the *Chicago Sun* reported, were said to be "in a very explosive frame of mind" and were "not going to be content to accept any 'shush-shush way of meeting the problem.'" An interracial delegation of fifty northern activists and clergy met with McNutt in Washington, pressing him without success to explain his actions and condemning him for his "paternalistic and insulting attitude" toward the delegation.⁴⁴ In New York, the Negro Labor Victory Committee held protest rallies at the Abyssinian Baptist Church, while in the Midwest, Alexander Saxton, secretary of the Chicago Negro Labor Win the War Conference, pledged his Sub-Committee on Railroad Employment's support to Milton Webster and the FEPC. In alliance with the All-Chicago Committee against Discrimination, Saxton's group scheduled mass meetings and directed petitions and telegrams of protest to President Roosevelt. "Everything depends now on your action," Saxton wrote Webster. "We urge you not to resign in individual protest" but instead "carry the issue to the American people."⁴⁵

Milton Webster and A. Philip Randolph drew upon the organizational infrastructure of the March on Washington Movement and the BSCP's Provisional Committee to publicize the FEPC's cause and to renew pressure on the government. In late January 1943, a Provisional Committee-sponsored mass meeting at the Vermont Avenue Baptist Church in Washington, D.C., brought out fifteen hundred people to protest McNutt's cancellation of the railroad hearings. A week later, a "Save the FEPC" conference, also sponsored by the Provisional Committee, attracted the support of forty-two organizations, which sent 150 delegates to Washington to discuss ways of "saving and preserving the independent status of the FEPC" and pursuing the fight to prevent "Order 8802 from becoming a scrap of paper." Not surprisingly, black railroad unions—the BSCP, its Provisional Committee, the Joint Council of Dining Car Employees, the UTSEA, and the independent ACRT and IARE—were well represented. In addition, participants in the two-day affair included large interracial unions such as the UAW and a wide range of liberal, civil rights, and religious organizations, such as the ACLU, the Socialist party, the Federal Council of Churches, the Washington Urban League, the NAACP, the Baptist Ministers Conference, and the National Negro Congress. The conference concluded by insisting that the railway hearings be rescheduled, that the FEPC be granted an adequate budget, that the FEPC be removed from the WMC, and that its initial independent status be restored.⁴⁶

For months following McNutt's controversial move, the Roosevelt administration deliberated the FEPC's future while powerless and frustrated committee members awaited word of its fate. "My feeling is that this question is becoming one of the sorest places in the whole business of the home front," conceded presidential aide Jonathan Daniels in January 1943. "No action with regard to the FEPC is possible which does not involve some continuance of agitation and friction. A policy of postponement of action now will rather increase than minimize the emotions already aroused." It was the administration's fear of mounting criticism from African-American and liberal groups that prompted the White House to devise a plan for a thorough reorganization of the FEPC. Roosevelt's Executive Order 9346 established a new FEPC and appointed a six-member board with Monsignor Francis J. Haas, previously with the National Labor Relations Board, as chair. Earl Dickinson, a Chicago African American who was one of the most vocal and radical members on the original committee, was not reappointed. The reorganized committee was removed from the WMC and McNutt's oversight and granted independent status in the Office of Economic Management, answerable to the president. In addition, the FEPC's budget was increased to half a million dollars, and the opening of numerous field offices was authorized. Many viewed these developments as a considerable victory. With its new lease on life, the FEPC prepared for the long-awaited railroad hearings.[47]

The September 1943 railroad hearings represented the showdown that black activists and rank-and-file railroad workers had long waited for. Days before the hearings opened, large numbers of black firemen prepared for the hearings at the Vermont Avenue Baptist Church in Washington, D.C., under the auspices of the BSCP's Provisional Committee, while twenty black newspaper editors descended on the nation's capital for conferences with FEPC officials. On September 15, black and white spectators filled the Department of Labor auditorium. With white railroad brotherhoods boycotting the four days of hearings, it was left to railroad attorneys to deny or justify discriminatory practices under relentless questioning by the FEPC's legal counsel. Most of the testimony came from black workers themselves, who put a human face on the tragic toll that union and workplace discrimination had taken on their lives.[48]

Although the industry's overall record of discrimination was on trial during the hearings, FEPC investigators made the plight of southern black firemen, brakemen, and switchmen the centerpiece of their case against the railroads and the unions. Counsel Bartley C. Crum, Charles Houston, and Harold Stevens targeted the Southeastern Carriers Conference Agreement of 1941, which one FEPC investigator termed the "ultimate in all discriminatory agreements" aiming at the "total elimination of colored men as firemen." In 1940, the Brotherhood of Locomotive Firemen and Enginemen (BLFE) had served notice on twenty-one railroads of its intention to negotiate a contract that would reserve all diesel jobs for "promotable" (i.e., white) men; give preference to promotable men on all new or changed runs; and limit the percentage of nonpromotable men to 50 percent on each division. (A "new run in railroad terminology is not a run that has never existed before," one FEPC official later learned, but was rather "one in which the starting time of a job has been changed as little as twenty minutes or twenty miles.") With NMB officials playing a key role, the parties signed a contract in February 1941 that almost instantly resulted in black demotions and furloughs.[49]

The impact of the 1941 Southeastern Carriers Conference agreement on black employment had been immediate; in the words of the *Chicago Defender,* the "wholesale dropping of Negro workers became the order of the day."[50] In Birmingham, Bester William Steele found himself removed from a desirable job. Steele worked in the Louisville and Nashville (L&N) railroad's passenger pool, along with one white and four other black firemen. In April 1941, the railroad reduced the mileage covered by the pool; under company rules, the change technically meant that all passenger pool jobs were now considered vacant. Together, L&N supervisors and BLFE officers concluded an agreement disqualifying blacks from those jobs and replaced the black firemen with whites, all of whom possessed less seniority than Steele. As a result, Steele was out of work for sixteen days. He was then assigned to more arduous, longer, and less remunerative work in local freight service, "where he was again displaced by a junior white firemen and assigned to work on a switch engine—"still harder and less remunerative."[51] However unpleasant the short-term consequences of management, white brotherhood, and government collusion, the long-term consequences were worse. Their secret and public agreements, particularly those barring blacks from diesel engines, were nothing less than an occupational death sentence for African-American firemen.

Black firemen were not alone in presenting their case to the FEPC. Among the sixty witnesses who attended the hearings were dining car waiters, brakemen, switchmen, and railroad car cleaners who testified to the specific forms of discrimination members of their job groups confronted. Before becoming a flight instructor with the U.S. Army, William C. Raines, a college graduate with a year and a half of law school, had spent his summers as a New York Central waiter. When vacancies for brakemen were posted, he applied along with two whites. Despite his familiarity with the work—he had spent two years as a porter brakeman before attending law school—his application was rejected, while the whites, one of whom admitted he had "never been on a train" before, were instantly hired. Employed in the Knoxville, Tennessee, yards of the Southern railroad since 1912, William K. Jones unsuccessfully applied for a foreman's position on a switchmen's crew in 1937; his manager gave the job to a junior white man instead. In his yard alone, some 243 whites, and only 6 blacks, had been hired as switchmen since 1937. New York Central laborer John W. Brooks of Chicago had been hired to grease and wash locomotives; finally promoted to hostler, he held his new job for only five days before the white firemen's brotherhood pressured the company into removing him.[52]

The September 1943 FEPC hearings not only put a human face on the long history of employment discrimination suffered by African-American railroaders but laid out a detailed case on its causes and consequences as well. Black workers like Bester Steele spoke powerfully to the personal hardships they endured, offering stories "full of pathos and drama," in one black observer's words. Economist Herbert Northrup, then serving on the National War Labor Board staff, left little to the imagination in his minute reconstruction of the decades-long efforts of whites on railroad after railroad to block black advancement and reduce black employment as well as the antiblack role played by federal agencies and railway labor law. FEPC officials and witnesses similarly testified to the moral, political, and military implications of black exclusion. Railroad companies' refusal to hire black workers during a period of severe labor shortages on the homefront exacerbated manpower problems that weakened the war effort; equally important, the denial of equal job opportunities to blacks "stultifies our moral leadership of the democracies and provides strong material for Axis propaganda against us," chief FEPC counsel Crum asserted in his opening. Clyde Miller of the Institute for Propaganda Analysis concurred, testifying that the exploitation of American racial practices was "one of the strongest weapons in the hands of Hitler." Racial and religious prejudice, Crum concluded, was a "cancer in our American civilization."[53]

By the end of the four days of testimony, the FEPC and the dozens of black witnesses had presented their case to the nation. There was little question that the hearing was "perforce a one-sided affair," as Malcolm Ross, who would assume the chairmanship of the FEPC shortly after the hearings, observed. "With the [white] unions absent and the railroads standing on their opening statement and three brief cross-examinations, the testimony became a repetitious story of Negro jobs lost and promotions refused." However repetitious the story, the irrefutable evidence constituted solid ammunition for the FEPC, black railroaders, and their liberal allies in the months to come. But while several railroads—including the Union Pacific, the Virginia, and the New York Central—expressed a willingness to investigate their minority workers' complaints and to upgrade blacks and Mexicans to specified positions when possible, most simply ignored the hearings and refused to cooperate with the FEPC.[54]

Matters came to a climax less than three months after the September 1943 hearings when the FEPC issued its "Findings and Directives," a series of scathing condemnations of union and company racial practices. While the white brotherhoods simply ignored them, the response of most railroads charged with discrimination was swift and direct: on December 13, a large group of railroads jointly rejected the directives outright. "It is wholly impractical, and indeed impossible, for these railroads to put into effect your Committee's Directives," their letter to the committee declared. "Any attempt on their part to comply . . . for instance, to promote Negroes to locomotive engineers or train conductors, would inevitably disrupt their present peaceful and cooperative relations with their employees, would antagonize the traveling and shipping public served by them, would substitute conditions of chaos for the present condition of harmony, would result in stoppages of transportation, and would most gravely and irreparably impair the whole war effort."[55] The railroad industry—and, through their silence, the white brotherhoods, the railroads' partner in discrimination—had thrown down the gauntlet. The issue that the *Pittsburgh Courier* had presciently raised in September was now starkly joined: either the racist, collusive agreements "are knocked down . . . and thousands of Negro workers are given new jobs and upgraded to higher skills and higher pay, or else the hearings will end in findings and decisions—big in words and small in deeds."[56] The moment of resolution had finally arrived.

The railroads' response did not come as a surprise to FEPC officials. Over the previous two years, most railroad executives had expressed no sympathy with the agency's goals, had given no indication of their desire to cooperate with the committee's investigation, and generally opposed FEPC meddling in their internal affairs. The views they expressed on race and on black workers' abilities should also have given pause to FEPC officials. Agency field representative Frances X. Riley interviewed numerous company personnel in 1942 and got more than an earful. The "Southern 'nigger' is entirely different from the Northern 'nigger,'" Riley's informants explained, in that the "Southern Negro has never gone to school or . . . has never gone far enough to absorb more than the bare rudiments of writing"; hence, he was unable to "read and interpret train orders," and "knowledge needed to run an engine is beyond the mental powers of a Southern colored man." Moreover, knowing their "place" in southern society meant that blacks were "psychologically unequipped to accept responsibility" as engineers or conductors. Even if they could accept such responsibility, the "social organization of the South" was such that it would "not permit a Negro to be in any supervisory capacity especially where a subordinate employee is white."[57]

Even the best southern employers—the paternalists, Riley called them—offered little to blacks. John Wilkes, president and general manager of the Jacksonville Terminal Company, was "one of the outstanding bulwarks of paternalism extant in the South today." Yet he employed no black engineers or conductors, had hired no black firemen since 1927, and had embraced percentage agreements not only to preserve black jobs but to guarantee an adequate supply of white labor as well. "My impression of Mr. Wilkes was that he had the utmost respect of the Negro as a railroad employee and the utmost contempt of him as an individual."[58] On his return to Washington, Riley summarized his discussions with various railroad executives. "Every single official to whom I talked," he reported, "either used segregation as a synonym for discrimination or else failed or refused to comprehend exactly what we were doing even after repeated explanation."[59]

But railroad managers had understood precisely what the FEPC wanted. When served with detailed charges of discriminatory practices weeks before the September 1943 hearings, they responded at considerable length, defending themselves and rejecting FEPC complaints. Managerial participation in employment discrimination extended well beyond any real or hypothetical economic benefits the railroads might accrue from keeping their labor force divided along racial lines; their resistance to change was rooted in deeply held beliefs about the innate abilities of blacks, the character of the racial order, potential white responses to any upgrading of black workers in the occupational hierarchy, and the industry's responsibilities in an era of changing racial expectations. "The operation of railroads in the South requires the management to observe the [region's] customs, manners and racial, social and economic conditions," explained Thomas W. Davis, the general solicitor for the Atlantic Coast Line railroad. That meant respecting, not challenging, racial hierarchies, especially in the workplace. Should a black be promoted and placed in a position of authority over whites, Davis predicted, the result would be nothing less than "discord, discontent and in all probability . . . boycott and serious trouble with the [white] members of the crew."[60] Such disruption, particularly during wartime, was just not acceptable.

Pragmatic considerations of work-crew harmony aside, rail managers issued a broader challenge to the FEPC. Should—or could—the FEPC impose its vision of a social order on an unwilling people? For southern rail managers, the answer was an obvious no. Following a line of reasoning that would find repeated echoes in the 1950s and early 1960s from opponents of integration, L&N vice president and general manager W. E. Smith insisted, "Human nature can not be changed by a stroke of the pen, nor by any law or order, no matter what dignity or force such law or order may have. To force the railroad into a program of reforming the attitudes and prejudices of the dominant forces of society . . . would bring about greater problems than now exist and would make it impossible for the railroad to serve the best interests of that society." Progress was being made, managers insisted, but it could not be imposed by outsiders who neither understood the region's troubled past nor appreciated its current problems. For the railroads to submit to the FEPC's directive to upgrade black workers to positions of authority—"on an Eutopian [sic] concept of equality"—would endanger blacks, disrupt transportation, and hurt the war effort.[61]

With the southern railroads' firm rejection of the FEPC's directives and authority in December 1943, the stage was set for political confrontation. The FEPC's opponents wasted no time in stepping up the pressure. Mississippi Democratic congressman John Rankin urged the abolition of the FEPC from the floor of the House of Representatives, declaring it to be a "rump organization without any legal authority," composed of a "bunch of crackpots." Just weeks later, in early January 1944, Virginia congressman Howard W. Smith, an antilabor and antiblack Republican, announced that his Special Committee to Investigate Executive Agencies would hold hearings into alleged abuses by the FEPC. Smith subpoenaed many of the agency's records and launched his own public crusade against its efforts. Smith's railroad hearings, held in March 1944, provided a sympathetic forum for railroad executives and white brotherhoods to explain their policies and denounce the FEPC and the forces supporting it.[62]

More important, however, was President Roosevelt's response to the FEPC's certification of the railroad cases. Unable to compel compliance, in early 1944 the FEPC had referred the case to Roosevelt for further action.[63] The outcome dashed the hopes of black railroaders, disappointed their allies, and provided satisfaction to railroad managers and white brotherhood officials who had stood up to the FEPC. In the first week of January 1944, Roosevelt postponed any fundamental action on enforcing the FEPC directives, displacing the issues they raised onto a new committee that would investigate the merits of the case. The three-member Stacy committee, headed by Judge Walter P. Stacy of North Carolina, was charged by the president with resolving the "impasse" brought about by the FEPC. "Obviously in such a complicated structure as the transportation industry," the president informed Stacy, "we cannot immediately attain perfect justice in terms of equal employment opportunities for all people." Yet "all Americans at this time should be anxious to see to it that no discrimination prevents the fullest use of our manpower in providing the strength essential to the major military offensive now planned."[64] The committee's official task, then, was to reconcile these seemingly irreconcilable beliefs. Toward that end, it was to review the FEPC findings and directives and find some way to reach a peaceful solution acceptable to all parties.[65]

The Stacy Committee was no FEPC, nor did its members view themselves as allies of the fair employment advocates. To the contrary, its chairman shared the view of the railroad industry that the FEPC possessed no authority to compel compliance and that its directives could not be sustained as a matter of law. The "FEPC's embarrassment arises," Stacy reflected in 1945, "not from our inability to carry out their wishes, but from their assumption of power which has been challenged and which they may not have." The Stacy Committee's own approach could not have been further from that of the

FEPC. Over the course of 1944, it conducted four sets of unpublicized and nonconfrontational meetings with railroad and white brotherhood representatives in an effort to "find a reasonable accommodation" within the framework of their collective bargaining agreements. Not a single black railroader or black union representative was consulted or called upon to participate in the discussions.[66]

Nor was any progress made. In November 1944 the committee concluded that the *Tunstall* and *Steele* cases then pending before the Supreme Court, which raised the issue of the legality under the Railway Labor Act of white unions bargaining against black interests, made any committee action unnecessary and unwise. In December, the Supreme Court handed counsel Charles Houston two related legal victories when it declared invalid the 1941 Southeastern Carriers' Conference agreement. Early in 1945, Houston formally asked Stacy to recommend compliance with the FEPC railroad directive, since the two rulings gave credence to the FEPC's earlier findings. Stacy replied that he did not intend to take any action to resolve the ongoing impasse between black railroaders and the FEPC on the one side, and the rail companies and white brotherhoods on the other. Since the drama had now shifted from the political to the judicial arena, there was little need for further action on his committee's part. "Presumably a new contract will be negotiated in the light of these decisions," Stacy noted. "Should federal assistance be needed, properly the services of the National Mediation Board"—a body long hostile to black workers' requests—"would be invoked by one or more of the parties." The Stacy Committee did little more. By August 1945, the NAACP demanded that President Harry S. Truman dismiss the committee, which had yet to make public recommendations or issue a report. In its place, the NAACP called on the new president simply to implement the original FEPC directives.[67]

By then, however, the wartime crisis that had prompted the FEPC's creation in the first place and afforded black railroaders and their allies the opportunity to challenge union and employment discrimination so publicly had passed. The FEPC railroad directives were never implemented. For all of the publicity and moral capital it generated, the FEPC ultimately affected the jobs of relatively few black workers. Southern black firemen, brakemen, and train porters saw virtually no concrete benefits from the spotlight the committee had cast on the pervasive racist practices in the industry. Its case against the railroad industry and its white unions, the FEPC concluded in its final report in 1946, "must be counted among the Committee's outstanding failures."[68] In their head-to-head confrontation with recalcitrant railroad managers and unions, the FEPC and black railroaders lost decisively.

The unsuccessful efforts of black activists and committed FEPC personnel to crack the walls of employment and union discrimination in the railroad industry bear out the pessimistic assessment of Willard Townsend, the CIO's highest-ranking black official and president of the United Transport Service Employees. The "FEPC was created not out of a keen desire to insure the full participation of negroes in the war employment," he argued in December 1943, just as the conflict between the FEPC and the railroads was coming to a head, "but rather out of the political necessity on the part of the present administration to placate the growing insistence of the Negro communities for greater opportunities in the field of war employment."[69] Blacks were not the only constituency the administration had to placate; southern politicians, large white railroad unions, and powerful railroad companies all objected to FEPC intrusion into the customary racial practices of the transportation industry. The Roosevelt administration was unwilling to disrupt the operation of an industry so vital to the successful prosecution of the war. The FEPC had "survived the onslaughts of 1942 and 1943, in the final analysis," as historian Merl Reed demonstrates, because "work as a civil right had become a moral issue too powerful to ignore." But the Roosevelt administration's changing positions on railroad discrimination revealed that work as a civil rights issue had also become a political issue that was too powerful to ignore. At a minimum, it had to be handled with the utmost care. The railroad brotherhoods' and their employers' greater disruptive capacity meant that, when push came to shove, black railroaders' demands for justice would be sacrificed on the altar of industrial peace.[70]

Yet the struggles to save the FEPC, prepare for the railroad hearings, and establish a permanent FEPC in the postwar era focused black workers' energies on concrete goals, allowing them to establish greater links between organizations and providing them with organizing tools for recruiting new members and publicizing their cause. The Provisional Committee to Organize Colored Locomotive Firemen, the International Association of Railway Employees, and the Association of Colored Railway Trainmen all contributed to and supported the FEPC investigations; all made extensive use of the information generated to bolster their own positions locally and to challenge the discrimination they faced in the courts. The tremendous political energy expended at the grassroots and union leadership levels focused unprecedented public attention on the plight of black railroaders and enabled the FEPC to get as far as it did.

7

The Politics of
Fair Representation

Despite the publicity focused on patterns of systemic discrimination in the railroad industry by the Fair Employment Practice Committee (FEPC), the problems confronting black operating craft workers only intensified over the course of the early 1940s. In their campaign to preserve their jobs and protect their seniority, black railroaders turned not only to the FEPC but to the courts as well, launching a series of legal campaigns that would eventually make labor law and civil rights history. But a strategy based on litigation was not without its drawbacks. Discriminatory agreements were "so numerous and apply to so many railroads that to invalidate them by litigation would require a multiplicity of suits and the expenditure of much time and money," the FEPC concluded pessimistically in its final report in 1946.[1] African-American railroaders' pursuit of the "courthouse route" in the 1940s and 1950s also involved the metamorphosis of the politics of fair employment into a politics of fair representation. The broad, bold themes of fair employment that resounded loudly through the war years—of the inherent justice of black workers' claims and of the inequity of racial discrimination in employment—were eclipsed by the narrower legal reasoning and technical language demanded by the litigative approach. While black workers won tangible, if limited, gains, the legal terrain on which they fought proved to be a much shallower one on which to make their stand than the political grounds of the FEPC. Given the shifting political currents of the era, however, the narrower legal path was often the only viable one open to them.

Black railroaders had turned to the courts for the redress of their grievances in the decade before World War II. By the late 1930s, new restrictions on their employment and new assaults on their seniority rights intensified black workers' interest in a legal approach. Two of the independent black associations—the International Association of Railway Employees (IARE) and the Association of Colored Railway Trainmen and Locomotive Firemen (ACRT)—retained noted civil rights attorney Charles Hamilton Houston to advocate their cause. For over a decade, Houston and his associates diligently chipped away at the legal edifice sustaining employment discrimination. But their early foray into railroad labor law to test the legality of overtly discriminatory contracts in federal court met with no success. Houston, his partners, and his clients all learned important lessons from their failures, however, which led them to new strategies that would eventually bear significant fruit.

When he began his legal work on behalf of the IARE and the ACRT in the late 1930s, Houston had familiarity, but no experience, with southern black railroaders' problems. His father, William L. Houston, was a prominent attorney in Washington, D.C., who served as counsel for the Railway Men's International Benevolent Industrial Association during the World War I era. After graduating from Harvard Law School, Charles joined his father in founding the firm of Houston & Houston in 1924, the same year he joined the Howard Law School faculty. For the next decade and a half, his energies were absorbed by a wide variety of projects. From 1929 to 1935, he served as vice-dean of the Howard Law School, transforming legal education there and training a new generation of socially committed and activist attorneys. From 1935 to 1938, he was special counsel for the NAACP, pursuing cases against educational discrimination. His experience with trade unions and labor law, however, remained slim.[2]

In 1939, the ACRT and the IARE retained Houston, now back in private practice, to launch a crusade against employment and union discrimination. Houston learned quickly on the job, and that crusade would absorb much of his attention until his death in 1950. His first important test case of the legality of overtly discriminatory contracts was *Teague v. Brotherhood of Locomotive Firemen and Enginemen and the Gulf, Mobile, and Ohio Railroad*. Ed Teague, a resident of Louisville, Mississippi, and a fireman with over three decades of experience, was displaced from his run by a junior white fireman in May 1938 when his employer, the Gulf, Mobile, and Northern railroad, placed a mechanical stoker-fired engine on his run. The displacement was the result of a "secret fraudulent compromise agreement" signed in January 1938 between the company and the white Brotherhood of Locomotive Firemen and Enginemen (BLFE), which provided that whites would receive preference on engines when mechanical stokers were installed. Teague had received no notice of the agreement, and the company ignored his protest. The complaints of his union, the IARE, and the local NAACP branch to the BLFE, the National Mediation Board (NMB), and the National Railroad Adjustment Board (NRAB) were similarly ignored. On Teague's behalf, Houston charged that the black firemen's Fifth Amendment right to due process had been violated by the Railway Labor Act. The courts, however, ruled that there was no federal issue involved and that the seniority rights that Teague alleged had been violated were contractual, not federal, in nature. Deciding against an appeal, Houston cast about for a more promising test case.[3]

The discriminatory Southeastern Carriers' Conference agreement of 1941, brokered by the NMB between the white firemen's brotherhood and twenty-one railroads, proved a clearer and ultimately more successful target. At Houston's urging, IARE officials on black Louisville and Nashville (L&N) railroad workers' behalf dispatched protests to the NMB, the NAACP, and the railroad's management, objecting to the rule against employing "non-promotable" (black) men as "the most unfair act ever practiced by the Company." That spring the railroad's personnel department held a series of conferences with the black unionists. The fact that the meetings took place was significant since the IARE was not a recognized organization. But they produced no satisfactory results. Company officials and white union delegates even suggested that any black who filed suit against them might be fired.[4]

Houston rejected any approach to the NMB as a "waste of time." The Southeastern Carriers' Conference agreement was simply illegal; "it was born in iniquity and conceived in sin," he insisted. Since the NMB had approved the agreement with full knowledge of blacks' objections to it, the board "could not be expected to repudiate its own action." As he prepared to file suit against the agreement, Houston further advised his clients that there "is no use being frightened away from defense of your rights. Some risk has to be taken, whichever way the matter goes. If you fight, you take a risk. If you stand still, you take a risk. Since your rights are being taken away while you do nothing, you can hardly lose more by fighting than you are losing standing still."[5] Bester William Steele put himself forward as plaintiff. In late August 1941, the suit was filed in an Alabama court.

Steele was not simply an aggrieved black employee; he was a long-standing railroad worker and labor activist in Birmingham. Fifty-four years old in 1941, he had first worked for the L&N in 1904 and briefly for the Atlanta Great Southern two years later. After spending two years in a floating gang in the Birmingham shop, he began work as a locomotive fireman on the L&N in 1910. When the Southeastern Carriers' Conference agreement came into effect, Steele was general chairman of the Birmingham IARE. The 1941 agreement and the legal challenge to it became an organizing tool in the hands of Steele and other IARE officers. Over the next decade of legal maneuvering, Steele remained a committed activist, representing his men not just in court but in negotiations with company and white brotherhood officials, until his death in 1955. As an ardent supporter of the IARE, Steele rebutted efforts of the BSCP's newly formed Provisional Committee to Organize Colored Locomotive Firemen to sign up new members at the IARE's expense. Indeed, Steele saw his suit not only as a challenge to discriminatory contract provisions but as a vehicle to attract black railroaders to the IARE. With that aim in mind, he viewed any efforts by the BSCP to enroll black firemen in its Provisional Committee as unwarranted and hostile territorial encroachment.[6]

Over the next three years, the case of *Steele v. L&N & BLFE* wound its way through the judicial system. Houston sought damages for the past violations of Steele's rights under the Southeastern Carrier's Conference agreement and an injunction against future violations of black firemen's seniority. On January 13, 1944, only months after Steele and other black railroaders had publicized their plight before the wartime FEPC, the Alabama Supreme Court upheld a lower court's dismissal of Steele's suit. As in the 1941 Teague ruling, the Alabama court found no constitutional issue involved and rejected the charge of Fifth Amendment violations. Seniority rights rested solely on contracts between private parties; the Fifth Amendment related only to government action, not actions carried out by private individuals. Where Steele's attorneys held that the white brotherhood "was under a duty to give the minority employees, non-members of the Brotherhood, notice of any action to be taken which would in any manner detrimentally affect their seniority rights," the court found no such duty at all.[7]

Almost one year after the Steele litigation commenced, another locomotive firemen, Tom Tunstall, initiated legal action against the BLFE and his railroad, the Norfolk Southern, when he lost his passenger run between Norfolk and Marsden, North Carolina, to a junior white fireman. Like Steele, Tunstall was a veteran railroader (his seniority dated from 1914) and a labor and civil rights activist. He was a member of both the ACRT and the NAACP's Norfolk chapter. Tunstall's case in large measure followed Steele's, charging the white brotherhood with being "persistently hostile" to blacks by seeking to drive them off their jobs under the terms of the 1941 Southeastern Carriers' Conference agreement. Specifically, Tunstall's attorneys—again Houston and his partner, Joseph Waddy, with black Virginia attorney Oliver Hill— sought $25,000 in monetary damages for the discrimination Tunstall faced, an injunction restraining the white brotherhood and the railroad company from enforcing discriminatory contract provisions, and a declaratory judgment that the BLFE was obliged to represent its minority members with fairness. Over the next two years, Tunstall and the ACRT found lower courts as unresponsive as would Steele and the IARE. In April 1943, Judge Luther B. Way of the Federal District Court in Norfolk dismissed the case on the grounds that the Railway Labor Act offered no provisions for the protection of minority members against the actions of the majority. The U.S. Fourth Circuit Court of Appeals in Richmond upheld the lower court's ruling in early January 1944, just three days before the Alabama Supreme Court rejected Steele's appeal. The ruling in *Teague* apparently prevailed: the federal courts had no jurisdiction over the case to afford relief, since the injury to Tunstall was the result of allegedly wrongful acts by the defendant brotherhood and railroad, not one "arising under the laws of the United States."[8] With the FEPC unable to do anything more than spotlight discrimination and the courts unwilling to consider racial exclusion in their rulings on the Railway Labor Act, the fate of black firemen appeared sealed.

The situation changed abruptly in December 1944, however, when the Supreme Court reversed not only the lower court decisions but its own previous stance in cases of racial discrimination under the 1934 Railway Labor Act. Houston had argued the *Steele* and *Tunstall* cases before the Supreme Court in November, and the Court rendered its decision only a month later. In the single most significant decision it would ever issue on the question of race and railroad labor, the Court held that the Railway Labor Act implicitly imposed a "duty of fair representation" on the exclusive bargaining agent— in this case, the BLFE. The act had conferred tremendous power on the union, the Court declared, clothing it "with power not unlike that of a legislature which is subject to constitutional limitations on its power to deny, restrict, destroy or discriminate against the rights of those for whom it legislates and which is also under an affirmative constitutional duty equally to protect those rights."[9]

The Court was clear about what the act explicitly permitted and what it implicitly did not. First, it granted exclusive bargaining power to the designated agent. Second, it placed no restrictions at all on the union's right to establish its own membership guidelines; the BLFE could legitimately exclude blacks if it wanted to. But Congress had not intended to "confer plenary power upon the union to sacrifice, for the benefit of its members, rights of the minority of its craft." Since black nonmembers could not negotiate individually or collectively with management, black nonmembers possessed "no means of protecting their interests or, indeed, their right to earn a livelihood by pursuing the occupation in which they are employed" if the recognized union chose to discriminate against them.[10]

The union, the Court concluded, could not discriminate through its contracts on racial grounds. The act designated the union to be the representative of all members of its craft or class, regardless of their union status. For the Court, the act imposed "upon the statutory representative . . . at least as exacting a duty to protect equally the interests of the members of the craft as the Constitution imposes upon a legislature to give equal protection to the interests of those for whom it legislates. Congress has seen fit to clothe the bargaining representative with powers comparable to those possessed by a legislative body . . . but it has also imposed upon the representative a corresponding duty . . . to exercise fairly the power conferred upon it in behalf of all those for whom it acts, without hostile discrimination against them." Discrimination had to be based on "differences relevant to the authorized purposes of the contract." Discriminations "based on race alone are obviously irrelevant and invidious." In a concurring opinion, Justice Frank Murphy went much further: "The utter disregard for the dignity and the well-being of colored citizens shown by this record is so pronounced as to demand the invocation of constitutional condemnation," something the Court had failed to do. "To decide the case and to analyze the statute solely upon the basis of legal niceties, while remaining mute and placid as to the obvious and oppressive deprivation of the constitutional guarantees, is to make the judicial function something less than it should be."[11]

"Every single proposition we have advocated for five years was adopted by the United States Supreme Court," Houston proudly informed his clients.[12] Black leaders, editors, and journalists were jubilant. The decision was "another milestone in the legal struggle to break down discrimination against Negro Americans," concluded NAACP special counsel Thurgood Marshall. The Supreme Court had delivered black firemen from "threatened economic slavery," the *Baltimore Afro-American* proclaimed, while the *Chicago Defender* believed that the Court had "discovered that whatever is segregated and Jim Crowed cannot be equal in the true sense . . . It opens the way for striking new powerful blows against Jim Crow in American life."[13] Swept up in the rhetorical exaggerations following the decision, Houston himself suggested that the decisions would go a long way toward the "democratization" of the railroads and would have a "favorable effect" on antiblack unions.

Houston also believed that the FEPC and the "agitation" over the black firemen's plight "served as a background preparing the way for the court's decisions." But *Tunstall* and *Steele* were not isolated decisions, for the Supreme Court ruled earlier that same year on behalf of black plaintiffs in *Smith v. Allwright,* outlawing the white primary in Texas. More than wartime protest and politics were involved. The changing composition of the Supreme Court—in particular, the appointments of Hugo Black, Stanley Reed, William O. Douglas, Felix Frankfurter, Frank Murphy, and Harlan Fiske Stone in the late 1930s and early 1940s—contributed to its shifts on racial issues. "Most of the justices who served on the Court in the early 1940s were personally sympathetic, to varying degrees, to the legal positions asserted by the NAACP, and none had strong objections based in constitutional theory to acting in a manner consistent with their inclinations," argues legal historian Mark V. Tushnet.[14] Whatever the sources of the new judicial responsiveness, Houston resolved to press the advantage. There would be a "rush to the courts" by the remaining thousands of firemen who were suffering under the 1941 contract. "We intend to file suits on every single railway company that is a party to the southeastern agreement," he declared on behalf of the ACRT and the IARE. "We intend further to enjoin the brotherhood if it attempts to bargain just for its members to the exclusion of Negro employes of the craft."[15]

Not all African Americans responded enthusiastically to the Supreme Court's rulings in *Steele* and *Tunstall*. Marjorie McKenzie, a *Pittsburgh Courier* columnist, was one of the few commentators to note the decisions' limitations. The "widespread acclaim" over the *Tunstall* and *Steele* railroad cases rested on the fairness of "representation, not membership," she wrote. The rulings gave black firemen the green light to petition the federal courts for equitable relief if the union in their craft—which remained their legal representative while still excluding them—represented them inadequately. They created a "legal obligation and a framework within which important protection is provided," she argued, but "the fundamental issue of open membership in labor unions is still before us." The Court settled the case in part on the "simple application of the law governing fiduciary relationships." But could the all-white brotherhoods in the future provide fair representation? At a minimum, their "activities will require constant policing to prevent their accomplishing, indirectly, what the court has told them they may not do." But because black firemen remained "outside the union, unable to know until too late, or to supervise matters affecting their interests," the task would prove difficult. Echoing McKenzie's analysis were black union officials in AFL and CIO railroad service unions. If the "ultimate effect" of the Court's rulings was to force the BLFE to represent blacks to protect itself against damage suits, "no good will be achieved," concluded Richard Smith of the Joint Council of Dining Car Employees. "It will be like having a lawyer working against you behind your back."[16]

Houston, of course, was hardly blind to the limitations of his victory; rather, he had consciously left the membership issue off his legal agenda, and the Court explicitly stated that exclusionary membership policies were legal. Justifying his limited approach, Houston argued that it "may be best that we do not bite off too much at one time but it seems to me that the ground work has now been laid so that in the near future we will be in position to challenge the right of the railroad unions to represent the craft or class at all as long as it excludes Negroes from membership."[17]

That time came in the late 1940s, when Houston argued that the "abstract right of fair representation is not enough" and that "to insure fair representation the nonmember minority worker must have the same participation" in the election of union officers as whites. On behalf of Cyrille Salvant, a Mobile fireman and IARE officer, Houston sought injunctive relief against the enforcement of a discriminatory contract provision on the grounds that blacks had neither been given notice of, nor invited to participate in the formulation of, the harmful proposal. Since the BLFE had, in effect, deprived Salvant of his civil and property rights without due process of law, Houston called on the courts to prevent the BLFE from further representing his client so long as blacks were denied full participation in the collective bargaining process. Houston got his desired injunction in *Salvant v. Louisville and Nashville Railroad,* but he failed to prompt the courts to open the BLFE to any black involvement. Even if he had, the organizations he represented—the IARE and the ACRT—harbored little desire to merge into the much larger, more powerful, and hostile white brotherhoods. At best, they preferred an approach that would allow them to bargain for themselves. Following Houston's death in 1950, the task of overturning exclusionary unionism would be assumed by A. Philip Randolph's rival Provisional Committee to Organize Colored Locomotive Firemen.[18]

Throughout World War II and the immediate postwar years, white firemen in the railroad industry expended considerable effort to disguise their discriminatory agenda. "The employment of firemen is a most delicate matter, especially at this time," confessed a member of the Seaboard Air Line's brotherhood grievance committee to a local brotherhood chairman, for "the labor market is shrinking, various groups are putting pressure on us in behalf of the colored firemen, [and] at this time we have at least two suits facing us." The course of action proposed was to "be most tactful in our handling of this subject." "If we can get through this war," he concluded, "I feel we are out of the woods with the colored question, but until then lets [*sic*] be careful."[19] It was hard to be careful, however, when the southern white rank and file remained anxious about job loss, when blacks were persistent in demanding runs on diesel engines, and when railroad managers were not above manipulating racial tensions.

By 1947, the legal writing was on the wall. The final resolution of the *Tunstall* case, the granting of a temporary injunction on behalf of black railroaders in the *Hinton* case, and the impending trial of *Graham v. Southern Railway* all drove home the point to BLFE officers that the old ways were crumbling. BLFE attorney Harold Heiss informed his clients that the court hearing the *Graham* case "appears to be imbued with the conviction that the Southeastern Agreement was prompted purely by racial considerations and that its invalidity is a foregone conclusion." Early the following year, another brotherhood attorney laid out the obvious. In the six suits filed against the BLFE since August 1942, the BLFE had thus far lost all of them. The future held little promise of change, for there was "every reason to expect the same results" in other suits still pending. His advice was to the point: the BLFE had to act promptly to "conform the existing agreements to the requirements of the courts" in order to avoid a "flood of new litigation (wherein the Brotherhood can expect scant sympathy from the courts)," further injunctions, and possible damage awards of a "very considerable sum." The white brotherhood's acting general chairman had no trouble understanding the legal trouble his union was in. "We are getting the worst of it from the Courts," he admitted, "and we should do something as soon as possible to try to salvage as much out of the deal as we can."[20]

The blatant discrimination that had formed the cornerstone of the BLFE's early strategy made for too easy a target by the late 1940s. And yet instead of accepting the courts' judgment and representing African Americans without prejudice, BLFE leaders sought an alternative approach to minimize the damage and accomplish their traditional ends. The Seaboard Air Line—one of the many lines to find itself sued by black firemen—was of a similar mind and put the ball in the union's court, making it clear to brotherhood vice-president W. E. Mitchell that it would be "glad to hear our thoughts on this subject . . . [and] give serious consideration to any proposal from our Brotherhood, which would take care of the non-promotable firemen, thus protecting the carrier (and the brotherhood) against the existing and potential litigation."[21]

In a contrived reversal, the BLFE now proclaimed a change of heart, proposing to drop all racial restrictions in their contracts and champion complete workplace equality, though not union membership. Not only would percentage agreements be eliminated, but so too would the distinction between promotable and nonpromotable men. All firemen—black and white—would be subject to the identical opportunities, limitations, responsibilities, and rules. All firemen would have to stand for promotion to engineer; failure to pass the requisite exams would result in dismissal. What the BLFE called "equality" black firemen denounced as "forced promotion."[22]

In the hands of BLFE officials, the idea of equality became a weapon for them to accomplish traditional discriminatory goals. Under the BLFE proposal, equality would be instantly granted. No one—neither white firemen, black firemen, nor the courts—doubted what the results of such equality would be. Without opportunity to prepare for qualifying exams, large numbers of black firemen would rapidly lose their jobs.[23]

Black railroaders, some represented by Houston and others by Randolph's Provisional Committee, turned to the courts to block the latest assault. This time, however, they were placed in the politically awkward position of arguing against equality of treatment. Older black workers had for decades been considered "nonpromotable"; no one—the black firemen included—had ever believed that they would one day become engineers. Some were barely literate. Yet there was no question that they had provided, and continued to provide, wholly adequate service in the job category in which they worked. Although black firemen would eventually succeed in having the forced promotion rule permanently enjoined, their arguments against "equality" would come back to haunt them over the course of the next decade.

Nowhere was the politically problematic nature of the black firemen's case better revealed than in the arguments of the U.S. District Court for the Eastern District of Virginia. For his earlier decisions in several civil rights cases, Judge Sterling Hutcheson had earned the support of the black press, which credited his "steadily expanding" stature for bringing "dignity and prestige to a United States court."[24] In the *Rolax* case in 1950, however, a narrow reading of the Railway Labor Act and the facts of the case led Hutcheson to side with the white brotherhood. The central issue was whether the brotherhood had fairly represented black firemen or whether it had used its power unfairly to discriminate against them. Hutcheson acknowledged but dismissed the white brotherhood leaders' long-standing antiblack rhetoric as some "unfortunate expressions." More to the point, he accepted the brotherhood's assertion that the firemen's position was needed to prepare potential locomotive engineers. Because of the past custom of promoting only whites, black firemen accumulated significant seniority that—if percentage agreements were abolished—would make it difficult for whites to gain the necessary training. "Unless some plan is worked out by which this experience can be acquired," Hutcheson inquired, "where are future engineers to be found?" Forced promotion through the abolition of the distinction between promotable and nonpromotable men would provide one solution, but blacks rejected such an approach, which carried with it risk of less desirable assignments or, even worse, dismissal if they failed to pass an examination. Since a "large majority of these men have spent the greater portion of their lives in the service of the railroad" and many were "advanced in age," such an arrangement "would put some of them out of work and without qualifications for other positions." That, however, was a necessary price they would have to pay: "one who exercises a right," Hutcheson wrote, "must be charged with the responsibility which accompanies that right." Although black firemen had every right to be worried, that simply was not Hutcheson's problem.[25]

Returning to the plaintiffs' contention that the brotherhood had the duty to consult with them in advance of making the demand on the railroad, Hutcheson upheld the prevailing, narrow definition of labor representation.

However desirable consultations might have been, the union had no obligation to consult with its white members or black nonmembers. Blacks' advice was sought no more "than was the advice of the individual members of the Brotherhood" on other issues. The plaintiffs' request for membership in the brotherhood was quickly rejected. "They insist upon full equality in reaping the benefits of seniority while resisting any effort to place upon their shoulders the responsibilities which accompany that right." Hutcheson denied the plaintiffs' request for an injunction blocking the forced promotion rule. As far as he was concerned, black firemen would have to pay the full price of the equality that they had presumably been demanding all along: their jobs. Hutcheson's reasoning was "unsound, specious and prejudicial," Randolph complained. The *Rolax* decision "puts another big stumbling block on the road colored firemen must travel to win their rights."[26]

Fortunately for southern black firemen, no other court followed Hutcheson's route of divorcing the theoretical issue of equality from the real context of inequality. In *Mitchell v. Gulf, Mobile and Ohio Railroad Company*, Provisional Committee member Matt Mitchell and several other black firemen similarly brought suit to secure their seniority rights and access to diesel jobs, charging the BLFE with discrimination. Since the railroad was 100 percent dieselized by the late 1940s, "most of the Negro firemen were sitting at home unemployed." Black railroaders again made it clear that they were not interested in promotion to engineer, although they wanted full access to diesel engines as firemen.[27]

District Court Judge Clarence Mullins of the Northern District of Alabama flatly rejected the BLFE's arguments and Hutcheson's earlier conclusions. The Supreme Court on three occasions (in *Steele, Tunstall,* and *Graham*) made clear that the Southeastern Carriers' Conference agreement was discriminatory, and black firemen's rejection of the forced promotion rule was not unreasonable. While "at first blush" it appeared fair, the forced promotion rule was "but to keep the word of promise to the ear and break it to the hope"; it was "deceptive and a mere illusion," since the older black firemen would lose their jobs. Rejecting the forced promotion rule was "merely an act of self-defense on their part."[28]

The Gulf, Mobile, and Ohio railroad had immediately understood and objected to the implications of the forced promotion rule. In its place, the railroad offered an alternative proposal designed to allow its black firemen to retain their jobs and exercise their seniority without restriction until they each retired. The BLFE turned down the counterproposal in March 1948. "It is a wry anomaly that the Railroad was more concerned about its Negro firemen than the Brotherhood which was under a fiduciary obligation to represent them," observed Judge Mullins. Thus, blacks' rejection of the forced promo tion rule did not, in the court's view, amount to a failure to do equity, while the brotherhood's adoption of this rule did not constitute "fair representation of these old Negro men who, for 20 to 40 years, did backbreaking work on steam locomotives." Further, although all of the road's black firemen had been excluded from the Gulf, Mobile, and Ohio's diesel engines—the only kind the railroad now ran—the brotherhood had not protested at all: "Its conspicuous failure to seek any relief for Negro firemen in such a situation not only indicates its satisfaction with their total exclusion, but also makes manifest that it is pleased to have its own members enjoy these preferred runs." Mullins ruled decisively on behalf of black firemen.[29]

By 1952, black firemen had more or less emerged victorious in their legal struggles against the white brotherhood and various southern railroads in preserving their jobs and respecting their seniority. The Provisional Committee to Organize Colored Locomotive Firemen and the BLFE reached a final agreement in December 1951, stipulating that the various temporary antidiscrimination injunctions be made permanent. The white union paid $30,000 in monetary damages to the Provisional Committee; and through the exercise of straight seniority, black firemen quickly secured many of "the cream runs on Southern railroads."[30] Discriminatory treatment did not end overnight, however, and black firemen and other railroaders continued initiating legal action to fight the white brotherhoods' inroads upon black jobs. The changes were, nonetheless, dramatic. Although the fight for "first-class industrial status" was hardly over, the Provisional Committee announced that the "shackles of racial-economic discrimination that denied and prevented" black firemen from exercising their seniority rights had been "broken and cast aside."[31]

Turning toward the future at its 1952 annual conference—held as its "Victory Conference"—the Provisional Committee mapped out an agenda for future action. It intended to establish classes for black firemen in the operation of diesel engines; monitor the white brotherhood to ensure its fair representation of black nonmembers; press for employment of blacks as new firemen; and undertake an educational and possibly legal campaign to alter the white brotherhood's policies so as to "secure bona-fide membership" for blacks.[32] Over the next decade, black firemen accomplished the first two objectives. In 1946, Provisional Committee members had complained of "patterns of discrimination" that "varied among divisions of the same railroad and from yard to yard." But by 1953, black firemen on the Georgia railroad were reporting that the "Negro Fireman problem . . . is better than it has ever been in the history of it," with blacks receiving the same training as whites and with the first black qualifying for a diesel job. An internal study conducted for the Provisional Committee in 1954 observed vast changes: The "anti-discrimination injunctions are effective in practice," its investigator found. The cases of discrimination that were uncovered, Provisional Committee attorney Joseph Rauh concluded, were "more or less isolated incidents rather than a pattern of systematic discrimination." But the last two objectives—new hires and union membership—proved virtually impossible to accomplish. The fact that the railroad industry was generally contracting during those years meant that companies were hiring relatively few new men; those it needed could be drawn from the expansive ranks of the furloughed.[33] The membership goal required either that white firemen voluntarily open their doors to blacks or that Congress or the courts force them to do so. As black firemen would later learn, white firemen, politicians, and jurists were unwilling to take that final step.

Although the courts remained the primary arena in the battle over employment and union discrimination, black labor activists had two opportunities to press their case before Congress in 1949 and 1950. The 1949 congressional hearings on a federal fair employment practices act were the culmination of over a half-decade of black and liberal advocacy of such a law. Charles Hamilton Houston (who was then the general co-counsel for the Negro Railway Labor Executives Committee, composed of a variety of independent black railroad unions), Willard Townsend of the United Transport Service Employees of America (UTSEA), Theodore Brown of the Brotherhood of Sleeping Car Porters (BSCP), the NAACP's Clarence Mitchell, and others testified aggressively on the need for a federal law that would bar discrimination by unions and employers alike. Like the earlier campaign for a permanent FEPC, these hearings produced no law and merely served as a sounding board for black labor officials and their allies to expose further the racist track record of the white railroad brotherhoods and numerous AFL affiliates.[34]

Black railroaders' second chance came the following year during congressional hearings on amending the Railway Labor Act to permit the closed shop. Like their white counterparts, many black trade unionists had no trouble with requiring union membership as a condition of employment: both white and black members experienced the classic "free rider" problem, in which non–dues-paying nonmembers received the same benefits as dues-paying union members. Workers who had "put down their hard earned dollars and suffered the discharge to build their unions," the BSCP's *Black Worker* argued, "deserved the union shop to eliminate the 'free Riders' who were enjoying the fruits of their struggles." More important, however, was the issue of union and job security that the union shop would provide.[35] With the passage of the amended act in January 1951, the BSCP reaped tremendous organizational advantages. By August of that year, the Pullman Company signed a union shop agreement with the BSCP, requiring each porter, maid, attendant, and busboy on its payroll to enroll in the brotherhood within sixty days or face dismissal. This brought welcome relief to the black union from the organizational and financial burdens of having to recruit new members continually.[36]

Unlike their white counterparts, black activists were initially uncomfortable with the amended Railway Labor Act because of the power it gave the white brotherhoods. Supporting the bill "as far as it goes," George L.-P. Weaver, assistant to Willard Townsend, insisted that the bill include a section to protect railroaders who were barred from union membership because of race. The legislation specified that no union shop agreement would result in the discharge of employees "to whom membership is not available"—that is, blacks barred from union membership in the white brotherhoods could retain their jobs. Weaver found this protection unacceptable. Rather, he proposed to deny the union shop to any union that discriminated in its membership policies. "You cannot have a closed shop with a closed union," he declared. The BSCP's Director of Research, Theodore E. Brown, concurred: Since "no other group has been able to accomplish the desired democratic objective"—neither the wartime FEPC nor the courts—the "extent to which some lilywhite unions will go to deny economic equality to workers because of their color should be corrected by this Congress." The union shop and dues check-off provisions should be available only to unions that admitted blacks to full union membership "without any restrictions whatsoever." Joseph Waddy, representing the IARE, the ACRT, the Colored Trainmen of America (CTA), and the Negro Railway Labor Executives Committee, an umbrella group, went even farther, demanding that any discriminating railroad union be denied not only the union shop and check-off provisions but also any provisions of the Railway Labor Act—the very position that C. W. Rice had taken in his congressional testimony eleven years earlier.[37]

The previous year, the BSCP had advanced a proposition similar to Waddy's, urging Congress to "outlaw discrimination based on race, creed, color or national ancestry, by denying the application of the law and services of any Board established to administer provisions of the labor law, to any union and or company, which denies Negroes and other citizens of minority status the right to participate as equals without discrimination in collective bargaining procedures." In 1950, with the prospect of winning a union shop provision that promised considerable benefits for the union, BSCP leaders narrowed their focus to ensuring that passage of such a provision would not harm black railroaders. Shortly before the amendment's passage, the BSCP promised to develop a "comprehensive program for the abolition of segregation and discrimination in the railroad unions and the railroad industry" later. The BSCP cooperated with George Harrison, the Brotherhood of Railway and Steamship Clerks' president and leader of the drive for the union shop bill, to ensure its passage, provided that it did not harm black workers.[38]

The amendment that Congress approved in early 1951 was at best a mixed victory for black railroaders. Some benefited and some did not, but the larger principle of nondiscrimination was subordinated to the institutional needs of larger unions. The drafters of the legislation included no provision banning the union shop to racist unions. Instead, the legislation retained its initial provision barring white unions under the closed shop from forcing the dismissal of non–union members who were ineligible for union membership because of their race. Thus Congress both strengthened the hand of the white brotherhoods while offering limited statutory protection to black nonmembers. For largely black unions with no real white competition, such as the BSCP, the amendment was a solid victory; for the black firemen who were members of the BSCP's Provisional Committee, it was no victory at all, but merely a freezing of the status quo.[39]

With Congress unwilling either to support fair employment legislation or to insist that white unions admit blacks to membership, black railroaders again turned to the judiciary. The courts had repeatedly upheld black workers' challenges to traditional and new discriminatory practices, although the process was slow and often imperfect. Now black railroaders confronted their final barrier to fair representation: membership. Could a union exercise its duty of fair representation while excluding members of its craft solely on the basis of race?

By 1948, Randolph had declared that black firemen would accept no compromise short of full union membership in the BLFE. Over the course of the 1950s, Randolph's Provisional Committee spearheaded the effort to break open the brotherhood, forcing the admission of African Americans on the simple ground that the brotherhoods by definition could not represent blacks fairly if they continued to exclude these workers from membership.[40] For decades Randolph had been hammering away against the racial practices of his fellow AFL union leaders, and in the 1940s and 1950s he singled out auxiliary and biracial union arrangements for condemnation. Randolph's goal was nothing short of integration; he had no sympathy with black unionists who wished to maintain their own distinct organizations. A subsidiary of the porters' union, the Provisional Committee took its cues from Randolph, who never hesitated to provide direction; and it was the Provisional Committee that would pursue the test case in the long campaign to mandate union desegregation through the law.

The case failed. If the courts' indignation over racial discrimination could be heard clearly in *Steele*, their impatience with continued litigation over discrimination was evident in *Oliphant*. The membership case bore the name of

Lee Oliphant, a black fireman and local chair of the Provisional Committee to Organize Colored Locomotive Firemen in Macon, Georgia. The Provisional Committee's attorneys argued that the BLFE continued to discriminate; the court accepted the white union's assertion that no discrimination had taken place, only "legitimate practices used by most unions for reasons other than discrimination." The ghost of the forced promotion rule continued to haunt the black firemen, however, for the court found that the most "basic action of discrimination, from which all others necessarily followed, was the rule" that blacks may not become engineers. Yet black firemen had secured injunctions to halt the removal of the "obstacle of nonpromotability." The U.S. District Court hearing the case thus found the factual issues of discrimination irrelevant.[41]

Once again the court considered and rejected claims of Fifth Amendment due process violation. There was no federal action involved in employment discrimination, save for the certification of the union as the exclusive bargaining representative. But Congress did not bar blacks from the BLFE; the BLFE did. It was never the intent of Congress to require white unions to admit blacks as a condition of certification. Earlier in the decade, Congress had rejected such a path during debates over the union shop amendment to the Railway Labor Act. The act's original and continuing purpose was the promotion of industrial peace, a goal that would have been undermined had Congress required the admission of blacks into white unions. The white brotherhood was ultimately a private association, not a governmental agency. Hence the court found insufficient federal action for it to declare the Railway Labor Act an unconstitutional deprivation of liberty or property. Black workers who continued to feel that union exclusion undermined fair representation should look to Congress, not the courts, for change.[42]

The Sixth Circuit Court of Appeals sustained the district court's ruling, resolving any doubt about the BLFE's status as a "private association, whose membership policies are its own affair." It also added one final argument against integration. The Railway Labor Act itself provided for no direct control over the union selected by the majority of the craft or class. The act only provided that an individual could vote for or against the agent in a representation election. To preserve industrial tranquillity, the act took from the individual employees the "right to negotiate their own contracts of employment." White members and black nonmembers alike had little control over the day-to-day functions of the brotherhood. Notwithstanding the charges of discrimination, the appeals court found that "we are really concerned only with ascertaining the rights of any person who, for any reason, finds himself in a minority or out-voted status." On that score, the importance of a smooth-running system of labor relations designed to promote industrial peace outweighed the grievances of individuals.[43]

Undeterred by these setbacks, supporters of union integration prepared for the next phase of the struggle: an appeal to the Supreme Court. The "issue in this case is so big, far-reaching, significant and vital," Randolph wrote to Milton Webster, "that the final decision on it should be rendered by the highest court of the land." The Provisional Committee's attorney, Joseph Rauh, was not surprised at the outcome: "we have always known that only the Supreme Court would take the big plunge of holding that unions may not bar Negroes," he informed Randolph. But Randolph's and Rauh's hope was not to be realized, for the following year the Supreme Court denied certiorari and allowed the appeals court ruling to stand. The courts had finally resolved the significant issue of union exclusion and segregation in favor of the white brotherhoods.[44]

Absent specific legislation barring discrimination in union membership, the courts maintained the dual fictions that trade unions were private associations whose admission standards were their own affairs and that membership and participation in union affairs were irrelevant to a union's ability to negotiate fairly. The earlier *Steele* decision, labor law scholar Karl Klare has argued, rested on a fundamentally conservative and nonparticipatory conception of the collective bargaining process. Klare's analysis holds even more true in *Oliphant.* The court refused to grant black railroaders, just as it had refused for whites, the right to object to undemocratic union policies, even though blacks were excluded and whites were not. Denying decades of experience, the court concluded that exclusion did not mean black nonmembers could not be fairly represented by whites. Reverting to the pre-*Steele* arguments of the *National Federation of Railway Workers v. NMB* of 1940, the court insisted that whites could represent blacks; to insist that only blacks could represent blacks would itself constitute discrimination. The courts' sanctioning of black exclusion reflected less an overt endorsement of the white unions' racial perspectives than an embrace of a collective bargaining model that privileged stability over potential turmoil and autocratic leadership over democratic participation.[45]

The legal cases themselves became a means for black railroad associations to win new members or retain old ones. Their victory in the *Steele* and *Tunstall* cases in 1944 allowed the independent IARE and the ACRT to claim that they had made real progress in protecting black firemen's rights; the independent's failure in *Rolax* and the Provisional Committee's victory in *Mitchell* enabled those affiliated with the BSCP to claim that their approach was the wiser one. That the Provisional Committee and the independents followed the same overall strategy did little to lessen the animosity between them and served only to intensify the factional rhetoric that masked their similarities

The independent associations had more at stake in the struggle for the allegiance of southern black firemen than did the Provisional Committee and Randolph, who commanded a national spotlight, access to liberal allies, and a proven and popular union's resources. Bester William Steele, the Birmingham plaintiff in the historic 1944 case against the Southeastern Carriers' Conference agreement, adamantly stuck to the IARE and lambasted the Provisional Committee's intrusion onto his union's turf. It was hard to avoid the conclusion that the Provisional Committee was following in the footsteps of the independents. "What has become of the Provisional Committee's 'Gospel' that the courts could not do us any good?" Steele asked. "Now they are seeking salvation from the same courts they preached against." Even Randolph's choice of allies served as grist for Steele's rhetorical mill. "Most of the Provisional Lawyers are white men and the money is comming [*sic*] from you and other Negroes to pay those lawyers. Do you think that a white man is going to work for you against his own color. Don't be so weak to even imagine such a thing." Appealing to racial pride, Steele did not need to remind his fellow IARE members that the independents' attorneys, Charles Houston and Joseph Waddy, were African American.[46]

Houston did far more than offer legal representation for his clients in the black independents; by the late 1940s, he actively sought to shape them into a more effective, coordinated movement. In October 1947, he floated the idea of a committee composed of the presidents of black railway unions, and by March 1948 he had succeeded in recruiting five organizations into the Negro Railway Labor Executives Committee (NRLEC), a body designed to coordinate black railroaders' legal campaigns against employment discrimination. Three of the groups were Houston's clients—the ACRT, the Colored Trainmen of America (CTA), and the IARE. The fourth was the obscure Savannah-based Southern Federation of Colored Locomotive Firemen's Union (SFCLFU), which came into being in 1939. The only non-southern, non–operating craft union on the committee was the Chicago-based Dining Car and Railroad Food Workers Union (DCRFWU), which was founded by Communist members expelled from the AFL's Joint Council of Dining Car Employees in 1947. The NRLEC brought together black activists who stood outside the national labor movement and who shared a distaste for the AFL, the white brotherhoods, and Randolph.[47]

Houston and his partner, Joseph Waddy, used NRLEC meetings to foster greater cooperation among the independent associations and raise funds to pursue the numerous legal cases they were bringing against southern railroads and the white brotherhoods. The organization's official goals included the protection of black railroaders' seniority and the opening up of all jobs in the railroad industry to black workers. Using the NRLEC as an organizational base, Houston and Waddy also advanced a legislative agenda, testifying before Congress in support of fair employment legislation and against discriminatory aspects of the Railway Labor Act. Seeking to collect and disseminate information about black railroaders, the committee irregularly published a newsletter, the *Negro Railway Labor News,* from 1948 to 1950, under the editorship of the left-wing DCRFWU. The newsletter aimed at fostering a sense of unity among the independents, provided coverage of a variety of legal cases involving black railroaders, and relentlessly criticized the industry's racist practices. Exposure to the communist-influenced DCRFWU led leaders of some of the black independents to participate in broader civil rights conferences and organizations on the national level.[48]

The *Negro Railway Labor News* also sought to bolster the independents' legitimacy by criticizing A. Philip Randolph. The "time has come to take our gloves off and talk a little about Mr. A. Phillip [*sic*] Randolph and his Provisional Committee," the *News* editorialized in the summer of 1949. Randolph's misdeeds were many. "At a time when unity is desperately needed among all Negro operating men," it charged, the Provisional Committee "tries to sow suspicion and division among the *organized* men in the transportation section of the industry." Randolph's group had signed weak contracts with railroads and disseminated false information. "There is some Napoleon in the man and he insists that he's doing the job of fighting discrimination all by himself. The facts are, however, that on a dozen fronts the Negro Operating Unions are churning up the campaign for equality while Mr. Randolph talks big and does harm." The *News* reflected the opinions of not only the small CP-dominated dining car union and the southern independents but of Houston himself. "To my mind," he told his clients in 1948, "Randolph has done us no good as far as the Transportation men are concerned . . . Randolph has never given us anything . . . We cannot follow Randolph because he is wrong."[49] Such claims reflected less the actual differences separating Randolph from the independents—there were few—than the broader, unresolvable organizational and personal divide between a nationally prominent organization with ties to white labor and localistic bodies that valued their autonomy, espoused racial pride, and kept their distance from all white unions. Houston's death in 1950 and the subsequent dissolution of the NRLEC did nothing to mend the rift between the Provisional Committee and the independents, despite their similar goals.

The white brotherhoods' campaign against black railroaders in the 1930s and 1940s was not limited to the firemen's craft alone. They also waged an all-out assault against African-American train porters. The position of train porter (also known as porter brakeman) was similar to that of brakeman, with several differences. Train porters would work only on the front end of passenger trains, rear-end braking jobs being reserved for white brakemen. They engaged in a small amount of on-board service work—cleaning cars and assisting passengers in particular. The service work, however, occupied little more than 5 percent of their time, their main job being braking work. Train porters received a smaller wage than brakemen, and their ranks were 100 percent African American. Most train porters considered themselves brakemen. "We have to buy the same quality material, same style uniform as that of the white trainmen, who are flagmen on the rear end of the train," explained Missouri Pacific train porter J. McDonald of Poplar Bluff, Missouri. "We also have to have standard watches and have them inspected as required as that of the flagmen. We stand the same examination."[50] Why, then, should they be treated differently than their white counterparts?

During World War I, the U.S. Railroad Administration had reclassified these black workers by the labor they performed, calling them brakemen and granting them brakemen's pay. But the postwar era saw the restoration of the prewar differentials in title, pay, and status. The outbreak of World War II produced no repeat of the earlier occupational reclassification and wage equalization, but it did generate similar complaints from the train porters, who again expressed their dissatisfaction with the discriminatory state of affairs. The "use of the very term 'porter' in the 'Train Porter' category," L. W. Fairchild contended, "has a tendency to lessen the value of this group of workers." Train porters "are required to qualify and perform daily all of the duties required of train brakemen." The nonpromotability clause, which prohibited train porters from standing for promotion to conductor, held blacks "within the confines of a low paid position." For Fairchild, the leader of a small, independent black union, appeals to the powerful constituted one of the few options available. "There is but one solution for correcting this evil," he informed FEPC investigators: "that the President of the United States will 'as a matter of war emergency' suspend all racial discrimination on public carriers."[51] Such dramatic declarations were not on the president's agenda, however.

In 1939, BRT officials targeted the Atchison, Topeka, and Santa Fe railroad (Santa Fe), claiming that black porter brakemen were performing work that contractually belonged to the brakemen. The white brotherhood brought the case to the National Railroad Adjustment Board (NRAB), requesting a ruling and reimbursement to individual white brakemen who, it claimed, should have had the jobs held by blacks. Two years later, on April 20, 1942, the NRAB sustained the whites' claim and ordered the Santa Fe to dismiss its train porters and replace them with brakemen. The position of train porter, which had existed on the Santa Fe since 1899, was simply abolished. The Santa Fe immediately appealed the award, but two years later, when no further action by the NRAB had been taken, the company relented under white union pressure and began demoting or furloughing its black workers. Only because of the wartime shortages of labor—including shortages of white brakemen—was the company allowed to carry out the shift gradually.[52]

Thus began black train porters' decade-long struggle to preserve their jobs. When the award was announced, their level of organization was low; they had, in the words of their attorney, only a "little Association, without any rules or regulations." Retaining black Chicago attorney Richard Westbrooks, Santa Fe train porters suggested he form them into a union. Westbrooks recommended the BSCP, which stepped in to coordinate their strategy because, in Randolph's words, "we believe it is morally unjustifiable for any organization or any individual to use its or his power to take bread and meat out of the mouths of children, and that is what is being done by the Brotherhood of Railroad Trainmen. And they are doing it because the children are black, and that makes it doubly despicable."[53] The moral issue aside, adopting the train porters' cause as its own fit well into the BSCP's larger strategy of organizing all black railroaders.

Santa Fe train porters were only the first to feel the full weight of the BRT's campaign, for Fairchild was correct when he warned in 1943 of a BRT "conspiracy." On the Missouri-Kansas-Texas (M-K-T) railroad, the BRT demanded in 1946 that the company end its six-decades-long tradition of employing blacks as front-end brakemen, repudiate its 1928 contract with its black workforce (now represented by the BSCP), and install whites in positions held by blacks. Like the Santa Fe, the M-K-T bowed to the BRT in the face of "threats and intimidation," even though it had no complaints against its black workforce. That same year, a BRT strike threat forced the St. Louis–San Francisco railroad (the Frisco) to demote and discharge 111 train porters, who were members of the small, independent Brotherhood of Trainmen, Brakemen, Porters, Switchmen, Firemen and Railway Employes.[54]

In each case, black workers turned to the courts for redress; in each case, the courts provided it; in each case, that redress took years to secure as the cases went through the inevitable appeals process. With the BSCP's financial and public relations backing, attorney Richard Westbrooks secured a temporary injunction in November 1944 blocking the implementation of the 1942 NRAB award; in 1948, a Circuit Court upheld the decision to void the award; and in 1949, the U.S. Supreme Court rejected the BRT's appeal for review. With the BRT's appeals exhausted and the legal path clear, the original District Court judge, Walter J. LaBuy of Chicago, made the injunction permanent in 1950. The "only thing that is keeping these men on their jobs," Milton Webster testified the following year, "is the action of the courts."⁵⁵ The other two cases followed a somewhat similar trajectory. A Missouri district court issued a temporary injunction against the 1946 order to replace train porters on the M-K-T; an appeals court reversed it on the grounds that the BSCP had failed to exhaust all available remedies—that is, it had not filed its case with the NRAB or the NMB. When the Supreme Court upheld the appeals court ruling, the BSCP did what it was told: it exhausted the available remedies. Predictably, the National Mediation Board hearing in August 1948 proved unable to reconcile the train porters and their white opponents, who refused to participate except as spectators; the NMB next recommended mediation, which the BSCP accepted and the BRT rejected. Now at an impasse, the BSCP returned to court with more favorable results. By 1950, the injunction had been upheld on appeal, and the M-T-K train porters' jobs were saved.⁵⁶

The independent Frisco train porters' union won a comparable, but further-reaching, victory. "Hell has broken loose on the Frisco," Houston and Waddy reported in September 1948. "Management is firing some train porters . . . and changing all others over to chair car porters—putting white brakemen in their place."⁵⁷ But faced with a suit by black workers for heavy financial damages, the BRT canceled its agreement with the railroad in 1949. Two years later, an appeals court weighed in on the side of Simon Howard and other black Frisco train porters. "It is plain that the position of train porter has had existence only because of the braking duties attached to it," stated the court. The BRT, through its agreement with the Frisco, had "reached out to take over, by forced action, without regard to basis the entire positional field of another craft, with the industrially inevitable, and so legally intended, result that a 40-year established and recognized craft would be pushed off the Railway and cease to have existence." White brakemen had no inherent right to train porters' positions; only a strike threat had moved the railroad to accede to the proposed "forced confiscation." The new contract sanctified "predatory seizure and appropriation, by one railroad craft, of another's entire and 40-year positional field." Since no real change in duty or skill was involved, the court concluded that the BRT was simply assimilating the train porters' position through a "change in nomenclature." This line of reasoning led the court to a dramatic conclusion: because brakemen's and train porters' jobs were essentially the same, the BRT had the obligation to protect "the historic and craft-orphaned holders of the positional field in their previous job rights." That is, the court imposed on the brakemen the same duty of fair representation that the Supreme Court had ruled in *Steele*. The court directed the trial court that had first heard the case to issue a permanent injunction blocking the agreement to consolidate the two crafts.⁵⁸

The Supreme Court concurred, finding that the 1946 agreement merely culminated a quarter-century "program of aggressive hostility" toward blacks in train service. The train porters' case differed from *Steele* in but one fundamental respect: Steele was unquestionably a member of the craft of locomotive firemen and the BLFE was required to represent him fairly. Train porters, however, were members of a traditionally "distinct" craft and had their own union to represent them. White brakemen had argued that this distinction was everything; since the BRT had discriminated only against train porters and not "minority members of its own craft,'" it "owed no duty at all to refrain from using its statutory bargaining power so as to abolish" the black porters' jobs and "drive them from the railroad." The justices rejected this reasoning. Speaking for the majority, Justice Hugo Black concluded that the only reason train porters were "threatened with loss of their jobs" was "because they are not white." Stepping back from the circuit court ruling that the train porters were in fact brakemen, Black directed the "disputed questions of reclassification" to the NMB. At the same time, he pushed the logic of *Steele* well beyond its earlier limits to a particular craft. The Railroad Labor Act prohibited authorized unions from "using their position and power to destroy colored workers' jobs in order to bestow them on white workers," he declared. The racial discrimination contained in the BRT's contract was "unlawful" regardless of the black workers' classification. Bargaining agents enjoying the "advantages" of the act's provisions, then, "must execute their trust without lawless invasions of the right of other workers."[59] The train porters' jobs, at least for the moment, were safe.

The *Howard* ruling was surprising, given the legality of discriminatory behavior by private parties on the one hand and the court's reluctance to intervene in administrative decision making (such as bargaining unit determinations) on the other. By taking the unusual step of rejecting the long-standing jurisdictional distinction between the crafts, however, the Court found its opening and took it. "It is not on the narrow legal grounds of statutory interpretation and induction that we shall find support for this conclusion of the majority," one legal scholar observed shortly after the ruling. Rather, the majority followed "in the great tradition of the Court of looking past the 'labels' to the substance." But aside from "a few vague ambiguities," the Court avoided the larger constitutional issues "suggested by the facts." None of the justices "saw fit to avoid a maze of tortured reasoning by means of a clear-cut and decisive constitutional pronouncement."[60] At no point in the 1950s or early 1960s did the Court deviate from its statutory approach to railroad labor law cases, in which it scrutinized the particular facts while remaining silent about the discriminatory effects of the Railway Labor Act and the white unions it empowered. As long as the Court treated unions as private institutions, it would issue no declarations on the constitutionality of discrim ination, only moral condemnations in its better moments and acquiescence to discriminatory conduct in its weaker moments. Railroad labor law cases would simply remain trapped in a "maze of tortured reasoning."[61]

By the late 1950s, the legal challenges initiated by southern black firemen and train porters brought into sharp conflict two distinct goals: racial equality in the workplace and the labor movement, and the maintenance of a smooth-running system of industrial relations. Willing to address some of the most egregious inequities perpetrated by white unions, the courts ultimately proved unwilling to disrupt the fundamental rules governing union membership and the determination of craft. In stopping short of granting blacks membership in the BLFE or declaring class and craft distinctions irrelevant, the courts were not merely closing their eyes to blatant racial injustice by maintaining the illusion that unions were private associations or that crafts were precisely definable, valid, immutable categories. The white backlash and social disruption in the years immediately following the 1954 *Brown v. Board of Education* decision prompted the courts to adopt a slower approach to racial change. But they were also upholding a system of labor relations designed to maximize the institutional integrity of union officials, minimize the input of the rank and file, reduce workplace conflict, and ensure industrial stability. Forcing union integration or collapsing craft distinctions would undoubtedly precipitate workplace conflict, which would heighten racial tensions and would contravene the very purpose of the Railway Labor Act: to preserve industrial tranquillity. When pressed to choose, the courts increasingly followed the minimalist path, choosing stability over equality.

Just as proponents of educational desegregation learned in the 1950s, court-imposed solutions were costly, time-consuming, and imperfect. Employment discrimination cases slowly wound their way through the judicial system in the 1940s, 1950s, and 1960s, addressing local variations as well as other obstacles that the white brotherhoods threw in the way of black railroaders. Without a doubt, these cases established important principles that undermined the legitimacy of racist practices. In effect, though, they eroded only at a glacial pace both existing and new practices designed to thwart the job rights of black firemen and brakemen. The realities of staunch white union hostility and the legal structure governing labor relations in the railroad industry had made "striking . . . through the courts"—in the words of some left-wing labor activists—the only plausible path for black railroaders to take. But the results, while they were a decisive break with the past, were less than satisfactory.[62]

Ultimately, mid-twentieth-century black railroaders preserved their jobs through their vigilant defense of seniority rights. In highlighting and publicizing a complex and invidious system of racial inequality on the job and in the union movement, their struggles contributed directly to the establishment of legal principles that undermined, if not overturned, workplace and union discrimination. Considering the forces arrayed against them, these limited and largely unheralded achievements were no small feats.

But occupational preservation and circumscribed judicial victories came at an inauspicious moment for African-American railroaders hoping to build on their success in the realm of litigation. On the eve of his retirement from the presidency of the Association of Railway Trainmen and Locomotive Firemen (formerly the ACRT) in 1958, Samuel H. Clark could conclude that the opportunities for black railroaders "are more permanent now than ever before in every way but hiring."[63] But these men, long-standing employees entering their later years, were relatively few in number. Their decades-long struggle had virtually no impact on new hires, and few new black workers were replacing their retiring predecessors. The elimination of barriers to black employment and advancement on the job would benefit African-American workers only if there was employment to be had. The problems confronting black railroaders were rooted not merely in the persistence of discrimination but in the dire economic straits in which the industry found itself.

By the mid- to late 1950s, the American railroad industry was contracting, not expanding, and cutting jobs, not creating them, leaving a large number of railroaders on the furlough list. When business picked up and companies required additional labor, they would follow seniority rules and draw from the list of furloughed men, who, given the long history of racial exclusion, were virtually all white in most job categories. Only when the furlough list had been exhausted would blacks be considered for employment. Thus, in principle, the judicial rulings of the 1940s and 1950s undermined racial barriers and promoted civil rights in employment; in practice, blacks won the right to stand at the back of a very long queue awaiting employment. "It is a matter of history," Randolph conceded in 1960, "that whenever there is any contracting in employment the black man is the first and the hardest hit."[64]

The post–World War II crisis in railroad employment reflected the industry's further decline, continuing a trend that had begun in the 1920s. Although railroads experienced a temporary revival during World War II, intensified competition from the interstate trucking industry and the airlines took a heavy financial toll on freight traffic and revenue. Passenger service suffered even more, as intercity buses, airplanes, and the automobile eventually inflicted irreparable harm. One Interstate Commerce Commission examiner predicted in 1958 that the railroad passenger coach might "take its place in the transportation museum along with the stagecoach, the sidewheeler, and the steam locomotive" within a decade. Although this obituary for rail travel proved premature, by 1965 only a little more than a third of the rail network in the United States was providing passenger service. Even the century-old Pullman Company ended its sleeping-car service in 1969. Only the creation of quasi-public Amtrak by the Rail Service Passenger Act in October 1970 kept passenger service on life support. As railroad revenues declined, so too did railroad employment, suffering a 32 percent drop between 1950 and 1960. Between 1960 and 1968, the number of railroad jobs further declined, from 909,000 to 683,000. The postwar period constituted, in railroad historian John Stover's words, "bleak years for the American who wishes to travel by rail." The same could be said for many of those who worked on the rails.[65]

Black railroaders' fortunes were eclipsed not only by the industry's decline but also by heightened racial conflict during the 1950s and 1960s. In 1954, the same year that the Provisional Committee's internal study found the courts' antidiscrimination injunctions highly effective, the Supreme Court declared racial segregation in schools to be unconstitutional. The following year in Alabama, the Montgomery Improvement Association launched the modern civil rights movement, with thousands of blacks boycotting that city's buses for over twelve months. Quickly and dramatically, the civil rights struggle centered on desegregation in transportation, education, and public accommodations and spread to voting rights in the early 1960s. The southern white backlash was quick in coming. With white communities actively resisting further black advances, southern politics polarized sharply and racist violence intensified, setting the stage for southern blacks' final assault against Jim Crow.

As the South became a battleground between proponents of black freedom and defenders of Jim Crow, few outside the railroad industry itself noticed either black railroaders' progress or the problems that continued to plague them. These workers' invisibility in these decades of bitter conflict—both to contemporaries and to historians—is understandable. By the 1950s, relatively few African Americans were involved in workplace struggles on southern railroads. The severe contraction of the railroad industry suggested that, unlike textiles or steel, it would play only a small role in the subsequent conflicts over black employment. In contrast to the charged response of many white southerners to such celebrated civil rights victories as the *Brown* decision, the integration of public schools in Little Rock, Arkansas, the student lunch counter sit-ins, and the freedom rides, black railroaders' courtroom gains provoked neither much national press coverage nor overt, organized hostility from the white brotherhoods.

For well over a generation, black railroaders had engaged in forms of civil rights activism over workplace and, in some cases, community issues. For unions of Pullman porters, dining car waiters, and red caps, whose center of organizational gravity lay in such northern and western cities as New York, Chicago, and Oakland, the struggle was explicitly about equality—in the workplace, the labor movement, and American society. In the post–World War II era, black activists in these unions provided money, institutional links to northern white liberal organizations, and in some cases personnel to the new southern church- and student-based civil rights movement. Operating in the Jim Crow South, African-American firemen and brakemen only rarely made explicit the connection between efforts to secure rights on the job and the broader movement for racial advancement, even as their associations waged aggressive and often successful campaigns against workplace-based racial inequality in the courts; indeed, few would have called themselves civil rights activists before the 1950s. These increasingly elderly black firemen and brakemen watched largely on the sidelines as supporters of a new civil rights movement mobilized black communities around the abolition of segregation in public transportation, accommodations, and services on the basis of mass protest and mobilization. But, like their counterparts in the railroad service industry, these black union and civil rights pioneers could take considerable pride in the groundwork they had laid for the rise of the new movement, which challenged and ultimately triumphed over Jim Crow.

8

Black Railroaders in
the Modern Era

The judicial victories of the 1940s and 1950s did little to alter the grim prognosis for the future of African-American railroaders. Blacks were "rapidly passing out of the operating departments" of the railroad industry, testified A. Philip Randolph in 1962 before a congressional subcommittee on the need for fair employment legislation. "In the South today, most of the railway yards have been practically transformed from black to white." He might have added that few blacks at all were to be found as firemen and brakemen in the North, and that no black anywhere had yet been employed as a locomotive engineer or conductor. The "lily-white, anti-Negro policy of the Big Four railway unions" had taken a heavy toll on the ranks of black railroaders. "Negro railway workers throughout the South . . . [were] victims of a traditional policy of job discrimination" made possible by the "collusion between railway management and the operating brotherhoods," added NAACP labor secretary Herbert Hill. It appeared that the "raw, grim and unholy war upon black rail firemen by an arrogant white chauvinistic firemen's Brotherhood"—as Randolph put it almost a decade before—had been won.[1]

The picture may have been bleak, but it was not hopeless. Two years before Randolph and Hill mourned the imminent passing of the black railroaders, twenty-year-old James A. Reed was hired as a fireman by the Illinois Central Railroad in Hattiesburg, Mississippi. Reed came from a railroad family: Isaiah Reed, the great-uncle who raised him, had worked for the Illinois Central as a brakeman for forty years. On the basis of the elder Reed's recommendation (family ties still greatly influenced railroad hiring practices for whites and blacks), James was hired after his freshman year at Tougaloo College. He soon became secretary of the local lodge of the International Association of Railway Employees (IARE). At work, the escalating southern civil rights movement was a constant source of whites' anxious conversation. Reed would "hear it, every day, about the Freedom Riders, what they should do to them," and how everything was all right in Mississippi, how "we treat our colored right." He held his tongue with them, but to his black co-workers Reed revealed his ambitions.[2]

At an IARE meeting in the early 1960s, Reed remarked, "One day I may want to be an engineer"; judging from the white men he worked with on a daily basis, Reed believed he could "do the work with one hand tied behind my back and blindfolded." Older black railroaders chided him for such thoughts. "Don't talk like that, don't even think like that," a fellow IARE member warned him. "All you gonna do is cause problems." The idea of black occupational advancement was unthinkable not only to whites but to many black railroaders as well.[3]

After a three-year stint in the U.S. Army, Reed resumed his work on the railroad in 1965 with his seniority intact. The black civil rights movement in Mississippi had had a dramatic impact on national politics and public policy by the mid-1960s and on race relations in Mississippi as well. In 1965, Reed cast his first vote in an election. The following year, as a result of the passage of the 1964 Civil Rights Act, the Illinois Central had to allow Reed and another black fireman, Eddie Smith, to stand for promotion from fireman to engineer. Thus, as a result of national political changes, Reed finally got the chance to realize his ambition.[4]

Reed and his fellow new black engineers did not have an easy time of it, however. White Mississippi workers' resentment was palpable. "'I don't see why they want to do this,'" Reed recalled white co-workers as saying, for "'they have the best jobs in the world because they don't have to do a damn thing, just ride the engine.'" The mindset of whites was "any time they would hire black that was taking a white man's job." Management would not force white engineers to train Reed, and the only white engineer willing to do so earned the reputation as "a nigger lover." But in 1967, the persistent Eddie Smith and James A. Reed became the first two African-American locomotive engineers on the Illinois Central and were among the first blacks in the nation to be promoted to that position. Later that year, they joined the formerly all-white Brotherhood of Locomotive Engineers (BLE). Nor were Reed and his friend Eddie Smith alone in their achievements, for numerous railroads across the nation had begun promoting blacks to engineer, and those new black engineers also joined the BLE.[5]

In gaining promotion into the engineers' craft and entry into the white engineers' brotherhood, these young southern black men accomplished what had appeared impossible only a few years before: the shattering of rigid color bars in the American labor market and in the labor movement. Since the origins of American railroading over 130 years earlier, white workers' and managers' assumptions of African-American intellectual inferiority and lack of moral character and of the inappropriateness of placing blacks in positions demanding responsibility and supervision served as convenient, and enduring, rationales for excluding blacks from such jobs as engineer and conductor. Now, with the Civil Rights Act in force and individual black workers asserting their right to stand for promotion, what had been unthinkable to most whites and even many blacks had become a reality. The act prompted another dramatic break with the past, forcing the white engineers' brotherhood to terminate its century-long ban on nonwhite membership. Under federal pressure, this bastion of white workers' supremacy could not stave off integration.

But how were African-American workers to exercise their new legal rights in a job market that had little use for any new workers, much less those previously barred from it? This was a question that few had an answer to or even confronted. Instead, northern liberals in the postwar years concentrated on dismantling institutional barriers to black employment and advancement. While Congress passed no fair employment legislation following World War II, a number of northern and western states did. State fair employment laws—which had been passed by the legislatures of Massachusetts, New Jersey, New York, Oregon, Rhode Island, and Washington by the early 1950s—prohibited employment and union discrimination on the basis of race. The New York State Commission against Discrimination (SCAD), created by 1945, was considered one of the most active and effective. When it came to the railroad industry, however, its efforts were less than promising.[6]

Pursuing an "all-out attack" on discriminatory practices, the New York SCAD had forced over thirty unions by 1947 to remove or suspend their "No Negroes Allowed" rules covering workers in New York. The lone holdout was the Brotherhood of Locomotive Engineers, which opposed the initial fair employment law by claiming that it would force employers to hire minority workers against their better judgment and would "tear down the foundation" on which the BLE was founded, forcing its members to "fraternize" with the very people it had previously excluded. However, to avoid legal sanctions, by 1948 even the BLE had consented to refrain from applying its antiblack provisions within the state. Following conferences with SCAD commissioners, railroads operating in New York also agreed to hire and promote without bias. Satisfied, SCAD adopted a "wait and watch" approach.[7]

Promises like these, of course, meant little if companies were not hiring. Despite assurances of nondiscrimination from management and unions, SCAD discovered that by 1953 there had been "no employment in practically any of the various job categories in which Negroes had never been employed." Yet the railroad labor market was not static: periodic upswings in the demand for labor, coupled with the normal resignation or retirement of some workers, meant that companies occasionally did hire. Through the early 1950s, railroads drew on the long list of men earlier furloughed from service, ensuring that whites, not blacks, would gain work. When SCAD commissioners concluded that the furlough lists were about to be exhausted and anticipated the hiring of new workers in 1953, it reconvened white employers and union officers to secure their renewed commitment to policies of nondiscrimination.[8]

Even then, promises were broken, demonstrating that official policy was not necessarily observed by subordinate officials. When African American Louis Tribble entered the employment office of the Pennsylvania railroad in early April 1953 to apply for a brakeman's job, he noticed two whites filing an application for the same position. The white men were hired, but Tribble received only a lecture on the disadvantages of the job: the work was not steady and might require working outside of New York City, he was told. When he insisted on filing his application anyway, he was informed that there were no more vacancies. Leroy Hall and Charles Morris had similar experiences. Their brakeman's applications were rejected while those of whites were accepted. Prompted by a local Railroad Employees Association against Discrimination, an informal group composed of employees of the New York Central, the Pennsylvania, and other regional railroads, the three men decided to file complaints with SCAD.[9]

In the course of its investigation, SCAD learned that the Pennsylvania railroad employed no blacks among its 685 passenger trainmen (brakemen) and 2,180 freight trainmen, and that over a three-month period in 1953 the railroad had hired 61 new brakemen, all of whom were white. Finding probable cause to support the charge of racial discrimination, SCAD commissioners followed the letter of the law by calling a meeting with Pennsylvania railroad officials to seek conciliation. The three black complainants were able to satisfy the "ordinary physical and educational requirements for brakemen," Commissioner Elmer Carter informed the Pennsylvania officials, and none of the three were "crackpots" or were "offensively aggressive." SCAD recommended that the company give the complainants physical exams and, if they passed, offer them the next available jobs. It also recommended that the company send written directives to all hiring and supervisory personnel reiterating the railroad's policy to comply fully with the antidiscrimination law and that the company cooperate with the commission by providing information about its record of hiring blacks in the future. The Pennsylvania railroad agreed. The result of this perseverance was that Charles Morris, one of the three complainants, became the railroad's first black brakeman on October 7, 1953. Several months later, he was admitted to Lodge 706 of the Brotherhood of Railroad Trainmen.[10]

Morris's breakthrough notwithstanding, progress was slow. Part of the problem rested with the individual case method followed by SCAD, requiring individuals who believed they had suffered discrimination to file complaints with the commission. After investigation and conciliation efforts,

SCAD could order railroads to hire the particular individuals, but could do little to alter broader patterns of employment. While the Pennsylvania railroad consented to begin hiring a small number of black brakemen, its subsidiary, the Long Island railroad, dragged its feet, refusing to give interviews, application forms, or physical exams to black applicants, keeping SCAD "at arms [sic] length," and offering it less than full cooperation. Eventually, in January 1955 the railroad announced a change of heart. John J. Gaherin, personnel manager for the Long Island railroad, informed a SCAD commissioner that he "meant it" when he said that it was "going to be their policy not to discriminate." His company was "doing business in a cosmopolitan area containing a 'mixed group'" and was "'legally and morally' obligated to take a new position." But, he added, "it had to be a 'slow evolution,'" for a company that hired and promoted blacks in train service would encounter numerous obstacles from employees and unions. The best policy of integrating blacks into train service, the railroad believed, "was to go slowly and quietly and to select the best possible candidates for promotion or for initial employment."[11]

Just how slowly the company would go was revealed in a study of railroad employment for a three-month period in 1957 jointly conducted by the New York SCAD and its counterpart, the New Jersey Division against Discrimination. Of all railroad jobs, those in the operating department offered the fewest jobs to blacks. The study found that only 118, or less than one percent, of the 20,900 operating jobs—including those of brakemen and flagmen, firemen and helpers, conductors, and engineers—were held by blacks; and all but 5 of these black workers were employed by a single railroad. Furthermore, most of the black workers were yard workers. Of the 118 black employees, 70 were yard brakemen and helpers (out of a total of 4,706), 43 were yard conductors and yard foremen (out of 1,832), and 3 were switchtenders and hostlers (out of 1,306). Only one worked as a road passenger brakeman (out of 658), and one as a road freight engineer or motorman (out of 897). Progress was spotty and uneven at best, and virtually nonexistent at worst.[12]

However gradual or imperceptible, change finally came to the white railroad brotherhoods, those staunch upholders of white supremacy and racial exclusion. By the early 1960s, their almost century-long racial policies had begun to erode. Their abilities to use their bargaining power against blacks was diminished, if not eliminated, by the Supreme Court rulings in *Steele* and *Tunstall* in 1944. Those judicial decisions imposed the duty of fair representation on the legally certified bargaining agent, while subsequent legal cases brought by black railroaders made certain forms of discriminatory behavior too expensive to continue. Although the Supreme Court upheld the legality of racial membership restrictions in 1959 in *Oliphant,* liberal public opinion and institutional intolerance of such practices rendered them vulnerable. When the BRT sought admission into the AFL-CIO, Randolph's continued blistering attacks on the brotherhood's racial practices made its admission problematic. In 1960, the trainmen's union voted to drop its ban against nonwhites; the Brotherhood of Locomotive Firemen and Enginemen did the same in 1961. With the passage of the Civil Rights Act of 1964, discrimination in union membership became illegal, leading even the Brotherhood of Locomotive Engineers to remove its prohibition against African-American members.[13]

For Randolph, such welcome sea changes in the railroad brotherhoods' constitutions was a vindication of his long crusade against subordinate auxiliary locals and exclusionary unions. At the same time, he recognized the immediate danger of black integration into the enemy camp, for white railroaders had hardly abandoned their antiblack animus. With the removal of their color bars, he predicted, the white trainmen and firemen "will make a bid" for black members, "and it is natural that these Negro operating employees will be inclined to join these unions. This situation will strip most of the existing Negro railway unions . . . very largely of their membership." But formal integration into white trade unions was not the same thing as achieving equality in the labor movement. Black workers needed to remain vigilant against potential infringement of their rights by whites who had only reluctantly, and under duress, admitted blacks into their association. The Provisional Committee hoped to monitor the firemen's brotherhood for any signs of discriminatory behavior in the hopes of protecting black workers' interests.[14]

Two challenges—the overall contraction of employment and the likelihood that the white brotherhoods would attempt to enroll black members—led Randolph once again to urge the unification of black railway workers as a means of self-protection. The "Negro railway labor organizations will either merge to survive," Randolph predicted, "or not unite and perish."[15] Little had changed in his thinking on the subject since the late 1930s: black associations of southern firemen, brakemen, and yardmen remained "too small financially, and organizationally too weak, to maintain independent units to do an effective job for the Negro railway employees," he believed. Indeed, only 411 black workers held contracts under the IARE and only 356 under the Association of Railway Trainmen and Locomotive Firemen (formerly the Association of Colored Railway Trainmen and Locomotive Firemen); another 125 of its members were not covered by contracts. As for the Texas and Louisiana-based Colored Trainmen of America (CTA), its locals were "dying by degree," its president admitted in 1960. By the mid 1960s, it represented no more than several hundred Missouri Pacific brakemen and firemen. But whatever their weaknesses, the black independent associations Randolph be-littled were no more willing to follow the Brotherhood of Sleeping Car Por-ters (BSCP) leader in the 1960s than they had been in the 1940s, and this fact led to the collapse of Randolph's dream of unifying black southern firemen. When an informal merger of the independent black associations finally took place in 1961, Randolph's Provisional Committee was not in-volved; the old acrimony and organizational rivalry had proved insurmount-able. Nor did all independent black associations affiliate with one another. The ACRT and the IARE joined forces, but the CTA voted unanimously to stand apart. Organizational jealousy and provincialism deprived southern black firemen and brakemen of whatever limited strength in numbers they might have achieved, ensuring the organizations' further decline.[16]

The otherwise positive changes in the racial climate proved fatal for the in-dependents. Precisely as Randolph had anticipated, the white brotherhoods' elimination of the color bar meant that whatever jurisdictional boundaries had been erected by race came tumbling down, taking the independent black associations with them. By 1966, the BRT was inviting black workers to join its locals. Despite the long history of exclusion, BRT membership held some attraction for blacks. Black CTA members had long earned less than their white BRT counterparts. In freight service, for instance, blacks were paid $2.10 a day less than whites in the early 1960s; when the BRT won a wage in-crease in 1964, the Missouri Pacific refused to raise black wages because CTA members technically were not a party to the agreement. Only a National Me-diation Board (NMB) order in 1966 phased in increases for blacks to equal-ize wages. The BRT was more powerful because it was a vastly larger associa-tion than the CTA; it represented all Missouri Pacific railroad brakemen and yardmen except the 195 black workers in the DeQuincy and Kingsville divi-sions. When the BRT finally set its sights on the small black union's member-ship, there was little the CTA could do to stave off its collapse.[17]

The CTA attempted to swim against the tide of racial change in the 1960s. Its leaders feared—unjustifiably, it turned out—that a BRT takeover would spell the end of black jobs through the merging of seniority districts, which would allow more senior whites to displace African Americans. Appeals based on the CTA's "unique history," its members' understandable distrust of white workers, and the potential negative consequences of BRT affiliation were not convincing, either to government officials or to black workers. The BRT challenged the CTA to represent black workers on the Missouri Pacific divisions, submitting to the NMB authorization cards from just over 50 per-cent of the men in question. NMB policy favored a "carrier-wide" policy of representation, with one union representing all workers in a craft or class on a given railroad. With the BRT representing 2,706 brakemen and yardmen on the Missouri Pacific plus half of the black employees on the DeQuincy and Kingsville divisions, the NMB certified the BRT as the bargaining agent without an election. After experiencing considerable difficulty in assembling its remaining members, the CTA met for the final time on March 30, 1969, to dissolve itself formally.[18]

The shifting racial and economic winds of the 1950s and 1960s affected even black service unions affiliated with the AFL-CIO. Both porters and red caps worked in dying trades, and the steady loss of jobs—and, in the case of Pullman, the demise of the company—meant that the BSCP and the United Transport Service Employees of America (UTSEA) represented a dwindling number of aging men. Neither union could sustain itself financially. In 1972, the 1,700 members of the UTSEA voted to merge with the Brotherhood of Railway and Airline Clerks (BRAC), the larger white union whose racial policies it had fought in the 1930s and 1940s. With the merger came the closing of the red caps' union office; their former officers became BRAC staffers.[19]

The prospect of union mergers was hardly a pleasing one. "Every effort ought to be made to maintain at least one international" union within the AFL CIO "which is under Negro leadership and control," C. L. Dellums, Randolph's successor as president of the BSCP, recommended in the same year as the CTA's formal dissolution. Advocating a "free and independent Negro voice in the labor movement" in an era of economic decline on the railroads proved an increasingly difficult task. By 1971, the BSCP's membership had fallen to less than 1,000 in the United States, most of whom were employed by the new Amtrak. "We are on the verge of losing our identity, not because of anything we have done or have failed to do," Dellums noted, but because "[we] are victims of the times." In 1978, the effort to "Save the Brotherhood" came to an end when financial and organizational exigencies forced the BSCP to follow the UTSEA's course of action by merging with the larger BRAC. Only the Joint Council of Dining Car Employees, already affiliated with a larger union of culinary and hotel workers, survived, albeit with a shrunken membership.[20]

African Americans' unprecedented, if gradual, breakthroughs in railroad employment previously reserved for whites and the eventual integration of the industry and its unions was largely the product of the Civil Rights Act of 1964 and blacks' efforts to use the openings the law afforded. Coming on the heels of the civil rights movement's Birmingham campaign, the March on Washington for Jobs and Freedom, and the assassination of President John Kennedy in 1963, the act outlawed discrimination in public accommodations, bringing an end to the era of legalized Jim Crow. Title VII of the act declared unlawful discrimination in hiring on the basis of race, color, religion, sex, or national origin, as well as any attempt to "limit, segregate or classify" workers so as to "deprive or tend to deprive" them of employment opportunities; it similarly declared unlawful racial discrimination by trade unions. The act created a five-member bipartisan Equal Employment Opportunity Commission (EEOC) with the power to investigate complaints of discrimination, issue findings of probable cause, and seek conciliation. What the EEOC could not do was issue "cease and desist" orders against offending parties or file antidiscrimination suits in court; that was the price the act's backers had to pay to secure select Republican support in Congress. Under the compromise, the EEOC could only refer cases to the Justice Department for further action once it had documented a "pattern or practice" of systemic discrimination or, more commonly, authorize legal suits by the individual complainants. (In 1972 Congress authorized the EEOC to file its own suits.) On July 2, 1965, the antidiscrimination employment statute became effective, and the fledgling EEOC began its efforts in earnest.[21]

For black railroaders, Title VII and the EEOC proved to be slow, imperfect vehicles for challenging past and continuing discriminatory practices, securing black employment rights, and promoting black employment. The EEOC's goal was to eradicate barriers to occupational entry and promotion, but it had little to say about employment itself. In historian Judith Stein's words, Title VII "separated the notion of discrimination from the more powerful causes of black unemployment." This was particularly true in the railroad industry: after 1965, the EEOC and the courts eliminated some obstacles to black advancement by questioning racist job classifications, overturning discriminatory seniority systems, and the like. But the collapse and demise of most of the railroads' passenger service and the dramatic postwar contraction in other jobs meant that the number of blacks who gained from the rulings was small. Because the railroad industry had few job opportunities to offer, the EEOC directed more of its attention to other industries, such as textiles and steel. In addition, the fact that the ultimate resolution of employment and union discrimination cases would take place in the courts ensured that defendant unions and firms would resort to costly legal maneuvers and technicalities to delay the eventual outcome of their cases. Five years after Title VII became law, EEOC chairman William H. Brown III found "the statistics on [railroad] employment of minorities unacceptable."[22]

The cases of Joe Vernon Sears and Earl Love illustrate the legal effectiveness of the Title VII suits and their ultimate irrelevance in the lives of at least some black railroaders. Born in 1914, Sears grew up in Newton, Kansas, where his father worked as a boilermaker with the Santa Fe railroad. Following a brief stint as a red cap at Newton's train station, he was hired as a chair car attendant by the Atchison, Topeka, and Santa Fe railway in 1936. That same year, Sears passed the requisite exams and became a train porter, a position that combined some cleaning tasks with a brakeman's duties. Over the years he occasionally applied for a brakeman's position, only to be told that "you can't become a brakeman until your skin changes color." By the early 1940s, the white Brotherhood of Railway Trainmen escalated its campaign against the use of train porters, claiming that all braking work should be performed by bona fide (white) brakemen. In 1946, the black Santa Fe workers affiliated as a local of the Brotherhood of Sleeping Car Porters, which then turned to the courts to block the BRT's efforts to replace black train porters with white brakemen; Sears served as the president of the train porters' Kansas City local for two years in the late 1940s. The BSCP held the line until 1959, when the National Railroad Adjustment Board (NRAB) ruled that only those train porters holding seniority prior to April 1942—the date of an earlier NRAB ruling giving brakemen jurisdiction over train porters' work—could retain their positions performing head-end braking work. Train porters hired after April 1942 were effectively displaced, demoted to the position of chair car attendants. Because he began work in 1936, Joe Sears was one of a small and aging group of train porters who managed to keep their jobs. Yet by the mid-1960s, the railroad's employment cutbacks had relegated even Sears to the ranks of chair car attendants.[23]

Sears's long pent-up anger against being denied promotions and his confinement to a service classification reserved only for blacks eventually exploded as he watched coverage of the civil rights struggle on television. Sears described himself as "brainwashed" in the 1950s and early 1960s. "We knew what we were supposed to do and how to act," Sears recalled. But that changed. As the Watts riot engulfed portions of Los Angeles in flames, Sears wrote a letter to the Santa Fe, again requesting a brakeman's job. The company refused on the grounds that he was too old. In March 1966, Sears filed a formal complaint against the United Transportation Union (the UTU, which represented the brakemen, had absorbed the BRT) and the Santa Fe railroad with the Kansas Commission on Civil Rights in Topeka. Seven months later, one of the state civil rights commissioners accepted a job with the new EEOC, and took Sears's case with him. In May 1968, the EEOC found probable cause that Sears's civil rights had been violated and in October 1972 informed Sears that he could sue under the Civil Rights Act's Title VII. At this point, Sears was working as an Amtrak porter and was only three years away from retirement.[24]

The class action suit of Joe Vernon Sears and seventy-two other train porters went to trial in 1978. U.S. District Court Judge Wesley E. Brown concluded that the black train porters were indeed victims of racial discrimination and held the Santa Fe management and the UTU equally responsible. While the company had settled with the porters earlier, the UTU found itself liable to pay $8.5 million in damages and fees. Only in December 1984, after an appeals court upheld the judgment, did the seventy-year-old Sears and his fellow porters finally receive payment for damages, which averaged roughly $85,000 per worker. The following year, Judge Brown ruled against Santa Fe chair car attendants in a similar class action suit, contending that the Santa Fe's seniority system, which forced attendants to give up their seniority if they became brakemen, was not discriminatory. Three years later, an appeals court disagreed; by 1993, the UTU was forced to pay $15.5 million to 120 attendants and the survivors of 80 more. Over a quarter century after Joe Sears filed his complaint with the Kansas Commission on Civil Rights, the Santa Fe's black train porters and chair car attendants had been vindicated.[25]

Earl Love, a veteran Pullman porter based in Denver, turned to the EEOC and the courts to challenge the long-standing Pullman practice of employing black "porters-in-charge" instead of white conductors, at a rate of pay substantially less than that of conductors. The Pullman Company hired white men off the streets as conductors, Love charged, never giving blacks the opportunity to advance to that position. Love filed a complaint with the Colorado Civil Rights Commission in 1963, only to have it dismissed in 1965 when he turned down a Pullman offer of promotion. To become a conductor, Love would have had to forfeit the forty years of seniority protection he had earned as a porter and begin at the bottom of the conductor's seniority roster. Given the number of white conductors who had been furloughed, Love would have been promoted into a job category in which there was no work. His promotion, then, entailed his accepting a layoff. In 1966, Love filed his complaint with the EEOC, which proved unable to secure Pullman's compliance. In 1968, Love and other porters-in-charge filed a class action suit against the Pullman company.[26]

Twelve years after Love's first complaint to the Colorado Commission, in 1975, the courts ruled on behalf of the porters-in-charge. "While many porters-in-charge did not request promotion to conductor, apparently because they felt it would be futile, some did seek promotion," U.S. District Court Judge Alfred A. Arraj noted. But Pullman employed no black conductors until 1967. The evidence indicated that "Pullman maintained racially segregated job classifications and that promotions of qualified employees were foreclosed on racial grounds." Rejecting Pullman claims that the general decline in railroad service meant that there were few if any jobs to fill, Arraj insisted that "the burden of the depressed economic condition of Pullman cannot be borne disproportionately by blacks." The cessation of Pullman service in 1969, however, meant that the very job classifications of porter, porter in charge, and Pullman conductor were things of the past; no one could be promoted into a job category that no longer existed. In 1979, 1,293 black men who had worked as porters-in-charge during and after 1965 (when the Civil Rights Act became effective), their families, and their attorneys received a $5.5 million settlement.[27]

Black train porters and Pullman porters' use of the EEOC and Title VII came too late to effect any material change in their employment prospects. For black workers still in the industry, however, the EEOC and the courts at times influenced their ability to exercise seniority rights and enhanced their prospects for promotion. The federal government's case against the Jacksonville Terminal Company, for instance, proved dramatic and far-reaching. Owned by three major railroads, the terminal had suffered a severe reduction in services, expenditures, and labor force size since World War II; by 1969, 275 whites and 257 blacks worked in some 102 separate job categories. Many of those categories had been, and continued to be, racially exclusive, and workers were represented by largely segregated unions. Transfer rights were highly limited; while there were 35 seniority rosters, workers could only bid for promotion within their own roster, that is, their seniority could not be used when bidding for a job listed on another roster. While this had the practical and desired effect of discouraging job hopping and promoting employment stability, the U.S. Court of Appeals for the Fifth Circuit also concluded that it froze blacks into the lowest-level jobs and protected whites in the higher-paying ones. Furthermore, the arbitrary administration of a personnel exam with little relationship to future job performance allowed company officials to favor whites over blacks, and the terminal's thirty-two toilet, locker, and shower facilities were designated according to craft, effectively segregating workers by race.[28]

The Fifth Circuit Court insisted that the long history of racial discrimination at the terminal was central to understanding black exclusion and that events occurring after Title VII became law must "be considered in light of relevant employment history and the total employment picture." Drawing on a recent Fourth Circuit Court decision, it further insisted that "practices, policies or patterns, even though neutral on their face, may operate to segregate and classify on the basis of race at least as effectively as overt racial discrimination." This meant that the terminal's exams and the overall seniority system, which erected impediments to intercraft and interclass transfers, were in fact perpetuating prior racial discrimination. To say that "the Terminal's seniority systems may well exclude a lifetime of black workers from higher paying crafts and classes is not conjectural hyperbole," the court argued. Thus, the terminal's seniority system was "neither *bona fide* nor a business necessity" two statutory exceptions to Title VII. The Circuit Court or dered the abolition of the discriminatory tests, the integration of restrooms, and the admission of blacks into specified white UTU locals, and also demanded that the seniority system be modified. Black terminal workers would be allowed to use their terminal seniority dates when bidding (once) on any job outside of their craft or class designation; they would no longer have to give up all previously acquired seniority to start at the bottom of a new list. Under the *Jacksonville Terminal* ruling, the court thus facilitated limited black advancement in an otherwise constricting labor market.[29]

Two years later, in the 1973 case of *Robert Rock et al. v. Norfolk & Western Railway Company and UTU, et al.,* the courts concurred with black Norfolk and Western (N&W) yard workers that company and union policies violated Title VII. With few exceptions, blacks worked at the N&W's Norfolk, Virginia, Barney yard, while whites worked at its much larger CT yard, with each yard possessing its own, racially distinct UTU local. Even after the passage of the Civil Rights Act, the company continued to hire largely along racial lines by relying on "word of mouth" and "nepotistic" hiring practices. Since seniority attached only to the yard in which these men worked, blacks were excluded from the more diverse and numerous opportunities in the CT yard. The U.S. Court of Appeals for the Fourth Circuit rejected the N&W's "business necessity" defense for maintaining separate seniority rosters, finding that the work in the CT yard did not require "greater and more specialized skills," as the company maintained. In 1973 the court ordered the merger of the segregated UTU locals and the creation of a single terminal seniority roster that preserved the rights of current employees—no white would be displaced from his job—but allowed blacks to bid for future vacancies in both yards.[30]

Black advances in employment came slowly during the 1960s and 1970s. The legal approach often resembled a siege more than a full-scale frontal assault, for the process of EEOC investigation, attempted conciliation, and eventual legal suits by the government or aggrieved black workers were drawn out and time consuming. Yet for many black workers, civil rights laws and the EEOC provided an effective mechanism for breaching the walls of racial discrimination in employment and the trade union movement. The enduring legacy of racial subordination and the intensity of white opposition to racial change suggest that without these federal resources, black workers' individual and collective advancement would have been virtually impossible.[31]

The civil rights revolution may have cracked the century-long barrier to black advancement in the railroad industry, but the individual black railroaders who benefited still faced the indifference of their supervisors and the open hostility of white coworkers. Blacks' entry into all-white crafts invariably generated workplace racial tensions. While black railroaders were the beneficiaries of the Civil Rights Act's Title VII, the integration process was often difficult and could leave personal scars. What trials they endured, they suffered largely alone, for their numbers were few and civil rights associations had many other pressing struggles to handle. Race relations on and off the job were varied, reflecting not only the industry's racial past but also the personal idiosyncrasies of white workers and managers, the commitment to integrating and advancing black workers by supervisors and union officials, and the racial characteristics of the communities to which blacks traveled and in which they worked.

For two decades, from 1972 to 1992, Herman Autry worked as a Southern Pacific (SP) engineer out of Houston, Texas. His father's jobs as an SP motorman and operator of a forklift and heavy crane exposed Autry to the world of railroading early in his life. Following a summer working as a machinist's apprentice in 1964, he attended Grambling State University. He returned to the SP after his graduation in 1968 and became an apprentice electrician. When he was furloughed the following year, the SP rehired him as a locomotive fireman, essentially a training position for engineer. Three years later, after acquiring the necessary experience and passing the requisite exams, he was promoted to engineer.[32]

Autry's progression from apprentice to fireman to engineer was marked by considerable racial conflict. By the time he returned to railroad service in 1968, the walls separating the segregated restrooms had come down, but the attitudes of whites toward blacks remained firmly intact. "It was very, very difficult," Autry recalled of his years as a fireman, for his white coworkers "did everything they could to get me fired." In 1971, Autry got into a fight with a white fireman with less seniority when the white man started using racial epithets, saying "nigger this and nigger that." Autry "beat him up pretty bad"; the incident dogged him. Six months later, Autry was assigned to work with the beaten fireman's father, an engineer. "I was just sitting down there, waiting for him to move," Autry recounted, when the engineer "jumped up and grabbed a hammer and said he was going to whoop my ass, to knock me in the head with the hammer because I was a nigger and I didn't know my place." Autry jumped off the engine and returned to the call board room, where the assistant superintendent fired him. "He fired me because I was a fireman and I was black." Only because another white engineer stood up for Autry did the company hold an investigation; only when another white fireman who witnessed the incident testified to what had actually transpired did the company reinstate him.

But little changed on the job. Almost always the sole African American on his train, Autry viewed his crewmates, many of whom were in their sixties and had worked on the railroad for as many as forty years, as "backward"; the white railroad workforce "wasn't ready for the integration." In fact, white co-workers on his five-man crew regularly engaged in verbal abuse; "they'd talk bad" and would "call you all kind of names." "And you had to take that stuff," he remembered. "You just had to learn to overlook it." When a train would make a stop in various small Texas towns, the white engineer would order Autry to perform extra work on the engine while the rest of the white crew went to eat. Autry learned to bring his lunch and eat on the engine by himself. Not only was he ostracized on the engine, but whites provided him with no training. Being a fireman involved gaining hands-on experience in running a train. But the SP (like other roads) did not force white engineers to train black firemen. "So out of probably three years," Autry "actually didn't touch [or] run the trains . . . I didn't have not one white brother let me run the train for three years." Whatever he learned, he had to learn on his own. When he finally became a locomotive engineer in 1972, it was by "God's will and the little skills that I had learned just by watching" that got him through his first trip. "I just had to figure out everything myself."

Eddie Lee Jenkins III was another African American who was among the first to break occupational barriers in the railroad industry. A newspaper advertisement led Jenkins to apply for a brakeman's position with the Louisville and Nashville railroad in 1966. Convinced that the men grading application tests were biased against blacks, Jenkins determined to confuse his graders by neglecting to indicate his race on paper. His plan worked. On the day of his first trip as a brakeman, a white worker sweeping out the engine remarked, "I didn't know that L&N was hiring niggers now." "Something must be wrong with you," Jenkins responded, pointing out that he, an African American, had been hired as a brakeman while the white man insulting him was merely pushing a broom. With the white engineer and fireman laughing loudly, the white sweeper walked off the engine, humiliated.[33]

But Jenkins, who became a conductor in 1967, was subsequently in for his own share of humiliation. Even when white workers were not harassing him, his job took him to places where local racial custom proved difficult to endure. When his train stayed overnight in a virtually all-white town, Jenkins was unable to find a place to sleep. The local hotel where railroaders stayed claimed no vacancies when Jenkins inquired about a room, directing him instead to a small garage. Jenkins later demanded that the owner provide him with proper lodging. "Now we're all on the same crew and I want you to understand that I ain't going to put up with that mess," he insisted. "Now you put my crew in the motel, you put me in the motel." The hotel then provided Jenkins with the accommodations he had demanded.[34]

Dave Leftridge, who became an engineer on the Chicago and North Western in 1974, similarly found himself traveling into racially hostile territory.

When he first stayed in South Pekin, Illinois, the railroad posted a security escort from the train to the motel "because the townspeople didn't want blacks in their town." Working temporarily in management in the mid-1970s, Leftridge was transferred to Fremont, Nebraska, a town with few black residents. White railroad workers would "send out letters for applications to the KKK and would leave [them] around the yard," he recalled; another time he found a watermelon on top of his car. A simple shopping trip for groceries was painful, for local whites would "act like I was a Martian or something." What put a "dagger" in his heart was the cold treatment his young daughter received from other children. Leftridge quickly transferred to Minneapolis.[35]

Despite persistent racial hostility, the removal of many of the legal barriers to black advancement did alter race relations on the railroads. Even black railroaders who reported early hostile racial encounters observed some degree of improvement over time. The "climate had begun to change," Autry concluded. The railroad still had some leftovers who would say, "Well, no nigger would never pull me on no train." But by the 1980s, there "wasn't a whole lot of racial problems out there" on the road. "We were pretty much well integrated," and some whites even "got to be friends" with their black coworkers. In 1972, Autry left the UTU to become one of the first blacks to join the BLE after being recruited by a white engineer. Other black engineers "didn't have anything kind to say about the BLE. They thought I was crazy" for joining it. But, he insisted, "no one really bothered me. I was just a regular union member." With as little as 5 percent of the membership black, Autry was twice elected president of his BLE lodge in the 1980s and served as the second vice-chairman for the Texas BLE's state legislative division.

Black engineer James A. Reed recounted a comparable shift in workplace race relations in recent decades. Following an accident with a switch engine in the Gulfport roundhouse on his third night as an engineer, the glee of his white coworkers was visible on their faces. Whites "made a joke about it," Reed remembered. "They're gonna sell tickets" to see him back into the roundhouse again. Despite such attitudes, Reed concluded that quitting the railroad would be "playing into their hands." The pay was good, the hours short, and he felt a sense of obligation to his great-uncle. "I owed that to him and the others that were before me to make the very best of it," he resolved. Many of the diehards, the whites who gave him a hard time, eventually retired or died. Although older racial attitudes hadn't completely vanished, the younger generation of whites who entered the railroad service in the late 1960s and 1970s was more open. "I've been here a long time," Reed noted in 1996. "They accept me." From 1976 to 1980, Reed served as secretary-treasurer of his BLE local. Chicago native Dave Leftridge also felt accepted by fellow workers when he first hired out as a brakeman with the Chicago and

North Western in 1973. When he became an engineer, his low seniority rank prompted him to transfer to a better job in Iowa, where most of his fellow white coworkers were not familiar with blacks. Not only did he experience no racial problems on the job, he was elected local chairman of his BLE lodge by an overwhelmingly white membership.[36]

In being elected to union leadership positions by whites, Autry, Reed, and Leftridge were hardly representative of black engineers in the 1970s, 1980s, and 1990s. Similarly, their views of the substantive improvements in whites' racial attitudes on the job are not shared by all black railroaders. A common belief among black railroaders holds that only the pressure created by various court-ordered settlements and consent decrees has allowed the hiring and upgrading of black workers to continue. Indeed, since the late 1960s, numerous lawsuits and EEOC investigations have found persistent discrimination in the industry. In 1997, the Black Railroaders' Association of the Union Pacific railroad in Chicago, a group formed to support charitable work and educational advancement for black Chicago children, angrily took its members' multiple complaints of discriminatory treatment to the company's managers at a meeting mediated by Operation Push in Chicago, resulting in temporary improvements on the job. In 1996, black employees of Amtrak's maintenance-of-way and engineering divisions in the Boston area complained of the persistence of nepotistic hiring practices that kept blacks out of jobs. "Nigger jokes" remained a staple among white workers, blacks and white supporters of affirmative action were singled out and subject to harassment, and the assignment of blacks to the worst jobs remained a common practice. To one investigative journalist, Boston's Amtrak workplace appeared "more like the Old South than Boston." Charging racial discrimination and harassment, a class action suit on behalf of 5,000 African-American repair and track-laying workers in the Northeast was filed against Amtrak in 1998. That same year, a group of black Amtrak managers launched their own class action suit against the company for what they called its discriminatory hiring and promotion policies and for maintaining a hostile working environment. Black railroaders are "not catching up, we're still behind," observed Samuel M. Ledford, Jr., a Southern Pacific engineer from Tucson, Arizona, in 1997. Ledford, a member of a California railroad family whose own workplace experiences have been quite positive, pessimistically concluded that "we're going to be behind probably for another hundred years."[37]

Given the long and bitter history of racial exclusion and discriminatory treatment in the railroad industry, the persistence of racism among managers and white workers should hardly be surprising. Neither should the vocal protests lodged by today's African-American railroaders, for it was only through past protest that black workers have gotten as far as they have. Notwithstanding the examples of contemporary racial intolerance and obstacles to further black advancement, the railroad industry's recent changes have been nothing short of revolutionary. In little more than a generation, the skilled railroad labor force has undergone a dramatic racial recomposition. A new generation of black workers found jobs after decades of declining employment levels and progressed up the occupational ladder into previously all-white domains. Working-class race relations on the railroads have also altered radically: many white workers now accept blacks as coworkers and even as supervisors, and admit them with little friction—though often with little welcome—into their unions. Although this revolution remains incomplete, the tremendous achievement of black railroaders in the 1990s is the fruit of generations of civil rights activism in their industry and in the broader society. But, as many African-American railroaders can attest, the struggle for equality remains an ongoing one, requiring constant vigilance, commitment, and engagement.

Conclusion

In the first half of the twentieth century, African-American railroaders questioned the legitimacy of a system of employment discrimination that restricted them to menial, semiskilled, or service positions, a system that disregarded their workplace rights and rendered insecure what jobs they had. By the 1920s and 1930s, black workers challenged the legality and constitutionality of a system of labor law that denied them representation in the collective bargaining process and left them without effective protection on the job, a system that seemed to sanction white workers' encroachment on blacks' jobs. Although black railroad service unions depended on federal labor law for their success and even existence, black railroaders came to indict white managers, white workers, and the federal government for perpetuating discrimination in employment that threatened to wipe out their access to entire categories of valuable railroad work.

Black railroaders' experiences, while extreme, were not atypical of black labor in the nineteenth and twentieth centuries. Occupational barriers in virtually all industries were familiar to most black workers through the 1930s and, in many cases, well beyond. African Americans' concentration in service, semiskilled, and common labor positions was representative of their place in American industry generally until World War II. In their exclusion from the railroad industry's more skilled jobs as engineers and conductors, black railroaders' experiences resembled those of other blacks who found themselves frozen out of the chief skilled trades in the automobile, shipbuilding, and construction industries through the 1960s. The barriers to black occupational and economic advancement in the era before the Civil Rights Act of 1964 were perhaps most blatant in the railroad industry, but those barriers, while less explicit or impermeable, remained commonplace in much of American industry.

In the realm of trade unionism, the paths followed by black railroaders in some cases paralleled and in others deviated from those trod by black workers in other industries. The labor upheavals of the 1930s and 1940s engaged hundreds of thousands of African Americans, many of whom joined interracial unions committed to racial equality in theory and sometimes in practice. Railroad service workers—Pullman porters, red caps, and dining car cooks and waiters—were active participants in labor's crusade during the Great Depression. The labor relations regime established by New Deal labor law allowed them, like many CIO and AFL unions, to consolidate their position and win significant improvements for their members. Black operating craft workers, however, stood in a very different relationship to labor law and the labor movement: the 1934 amendments to the Railway Labor Act weakened their position and emboldened their white opponents. Unlike black railroad service workers or industrial workers, they found the doors of the revitalized House of Labor sealed shut. For them, organized labor resembled not a potential interracial movement but instead a hostile and predatory force.

Racial discrimination and exclusion in railroad employment and in railroad unions gave rise to civil rights challenges by black workers who were determined to overcome racial subordination in the workplace and the labor movement. In this, black railroaders may have been particularly prominent, but they were hardly alone. Long before the Freedom Struggle of the 1950s and 1960s, black workplace activists pressured their unions, confronted white workers, criticized their employers, pursued legal action, and engaged in shop floor activism in rail yards, in automobile and rubber plants, in shipyards and packinghouses, on the docks, and in steel mills. With or without the assistance of sympathetic white workers or black civil rights organizations, they contested inequality in the workplace, in the labor market, and in the labor movement. However they conceived of their struggles, they were as much civil rights pioneers as the men and women who later boycotted buses, sat in at lunch counters, registered voters, endured the fire hoses and police dogs, and marched for jobs and freedom.

From the mid-1960s on, the railroad industry and its unions, like much of American society, experienced a racial transformation that would have been unimaginable to either white supremacists or black activists of the 1950s and early 1960s. The impact of the modern civil rights movement on the fortunes of African-American workers, however, ultimately proved mixed. By the time black railroaders broke the color line in hiring, promotion, and union representation, their achievements came too late to provide an economic windfall to African-American communities. In earlier decades, high levels of unskilled and semiskilled railroad employment sustained many black communities by providing steady wages. But by the 1960s, railroads employed far smaller numbers of workers than in previous decades. Civil rights law simply could not mitigate the impact of the overall contraction of the railroad industry. Nor could it address the impact of the precipitous decline of other basic industries, such as steel and meatpacking, on aggregate levels of black employment. In late-twentieth-century America, the promise of the civil rights agenda was blunted by broader economic forces. This produced a paradoxical situation: while many African Americans have successfully broken through occupational barriers and entered the American middle class, many others have been left behind in decaying urban centers as capital has relocated to suburbs, rural America, the South, or overseas.

Yet black protest and civil rights employment law mattered. That African Americans James Reed, Herman Autry, Dave Leftridge, and Eddie Lee Jenkins could become locomotive engineers or conductors, join formerly all-white unions, and in several cases serve as brotherhood officers owed much to their individual persistence and willingness to bear substantial personal costs. But equally important in promoting their advancement was the new legal and political environment that made overt employment discrimination and union exclusion illegitimate and illegal. A generation earlier, World War II had undermined reigning racial orthodoxies and created a temporary political opening for proponents of black equality to assail employment discrimination through the FEPC. The civil rights movement of the 1960s too established a supportive ideological climate and provided concrete administrative and legal weapons for determined black workers to lay siege to the bastions of racism in industry and labor. By the early 1970s, their efforts yielded tangible results. While some white workers and managers resisted the changes, many others accepted the inevitable, and still others accorded black railroaders a modicum of respect. Beyond the outlawing of traditional racist practices, the civil rights era witnessed a profound alteration in white attitudes and behavior long held to be immutable.

Black railroad workers' occupational and associational breakthroughs were largely the result of legislative changes produced by the civil rights movement, whose indispensable groundwork had been laid by A. Philip Randolph, his Brotherhood of Sleeping Car Porters, and countless other people and organizations. But most members of the diverse, pioneering group of committed, pre-1960s black activists who fought employment and union discrimination—such leaders as Robert L. Mays, John Henry Eiland, Thomas Redd, Halena Wilson, Ishmael Flory, Solon Bell, Ernest Calloway, and Willard Townsend—have been forgotten by new black railroad workers and historians alike. Many Americans today might recall the name and deeds of A. Philip Randolph, but few recognize his role as the crucial link between an earlier generation of black pioneers anchored in unions and other formal institutions and a newer generation of grassroots black activists. Long threads barely visible today tie the achievements of late-twentieth-century black workers to the political initiatives of their predecessors in the first half of the century.

While the efforts of previous generations of railroad activists did not topple the system of employment or union discrimination, they did make its operation more difficult, publicize its injustices, and render it illegitimate among growing numbers of Americans. It took the civil rights movement of the 1960s to enact legislation that ultimately, if imperfectly, brought about the changes advocated by earlier railroad activists. It is difficult to overstate the magnitude of the changes they effected. The breakthroughs in railroad employment and in union membership were dramatic, the transformations in labor and race relations were pronounced, and the opportunities made available to a younger generation of black workers were unprecedented. For today's African-American railroad workers, those achievements constitute not the end of the line, but merely one stop on the much longer journey toward equality.

Notes

Prologue

1. Author's interview with Wynetta A. Frazier and Tony Berry, April 1, 1997, Chicago, Illinois.
2. *New Jersey Reformer News,* December 14, 1918, in *Tuskegee Institute News Clippings File* (Tuskegee, Ala.: Division of Behavioral Science Research, Carver Research Foundation, Tuskegee Institute, 1976), Reel 8.
3. Samuel C. Jackson, Comment on EEOC, Johnnie Nichols, et al. v. St. Louis–San Francisco Railway Co. and Brotherhood of Railroad Trainmen, case nos. 5-10-1521, 5-10-1778, 5-10-1779, 5-10-1780, 5-10-1781, July 15, 1966, in Pullman Company Archives, 04/01/02, Box 10, Newberry Library, Chicago.
4. *New York Times,* December 12, 1956.
5. On the developing scholarship on labor and race, see Joe William Trotter, Jr., "African-American Workers: New Directions in U.S. Labor Historiography," *Labor History* 35 (Fall 1994), 495–523; Eric Arnesen, "Up from Exclusion: Black and White Workers, Race, and the State of Labor History," *Reviews in American History* 26 (March 1998), 146–174.

1. Race in the First Century of American Railroading

1. Leon R. Harris, "The Railroads and the Colored Brother," *Railway Review* 76 (May 16, 1925), 889; Col. F. H. Johah, "A Tribute to the Old Time Roadmaster," *Railway Review* 73 (September 29, 1923), 464.
2. William Thomas White, "A History of Railroad Workers in the Pacific Northwest, 1883–1934" (Ph.D. diss., University of Washington, 1981), 165–167; Matthew E. Mason, "'The Hands Here Are Disposed to be Turbulent': Unrest among the Irish Trackmen of the Baltimore and Ohio Railroad, 1829–1851," *Labor History* 39 (August 1998), 253–272.
3. Mason, "'The Hands Here,'" 253–272; James D. Dilts, *The Great Road: The Building of the Baltimore and Ohio, the Nation's First Railroad, 1828–1853* (Stanford: Stanford University Press, 1993); David L. Lightner, *Labor on the Illinois Central Railroad, 1852–1900: The Evolution of an Industrial Environment* (1970; rpt. New York: Arno Press, 1977), 20–21, 29–39, 89, 102–118; 808, "Madison Records, April 10, 1903, "Lehigh Valley Maintenance Methods," *Railway Maintenance Engineer* 12 (June 1916), 165, "Welfare Work

among Maintenance Men," *Railway Maintenance Engineer* 15 (February 1919), 40–41; Thomas Bell, *Out of This Furnace* (1941; rpt. Pittsburgh: University of Pittsburgh Press, 1976), 20–21.

4. John P. Davis, *The Union Pacific Railway: A Study in Railway Politics, History, and Economics* (Chicago: S. C. Griggs and Co., 1894), 140; John Hoyt Williams, *A Great and Shining Road: The Epic Story of the Transcontinental Railroad* (New York: Times Books, 1988), 93–100; George Kraus, "Chinese Laborers and the Construction of the Central Pacific," *Utah Historical Quarterly* 37 (Winter 1969), 41–57.

5. W. Thomas White, "Race, Ethnicity, and Gender in the Railroad Work Force: The Case of the Far Northwest, 1883–1918," *Western Historical Quarterly* 16 (July 1985), 268, 273–277; Yuji Ichioka, *The Issei: The World of the First Generation Japanese Immigrants, 1885–1924* (New York: Free Press, 1988), 72–77; Yuzo Murayama, "Contractors, Collusion, and Competition: Japanese Immigrant Railroad Laborers in the Pacific Northwest, 1898–1911," *Explorations in Economic History* 21 (July 1984), 290–305; *Seattle Union Record*, April 27, June 8, 1900.

6. Jeffrey Marcos Garcilazo, "Traqueros: Mexican Railroad Workers in the United States, 1870 to 1930" (Ph.D. diss., University of California at Santa Barbara, 1995), 48–59; Victor S. Clark, "Mexican Labor in the United States," *Bulletin of the Bureau of Labor*, no. 78 (September 1908), 472, 477–482; James H. Ducker, *Men of the Steel Rails: Workers on the Atchison, Topeka, and Santa Fe Railroad, 1869–1900* (Lincoln: University of Nebraska Press, 1983), 27–28; Michael M. Smith, "Beyond the Borderlands: Mexican Labor in the Central Plains, 1900–1930," *Great Plains Quarterly* 1 (Fall 1981), 240, 243–244; Robert Oppenheimer, "Acculturation or Assimilation: Mexican Immigrants in Kansas, 1900 to World War II," *Western Historical Quarterly* 16 (October 1985), 432–444.

7. Robert S. Starobin, *Industrial Slavery in the Old South* (New York: Oxford University Press, 1970), 28; Howard D. Dozier, *A History of the Atlantic Coast Line Railroad* (1920; rpt. New York: Augustus M. Kelley Publishers, 1971), 158; Ulrich Bonnell Phillips, *A History of Transportation in the Eastern Cotton Belt to 1860* (New York: Columbia University Press, 1908), 149–150; Kenneth W. Noe, *Southwest Virginia's Railroad: Modernization and the Section Crisis* (Urbana: University of Illinois Press, 1994), 82–83.

8. Noe, *Southwest Virginia's Railroad*, 29; Dozier, *History of the Atlantic Coast Line*, 90; Phillips, *History of Transportation*, 149–150, 260, 273; Richard C. Wade, *Slavery in the Cities: The South, 1820–1860* (New York: Oxford University Press, 1964), 37; Starobin, *Industrial Slavery*, 28; Allen W. Trelease, *The North Carolina Railroad, 1849–1871, and the Modernization of North Carolina* (Chapel Hill: University of North Carolina Press, 1991), 162–163; Steven G. Collins, "Progress and Slavery on the South's Railroads," *Railroad History* no. 181 (Autumn 1999), 17–22.

9. James H. Brewer, *The Confederate Negro: Virginia's Craftsmen and Military Laborers, 1861–1865* (Durham: Duke University Press, 1969), 79–94; Clarence L. Mohr, *On the Threshold of Freedom: Masters and Slaves in Civil War Georgia*

(Athens: University of Georgia Press, 1986), 136–137, 140, 151, 163–165, 182; Robert C. Black III, *The Railroads of the Confederacy* (1952; rpt. Chapel Hill: University of North Carolina Press, 1998), 29; Ervin L. Jordan, Jr., *Black Confederates and Afro-Yankees in Civil War Virginia* (Charlottesville: University Press of Virginia, 1995), 65; Angus James Johnston II, *Virginia Railroads in the Civil War* (Chapel Hill: University of North Carolina Press, 1961), 128–129, 135–136, 225–226; Jeffrey N. Lash, *Destroyer of the Iron Horse: General Joseph E. Johnston and Confederate Rail Transport, 1861–1865* (Kent, Ohio: Kent State University Press, 1991), 24, 37, 64–65, 76–77, 85–86; Charles W. Turner, *Chessie's Road* (Richmond: Garrett & Massie, 1956), 45–56.

10. Herman Haupt, *Reminiscences of General Herman Haupt* (Milwaukee: Wright & Joys Co., 1901), 319; Francis A. Lord, *Lincoln's Railroad Man: Herman Haupt* (Rutherford, N.J.: Fairleigh Dickinson University Press, 1969), 91–92, 97–101; James A. Ward, *That Man Haupt: A Biography of Herman Haupt* (Baton Rouge: Louisiana State University Press, 1973), 121; George B. Abdill, *Civil War Railroads* (Seattle: Superior Publishing, 1961), 31, 41, 57, 82; Scott Reynolds Nelson, *Iron Confederacies: Southern Railways, Klan Violence, and Reconstruction* (Chapel Hill: University of North Carolina Press, 1999), 172–173.

11. Wayne Cline, *Alabama Railroads* (Tuscaloosa: University of Alabama Press, 1997), 74; Jonathan W. McLeod, *Workers and Workplace Dynamics in Reconstruction Era Atlanta. A Case Study* (Los Angeles: Center for Afro-American Studies, University of California, Los Angeles, 1989), 22, 26, 28–29, 33–34.

12. Cline, *Alabama Railroads*, 74; Trelease, *North Carolina Railroad*, 231–232; John F. Stover, *The Railroads of the South, 1865–1900: A Study in Finance and Control* (Chapel Hill: University of North Carolina Press, 1955), 57; Alex Lichtenstein, *Twice the Work of Free Labor: The Political Economy of Convict Labor in the New South* (London: Verso, 1996), 44.

13. William Cohen, *At Freedom's Edge: Black Mobility and the Southern White Quest for Racial Control, 1861–1915* (Baton Rouge: Louisiana State University Press, 1991), 85, 128–130, 139; Stover, *Railroads of the South*, 57; Robert Somers, *The Southern States since the War, 1870–71* (1871; rpt. University: University of Alabama Press, 1965), 159.

14. Lichtenstein, *Twice the Work*, 34–36; Edward Ayers, *Vengeance and Justice: Crime and Punishment in the Nineteenth-Century South* (New York: Oxford University Press, 1984), 191–193; A. Elizabeth Taylor, "The Convict Lease System in Georgia, 1866–1908" (master's thesis, University of North Carolina at Chapel Hill, 1940), 7–20.

15. Lichtenstein, *Twice the Work*, 41–49; Nelson, *Iron Confederacies*, 78–79, 169; *Proceedings of the Joint Committee Appointed to Investigate the Condition of the Georgia Penitentiary* (1870; rpt. New York: Arno Press, 1974), 75; Russell Duncan, *Entrepreneur for Equality: Governor Rufus Bullock, Commerce, and Race in Post–Civil War Georgia* (Athens: University of Georgia Press, 1994).

16. *Proceedings of the Joint Committee*, 27–28, 36–37, 43, 70–73, 90, 116–122; Lichtenstein, *Twice the Work*, 53; Taylor, "Convict Lease System," 11–12, 16–18.

17. Ayers, *Vengeance and Justice*, 191; Mark W. Summers, *Railroads, Reconstruction, and the Gospel of Prosperity: Aid under the Radical Republicans, 1865–1977* (Princeton: Princeton University Press, 1984), 32–46; *Missouri Republican*, December 23, 1885; *Mobile Register*, March 14, 1885; *Louisville Commercial*, June 17, 1886.

18. Board of Railroad Wages and Working Conditions (hereafter BRWWC), "In re: Maintenance of Way Employes," July 12, 1918, Transcripts of Hearings of BRWWC, June 3, 1918–August 1, 1920, Records of the BRWWC (hereafter BRWWC Transcripts), Box 2, 365, United States Railroad Administration (hereafter USRA), Record Group (hereafter RG) 14, National Archives.

19. "Difficulties of the Labor Problem in Southern Industries," *Manufacturers' Record* 48 (July 20, 1905), 10, 12. For one southern contractor's experiences with black labor during Reconstruction, see James A. Ward, ed., *Southern Railroad Man: Conductor N. J. Bell's Recollections of the Civil War Era* (DeKalb: Northern Illinois University Press, 1994), 57–60.

20. Brett Williams, *John Henry: A Bio-Bibliography* (Westport, Conn.: Greenwood Press, 1983), 12.

21. Harris quoted in Guy B. Johnson, *John Henry: Tracking Down a Negro Legend* (1929; rpt. New York: AMS Press, 1969), 17–19.

22. Vladimir Bogoraz, "The Black Student," in Olga Peters Hasty and Susanne Fusso, eds., *America through Russian Eyes, 1874–1926* (New Haven: Yale University Press, 1988), 115; Edward Hungerford, "Eating on the Train," *Harper's Weekly* 58 (March 21, 1914), 13; *Chicago Defender*, October 24, 31, 1914; Max O'Rell, *A Frenchman in America: Recollections of Men and Things* (New York: Cassell Publishing, 1891), 211.

23. Mrs. [Ethel] Alec-Tweedie, *America as I Saw It, or America Revisited* (New York: Macmillan Co., 1913), 364, 368.

24. John H. White, Jr., *The American Railroad Passenger Car* (Baltimore: Johns Hopkins University Press, 1978), 288; Sarah H. Gordon, *Passage to Union: How the Railroads Transformed American Life, 1829–1929* (Chicago: Ivan R. Dee, 1996), 78–91.

25. 1838 quote from James D. Porterfield, *Dining by Rail: The History and the Recipes of America's Golden Age of Railroad Cuisine* (New York: St. Martin's Press, 1993), 6, (see also 9, 116–117); Stewart H. Holbrook, *The Story of American Railroads* (New York: Crown Publishers, 1947), 214; J. Richard Beste, *The Wabash: Or Adventures of an English Gentleman's Family in the Interior of America*, vol. 1 (1855; rpt. Freeport, N.Y.: Books for Libraries Press, 1970), 109, 164; Whitelaw Reid, *After the War: A Tour of the Southern States, 1865–1866* (New York: Harper Torchbooks, 1965), 330.

26. Lesley Poling-Kempes, *The Harvey Girls: Women Who Opened the West* (New York: Paragon House, 1991), xiii, 28–47, 87; Holbrook, *Story of American Railroads*, 215–216; Jack Mullen, "America's Best-Fed Travelers," *Santa Fe Magazine* 37 (December 1943), 9–36; Merle Armitage, *Operations Santa Fé: Atchison, Topeka, and Santa Fe Railway System* (New York: Duell, Sloan & Pearce, 1948), 147–154.

27. Porterfield, *Dining by Rail*, 29–69; White, *American Railroad Passenger Car*,

311–342; Hungerford, "Eating," 12; *New York Times*, February 8, 1953; Richard Barnitz with Rufus Jarman, "They've Been Dining on the Railroad," *Saturday Evening Post* 226 (April 10, 1954), 32–33, 87–88.

28. William Fraser Rae, *Westward by Rail: The New Route to the East* (1871; rpt. New York: Arno Press, 1973), 51; White, *American Railroad Passenger Car*, 203–260; Peter T. Maiken, *Night Trains: The Pullman System in the Golden Years of American Rail Travel* (Chicago: Lakme Press, 1989), 8–11; Holbrook, *Story of American Railroads*, 317–328.

29. *Final Report and Testimony Submitted to Congress by the Commission on Industrial Relations*, vol. 10 (Washington, D.C.: Government Printing Office, 1916), 64th Congress, 1st session. Senate Document no. 415 (hereafter CIR, *Final Report* 10), 9623–9624.

30. Opie Read, "Caste of Negro Porters Defies Time and Change," *Chicago Journal*, May 30, 1918, in *Tuskegee Institute News Clippings File* (Tuskegee, Ala.: Division of Behavioral Science Research, Carver Research Foundation, Tuskegee Institute, 1976) (hereafter *TINCF*), Reel 8; Joseph Husband, *The Story of the Pullman Car* (Chicago: A. C. McClurg & Co., 1917), 155; Jack Santino, *Miles of Smiles, Years of Struggle: Stories of Black Pullman Porters* (Urbana: University of Illinois Press, 1989), 6–7; N. H. Hall, "The Art of the Pullman Porter," *American Mercury* 23 (July 1931), 335.

31. CIR, *Final Report* 10, 9553.

32. Julius B. Hinton, Oral History interview with Robert Hayden, November 20, 1989, in Oral History Interview Transcripts, Knights of the Rail: Boston African American Railroad Workers, 1977–1991, Collection Number 67 (hereafter Knights of the Rail Collection), Archives and Special Collections, Healey Library, University of Massachusetts at Boston; "Pullman Company—First in Travel Service," *Negro World Statesman* 2 (April 1947), 10; BRWWC, "In re: Sleeping and Parlor Car Porters," December 1, 1919. BRWWC Transcripts, Box 14, 50; Herbert O. Holderness, *The Reminiscences of a Pullman Conductor* (Chicago: n.p., 1901), 13; CIR, *Final Report* 10, 9551.

33. BRWWC, "In re: Sleeping and Parlor Car Porters," December 3, 1919. BRWWC Transcripts, Box 15, 218–219, 226.

34. Alec-Tweedie, *America as I Saw It*, 302; Collier, *America and the Americans: From a French Point of View* (London: William Heinemann, 1897), 179–181; Bernard Mergen, "The Pullman Porter: From 'George' to Brotherhood," *South Atlantic Quarterly* 73 (Spring 1974), 224–225.

35. *New York Age*, February 16, 1918; Hall, "Art of the Pullman Porter," 334.

36. Santino, *Miles of Smiles*, 74; Edward M. Swift and Charles S. Boyd, "The Pullman Porter Looks at Life," *Psychoanalytic Review* 15 (October 1928), 395; Railroad Wage Commission (hereafter, RWC), Sixth Hearing, February 8, 1918, Records of the BRWWC, Transcripts of Hearings of the Railroad Wage Commission (January–March 1918) (hereafter RWC 1918 Transcripts), Box 2, 811; BRWWC, "In re: Sleeping and Parlor Car Porters," December 3, 1919. BRWWC Transcripts, Box 15, 322; "Here are Pullman Porters in Review: The Pullman Traveler Knows Him Well," *Pullman News* 24 (April 1946), 9.

37. William August Crossland, "Industrial Conditions among Negroes in St.

Louis," *Studies in Social Economics* 1 (1914), 63; *Financial America,* August 24, 1917, in *TINCF,* Reel 6; BRWWC, "In re: Wages and Working Conditions of Conductors, Stewards, Waiters, Porters, and Other Dining and Sleeping Car Employees," November 14, 1918, BRWWC Transcripts, Box 5, 292–293; CIR, *Final Report* 10, 9654; *Chicago Broad Ax,* July 5, 1894. On red caps and tips, see Chapter 5.

38. P. A. Wagner, "Our Dining Car Department," *L&N Employes' Magazine* (September 1927), 20–21; "Introducing an L&N Ambassador," *L&N Employes' Magazine* (October 1931), 12–14; Lawrence W. Sagle, "Meals en Route," *Trains* (January 1941), 5, 11.

39. "Introducing an L&N Ambassador," 13; Roy Wilkins with Tom Mathews, *Standing Fast: The Autobiography of Roy Wilkins* (1982; rpt. New York: Penguin Books, 1984), 37; Fidel S. Barboza interview (n.d.), Knights of the Rail Collection, 2; Jimmy Clark interview, in David D. Perata, *Those Pullman Blues: An Oral History of the African American Railroad Attendant* (New York: Twayne Publishers, 1996), 107.

40. Cited in Porterfield, *Dining by Rail,* 114; Barboza interview, 5–6; Jimmy Clark interview, 107; BRWWC, "In re: Dining Car Conductors, etc.," September 20, 1919, BRWWC Transcripts, Box 13, 246; Hungerford, "Eating," 13.

41. Wilkins, *Standing Fast,* 41.

42. BRWWC, "In re: Dining Car Conductors," September 19, 1919, BRWWC Transcripts, Box 12, 220; BRWWC, "In re: Wages and Working Conditions of Conductors, Stewards, Waiters, Porters, and Other Dining and Sleeping Car Employees," November 14, 1918, BRWWC Transcripts, Box 5, 250–255, 270–271, 298–299; RWC, Sixth Hearing, 812; CIR, *Final Report* 10, 9626.

43. *Chicago Defender,* May 30, 1914.

44. BRWWC, "In re: Dining Car Conductors," September 19, 1919, BRWWC Transcripts, Box 12, 207–209, 213, 215–216; RWC, Tenth Hearing, February 14, 1918, RWC 1918 Transcripts, Box 3, 1463; "Economics," *Crisis* 3 (March 1912), 186; Holderness, *Reminiscences,* 136.

45. Theron Brown interview, n.d., and Dean Denniston interview, July 1988, Knights of the Rail Collection; BRWWC, "In re: Wages and Working Conditions of Conductors, Stewards, Waiters, Porters, and Other Dining and Sleeping Car Employees," January 6, 1919, BRWWC Transcripts, Box 7, 430, 451; BRWWC, "In Re: Dining Car Conductors, etc.," September 20, 1919, BRWWC Transcripts, Box 13, 253, 272; BRWWC, "In the Matter of Wages and Working Conditions of Sleeping Car, Parlor Car, and Dining Car Employees," November 22, 1918, BRWWC Transcripts, Box 6, 29; W. L. Reed, "All Right Cap," *Chicago Defender,* October 17, 1914. See also Wayne Cooper, *Claude McKay: Rebel Sojourner in the Harlem Renaissance* (1987; rpt. New York: Schocken Books, 1990), 78, 84–86, 98; Claude McKay, *Home to Harlem* (1928; rpt. Chatham, N.J.: Chatham Bookseller, 1973), 143, 145–147, 151, 160.

46. Charles Dickens, *American Notes for General Circulation* (1842; rpt. New York: Penguin Books, 1972), 111.

47. Barbara Y. Welke, "When All the Women Were White, and All the Blacks Were

Men: Gender, Class, Race, and the Road to Plessy, 1855–1914," *Law and History Review* 13 (Fall 1995), 261–316; Edward L. Ayers, *The Promise of the New South: Life after Reconstruction* (New York: Oxford University Press, 1992), 140–146; T. Thomas Fortune, "Rambles in the South," *New York Age*, May 10, 1890. On the hazards of Jim Crow travel, see Catherine A. Barnes, *Journey from Jim Crow: The Desegregation of Southern Transit* (New York: Columbia University Press, 1983).

48. *Norfolk Journal and Guide*, April 19, 1947; *Chicago Defender*, September 11, 1920, October 25, 1930, September 18, 1943; John LeFlore, "Dixie Railroads Jam Passengers in Prison Cars," *Chicago Defender*, April 7, 1945; George B. Morgan, "Waiters Give Own Race Raw Deal in Depot," *Chicago Defender*, August 4, 1923; Elmer Carter, "RR Porters Can Improve Travel," *Baltimore Afro-American*, November 6, 1943.

49. *Oklahoma City Black Dispatch*, January 20, 1920; *Washington Afro-American*, May 27, 1939; Elmer Carter, "Red Caps Resent Carter's Attack," *Baltimore Afro-American*, November 20, 1943.

50. *Washington Bee*, June 21, 1919; *Chicago Whip*, July 9, 1919; *Pittsburgh Courier*, August 11, 1923; *New York Age*, March 6, 1920; *Birmingham Reporter*, July 24, 1926; Claude McKay, *A Long Way from Home: An Autobiography* (1937; rpt. New York: Harcourt Brace & World, 1970), 8–9, 31; see also *Chicago Defender*, May 24, 1930.

51. Robert E. Turner, *Memories of a Retired Pullman Porter* (New York: Exposition Press, 1954), 110–111; McKay, *A Long Way from Home*, 31. On armed blacks in the South and North, see William M. Tuttle, *Race Riot: Chicago in the Red Summer of 1919* (New York: Atheneum, 1972), 210.

52. Altamont F. Bolt, Oral History interview, October 22, 1988, Knights of the Rail Collection, p. 10; Santino, *Miles of Smiles*, 71; Wilkins, *Standing Fast*, 41; Hall, "Art of the Pullman Porter," 335; Cooper, *Claude McKay*, 85.

53. William B. Thomas and Kevin J. Moran, "The Illusion of Aristocracy: Intra-Racial Divisions in a Racist Labor Market, 1910–1930," in Marcel van der Linden and Jan Lucassen, eds., *Racism and the Labour Market: Historical Studies* (Bern: Peter Lang, 1995), 237–262.

54. Bogoraz, "Black Student," 117–120, 125–126; "Pullman Service Means Education, Says Porter," *Pullman News* 3 (May 1924), 5; Benjamin E. Mays, *Born to Rebel: An Autobiography* (1971; rpt. Athens: University of Georgia Press, 1987), 39, 61–64; Harry Haywood, *Black Bolshevik: Autobiography of an Afro-American Communist* (Chicago: Liberator Press, 1978), 37–41, 88–90; Taylor Gordon, *Born to Be* (1929; rpt. Seattle: University of Washington Press, 1975), 82–92; CIR, *Final Report* 10, 9653; *Indianapolis Freeman*, January 11, 1890.

55. O. H. Kirkpatrick, *Working on the Railroad* (Philadelphia: Dorrance & Co., 1949), 115, 120–125. On the racial division of labor and the operating crafts, see also William A. Sundstrom, "Half a Career: Discrimination and Railroad Internal Labor Markets," *Industrial Relations* 29 (Fall 1990), 423–440.

56. James Samuel Stemons, "The Industrial Color-Line in the North," *Century Magazine* 60 (1900), 478; Unknown, "St. Augustine, Florida, *Railroad Trainmen's Journal* (hereafter *RTJ*) 18 (March 1901), 213–214; Starobin, *Industrial*

Slavery, 28; Walter Licht, *Working for the Railroad: The Organization of Work in the Nineteenth Century* (Princeton, Princeton University Press, 1983), 42, 65–69; Benn, "The Sunny South," *Locomotive Firemen's Magazine* (hereafter *LFM*) 11 (September 1887), 546–547; "Employment of Negroes on Railroads," *Monthly Labor Review* (November 1924), 16; Commission on Standard Workday of Railroad Employees, *Report of the Eight-Hour Commission* (Washington, D.C.: Government Printing Office, 1918), 413; Edward Aaron Gaston, Jr., "A History of the Negro Wage Earner in Georgia, 1890–1940" (Ph.D. diss., Emory University, 1957), 237–242.

57. C. J. Goff, "The Brotherhood in the South—The Negro Fireman Problem," *Locomotive Firemen and Enginemen's Magazine* (hereafter *LFEM*) 60 (June 1916), 681; *Report of the Eight-Hour Commission* (Washington, D.C.: Government Printing Office, 1918) 414; Jack, "The Negro Firemen," *LFM* 22 (January 1897), 58, 60; "Georgia Railroad Strike—The Negro as a Citizen," *LFEM* 47 (December 1909), 893; *Atlanta Journal,* June 25, 1909; "Grand Fork," *RTJ* 17 (June 1900), 506–507; W. E. B. Du Bois, ed., *The Negro Artisan: Report of a Social Study Made under the Direction of Atlanta University,* Atlanta University Publications no. 7 (Atlanta: Atlanta University Press, 1902), 115–116.

58. J. C. Clark to T. Morris Chester, April 29, 1886, President's In-Letters, J. C. Clarke, January 1–April 30, 1886, 1C5.2, Illinois Central Papers, Special Collections, Newberry Library; *Report of the Eight-Hour Commission,* 414; Lightner, *Labor on the Illinois Central,* 227–228; *Report of the Industrial Commission on Labor Organizations, Labor Disputes, and Arbitration, and on Railway Labor* 17, (Washington, D.C.: Government Printing Office, 1901), 217.

59. Paul Worthman, "Black Workers and Labor Unions in Birmingham, Alabama, 1897–1904," *Labor History* 10 (Summer 1969), 375–407; *Proceedings of the Twelfth Biennial Convention of the Brotherhood of Locomotive Firemen and Enginemen, Beginning June 6, 1910. St. Paul, Minnesota* (hereafter *BLFE 1910 Proceedings*) (St. Paul: McGill-Warner Co., 1910), 471; Ira De A. Reid, *Negro Membership in American Labor Unions* (New York: Alexander Press, 1930), 57.

60. Goff, "Brotherhood," 680; Timothy Shea, "Conditions of the Brotherhood in the South," *LFEM* 45 (September 1908), 408–409; "The Negro and the Labor Question," *LFM* 21 (July 1896), 4–6; *Report of the Eight-Hour Commission,* 272; *Report of Grand Lodge Officers, Brotherhood of Locomotive Firemen and Enginemen, Twelfth Biennial Convention, St. Paul, Minnesota, June 1910* (n.p., n.d.) (hereafter *BLFE Grand Lodge Officers 1910 Report*), 222, 478; *New York Evening World,* February 14, 1918, in *TINCF,* Reel 8.

61. R. C. Ransom, "Closing the Doors of Various Trades against Colored People," *Christian Recorder,* June 28, 1888. On the requirements for occupational advancement, see W. Fred Cottrell, *The Railroader* (Stanford: Stanford University Press, 1940), 18–19; Stephen Ray Henson, "Industrial Workers in the Mid-Nineteenth-Century South: Atlanta Railwaymen, 1840–1870" (Ph.D. diss., Emory University, 1982), 74, 120–123. For a closer analysis of the white brotherhoods' racial practices and ideologies, see Eric Arnesen, "'Like Banquo's Ghost, It Will Not Down': The Race Question and the American Railroad

Brotherhoods, 1880–1920," *American Historical Review* 99 (December 1994), 1601–1633.

62. Cottrell, *Railroader*, 18; Shelton Stromquist, *A Generation of Boomers: The Pattern of Railroad Labor Conflict in Nineteenth-Century America* (Urbana: University of Illinois Press, 1987), 105–106; Testimony of Sidney S. Alderman, March 2, 1944, *Hearings before the Special Committee to Investigate Executive Agencies,* House of Representatives, 78th Congress, 1st and 2nd sessions, Part 2, 2133–2134.

63. Charles B. George, *Forty Years on the Rail: Reminiscences of a Veteran Conductor* (Chicago: R. R. Donnelley & Sons, 1887), 175; *BLFE Grand Lodge Officers 1910 Report,* 181; *Seattle Union Record,* July 24, 1909; Chicago Commission on Race Relations, *The Negro in Chicago: A Study of Race Relations and a Race Riot* (Chicago: University of Chicago Press, 1922), 409.

64. RWC, Nineteenth Hearing, February 13, 1918, RWC 1918 Transcripts, Box 2, 1299–1300.

65. B. R. Lacy, Commissioner, *Seventh Annual Report of the Bureau of Labor Statistics of the State of North Carolina, for the Year 1893* (Raleigh: Josephus Daniels, State Printer, 1894) 103–105; Ducker, *Men of the Steel Rails,* 53–56, 113; Benn, "Sunny South," 546.

66. George, *Forty Years on the Rail,* 166; Justin D. Fulton, *Sam Hobart, the Locomotive Engineer. A Workingman's Solution of the Labor Problem* (New York: Funk and Wagnalls, 1883), 28; J. Harvey Reed, *Forty Years a Locomotive Engineer: Thrilling Tales of the Rail* (Prescott, Wash.: Chas. H. O'Neil, 1913), 14–15; R. A. Bennett, "The Negro Question," *LFEM* 48 (January 1910), 126–128; "Educational Training for Railroad Service," *RTJ* 18 (February 1901), 101–103.

67. M. E. Dowdy, Springfield, Mo., "The Negro Fireman," *LFM* 30 (March 1901), 441. Also in *LFM,* see Member of 76, Berkley, Va., "The Negro Problem," 33 (September 1902), 427; Dilar, "The Negro and Organized Labor in the South," 33 (September 1902), 436; C. E. Pane, "Negro vs. White Firemen," 27 (August 1899), 203–204.

68. *Constitution and General Laws of the Brotherhood of Locomotive Firemen* (adopted September 1888), 41, at the Department of Labor Library, Washington, D.C.; Reed C. Richardson, *The Locomotive Engineer, 1863–1963: A Century of Labor Relations and Work Rules* (Ann Arbor: Bureau of Industrial Relations, Graduate School of Business Administration, University of Michigan, 1963), 189; Lindsay, "Report on Railway Labor," 823, 839; Paul Michel Taillon, "Culture, Politics, and the Making of the Railroad Brotherhoods, 1863–1916" (Ph.D. diss., University of Wisconsin–Madison, 1997), 162–166.

69. *Parson's Weekly Blade,* June 30, 1894, July 21, 1894; *Topeka Weekly Call,* July 21, 1894; *Chicago Railway Times,* July 15, 1894.

70. *Parson's Weekly Blade,* July 21, 1894; *Kansas City American Citizen,* July 13, 20, 1894; *Cleveland Gazette,* June 30, July 14, 1894; *Lake County News,* June 28, 1894; *Indianapolis Freeman,* July 14, 1894; *New Orleans Daily Picayune,* July 10, 11, 1091, Holman Head, "The Development of the Labor Movement in Alabama Prior to 1900" (master's thesis, University of Alabama, 1955), 110

113; Eugene V. Debs, "The Negro Worker" (New York, 1923), 6–7, quoted in Philip S. Foner, *Organized Labor and the Black Worker, 1619–1981* (New York: International Publishers, 1981), 105.

71. "Historical Sketch of the Brotherhood of Locomotive Firemen and Enginemen," *LFEM* 54 (June 1913), 816; Kurt Wetzel, "Railroad Management's Response to Operating Employees' Accidents, 1890–1913," *Labor History* 21 (1980), 351–368; Edwin Clyde Robbins, *Railway Conductors: A Study in Organized Labor* (New York: Columbia University, Longmans, Green and Co., Agents, 1914), 123–155; Mary Ann Clawson, *Constructing Brotherhood: Class, Gender, and Fraternalism* (Princeton: Princeton University Press, 1989), 129–133.

72. Herbert R. Northrup, "The Negro in the Railway Unions," *Phylon* 5 (2nd Quarter 1944), 160; Taillon, "Culture, Politics," 166.

73. On the hazards of railroading, see John Williams-Searle, "Courting Risk: Disability, Masculinity, and Liability on Iowa's Railroads, 1868–1900," *Annals of Iowa* 58 (Winter 1999), 27–77. On labor conflict in the railroad industry, see Herbert G. Gutman, "Trouble on the Railroads in 1873–1874: Prelude to the 1877 Crisis?" *Labor History* 2 (Spring 1961), 215–235; O. D. Boyle, *History of Railroad Strikes* (Washington, D.C.: Brotherhood Publishing Co., 1935).

74. WLF, "Current Comment," *LFM* 27 (November 1899), 595; "Industrial and Commercial Barons," 5. In the *RTJ*, see "Wealth and Manhood," 16 (January 1899), 85–86; "The Slums," 15 (July 1898), 582; "Public Meeting of the Brotherhood of Railroad Trainmen, Fifth Annual Convention," 18 (June 1901), 495.

75. Canuck, "Immigration," *LFM* 33 (April 1897), 221; "Aliens in the Majority in Basic Industries," *Railroad Trainman* (hereafter *RT*) 37 (January 1920), 27; "A Million New Workers Each Year," *RT* 27 (June 1910), 513; "Immigration and What It Means," *RTJ* 19 (June 1902), 477.

76. "The Negro and the Labor Question," 4; "The Crime of Competition," *RTJ* 15 (November 1898), 917; "Starving Miners," *LFM* 13 (August 1889), 707; "Omens of Strife," *RTJ* 19 (July 1902), 553. In the *RTJ*, also see 16 (October 1898), 852; "Negro Domination," 16 (September 1899), 880; "Illinois Miners Win," 16 (December 1898), 1005–1006.

77. C. S. Daniel, "White Firemen Not Wanted," *LFEM* 58 (May 1915), 609; *BLFE 1910 Proceedings*, 464, 466, 472, 478; A. G. Walker, "McDonald, W. Va.," *RTJ* 20 (October 1903), 774–775.

78. Shea, "Conditions," 406; Lacy, *Seventh Annual Report of the Bureau of Labor Statistics of . . . North Carolina . . . 1893*, 103–104; *Report of the Eight-Hour Commission*, 339; Goff, "Brotherhood," 679–682; "Southern Region—Operating Conditions," *Railway Age* 66 (March 14, 1919), 594.

79. "The Georgia Railroad Strike," *LFEM* 47 (August 1909), 261.

80. Member Lodge 201, "Employment Conditions in the South," *LFEM* 57 (December 1914), 748. See also "The Negro Fireman Question," *LFEM* 59 (September 1915), 357–358; *BLFE Grand Lodge Officers 1910 Report*, 182; *Proceedings: Arbitration between the Eastern Railroads and the Brotherhood of Locomotive Firemen and Enginemen . . . 1913*, vol. 3 (New York: Hulse and

Allen, 1913), 2365; *Report of the Eight-Hour Commission,* 414–415; J. C. Hall, "Colored Firemen," *Locomotive Engineers' Monthly Journal* 33 (April 1899), 251–253; J. C. Hall, "The Negro Fireman and Promotion," *LFM* 27 (July 1899), 81–82; Robert L. Mays to W. S. Carter, July 8, 1919, and the affidavits of Thomas C. Jefferson and Walter Jones, in James Grossman, ed., *Black Workers in the Era of the Great Migration, 1916–1929* (Frederick, Md.: University Microfilms of America, 1985), Reel 9.

81. A White Fireman, St. Augustine, Florida, "Negro Fireman," *LFM* 27 (July 1899), 83; Goff, "Brotherhood," 680.

82. Ex-L&N Brakeman, "From the South," *RTJ* 16 (April 1899), 346; *Proceedings: Arbitration,* vol. 3, 2365–66. See also *New Orleans Daily Picayune,* April 6, 1913; Samuel T. Graves, "The Negro No Good," *RTJ* 17 (June 1900), 505–506.

83. "The Negro Firemen Problem," *LFM* 26 (May 1899), 539–542; "The Negro and the Labor Question," *LFM* 21 (July 1896), 4–6; "Negro Wages Must Go," *LFM* 26 (January 1899), 109–110; Frank W. Trainham, "Another Problem," *RTJ* 20 (February 1903), 136.

84. Southern Tallow Pot, "Organizing the Negro," *LFM* 33 (September 1902), 434; "Current Comment," *LFM* 25 (August 1898), 214–215; S. H. LaLonde, "The Negro Fireman," *LFM* 30 (March 1901), 440; IC Fireman, "Organized Labor and the Negro in the South," *LFM* 33 (September 1902), 428; Member Lodge 200, "The Negro in the South," *LFM* 33 (September 1902), 429. White brakemen engaged in a comparable discussion in the pages of the *RTJ.* See "Colored Labor in Organizations," *RTJ* 16 (November 1898), 912–914. On biracial unionism, see Eric Arnesen, "Following the Color Line of Labor: Black Workers and the Labor Movement before 1930," *Radical History Review* no. 55 (Winter 1993), 53–87.

85. Charles H. Houston, "Foul Employment Practice on the Rails," *Crisis* 56 (October 1949), 269–270; "The Labor Factor in Race Troubles," *Literary Digest* 27 (December 24, 1898), 740; "Union Meeting at Norfolk, Va.," *LFM* 26 (January 1899), 118–120.

86. M. W. Caldwell, "Civil Rights in Tennessee," *New York Age,* July 5, 1890.

87. *New York Age,* July 15, 1909; *Indianapolis Freeman,* July 31, 1909; *Houston Observer,* December 16, 1916, in *TINCF,* Reel 5.

88. *Birmingham Age-Herald,* August 14, 1891; *Mobile Register,* August 14, 1891. On the post–World War I violence, see Chapter 2; on violence during the Great Depression, see Chapter 3.

89. *Houston Post,* September 30, October 1, 3–5, 9, 10, 1890; *Galveston Daily News,* October 7, 8, 9, 1890; "The Trouble on the Houston and Texas Central R.R.," *LFM* 14 (December 1890), 1094–96; Herbert Hill, *Black Labor and the American Legal System: Race, Work, and the Law* (Madison: University of Wisconsin Press, 1985), 335–336.

90. *Proceedings of the Eleventh Biennial Convention of the Brotherhood of Locomotive Firemen and Enginemen Beginning September 14th, 1908, Columbus, Ohio* (Columbus: Berlin Printing Co., 1908), 619–620, 865; "Georgia Railroad and Atlanta Terminal," *Report: President: Brotherhood of Locomotive Firemen and En*

ginemen, Twelfth Biennial Convention, St. Paul, Minnesota, June 1910 (n.p., n.d.) 290–311; F. S. Foster, "Georgia Railroad Strike—Mistaken Ideas of the Press," *LFEM* 47 (November 1909), 740. For selected secondary treatments of the strike, see Hugh B. Hammett, "Labor and Race: The Georgia Railroad Strike of 1909," *Labor History* 16 (Fall 1975); John Michael Matthews, "The Georgia 'Race Strike' of 1909," *Journal of Southern History* 40 (November 1974), 613–630. For a sample of contemporary coverage, see *Nation* 89, May 27, June 3, July 1, 8, 1909; "New Kind of Race War in Georgia," *Literary Digest* 38 (June 5, 1909), 949–950; "The Negro's Right to Shovel Coal," *Literary Digest* 39 (July 10, 1909), 41–42; "The Georgia Railroad Strike," *Outlook* 92 (June 5, 1909), 310–312; "The Georgia Strike Arbitration," *Harper's Weekly* 53 (July 3, 1909). For a sample of the response of the black press to the strike, see *Atlanta Independent*, May 29, June 5, 12, 26, July 3, 1909; "Significance of Atlanta Strike," *Colored American Magazine* 16 (June 1909), 382–383.

91. "The Georgia Railroad Strike," *LFEM* 47 (August 1909), 261–262. On race relations and labor in Georgia, see Clifford M. Kuhn, Harlon E. Joye, and E. Bernard West, *Living Atlanta: An Oral History of the City, 1914–1948* (Atlanta: Atlanta Historical Society and the University of Georgia Press, 1990). On the importance of seniority on the railroads, see Dan H. Mater, *The Railroad Seniority System: History, Description, and Evaluation* (Chicago: University of Chicago Libraries, 1941).

92. "The Negro Fireman Situation," *LFEM* 47 (August 1909), 284–285; F. S. Foster, "Georgia Railroad Strike—Mistaken Ideas of the Press," *LFEM* 47 (November 1909), 740; *BLFE 1910 Proceedings*, 290–311.

93. "Report of International President Cincinnati, New Orleans and Texas Pacific Railway. 'Negro Question,' Resulting in Strike," *Quarterly Report of the International Officers, Brotherhood of Locomotive Firemen and Enginemen* no. 4 (April 1, 1911), 84–85; "Firemen's Strike on the Queen and Crescent," *Railway Age Gazette* 50 (March 24, 1911), 703–704; *Commercial Tribune*, March 17, 1911; *Louisville Courier-Journal*, March 18, 1911; "Strike on the Queen and Crescent," *LFEM* 50 (April 1911), 519–520; *Crisis* 1 (April 1911), 7–8; "STRIKE: Statement of the Firemen's Position in the Strike Now on the CNO&TP Ry.," File 42, Erdman Act Case Files, Records of the National Mediation Board, Record Group 13, Washington National Records Center, Suitland, Md. (hereafter Erdman Act Case Files); *Chattanooga Daily Times*, March 10, 24, 1911.

94. *Cincinnati Commercial Tribune*, March 7, 1911; "Strike on the Queen and Crescent," *LFEM* 50 (April 1911), 520; "Report of International President," 94; *Louisville Courier-Journal*, March 15, 1911; "Firemen's Strike on the Queen and Crescent," 703. For contemporary accounts of the strike, see "General News Section," *Railway Age Gazette* 50 (March 17, 1911); "Q&C Firemen's Strike Settled," *Railway Age Gazette* 50 (March 31, 1911), 803; "Settlement of Queen and Crescent Strike," *LFEM* 50 (May 1911), 655–657; *Louisville Courier-Journal*, March 10–16, 18–21, 23, 26, 27, 1911; *Louisville Times*, March 10, 11, 13–18, 21, 23–25, 1911; *Chattanooga Daily Times*, March 9–16, 18–21, 23, 26–27, 1911; *Cincinnati Commercial Tribune*, March 7–18, 21–26, 28, 1911; *Birmingham Age-Herald*, March 10, 26, 1911; *Cleve-*

land Press, March 13, 1911; Sterling D. Spero and Abram L. Harris, *The Black Worker: The Negro and the Labor Movement* (1931; rpt. New York: Atheneum, 1969), 291–292.

95. "Firemen's Strike," *Crisis* 2 (May 1911), 16; "Settlement," and "Memorandum of Agreement, March 25th, 1911," in File 42, Erdman Act Case Files.

96. *Jackson Daily Sun,* quoted in "Settlement of Queen and Crescent Strike," 657, and in "Report of International President," 101; "Firemen's Strike," 16.

97. "Would Have Laws Passed by Our Legislative Bodies Barring the Negro from Train Service," *LFEM* 47 (November 1909), 750; Gaston, Jr., "History of the Negro Wage Earner," 240; *Atlanta Constitution,* July 17, 1914, in *TINCF,* Reel 3.

98. "Jockeying Negroes Out of Jobs," *Crisis* 2 (October 1911), 224; *Savannah Morning News,* June 30, 1909; "Full Crew Law," *Texas Railway Journal* 13 (June 1909), 2; *Baltimore Trades-Unionist,* April 10, 1915; *Crisis* 3 (November 1911), 9; *Norfolk Journal and Guide,* April 13, 1929; Spero and Harris, *Black Worker,* 306–307.

99. The Grand Rapids and Indiana railroad responded by converting their black train porters into "full-fledged brakemen, with a brakeman's badge and uniform." *Indianapolis Freeman,* June 5, July 31, 1909. Full crew laws often involved workers' legitimate safety concerns, not race. See "Railroad Legislation on Full Crew, Personnel, and Train Lengths," *Monthly Labor Review* 50 (June 1940), 1429–34.

100. *New York Age,* March 13, 1913; *McDowell Times,* March 12, 1915; "The New York 'Full-Crew' Law Has Gone into Effect," *Square Deal* 13 (October 1913), 203; *Chicago Defender,* January 31, April 18, 1914; June 25, 1921.

101. *BLFE 1910 Proceedings,* 222; *Quarterly Report of the International Officers, Brotherhood of Locomotive Firemen and Enginemen* no. 6 (October 1, 1911), 160–177; "Discrimination against White Trainmen," *RT* 36 (November 1919), 804; "Circular of Instructions," *RT* 37 (May 1920), 304; *Report of the Eight-Hour Commission,* 413; Reid, *Negro Membership in American Labor Unions,* 57.

102. Stemons, "Industrial Color-Line in the North," 477–478.

2. Promise and Failure in the World War I Era

1. John H. Dailey to J. J. Forrester, August 26, 1919; Freight Handlers Union no. 16700 Committee to Forrester, September 14, 1919, in Records of the Division of Labor, Case Files of G. W. W. Hanger, Assistant Director, Division of Labor, 1918–1920, Entry 86 (hereafter Hanger Case Files), File no. 878, Records of the United States Railroad Administration (hereafter USRA), Record Group 14, National Archives, Washington, D.C.

2. John H. Dailey to G. W. W. Hanger, October 2, 1919; Hanger to J. J. Forrester, October 8, 1919; Forrester to J. A. Franklin, October 31, 1919, and November 25, 1919; Oliver Johnson to Hanger, January 26, 1920; Forrester to Hanger, February 11, 1920; Hanger to Johnson, February 17, 1920, in Hanger Case Files, File no. 878.

3. George Segor to Walker D. Hines, May 24, 1919, in Records of the Division of

Labor, Subject Classified General File for the Division of Labor, 1918–1922, Colored Employes, File E-38-11 (hereafter E-38-11), Box 64, USRA, RG 14.

4. E. R. Lewis, "Holding Labor on Railroad Work: Alleviating the Labor Shortage," *Railway Maintenance Engineer* 12 (June 1916), 169; "Scarcity of Track Labor," *Railway Engineering and Maintenance of Way*, n.s., 12 (February 1916), 1; W. E. B. Du Bois, "The Migration of Negroes," *Crisis* 14 (June 1917), 65; "A Year of Prosperity for Railway Labor," *Railway Age* 66 (January 3, 1919), 37; Board of Railroad Wages and Working Conditions (hereafter BRWWC), "In re: Maintenance of Way Employes," July 12, 1918, Transcripts of Hearings of BRWWC, June 3, 1918–August 1, 1920, Records of the BRWWC (hereafter BRWWC Transcripts), Box 2, 323–326, USRA, RG 14.

5. James R. Grossman, "Black Labor Is the Best Labor: Southern White Reactions to the Great Migration," in Alferdteen Harrison, ed., *Black Exodus: The Great Migration from the American South* (Jackson: University Press of Mississippi, 1991), 57–60; Emmett J. Scott, *Negro Migration during the War* (New York: Oxford University Press, 1920), 72–85; *McDowell Times*, August 11, 18, 25, September 29, 1916, June 27, 1917; "The Horizon: Industry," *Crisis* 13 (December 1916), 89; *Savannah Morning News*, November 26, 1916; April 5, 1918; *Norfolk Journal and Guide*, January 27, 1917; *Chicago Defender*, March 24, 1917; *Black Dispatch*, May 31, 1923 *New Orleans Times-Picayune*, August 25, 1916; *Crisis* 12 (October 1916), 297.

6. *McDowell Times*, August 25, 1916; December 8, 1916; *New York Age*, July 27, 1916; August 24, 1916; *Afro American*, July 16, 1919, in *Tuskegee Institute News Clippings File* (Tuskegee, Ala.: Division of Behavioral Science Research, Carver Research Foundation, Tuskegee Institute, 1976) (hereafter *TINCF*), Reel 11; *Southwestern Christian Advocate*, September 7, 1916; *Norfolk Journal and Guide*, February 24, 1917; Cindy Hahamovitch, *The Fruits of Their Labor: Atlantic Coast Farmworkers and the Making of Migrant Poverty, 1870–1945* (Chapel Hill: University of North Carolina Press, 1997), 86.

7. *New York Age*, July 20, 27, 1916, April 5, 1917; *Atlanta Independent*, June 30, 1917; "Migration and Help," *Crisis* 13 (January 1917), 115. See also *Houston Observer*, July 21, 1917, and *Indianapolis Freeman*, October 13, 1917, in *TINCF*, Reel 6.

8. *Chicago Defender*, March 7, 1917; *New York Age*, March 15, 1917; Omaha, Neb., n.t., March 4, 1917, in *TINCF*, Reel 6; W. Thomas White, "Railroad Labor Relations in the Great War and After, 1917–1921," *Journal of the West* 25 (April 1986), 37.

9. "Women Successful in Railway Work," *Literary Digest* 59 (December 21, 1918), 65; Consumers' League of Eastern Pennsylvania, *Colored Women as Industrial Workers in Philadelphia* (n.p., 1919–1920?), 22; "The Horizon: Industry," *Crisis* 15 (December 1917), 87. See also "A Year of Prosperity for Railway Labor," *Railway Age* 66 (January 3, 1919), 37–42. On women's work in railroad yards and laundries, see the USRA's reports on working conditions, toilet facilities, and the racial characteristics of the labor force in James Grossman, ed., *Black Workers in the Era of the Great Migration, 1916–1929* (Frederick, Md.: University Microfilms of America, 1985), Reel 11.

10. Maurine Weiner Greenwald, *Women, War, and Work: The Impact of World War I on Women Workers in the United States* (Westport, Conn.: Greenwood Press, 1980), 114–115.

11. "Women Make Good as Railroad Employes," *Life and Labor* 10 (March 1920), 93; Mary E. Jackson, "The Colored Woman in Industry," *Crisis* (November 1918), 16; "The Horizon: Industry," *Crisis* 15 (December 1917), 87. See also *Baltimore American,* August 9, 1918, *Chicago News,* July 13, 1918, and *St. Louis Post Dispatch,* May 11, 1918, in *TINCF,* Reel 8; *Southwestern Christian Advocate,* October 31, 1918; Kimberley L. Phillips, *AlabamaNorth: African-American Migrants, Community, and Working-Class Activism in Cleveland, 1915–45* (Urbana: University of Illinois Press, 1999), 72–75.

12. "Women Successful in Railway Work," 65; *Daily Herald,* March 16, 1918, in *TINCF,* Reel 8. On black and white women's turnover, see Women's Bureau, U.S. Department of Labor, "Hours and Conditions of Work for Women in Industry in Virginia," *Bulletin of the Women's Bureau,* no. 10, March 1920 (Washington, D.C.: Government Printing Office, 1920), 29.

13. *National Baptist Union Review,* March 30, 1918, in *TINCF,* Reel 8.

14. BRWWC, "In re: Maintenance of Way Employees," July 13, 1918, in BRWWC Transcripts, Box 2, 402–405; BRWWC, "In re: Labor Conditions in Alexandria and Potomac Yards," June 11, 1918, BRWWC Transcripts, Box 1, 4.

15. Frank Haigh Dixon and Julius H. Parmelee, "Wartime Administration of the Railway in the United States and Great Britain," *Carnegie Endowment for International Peace Preliminary Economic Studies of the War* no. 3 (New York: Oxford University Press, 1919), 61–63; William J. Cunningham, "The Railroads under Government Operation: Part I, To the Close of 1918," *Quarterly Journal of Economics* 35 (February 1921), 297; Colin Davis, *Power at Odds: The 1922 National Railroad Shopmen's Strike* (Urbana: University of Illinois Press, 1997), 34–36; *Atlanta Independent,* December 29, 1917; Maury Klein, *Union Pacific: The Rebirth, 1894–1969* (New York: Doubleday, 1989), 225–226.

16. Keith W. Olson, *Biography of a Progressive: Franklin K. Lane, 1864–1921* (Westport, Conn.: Greenwood Press, 1979), 146; *Southwestern Christian Advocate,* January 3, 1918.

17. Walker D. Hines, *Director General of Railroads, Report to the President for Fourteen Months Ended March 1, 1920* (Washington, D.C.: Government Printing Office, 1921), 17; Frank Julian Warne, *The Workers at War* (New York: Century Co., 1920), 90–91; W. S. Carter, "What Federal Control Has Done for Labor," *Railway Maintenance Engineer* 15 (January 1919), 11; Davis, *Power at Odds,* 36–37; Olson, *Biography of a Progressive,* 146–147.

18. Jeffrey Haydu, *Making American Industry Safe for Democracy: Comparative Perspectives on the State and Employee Representation in the Era of World War I* (Urbana: University of Illinois Press, 1997), 96–97.

19. Cunningham, "Railroads," 331; William J. Cunningham, *American Railroads: Government Control and Reconstruction Policies* (Chicago: A. W. Shaw Co., 1922), 102–114; n.t., *Crisis* 16 (July 1918), 137; Carter, "What Federal Control Has Done," 11.

20. *Christian Advocate,* May 30, 1918, in *TINCF,* Reel 8; *New York Age,* June 1, 8,

1918; John F. Marshall to W. G. McAdoo, September 23, 1918; S. A. Padgett to McAdoo, May 30, 1918, E-38-11.

21. "Strike of Negro Brakemen, Georgia R.R. (File 6257)," *Reports of Grand Lodge Officers Year 1916* (n.p.: Brotherhood of Railroad Trainmen, 1917).

22. "The Horizon: Industry," *Crisis* 13 (December 1916), 89; "The Horizon: Industry," *Crisis* 15 (December 1917), 87; "The Horizon: Industry," *Crisis* 18 (September 1919), 252; *Houston Labor Journal*, October 27, 1917; *Houston Press*, August 14, 1917, in *TINCF*, Reel 6; *Houston Observer*, May 18, 1918, in *TINCF*, Reel 8; *Augusta Herald*, May 12, 1918, in *TINCF*, Reel 8; *Augusta Labor Review*, January 26, 1918.

23. *Birmingham Ledger*, October 3, 1918, *Birmingham Age Herald*, November 9, 1918, both in *TINCF*, Reel 8; John R. Shillady to R. M. Dunn, June 6, 1919, in John H. Bracey, Jr., and August Meier, eds., *Papers of the NAACP, Part 10: Peonage, Labor, and the New Deal, 1913–1939* (Frederick, Md.: University Publications of America, 1990) (hereafter *NAACP Papers*, Part 10), Reel 9. See also *Vicksburg Herald*, November 18, 1917, in *TINCF*, Reel 6; *Houston Observer*, May 18, 1918, in *TINCF*, Reel 8.

24. *Norfolk Journal and Guide*, September 22, 29, October 13, 1917; *Virginia Pilot and Norfolk Landmark*, September 12, 1917; in *TINCF*, Reel 6: *New York Age*, September 27, 1918; *Raleigh Independent*, September 15, 1917. C. J. Jones and W. H. Pack, Resolution, June 17, 1918 (received), and Assistant to the Director to C. J. Jones and W. H. Pack, June 22, 1918, in E-38-11; BRWWC, Railroad Wage Commission Fifteenth Hearing, February 25, 1918, BRWWC Transcripts, 2133–42.

25. Scott, *Negro Migration*, 55; "A Year of Prosperity for Railway Labor," *Railway Age* 66 (January 3, 1919), 37; "A Review of the Labor Conditions of 1918," *Railway Maintenance Engineer* 15 (February 1919), 63.

26. H. S. Jeffery to W. S. Carter, June 6, 1918, in E-38-11.

27. Hugh Porter to Walker D. Hines, August 30, 1919; M. L. Kennedy to Walker D. Hines, October 24, 1919; George W. Slater, Jr., to G. Haynes, February 1919; Louis J. Pierce to McAdoo, June 21, 1918, in E-38-11.

28. H. G. Williams to W. S. Carter, March 3, 1919; Arthur B. Hill to McAdoo, November 28, 1918; Butler W. Nance to Director General, February 4, 1919, in E-38-11.

29. Will Smith to McAdoo, October 24, 1918; Paul Barnsley, January 27, 1919; A. M. Harvey to McAdoo, June 21, 1918; Ralph A. Crawford to W. S. Carter, January 16, 1919; Jim Crockett to McAdoo, July 29, 1918 (received); W. M. Spaulding to W. S. Carter, July 1, 1918; J. C. Murphy to McAdoo, July 29, 1918; W. M. Henderson to Samuel B. Gompers, July 15, 1918; L. H. Brown to W. A. Ryan, June 26, 1918; Ralph A. Crawford to W. S. Carter, January 16, 1919, in E-38-11.

30. Chalmer Lowary et al. to McAdoo, August 19, 1918, in E-38-11.

31. H. J. Jackson, William Wyles, Jesse Gurley, Will Randall Merriwether to McAdoo, June 5, 1918, E-38-11. On workers' adoption of the language of patriotism and Americanism during the war, see Joseph A. McCartin, *Labor's Great War: The Struggle for Industrial Democracy and the Origins of Modern American Labor Relations, 1912–1921* (Chapel Hill: University of North Carolina Press, 1997).

32. J. W. Taylor to McAdoo, May 29, 1918; Wm. Spaulding to W. S. Carter, July 22, 1918, July 1, 1918; J. C. Murphy to McAdoo, July 29, 1918; Porters, Union Terminal Company, Dallas, to W. D. Hines, March 1919; M. L. Kennedy to Walker D. Hines, October 24, 30, 1919; W. E. Henderson et al. to McAdoo, October 16, 1918, in E-38-11.

33. *Louisville News,* March 9, 1918 (reprinted from the *New World*); *Augusta Labor Review,* July 6, 1918. On black labor activism during the war, see Eric Arnesen, *Waterfront Workers of New Orleans: Race, Class, and Politics, 1863–1923* (New York: Oxford University Press, 1991), 217–252; Earl Lewis, *In Their Own Interests: Race, Class, and Power in Twentieth-Century Norfolk, Virginia* (Berkeley: University of California Press, 1991), 48–61.

34. *Chicago Whip,* July 17, 1920; *New York Age,* February 7, 1920; Steven A. Reich, "Soldiers of Democracy: Black Texans and the Fight for Citizenship, 1917–1921," *Journal of American History* 82 (March 1996), 1482, 1490, 1504.

35. "Case of the Colored Freight Handlers," *American Federationist* 28 (August 1921), 638–639; *St. Louis Argus,* October 31, 1919; *Washington Tribune,* November 7, 1925; Monroe N. Work, ed., *Negro Year Book: An Encyclopedia of the Negro 1921–22* (Tuskegee: Negro Year Book Publishing Co., 1922), 35–36; John D. Finney, "A Study of Negro Labor during and after World War I" (Ph.D. diss., Georgetown University, 1967), 341–342; Ira De A. Reid, *Negro Membership in American Labor Unions* (New York: Alexander Press, 1930), 118.

36. *New York Age,* September 14, 1918; *Tampa Morning Tribune,* February 26, 1918; *New York News,* December 4, 1919; F. Boyd, "Previous Struggles of the Pullman Porters to Organize," *Messenger* 8 (September 1926), 283.

37. *Call,* June 24, 1918; *New York Age,* June 20, 29, 1918; *St. Louis Argus,* June 28, 1918; *Chicago Whip,* July 25, 1919.

38. Thomas L. Dabney, "The Union in the Dining Car," *Locomotive Engineers Journal* 61 (July 1927), 517, 571; *New York Age,* June 5, 1920; Samuel Enders Warren, "The Negro in the American Labor Movement" (Ph.D. diss., University of Wisconsin–Madison, 1941), 376–381; Rienzi B. Lemus, "A Successful Negro Labor Union," *Opportunity* 1 (May 1923), 21; Finney, "Study of Negro Labor," 348–349.

39. *Norfolk Journal and Guide,* June 24, 1919; "The Horizon: Industry," *Crisis* 18 (August 1919), 205.

40. *Chicago Defender,* January 31, 1914; *Savannah Tribune,* November 20, 1920, January 29, 1921; *New York Age,* January 4, 1919; *Kansas City Sun,* in *TINCF,* Reel 11; *Atlanta Independent,* July 5, 1919; John Pittman, "Railroads and Negro Labor" (master's thesis, University of California at Berkeley, 1930), 20c–d, in William H. Harris, ed., *Records of the Brotherhood of Sleeping Car Porters, Series A: Holdings of the Chicago Historical Society and the Newberry Library, 1925–1969,* Part 1: *Records of the BSCP, 1925–1969* (Bethesda, Md.: University Publications of America, 1990), Reel 9; Warren, "The Negro in the American Labor Movement," 368–371; Sterling D. Spero and Abram L. Harris, *The Black Worker: The Negro and the Labor Movement* (1931; rpt. New York: Atheneum, 1969), 314.

41. Spero and Harris, *Black Worker,* 311–312; Enders, "Negro in the American La-

bor Movement," 373; *Chicago Defender,* January 30, September 18, 1915, October 2, 1920; Reid, *Negro Membership,* 124; Chicago Commission on Race Relations, *The Negro in Chicago: A Study of Race Relations and a Race Riot* (Chicago: University of Chicago Press, 1922), 409–411. In a wildly exaggerated claim in 1919, the association announced its membership at 60,000. *St. Louis Argus,* July 18, 1919.

42. *Report of Proceedings of the Thirty-Eighth Annual Convention of the American Federation of Labor Held at St. Paul, Minn., June 10 to 20, Inclusive, 1918* (Washington, D.C.: Law Reporter Printing Co., 1918), 161, 263–264; Frank Morrison to John Fitzpatrick, January 2, 1919, in John Fitzpatrick Papers, Box 25, Chicago Historical Society (hereafter Fitzpatrick Papers); *Chicago Whip,* July 17, 1920; *New York Age,* June 5, 1920; *Tacoma News,* May 25, 1918, in *TINCF,* Reel 8; Warren, "The Negro in the American Labor Movement," 376–381.

43. *Birmingham Times Plain Dealer,* July 10, 1920, in *TINCF,* Reel 11.

44. Chicago Commission on Race Relations, *The Negro in Chicago,* 410; *Chicago Whip,* July 17, 1920; *Chicago Defender,* March 20, 1920; *Times Plain Dealer,* June 12, August 14, 1920, in *TINCF,* Reel 11; *St. Louis Argus,* October 29, 1920; *Brotherhood* (November–December 1920), in *TINCF,* Reel 11; "Report on Convention Held in Chicago . . . September 20, 1920 . . .," Fitzpatrick Papers.

45. *Times Plain Dealer,* October 2, 1920, in *TINCF,* Reel 11; *Chicago Defender,* January 29, 1921.

46. *Times Plain Dealer,* April 3, 1920, January 1, 1921, in *TINCF,* Reel 11; *Chicago Defender,* February 28, March 6, July 24, 1920; *Savannah Tribune,* February 19, 1921; *Birmingham Reporter,* July 15, 1922.

47. *Times Plain Dealer,* January 10, August 14, November 13, 1920, in *TINCF,* Reel 11; *Chicago Defender,* October 22, 1921; *Black Dispatch,* October 27, 1921; *Birmingham Reporter,* July 15, 1922; Saunders Redding, *The Lonesome Road: The Story of the Negro's Part in America* (Garden City, N.Y.: Doubleday and Co., 1958), 253. On blacks and the 1922 strike, see Davis, *Power at Odds,* 22–23, 29, 29–71, 118–119; "Railroad Strike," *Messenger* 3 (November 1921), 273; *Birmingham Reporter,* May 13, July 22, 29, 1922; *New York Age,* July 29, 1922; *Chicago Defender,* August 19, 1922.

48. Robert L. Mays, RMIBIA, Special Bulletin, All Locals, August 21, 1920, in Fitzpatrick Papers; *Times Plain Dealer,* November 7, 1920, in *TINCF,* Reel 11; *Savannah Tribune,* January 22, 1921; *Chicago Defender,* January 8, 29, 1921; February 4, 1922; *Buffalo American,* January 21, 1922.

49. *Chicago Defender,* March 6, 1920, April 15, 1922; *Brotherhood,* November–December 1920, in *TINCF,* Reel 11; *Chicago Whip,* October 30, 1920; *St. Louis Argus,* October 29, 1920; "Report on Convention Held in Chicago . . . September 20, 1920," Fitzpatrick Papers. At least some porters, the 3,000 members of the Pullman car porters' organization, Local Union no. 268, did join the AFL in Chicago. *Chicago Defender,* October 29, 1921. Brailsford Brazeal has argued that the Protective Union "was not a labor union; in some respects, it was more of a fraternal organization." Brailsford R. Brazeal, *The Brotherhood*

of Sleeping Car Porters: Its Origin and Development (New York: Harper and Brothers, 1946), 10–11.

50. *Chicago Defender,* June 5, 1920, January 15, 1921; *Savannah Tribune,* September 22, 1921; *Times Plain Dealer,* June 12, August 28, November 6, 13, 21, December 11, 1920, in *TINCF,* Reel 11; *Birmingham Reporter,* January 10, 1920.

51. *Chicago Whip,* October 2, 1920; *St. Louis Argus,* July 11, 1919; *Chicago Defender,* January 23, February 6, March 27, 1926.

52. *Pittsburgh Courier,* April 12, 1924.

53. "R. L. Mays: A Failure," *Messenger* 8 (March 1926), 78–79; "Mays and the Brotherhood," *Messenger* 8 (February 1926), 46, 52; *Chicago Defender,* January 23, February 6, March 27, June 19, 1926; "Open Forum," *Messenger* 8 (March 1926), 93–95; Frank Crosswaith, "The Pullman Company's Gold 'Lust' Twins," *Messenger* 10 (January 1928), 20–22; *Amsterdam News,* January 27, 1926.

54. *Chicago Defender,* September 6, 13, 20, 27, 1930; Robert L. Mays to Claude A. Barnett, October 27, 1928, in *Claude A. Barnett Papers, Subject Files on Black Americans, 1918–1967: Series C, Economic Conditions, 1918–1966, Part 3* (Frederick, Md.: University Publications of America, 1986), Reel 9.

55. *Chicago Defender,* March 27, 1926. Information on Mays's activities in the 1930s is based on author's interview with Truman Gibson, December 15, 1994. For more details on Mays's activities in the 1930s, see Chapter 4.

56. C. M. Kittle to B. L. Winchell, January 18, 1919; William Blackman and John A. Moffitt to W. S. Carter, January 22, 1919, in Hanger Case Files, no. 435.

57. *Memphis Commercial Appeal,* January 14, 15, 1919. In Hanger Case Files, no. 435, see William Blackman to G. W. W. Hanger, January 18, 1919; John A. Moffitt and William Blackman to W. S. Carter, January 22, 1919. For narrative accounts of the Memphis strike, see Spero and Harris, *Black Worker,* 295–299; Rambling Rattler, "Memphis, Tenn.—219," *Journal of the Switchmen's Union of North America* (hereafter *JSUNA*) 21 (April 1919), 213–214; *Memphis Commercial Appeal,* January 12–18, 1919; *Memphis News Scimitar,* January 13–17, 1919.

58. W. S. Carter to W. S. Lee, January 14, 1919; W. S. Carter to Director General et al., January 14, 1919, in Hanger Case Files, no. 435; "Illegal Strike, Memphis (Tenn.) Terminals," *Railroad Trainman* (hereafter *RT*) 36 (March 1919), 200.

59. *Memphis News-Scimitar,* January 14, 1919; *Memphis Commercial Appeal,* January 14, 1919.

60. "Labor's Peril: Greater Dangers Have Never in the Nation's History Confronted the Workers of the United States," *Brotherhood of Locomotive Firemen and Enginemen's Magazine* (hereafter *BLFEM*) 62 (June 1, 1917), 3.

61. In *BLFEM,* see W. S. Carter, "The Negro Question," 62 (June 15, 1917), 9; "Railroads Eager to Employ Negroes in Train Service," 63 (August 15, 1917), 11; W. S. Carter, "The War, the Railroads, and Our Brotherhood," 64 (January 15, 1918), 12–14; "Scheme to Install Cheap Labor in Firemen's Jobs," 64 (January 15, 1918), 21.

62. C. M. Kittle to B. L. Winchell, January 18, 1919, and Illinois Central Railroad Company, "Misunderstanding between Officers of the Brotherhood of Railroad Trainmen, and the Officers of the Yazoo and Mississippi Valley Railroad, on Seniority Rules" (hereafter IC, "Misunderstanding"), in Hanger Case Files, no. 435; D. R. Goldsby, "Memphis, Tenn." *Railroad Trainmen's Journal* (hereafter *RTJ*) 17 (May 1900), 412–413; S. J. Whitaker, "Memphis, Tenn.," *RTJ* 16 (November 1899), 1040. On labor and race in Memphis, see Michael Honey, *Southern Labor and Black Civil Rights: Organizing Memphis Workers* (Urbana: University of Illinois Press, 1993), 16; Kate Born, "Organized Labor in Memphis, Tennessee, 1826–1901," *Western Tennessee Historical Society Papers* 21 (1967), 77–78.

63. "From Assistant President J. B. Connors," *JSUNA* 21 (March 1919), 138–139; "Memphis, Tenn.—219," *JSUNA* 21 (April 1919), 213–215; "Memphis, Tenn.—219," *JSUNA* 21 (May 1919), 290; "Memphis Terminals (File 7260), Brotherhood of Railway Trainmen, *Reports of Grand Lodge Officers, Year 1919*, (n.p., n.d.), 91–93; *Memphis Commercial Appeal*, January 13, 1919; *Memphis News-Scimitar*, January 13, 14, 18, 1919; *Chattanooga Daily Times*, January 15, 1919.

64. Church quoted in William M. Tuttle, Jr., *Race Riot: Chicago in the Red Summer of 1919* (New York: Atheneum, 1970), 210.

65. B. L. Winchell to W. T. Tyler, January 30, 1919; C. M. Kittle to B. L. Winchell, January 18, 1919; W. S. Carter, Memorandum, March 22, 1919; IC, "Misunderstanding," in Hanger Case Files, no. 435.

66. "From Assistant President J. B. Connors," *JSUNA* 21 (March 1919), 138–139; BRT, *Reports of Grand Lodge Officers, Year 1919*, 93. In Hanger Case Files, no. 435: B. L. Winchell to W. T. Tyler, January 30, 1919; William Blackman and John A. Moffitt to W. S. Carter, January 22, 1919; A. E. Clift to William Blackman, February 6, 1919; W. S. Carter, Memorandum, March 22, 1919. "In Re: Switchmen's Strike . . . Statement of Facts from the Grievance Committee of the Colored Association of Railway Employees . . .," Papers of the NAACP, Library of Congress, Washington, D.C. (hereafter, NAACP-LC Papers), Box C272.

67. Hugh Reid, "The Labor Outlook for the Coming Year," *Railway Maintenance Engineer* 15 (February 1919), 43; "A Year of Prosperity for Railway Labor," *Railway Age* 66 (January 3, 1919), 37.

68. William Blackman and John A. Moffitt to W. S. Carter, January 22, 1919; Memorandum, W. S. Carter, March 22, 1919; H. H. Reed, Memorandum, March 25, 1919; IC, "Misunderstanding"; C. M. Kittle to B. L. Winchell, January 18, 1919, in Hanger Case Files, no. 435.

69. William Blackman to G. W. W. Hanger, January 18, 1919, in Hanger Case Files, no. 435.

70. E. D. Franis to Walker D. Hines, March 20, 1919; John McGinnis to Hines, March 20, 1919; C. C. Connolly to Hines, March 20, 1919, in Hanger Case Files, no. 435.

71. Timothy Shea to W. S. Carter, May 23, 1919, and Carter, Memorandum, March 22, 1919, in Hanger Case Files, no. 435; "Report of the President," BRT, *Reports of Grand Lodge Officers, Year 1919*, 101–103.

72. Lloyd L. Brown, *Iron City* (New York: Masses & Mainstream, 1952), 162; "Discrimination against White Trainmen," *Railroad Trainmen* 36 (November 1919); Spero and Harris, *Black Worker*, 299–301. Founded in Knoxville in 1912, CARE changed its name to the Association of Colored Railway Trainmen and Locomotive Firemen (ACRT) in the early 1920s; I use the acronym CARE throughout this chapter and the acronym ACRT in subsequent chapters. CARE boasted a southern membership of 4,000 men. BRWWC, "In re: Colored Association of Railway Employees," BRWWC Transcripts, June 15, 1918.

73. In Docketed Case File 138 (hereafter RLB Docket 138), Entry 56, Records of the Railroad Labor Board 1920–1926, Docketed Case Files, 1920–1926, Records of the National Mediation Board, Record Group 13 (hereafter Entry 56, RLB Records), Washington National Records Center, Suitland, Md.: J. H. Eiland to C. H. Markham, February 24, 1920; Eiland to C. H. Markham, March 26, 1920; L. C. Going to Eiland, June 2, 1920; Going and Eiland to R. M. Barton, et al., re CARE v. IC and Y&MV, June 2, 1920. In Docketed Case File 4092 (hereafter RLB Docket 4092), Entry 46, RLB Records: U.S. Railroad Labor Board (hereafter RLB), Bureau no. 3, ACRT v. IC and Y&MV, "Proceedings," June 18, 1924. See also Reid, *Negro Membership in American Labor Unions*, 56–58.

74. BRT, *Reports of Grand Lodge Officers, Year 1919*, 21.

75. On whites' failure to displace blacks, see James Hutton Lemly, *The Gulf, Mobile, and Ohio: A Railroad That Had to Expand or Expire* (Homewood, Ill.: Indiana University School of Business/Richard D. Irwin, 1953), 39–40.

76. Walter F. White, "Memorandum re Railroad Trainmen's Case, January 4th & 5th, 1920" (hereafter White, "Trainmen's Memorandum"), and White to John Henry Eiland, January 6, 1920, in NAACP-LC Papers, Box C414. Also see C. S. Lake to Daugherty, February 2, 1920, in Records of the Division of Operation, General Correspondence of C. S. Lake, Assistant Director, July 1919–March 1920, Entry 77, Box 1, USRA, RG 14.

77. W. S. Lovett to Walter F. White, January 27, 1920; John Henry Eiland to Walter F. White, January 24, 1920, in NAACP-LC Papers, Box C414. On B. L. Winchell, see "Southern Region—Operating Conditions," *Railway Age* 66 (March 14, 1919), 593; W. S. Carter, Memorandum, March 22, 1919, in Hanger Case Files, no. 435; "Seniority, etc., of White and Colored Trainmen," in BRT, *Reports of Grand Lodge Officers, Year 1919*, 101–107.

78. In NAACP-LC Papers: R. R. Church to James W. Johnson, January 17, 1919, Box C414; John Henry Eiland to Walter F. White, December 31, 1919, Box C319. Kate Born, "Memphis Negro Workingmen and the NAACP," *West Tennessee Historical Society Papers* 28 (1974), 98–99.

79. *Report of the National Association for the Advancement of Colored People for the Years 1917 and 1918: Eighth and Ninth Annual Reports* (n.p., 1919), 45; *New York Age*, December 12, 18, 1918; *Houston Observer*, December 28, 1918, in *TINCF*, Reel 8; *St. Louis Argus*, December 6, 1918.

80. In NAACP-LC Papers, see Press Release, January 21, 1919, Box C319; White to F. G. Antoine, January 12, 1921, and White to Clarence Darrow, March 0, 1921, Box C414; White to J. H. McConico, March 17, 1919, Box C319.

81. R. R. Church to James W. Johnson, January 17, 1919, NAACP-LC Papers, Box

C414; John Henry Eiland to W. D. Hines, January 26, 1919, in NAACP-LC Papers, Box C319; Eiland to C. H. Markham, February 24, 1920, in RLB Docket 138.

82. John Henry Eiland to U.S. Railroad Labor Board, February 9, 1920, in RLB Docket 138.

83. L. C. Going and John Henry Eiland to R. M. Barton, re *CARE v. IC and Y&MV,* June 2, 1920, in RLB Docket 138.

84. John Henry Eiland to C. H. Markham, February 24, 1920; Eiland to Markham, March 26, 1920, in RLB Docket 138.

85. Rufus Reed and W. A. Williams to T. W. Collins, W. E. Romine, and G. W. Griffin, March 1, 1920, NAACP-LC Papers, Box C272.

86. Rufus Reed and W. A. Williams to W. E. Brooks, October 20, 1919, NAACP-LC Papers, Box C272.

87. In Docketed Case File 2032 (hereafter RLB Docket 2032), Entry 56, RLB Records: U.S. Railroad Labor Board Bureau no. 3, Protective Order of Railroad Trainmen vs. Missouri Pacific Railroad Company, Docket 2032, Chicago, November 20, 1922, 5 (hereafter PORT v. MP Docket 2032); John Clark to Lewis Fairchild, "Statement," February 20, 1922, Exhibit no. 1. W. A. Williams and Rufus Reed to Mo. P. RR Officials, December 13, 1920, and Rufus Reed to B. F. Bush, A. Robertson, and J. F. Murphey, n.d. (likely late 1920 or early 1921), NAACP-LC Papers, Box C272.

88. W. A. Williams and Rufus Reed to Missouri Pacific Railroad Officials, December 13, 1920; Reed to B. F. Bush, A. Robertson, and J. W. Murphey, n.d. (likely late 1920 or early 1921), NAACP-LC Papers, Box C272.

89. In NAACP-LC Papers: A. Robertson to Julius Johnson and Rufus Reed, December 20, 1920, Box C414; T. W. Collins to Rufus Reed, November 28, 1920, Box C272.

90. In RLB Docket 138: L. C. Going to R. M. Barton, May 1, July 14, September 9, 22, 1920; RLB, November 4, 1921, Decision no. 307 (Docket 138); RLB, "Proceedings," June 18, 1924. See also *Norfolk Journal and Guide,* January 22, 1921.

91. RLB, "Proceedings," June 18, 1924, in RLB Docket 4092, 21; Decision no. 3524—Docket 4092, May 12, 1925, *Decisions of the United States Railroad Labor Board with Addenda and Interpretations, 1925* 6 (Washington, D.C.: Government Printing Office, 1926), 904; G. E. Patterson to J. J. Pelley, July 6, 1925, in Records of the Illinois Central Gulf Railroad, Selected Personnel Files, no. 5295, Box 8, Folder 13, Kheel Center for Labor-Management Documentation and Archives, Cornell University, Ithaca, New York.

92. PORT v. MP Docket 2032, pp. 5, 7, 14. See also: Lewis Fairchild to J. M. Egan, May 6, 1924, "Employes Petition, to Re-Open Negotiations . . ." (hereafter Fairchild, "Employes Petition"), in RLB Docket 2032.

93. PORT vs. MP Docket 2032, 11, 16; Fairchild, "Employees Petition"; Decision no. 2891—Docket 2032, February 3, 1925, *Decisions of the United States Railroad Labor Board, 1925* 6, 162–163.

94. "Report of the President W. G. Lee," *Reports of Grand Lodge Officers. Year 1919,* 104; John Henry Eiland to R. R. Church, May 9, 1921, NAACP-LC Papers, Box C414.

95. *McDowell Times,* July 7, 1916; *Crisis* 12 (August 1916); *Chicago Whip,* March 13, 1920. Also see Walker James to the *Crisis,* March 8, 1921, NAACP-LC Papers, Box C414.

96. Nathan Hopkins, "'Get Off!'—Death Signal to Trainmen in the South," *Chicago Defender,* March 4, 1922. On the campaign of terror, see also *Chicago Defender,* June 4, 11, September 10, October 15, 1921, April 28, 1922; *Jackson Daily News,* September 21, 22, 1921; *New York Age,* August 6, 20, 1921; *Norfolk Journal and Guide,* September 24, 1921; *Birmingham Reporter,* December 3, 1921; "Discrimination," *Crisis* 23 (March 1921), 212.

97. Statement of brakeman Bob Grant, NAACP-LC Papers, Box C414.

98. Jesse Ficklin to J. H. Eiland, May 17, 1921, NAACP-LC Papers, Box C414.

99. John Henry Eiland to R. R. Church, May 9, 1921; Eiland to Church, May 11, 1921, NAACP-LC Papers, Box C414; Hopkins, "Get Off!"; *Jackson Daily News,* September 21, 22, 1921.

100. In NAACP-LC Papers, Box C414, see Walter White to J. H. Eiland, May 18, 24, 26, 1921; White to Interstate Commerce Commission, May 25, 1921; White to Attorney General, May 26, 1921; White to R. R. Church, May 26, 1921; Eiland to White, May 27, 1921; George B. McGinty to White, June 4, 1921; McGinty to White, June 6, 1921; R. P. Steward to White, May 31, 1921.

101. Spero and Harris, *Black Worker,* 314–315.

102. Judith Stein, *The World of Marcus Garvey: Race and Class in Modern Society* (Baton Rouge: Louisiana State University Press, 1986).

3. The Black Wedge of Civil Rights Unionism

1. *Atlanta Daily News,* March 25, April 4, 1944; *Chicago Defender,* April 8, 1944; text of Randolph's speech in *Black Worker* 10 (April 1944), 4; (May 1944), 4; (June 1944), 2; (July 1944), 4; (August 1944), 4; Michael Honey, *Southern Labor and Black Civil Rights: Organizing Memphis Workers* (Urbana: University of Illinois Press, 1993), 205–206.

2. E. J. Bradley to A. Philip Randolph, November 11, 1943, in *The Papers of A. Philip Randolph* (Bethesda, Md.: University Publications of America, 1990) (hereafter *APR Papers*), Reel 5; *Baltimore Afro-American,* November 13, 1943; *New York Age,* December 25, 1943; *Michigan Chronicle,* January 29, 1944; *Sunday Chicago Bee,* March 26, 1944; *Chicago Defender,* March 19, April 1, 1944; *Atlanta Daily World,* March 21, 1944.

3. BSCP Press Release, 1944, and E. J. Bradley to Randolph, March 10, 1944, in *APR Papers,* Reel 5.

4. On blacks' political migration to the Democratic party, see Nancy J. Weiss, *Farewell to the Party of Lincoln: Black Politics in the Age of FDR* (Princeton: Princeton University Press, 1983). On the rise of Depression-era civil rights activism, see Beth Tompkins Bates, "A New Crowd Challenges the Agenda of the Old Guard in the NAACP 1933–1941," *American Historical Review* 102 (April 1997), 340–377.

5. *Houston Informer and Texas Freeman* (hereafter *Informer*), May 1, 1937; *Min-*

neapolis Spokesman, April 1, 1932, November 25, 1938; St. Clair Drake and Horace R. Cayton, *Black Metropolis: A Study of Negro Life in a Northern City,* vol. 1 (1945; rpt. New York: Harcourt, Brace & World, 1962), 313; George McCray, "The Labor Movement: Gains in Union Membership," in Florence Murray, ed., *The Negro Handbook 1944* (New York: Current Reference Publications, 1944); Horace R. Cayton and George S. Mitchell, *Black Workers and the New Unions* (Chapel Hill: University of North Carolina Press, 1939), 409–415.

6. *New York Age,* March 18, 1915, December 21, 1916; January 26, 1924; *Chicago Defender,* July 24, 1926, May 25, 1935. Also, in *Tuskegee Institute News Clippings File* (Tuskegee, Ala.: Division of Behavioral Science Research, Carver Research Foundation, Tuskegee Institute, 1976) (hereafter *TINCF*), Reel 26: *St. Paul Echo,* May 29, 1926, and *Chicago Whip,* November 27, 1926. Beth Tompkins Bates, "The Brotherhood," *Chicago History* 25 (Fall 1996), 4–23.

7. *New York Age,* October 12, 1918, and May 6, September 2, 1922; James H. Hogans, "Pullman Porter News," *New York Age,* August 12, September 16, 1922; *Chicago Defender,* May 6, 1922, December 8, 1923. On Pullman and musical entertainment, see also *Pullman News* 1 (May 1922), 11; 1 (June 1922), 61; 2 (October 1923), 166; 3 (June 1924), 59; 3 (August 1924), 115, 123; 3 (September 1924), 153; 3 (October 1924), 186; 3 (November 1924), 219; 3 (March 1925), 340; 4 (May 1925), 21.

8. David Brody, "The Rise and Decline of Welfare Capitalism," in Brody, *Workers in Industrial America: Essays on the Twentieth Century Struggle* (New York: Oxford University Press, 1980), 55; James H. Hogans, "Pullman Porter News," *New York Age,* October 28, 1922, June 28, 1924; Thomas L. Dabney, "The Case of the Pullman Porters," *Locomotive Engineers Journal* 61 (January 1927), 19.

9. *Informer,* April 5, 1924; "Industrial Relations Department," *Pullman News* 3 (May 1924), 6; "Million Dollars Wage Increase for Porters and Maids," *Pullman News* 4 (March 1926), 357; Ashley L. Totten, "Why Pullman Porters Organized," *Interracial Review* 22 (November 1949), 169; F. Boyd, "Previous Struggles of the Pullman Porters to Organize," *Messenger* 8 (September 1926), 284; Arthur McWatt, "'A Greater Victory': The Brotherhood of Sleeping Car Porters in St. Paul," *Minnesota History* 55 (Spring 1997), 208–209.

10. *New York City World,* August 20, 1925, and *Amsterdam News,* September 2, 1925, in *TINCF,* Reel 23; William H. Harris, *Keeping the Faith: A. Philip Randolph, Milton P. Webster, and the Brotherhood of Sleeping Car Porters, 1925–1937* (Urbana: University of Illinois Press, 1977); Jervis Anderson, *A. Philip Randolph: A Biographical Portrait* (New York: Harcourt Brace Jovanovich, 1972), 168–169.

11. On Randolph's background, see Anderson, *A. Philip Randolph;* Benjamin Quarles, "A. Philip Randolph: Labor Leader at Large," in John Hope Franklin and August Meier, eds., *Black Leaders of the Twentieth Century* (Urbana: University of Illinois Press, 1982), 140–147.

12. A. Philip Randolph, "Pullman Porters Need Own Union," *Messenger* 7 (August

1925), 289; Randolph, "The Pullman Company and the Pullman Porter," *Messenger* 6 (September 1925), 312–314, 355–356; R. W. Dunn, "Company Unions à la Pullman," *Messenger* 7 (December 1925), 394–395; *New York World,* October 11, 1925, in *TINCF,* Reel 23.

13. A. Philip Randolph, "An Open Letter to Mr. E. F. Carry," *Messenger* 8 (January 1926), 10, 26; Randolph, "The Truth about the Brotherhood of Sleeping Car Porters," *Messenger* 8 (February 1926), 37–38, 61; A. Saggitarius, "Not Servitude but Service," *Messenger* 8 (November 1926), 324; Randolph, "The New Pullman Porter," *Messenger* 8 (April 1926), 109; Randolph, "Pullman Porters Need Own Union"; Randolph, "The Pullman Company and the Pullman Porter."

14. Frank R. Crosswaith, "Porters Smash a Company Union," *Labor Age* 17 (January 1928), 15–16; Benjamin Stolberg, "The Pullman Peon: A Study in Industrial Race Exploitation," *Nation* 122 (April 7, 1926), 235–237; "Randolph's Reply to Perry Howard," *Messenger* 7 (October–November 1925), 350–352.

15. Greg Leroy, "The Founding Heart of A. Philip Randolph's Union: Milton P. Webster and Chicago's Pullman Porters Organize, 1925–1937," *Labor's Heritage* 3 (July 1991), 27–31; Harris, *Keeping the Faith,* 42–48. On the Pullman Company's introduction of Filipino workers as an anti-union tactic, see Barbara M. Posadas, "The Hierarchy of Color and Psychological Adjustment in an Industrial Environment: Filipinos, the Pullman Company, and the Brotherhood of Sleeping Car Porters," *Labor History* 23 (Summer 1982), 349–373.

16. *Baltimore Afro-American,* October 17, 1925; *Washington Tribune,* October 31, November 14, 1925; *Chicago Whip,* December 19, 1925, in *TINCF,* Reel 23; Samuel E. Warren, "The Negro in the American Labor Movement" (Ph.D. diss., University of Wisconsin, 1941), 469–470.

17. Leroy, "Founding Heart," 27–28; Bates, "The Brotherhood"; Paul L. Caldwell, "Our Local Struggle to Organize St. Paul, Minnesota," *Messenger* 9 (January 1927), 25.

18. *Birmingham Reporter,* November 17, 1925; *Bolivar County, Mississippi Cotton Farmer,* November 28, 1925; *Pittsburgh American,* September 25, 1925; *Washington Tribune,* November 14, 1925, all in *TINCF,* Reel 23. In the National Urban League Records, Series 13, Box 82, Library of Congress (hereafter NUL-LC), see *Florida Sentinel,* October 24, 1925, and *Florida Enterprise,* October 25, 1925; H. N. Hall, "The Art of the Pullman Porter," *American Mercury* 23 (July 1931), 335.

19. A. Philip Randolph, "Ye Pioneer Brotherhood Men," *Messenger* 9 (April 1927), 129. The best study of the BSCP's construction of an alliance among black elites in the 1920s is Bates, "The Brotherhood." On black elites and unions in the 1930s, see August Meier and Elliot Rudwick, *Black Detroit and the Rise of the UAW* (New York: Oxford University Press, 1979).

20. A. Philip Randolph, "The Brotherhood and the Mediation Board," *Messenger* 9 (January 1927), 17, 19; *Houston Informer,* August 6, 1927; *Mixer and Server* 36 (November 15, 1927), 46.

21. *Washington Tribune,* March 5, 19 1926; *Amsterdam News,* March 3, 1926; *Birmingham Reporter,* March 6, 1926, *Chicago Defender,* June 19, 1926, all in

TINCF, Reel 26. On the Watson-Parker Act, see Robert H. Zieger, "From Hostility to Moderation: Railroad Labor Policy in the 1920s," *Labor History* 9 (Winter 1966), 35–36; Ruth O'Brien, *Workers' Paradox: The Republican Origins of New Deal Labor Policy, 1886–1935* (Chapel Hill: University of North Carolina Press, 1998), 137–140.

22. Harris, *Keeping the Faith;* Anderson, *A. Philip Randolph;* "The Pullman Porters' Attempt to Organize," *Information Service* 8 (February 9, 1929), 1–4, in *Claude A. Barnett Papers, Subject Files on Black Americans, 1918–1967: Series C, Economic Conditions, 1918–1966, Part 3* (Frederick, MD.: University Publications of America, 1986), Reel 9. See also the numerous articles on the 1928 strike threat in *NAACP Papers,* Part 10, Reel 22.

23. *Seattle Northwest Enterprise,* September 21, 1933; *Chicago Defender,* June 17, October 28, 1933; January 27, 1934; Sterling D. Spero and Abram L. Harris, *The Black Worker: The Negro and the Labor Movement* (1931; rpt. Atheneum, 1969), 448, 457, 460; Harris, *Keeping the Faith,* 152–182; Brailsford R. Brazeal, *The Brotherhood of Sleeping Car Porters: Its Origin and Development* (New York: Harper & Brothers, 1946), 95–100.

24. *Northwest Enterprise,* September 14, October 5, 1933; statement of A. Philip Randolph, *Railway Labor Act Amendments: Hearings before the Committee on Interstate and Foreign Commerce on H.R. 7650,* House of Representatives, 73rd Congress, 2nd sess. May 22, 23, 24, and 25, 1934 (Washington, D.C.: Government Printing Office, 1934), 111; Anderson, *A. Philip Randolph,* 216–220; Leo Troy, "Labor Representation on American Railways," *Labor History* 2 (Fall 1961), 311–315.

25. A. Philip Randolph, "The Story of the Brotherhood of Sleeping Car Porters," *APR Papers,* Reel 9; *Chicago Defender,* January 20, April 7, 14, 21, June 23, July 7, 14, September 15, 1934; Otto S. Beyer, "Collective Bargaining under the Railway Labor Act," *Labor Information Bulletin* 4 (February 1937), 1–3; Harris, *Keeping the Faith,* 181–189; Anderson, *A. Philip Randolph,* 217–230; "New Life to Porters' Union," *Crisis* 41 (September 1934), 269.

26. *Chicago Defender,* April 27, 1935; J. T. Reid, "Penn Terminal Notes," *New York Age,* June 1, August 24, 1935; Traveller, "Is 'George' Better Off in the Union?" *Baltimore Afro-American,* May 21, 1938; T. Arnold Hill, "Labor: The Pullman Porter—The Big Boss," *Opportunity* 13 (June 1935), 186; Victor Weybright, "Pullman Porters on Parade," *Survey Graphic* (November 1935), 572; *Chicago Defender,* February 9, March 16, May 18, June 15, July 6, July 13, 1935; A. Philip Randolph to Walter White, May 23, 1935, in *NAACP Papers,* Part 10, Reel 22.

27. *Northwest Enterprise,* October 17, 1935; A. Philip Randolph, "Pullman Porters Win," *Opportunity* 15 (October 1937), 299–300, 315; G. James Fleming, "Pullman Porters Win Pot of Gold," *Crisis* 44 (November 1937), 332–333, 338, 346; *Chicago Defender,* August 28, 1937; *Minneapolis Spokesman,* September 3, 1937; *Black Worker* 3 (October 1937), 1–2.

28. Fleming, "Pullman Porters Win," 332–333; *Chicago Defender,* September 18, 1937, September 17, 1938; Victor Weybright, "Pullman Porters on Parade," *Survey Graphic* (November 1935), 574.

29. Rienzi B. Lemus, "A Successful Negro Labor Union," *Opportunity* 6 (May

1923), 21; Thomas L. Dabney, "The Union in the Dining Car," *Locomotive Engineers Journal* 61 (July 1927), 517, 571; Lemus, "Negroes Not Communists," *Trenton Times,* November 11, 1925, in *TINCF,* Reel 23; Monroe Work, ed., *Negro Year Book: An Annual Encyclopedia of the Negro, 1931–1932* (Tuskegee, Ala.: Negro Year Book Publishing Co., 1931), 149–150; *New York Age,* June 5, 1920, March 1, 1924, January 31, April 4, 1925; *Informer,* July 16, 1927; *Pittsburgh Courier,* April 11, 1924, October 11, 1924, May 30, 1925, June 5, 1926; *Buffalo American,* June 4, 1925.

30. Rienzi B. Lemus to T. Arnold Hill, January 29, 1926; William Green to Lemus, March 31, May 22, 1926; Lemus to Green, May 18, 1926, all in NUL-LC, Series 4, Box 2; T. Arnold Hill, "The Dilemma of Negro Workers," *Opportunity* 4 (February 1926), 41; "Proceedings of the [HRE] Twenty-Fourth General Convention . . . August 8, 9, 10, 11, and 12, 1927," in *Mixer and Server* 36 (September 15, 1927), 46–52; "President's Report," in "Proceedings of the [HRE] Twenty-Fifth General Convention . . . August 12, 13, 14, 15, 16, and 17, 1929," in *Mixer and Server* 38 (September 15, 1929), 14–16; James H. Hogans, "Among Railroad and Pullman Workers" (hereafter Hogans, "ARPW"), *Baltimore Afro-American,* August 23, September 6, 1941.

31. Floyd C. Covington, "Union Styles: Black Labor in White Coats," *Opportunity* 9 (July 1931), 208–210; Charles L. Upton, "Railroad Clatter—Coast Doings," *California Eagle,* April 25, 1930, March 27, 1931; *California Eagle,* December 19, 1930, March 27, 1931; "Our Dining Car Employees' Division," *Catering Industry Employee* 43 (October 12, 1934), 31–32; "President's Report," *Mixer and Server* 38 (September 15, 1929), 13–14; "Proceedings of the [HRE] Twenty-Sixth General Convention . . . August 8, 9, 10, 11, and 12, 1932," in *Catering Industry Employe* 41 (September 12, 1932), 19.

32. Arthur Cyrus Hill, "The History of Dining Car Employees Unions in the Upper Midwest and the Impact of Railroad Abandonments, Consolidations and Mergers on Dining Car Unions" (master's thesis, University of Minnesota, 1968), 40–44; *New York Age,* March 9, 23, 1935, January 25, 1936; *Pittsburgh Courier,* December 8, 1934; *Baltimore Afro-American,* July 11, 1936, October 23, 1937; *Catering Industry Employee* 44 (December 12, 1935), 38.

33. *Black Dispatch,* September 24, 1935, in *TINCF,* Reel 50; *Baltimore Afro-American,* March 23, 1935, February 19, 1938; *New York Age,* March 23, 1935; Rienzi B. Lemus to Claude A. Barnett, August 4, 1934, in *Claude A. Barnett Papers,* Part 3, Series C, Reel 9; *Seattle Northwest Enterprise,* September 20, 1934.

34. *Seattle Northwest Enterprise,* July 19, 1934, September 19, 1935; *Baltimore Afro-American,* February 15, 1936, July 4, 1936, October 30, 1937; *Pittsburgh Courier,* October 10, 1936; *Black Dispatch,* February 19, 1938; author's interview with Truman K. Gibson, Jr., December 15, 1994; "Brotherhood of Dining Car Employees," in Florence Murray, ed., *The Negro Handbook* (New York: Wendell Malliet & Co., 1942), 138; *Catering Industry Employee* 45 (March 12, 1936), 39; 46 (January 12, 1937), 40–41; 46 (December 12, 1937), 36; 47 (January 1938), 40; Hogans, "ARPW," *Baltimore Afro-American,* April 9, 1938.

35. *Catering Industry Employee* 44 (April 12, 1935), 26, 47 (February 12, 1938),

35; author's interview with Ishmael Flory, January 13, 1994; "Proceedings First National Conference Dining Car Employees, Omaha, Nebraska, October 25–28, 1937," typescript, in *APR Papers,* Reel 9 (hereafter 1937 Proceedings); Flory, "First Anniversary of Joint Council of Dining Car Employees," *Catering Industry Employee* 47 (December 12, 1938), 43.

36. Author's interview with Ishmael Flory, January 13, 1994; 1937 Proceedings; Flory, "First Anniversary"; *Black Dispatch,* November 13, 1937; *Chicago Defender,* February 26, April 2, 1938; *Catering Industry Employee* 47 (January 12, 1938), 41.

37. Harold Preece, "Ishmael Flory Becomes Prominent Labor Leader," *Chicago Defender,* August 26, 1939; author's interview with Ishmael Flory, January 13, 1994.

38. *Chicago Defender,* March 10, 17, 1934; Ishmael Flory, "Flory's Own Story of Fisk!" *Chicago Defender,* March 23, 1924; "Fisk and Flory," *Crisis* 41 (April 1934), 111–112.

39. Edward H. Himes, "'A New Day for the Dining Car Worker,'" *Catering Industry Employee* 47 (October 12, 1938), 44; Ishmael Flory, "Short Subjects on the Streamlined March of Dining Car Employees," *Catering Industry Employee* 48 (August 12, 1939), 35; Flory and George E. Brown, "Report and Memorandum on Assignment by President Flore," *Catering Industry Employee* 47 (November 12, 1938), 41; Flory, "Railroad Labor and the National Mediation Board," *Catering Industry Employee* 48 (April 12, 1939), 40–41; "Vacation Fight On," *Dining Car Worker* (July 1942), 1; *Northwest Enterprise,* August 25, December 1, 1939; *Chicago Defender,* February 25, September 23, 1939; *Atlanta Daily World,* January 30, 1944; *Pittsburgh Courier,* April 15, 1950; "History of Struggle," *Dining Car Worker* (October 1942), 4.

40. Brazeal, *Brotherhood,* 39–43.

41. In the *Messenger,* see George S. Schuyler, "Blessed Are the Organized," 8 (November 1926), 347; A. Philip Randolph, "To the Brotherhood Men," 8 (November 1926), 325; Randolph, "Dialogue of the Old and New," 9 (March 1927), 94; Frank R. Crosswaith, "Crusading for the Brotherhood," 8 (June 1926), 173; Randolph, "State of the Brotherhood," 9 (February 1927), 55. See also *New York City World,* August 20, 1925, in *TINCF,* Reel 23; Melinda Chateauvert, *Marching Together: Women of the Brotherhood of Sleeping Car Porters* (Urbana: University of Illinois Press, 1998), 53–54, 59.

42. "National Negro Labor Conference," in Frederic Robb, ed., *The Negro in Chicago, 1779 to 1929* (Chicago: Washington Intercollegiate Club, 1929), 68–75, 198–199, in Special Collections, University of Illinois at Chicago; "Sixth Annual Statement of Achievements and Hopes of the Porters' Union," *American Federationist* 39 (March 1932), 302; *Black Worker* 2 (January 15, 1930), 4; 2 (February 15, 1930), 4; *Chicago Defender,* January 11, 25, February 1, 1930; *California Eagle,* January 9, 1931; Bates, "A New Crowd."

43. Lawrence S. Wittner, "The National Negro Congress: A Reassessment," *American Quarterly* 22 (Winter 1970), 883–901; Paula F. Pfeffer, *A. Philip Randolph, Pioneer of the Civil Rights Movement* (Baton Rouge: Louisiana State University Press, 1990), 31–43.

44. *Chicago Defender,* February 8, 15, 22, June 6, 1936; May 4, 1940; August 9, 1941; April 14, 22, 1944; *Sunday Chicago Bee,* September 10, 1944; Bates, "A New Crowd," 364–366.

45. *Seattle Northwest Enterprise,* September 22, October 6, 27, 1939, May 16, 1945, March 23, 1949; Frank Boyd to Milton Webster, August 4, 1941, in Papers of the Brotherhood of Sleeping Car Porters, Chicago Historical Society (hereafter BSCP-CHS Papers), Box 129; Quintard Taylor, *The Forging of a Black Community: Seattle's Central District from 1870 through the Civil Rights Era* (Seattle: University of Washington Press, 1994), 171–172; *Minneapolis Spokesman,* July 21, December 22, 1939, January 12, April 26, June 30, October 11, 1940, March 14, 1941, December 18, 1942, February 23, March 2, 14, April 13, August 31, 1945; David M. Colman, "On the Right Track: The Brotherhood of Sleeping Car Porters, the Dining Car Employees' Union Local 516, and the Ladies' Auxiliary to the BSCP, Black Labor Organizing in St. Paul, 1937–1950" (honors thesis, Macalester College, 1992), 113–122.

46. Halena Wilson to members, October 22, 1940 (Box 27), and "Chicago Auxiliary History" (1948) (Box 34) in International Ladies Auxiliary Papers, Papers of the Brotherhood of Sleeping Car Porters, Chicago Historical Society (hereafter ILAP-BSCP-CHS). The definitive treatments of the Auxiliary are Chateauvert's *Marching Together* and Paula F. Pfeffer, "The Women behind the Union: Halena Wilson, Rosina Tucker, and the Ladies' Auxiliary to the Brotherhood of Sleeping Car Porters," *Labor History* 36 (Fall 1995), 557–578.

47. Halena Wilson to "Sister," January 19, 1940 (Box 27) and Wilson to members, March 4, 1954 (Box 34), ILAP-BSCP-CHS; *Chicago Defender,* September 17, 1938; "Praise Auxiliaries," *Dining Car Worker* (May 1942), 3; "Ladies Auxiliary, Local 370, Hold Installation" and "Our Challenge" (June 1942), 3; Colman, "On the Right Track," 137–147, 155–157.

48. Dining Car Employees Union Local 370, New York City, Mimeographed Newsletter (August 1943), 3–4, in *Records of the Committee on Fair Employment Practice, 1941–1946* (Glen Rock, N.J.: Microfilming Corporation of America, 1971) (hereafter *FEPC Records*), Reel 10; *Pittsburgh Courier,* January 29, 1944.

49. *Chicago Defender,* October 7, 1944; *Northwest Enterprise,* December 1, 1943, August 23, 1944; *Pittsburgh Courier,* February 19, 1944, July 28, December 1, 1945; *Minneapolis Spokesman,* April 13, 1945; *Sunday Chicago Bee,* September 15, 1945; *Houston Informer and Texas Freeman,* October 23, 1943.

50. *Hearings before a Subcommittee of the Committee on Interstate Commerce, on S. 3798, "Supervision of Sleeping Cars,"* U.S. Senate, 76th Congress, 3rd sess., May 15, 16, and 17, 1940; *Chicago Defender,* June 8, 22, 1940; Hogans, "ARPW," *Baltimore Afro-American,* June 22, 1940; *Minneapolis Spokesman,* June 7, 1940; *Northwest Enterprise,* June 21, 1940. In Brotherhood of Sleeping Car Porters Papers, Library of Congress, Washington, D.C., Box 95, see W. S. Anderson to A. Philip Randolph, May 15, 16, 1940; Sherman Minton to Thomas Paterson, June 10, 1940; Randolph to Edward Keating, August 15, 1940; *Pullman Co. et al. v. Railroad Commission of Texas et al.,* No. 38 Civ A (1940), 33

F.Supp. 675. See also Pullman Co. v. Public Service Commission of South Carolina et al., No. 17788 (1961), 120 S.E.2d 214; *Pittsburgh Courier,* February 17, 1951.

51. Hogans, "ARPW," *Baltimore Afro-American,* November 21, 1942; Hogans, "Among R.R. Workers," Baltimore *Afro-American,* April 1, 8, May 6, July 1, 1944; *Chicago Defender,* August 15, 1942, March 4, April 1, 1944; *Pittsburgh Courier,* March 11, 1944, February 15, 1947; *Northwest Enterprise,* March 15, 1944; *Minneapolis Spokesman,* March 10, June 9, 1944. In *FEPC Records,* see "Before the President's Committee on Fair Employment Practice . . . Summary, Findings and Directives in Re Pennsylvania Railroad Company," November 1943 (Reel 10); T. A. Jackson, R. W. Smith, and George E. Brown to Malcolm Ross, March 3, 1944 (Reel 10); and Maceo W. Hubbard to George M. Johnson, Memorandum, March 29, 1944 (Reel 24). In Records of the Committee on Fair Employment Practice, Closed Cases, Region VI, Record Group 228, Box 73, National Archives and Records Administration, Great Lakes Region, Chicago, see W. S. Seltzer to Elmer Henderson, September 19, 1944; Harry H. C. Gibson to Henderson, November 22, 1944.

52. Abram L. Harris, "Why the Brotherhood of Sleeping Car Porters Should Organize under a Separate International Charter," 1930, in *NAACP Papers,* Part 10, Reel 22.

53. "President's Report," in *Mixer and Server* 38 (September 15, 1929), 15–16; Brazeal, *Brotherhood,* 133–138, 143–147; *Chicago Defender,* September 8, October 27, November 10, 1934; *Northwest Enterprise,* September 20, October 4, November 15, 1934; *Ontario Dawn of Tomorrow,* October 1934; Harris, *Keeping the Faith,* 199–201.

54. *Chicago Defender,* April 2, 1938; *Daily Worker,* April 8, 1938; *Pittsburgh Courier,* April 16, 1938; *Houston Informer and Texas Freeman,* April 16, 1938, May 20, 1939; *Dining Car Worker* (October 1942), 1; (March 1943), 1; Anderson, *A. Philip Randolph,* 9–10; Randolph quoted in Joseph F. Wilson, *Tearing Down the Color Bar: A Documentary History and Analysis of the Brotherhood of Sleeping Car Porters* (New York: Columbia University Press, 1989), 46.

55. *Seattle Northwest Enterprise,* July 8, 1938; Hogans, "ARPW," *Washington Afro-American,* August 20, September 3, 1938; *Chicago Defender,* August 27, 1938; C. L. Dellums to Thomas T. Patterson, January 20, 1939, in C. L. Dellums Papers, Bancroft Library, University of California at Berkeley, Box 2; *Pittsburgh Courier,* September 25, 1948.

56. Thomas T. Patterson to C. L. Dellums, August 17, 1942; Dellums to Patterson, December 11, 1945, in Dellums Papers, Box 2; *Chicago Defender,* November 30, 1940; *Report of the Proceedings of the Sixty-Ninth Convention of the American Federation of Labor Held at New Orleans, Louisiana, November 18 to 29, Inclusive, 1940* (Washington, D.C.: Ransdell, 1940), 509; *Report of Proceedings of the Sixtieth Annual Convention of the American Federation of Labor Held at Houston, Texas, September 18 to 23, Inclusive, 1950* (published at the direction of the AFL, 1950), 472–473.

57. *Report of Proceedings of the Forty-Ninth Convention of the American Federation of Labor Held at Toronto, Ontario, Canada, October 7th to 18th, Inclusive, 1929*

(Washington, D.C.: Law Reporter Printing Co., 1929), 216; *Chicago Defender,* October 13, 1934; *Report of the Proceedings of the Fifty-Fifth Annual Convention of the American Federation of Labor Held at Atlantic City, New Jersey, October 7 to 19, Inclusive, 1935* (Washington, D.C.: Judd & Detweiler, 1935), 807–809; *Report of Proceedings of the Fifty-Sixth Annual Convention of the American Federation of Labor Held at Tampa, Florida, November 16 to 27, Inclusive, 1936* (Washington, D.C.: Judd & Detweiler, 1936), 659.

58. *Report of Proceedings of the Sixty-Third Annual Convention of the American Federation of Labor Held at Boston, Massachusetts, October 4 to 14, Inclusive, 1943* (Washington, D.C.: Ransdell, 1943), 421–430; *New York Times,* July 10, 1935; Richard W. Smith, "Memorandum on Racial Discrimination," *Catering Industry Employee* 54 (December 12, 1944) 25–26; Smith, "Memorandum on Racial Discrimination," in *Claude A. Barnett Papers,* Series C, Part 3, Reel 9; *Atlanta Daily World,* December 2, 1944; John LeFlore, "AFL Race Bias Sings Negro Labor to CIO Unions, AFL Parley Told," *Chicago Defender,* December 2, 1944.

59. C. L. Dellums to Thomas T. Patterson, December 11, 1945; Patterson to Dellums, December 19, 1945; in Dellums Papers, Box 2; Hogans, "ARPW," *Washington Afro-American,* November 26, 1938; *Baltimore Afro-American,* November 9, 1940, May 9, 1942; *New York Times,* October 24, 1946.

60. Randolph quoted in Anderson, *A. Philip Randolph,* 295; P. L. Prattis, "The Horizon," *Pittsburgh Courier,* October 30, 1943.

61. Author's interview with Molly West, May 18, 1994; author's interview with Ishmael Flory, January 13, 1994; *Chicago Defender,* October 14, 21, 1939; HRE memorandum, November 2, 1939, in Dellums Papers, Box 23; Flory, "Wreck Scores Heavily among Dining Car Employees," *Catering Industry Employee* 48 (September 12, 1939), 33; *Chicago Defender,* April 10, 1940; Hogans, "ARPW," *Baltimore Afro-American,* December 9, 1939, January 13, 1940.

62. *Chicago Defender,* June 17, 1944.

63. *Michigan Chronicle,* April 20, 1946; *Norfolk Journal and Guide,* September 7, 1946; *Chicago Defender,* June 12, 1948; *Railroad Workers' Link* 1 (June 1947); 1 (July 1947); *Hearings before the Subcommittee to Investigate the Administration of the Internal Security Act and Other Internal Security Laws of the Committee on the Judiciary, on Subversive Influence in the Dining Car and Railroad Food Workers Union,* U.S. Senate, 82nd Congress, 1st sess., July 30, August 6, 10, 20, September 10, 14, and 25, 1951 (hereafter "Subversive Influence in the DCRFWU"), 18–20, 25–31.

64. *Diner* 1 (September 1947), in Colored Trainmen of America Papers, Houston Metropolitan Research Center, Houston, Texas; *Railroad Workers' Link* 1 (January 1947); 1 (February 1947); 1 (June 1947); 1 (July 1947); 2 (September–October 1947); 5 (January–February 1952); 6 (April 1952); *Norfolk Journal and Guide,* September 6, 1947; *Pittsburgh Courier,* September 6, 1947; *Negro Labor News,* October 18, 1947; *New York Times,* March 13, 1949; "Subversive Influence in the DCRFWU."

65. Chateauvert, *Marching Together,* 125–132; Hogans, "ARPW," *Baltimore Afro-American,* March 1, 22, August 23, October 11, 1941, December 12, 1942,

January 27, 1945; "Conference of Pullman Yard Forces and Car Cleaners," *Report of Proceedings of the Fifth Biennial Convention and Twenty-First Anniversary Celebration of the Brotherhood of Sleeping Car Porters, held at Chicago, Illinois, September 16th to 20th, Inclusive, 1946* (n.p., n.d.), 248–285; "This Is the Story," in *Journal: 8th Biennial Convention of the United Transport Service Employees, June 22–23–24–25, 1952, Hotel Manse—Cincinnati, Ohio* (n.p., 1952); *Dining Car Worker* (January 1943), 1; *Minneapolis Spokesman,* January 28, 1944; *Negro Labor News,* September 13, 1947; *Pittsburgh Courier,* February 26, 1944; *Sunday Chicago Bee,* May 25, 1947.

66. Horace R. Cayton, "Railroadmen," *Pittsburgh Courier,* July 26, 1941; George F. McCray, "Labor News," *Sunday Chicago Bee,* January 7, 1945.

67. Edward H. Hines, "A New Day for the Dining Car Worker," *Catering Industry Employee* 47 (October 12, 1938), 44; Matthew Josephson, *Union House, Union Bar: The History of the Hotel and Restaurant Employees and Bartenders International Union, AFL-CIO* (New York: Random House, 1956), 331–332.

4. Independent Black Unionism in Depression and War

1. Ernest Calloway, "Negro Rail Worker Developing a New Awareness of His Problems in the Industry," *Bags & Baggage* 3 (August 1939), 3; John T. Clark to T. Arnold Hill, September 21, 1934, National Urban League Records (hereafter NUL-LC), Series 4A, Box 2, Library of Congress, Washington, D.C.

2. A. Philip Randolph, "The Crisis of Negro Railroad Workers," *American Federationist* 46 (August 1939), 807; H. Roger Grant, *Erie Lackawanna: Death of an American Railroad, 1938–1992* (Stanford, Calif.: Stanford University Press, 1994), 17; Charles S. Johnson, "Negroes in the Railway Industry, Part II," *Phylon* 3 (2nd Quarter 1942), 198; Harry D. Wolf, "Railroads," in Harry A. Millis, ed., *How Collective Bargaining Works: A Survey of Experience in Leading American Industries* (New York: Twentieth Century Fund, 1942), 320–321; Ralph L. Woods, "You and I and the Railroads," *Survey Graphic* 25 (September 1936), 501.

3. Wolf, "Railroads," 321; *Daily Worker,* December 6, 1937; H. M. Douty, "Ferment in the Railroad Unions," *Nation* 135 (November 30, 1932), 526–527; black employment figures from Calloway, "Negro Rail Worker Developing a New Awareness," 3. For somewhat different figures, see Charles S. Johnson, "Negroes in the Railway Industry," *Phylon* 3 (1st Quarter 1942), 5; "Preliminary Summary Statement on the Employment of Negroes on Railroads" (July 21, 1933), NUL-LC, Series 6, Box 89.

4. "Summary, Findings and Directives in Re Illinois Central Railroad Company . . ." in *Records of the Committee on Fair Employment Practice, 1941–1946* (Glen Rock, N.J.: Microfilming Corporation of America, 1971), Reel 10 (hereafter *FEPC Records*).

5. Ibid.; Herbert Northrup, *Organized Labor and the Negro* (New York: Harper & Brothers, 1944), 52–54; Charles Hamilton Houston and Joseph C. Waddy to Committee on Fair Employment Practices, March 30, 1942, in *Papers of the NAACP, Part 13: The NAACP and Labor, 1940–1955, Series A* (Bethesda, Md.:

University Publications of America, 1992) (hereafter *NAACP Papers,* Part 13-A), Reel 10.

6. "Memorandum. Re: Colored Locomotive Firemen" (March 30, 1942), Records of the Brotherhood of Sleeping Car Porters, Library of Congress (hereafter BSCP-LC), Box 66; *Houston Informer and Texas Freeman,* February 6, 1932; Wolf, "Railroads," 318–339; Johnson, "Negroes in the Railway Industry, Part II," 196–200.

7. In Records of the Illinois Central Gulf Railroad Selected Personnel Files, no. 5295, Kheel Center for Labor-Management Documentation and Archives, Cornell University (hereafter IC Papers), Box 8: "Test Rights as Senior Employees," *Memphis World* (1933), Folder 13; J. C. Strickland, Jr., to G. E. Patterson, August 7, 1933, Folder 13; T. S. Jackson to David Hanover and Strickland, Jr., September 27, 1933, Folder 13; "Memorandum, Subject: Complaint made to Mr. Eastman by our colored employees on the Memphis Terminal, and other Southern Territory, May 8, 1934," Folder 12; "Memorandum, Subject: Complaint made to Mr. Eastman by our Colored Yardmen on the Memphis Terminal," Folder 12.

8. Houston and Waddy to Committee on Fair Employment Practices, March 30, 1942; Herbert Northrup, "The Negro in the Railway Unions," *Phylon* 5 (2nd Quarter 1944), 164.

9. "Memorandum. Re: Colored Locomotive Firemen"; Johnston vs. Atchison, Topeka & Santa Fe Railway Company et al., 225 ICC Rep. 519; Houston and Waddy to Committee on Fair Employment Practices, March 30, 1942.

10. Henry R. Lieberman, "White Railroad Firemen Squeeze Negroes, *PM,* November 4, 1941; Suzanne La Follette, "Jim Crow and Casey Jones," *Nation* 155 (December 19, 1942), 675.

11. Hilton Butler, "Murder for the Job," *Nation* 137 (July 12, 1933), 44; *Houston Informer and Texas Freeman,* April 2, 1932; Horace R. Cayton and George S. Mitchell, *Black Workers and the New Unions* (Chapel Hill: University of North Carolina Press, 1939), 439; Lloyd Brown, *Iron City* (New York: Masses and Mainstream, 1951), 163–164. On the "blackhand letter," see Walter White, memorandum: "Re: Killings and Assaults along the Illinois Central Railroad" (April 5, 1932), in John H. Bracey, Jr., and August Meier, eds., *Papers of the NAACP, Part 10. Peonage, Labor, and the New Deal, 1913–1939* (Frederick, Md.: University Publications of America, 1990) (hereafter *NAACP Papers,* Part 10), Reel 22.

12. L. R. Moloy and Clarence Booker to Walter White, February 17, 1932; "Memorandum Re Assaults on Negro Trainmen," June 23, 1932; and Memo to Mr. Wilkins from Mr. White, July 5, 1932, in *NAACP Papers,* Part 10, Reel 22; *Houston Informer and Texas Freeman,* February 27, April 2, 23, June 11, 1932; *Baton Rouge Morning Advocate,* March 13, June 7, 1932; *Chicago Defender,* April 9, 1932, May 28, 1932.

13. On the murder of Scott, see: *Houston Informer and Texas Freeman,* July 23, 1932. On Grant Johnson's and Frank Johnson's deaths, see *Baton Rouge Morning Advocate,* April 30, May 31, 1932, December 24, 25, 27, 1932; *Chicago Defender,* January 7, 21, 1933. On the Johnsons' role as blacks' representatives,

see Grant Johnson, Frank Johnson, and John Taylor to W. Atwill, June 6, 1930, in IC Papers, Box 8, Folder 1.

14. J. L. Harrington to A. D. Caulfield, June 8, 1934, and Jerry Cronin to Stanford, June 4, 1934, in IC Papers, Box 8, Folder 12; Cayton and Mitchell, *Black Workers*, 440–441; Northrup, *Organized Labor and the Negro*, 54–55.

15. Butler, "Murder for the Job," 44; Ira De A. Reid to the Editors, "Negro Firemen," *Nation* 137 (September 6, 1933), 272–273; M. Quigley to W. Atwill, September 28, 1931, in IC Papers, Box 8, Folder 5; L. R. Moloy to Walter White, February 29, 1932, in *NAACP Papers*, Part 10, Reel 22.

16. L. R. Moloy to Walter White, February 29, 1932, *NAACP Papers*, Part 10, Reel 22; *Houston Informer and Texas Freeman*, May 14, 1932; *Baton Rouge Morning Advocate*, May 31, 1932.

17. Walter White to Special Agents' Office, March 3, 1932; T. T. Keliher to Walter White, March 23, 1932, *NAACP Papers*, Part 10, Reel 22.

18. In *NAACP Papers*, Part 10, Reel 22: Nathan R. Margold to Walter White, April 2, 1932; White to Margold, April 5, 1932; Nugent Dodds to White, April 7, 1932; U.S. Attorney Ben F. Cameron to Will Alexander, April 19, 1932.

19. Patricia Sullivan, *Days of Hope: Race and Democracy in the New Deal Era* (Chapel Hill: University of North Carolina Press, 1996), 32; CIC quote from Neil McMillan, *Dark Journey: Black Mississippians in the Age of Jim Crow* (Urbana: University of Illinois Press, 1989), 313. In *NAACP Papers*, Part 10, Reel 22, see Walter White to Will W. Alexander, April 11, 1932; Alexander to White, April 14, 1932; Alexander Fitzhugh to Alexander, April 18, 1932, frame 738; Alexander to White, April 29, 1932; F. C. Willcoxon to Alexander, April 22, 1932.

20. Alexander Fitzhugh to Will W. Alexander, April 18, 1932, in *NAACP Papers*, Part 10, Reel 22; *Baton Route Morning Advocate*, December 24, 25, 1932.

21. *Baton Rouge Morning Advocate*, June 1, 4, 5, 1932; *Chicago Defender*, June 18, 1932; *Houston Informer and Texas Freeman*, July 9, September 3, 1932.

22. Chief Special Agent to W. Atwill, August 25, 1932; Memorandum, July 22, 1937, in IC Papers, Box 8, Folder 21.

23. Memorandum, July 22, 1937; Chief Special Agent to A. Atwill, August 25, 1932, in IC Papers, Box 8, Folder 21.

24. George Royan to T. T. Keliher, September 26, 1932; Chief Special Agent to W. Atwill, October 14, 18, 1932; memorandum, July 22, 1937; Special Agent George Royan to T. T. Keliher, January 18, 1933, in IC Papers, Box 8, Folder 21; Cayton and Mitchell, *Black Workers*, 444.

25. C. A. Tweedy to G. E. Patterson, September 26, 1934; undated memorandum, September 1934; memorandum, July 22, 1937, Box 8, Folder 21; C. R. Young to J. P. Farrell, July 23, 1937; Young to Burch, March 20, 1937, in IC Papers, Box 8, Folder 10.

26. Otto S. Beyer, "Collective Bargaining under the Railway Labor Act," *Labor Information Bulletin* 4 (February 1937), 1–3; P. Harvey Middleton, *Railways and Organized Labor* (Chicago: Railway Business Association, 1941), 73; Leonard A. Lecht, *Experience under Railway Labor Legislation* (New York: Columbia

University Press, 1954), 73–87; Leo Troy, "Labor Representation on American Railways," *Labor History* 2 (Fall 1961), 311–321.

27. Herbert R. Northrup, "The Appropriate Bargaining Unit Question Under the Railway Labor Act," *Quarterly Journal of Economics* 60 (February 1946), 260–261.

28. La Follette, "Jim Crow and Casey Jones"; Henry R. Lieberman, "White Railroad Firemen Squeeze Negroes," *PM,* November 4, 1941; "Preliminary Summary Statement on the Employment of Negroes on Railroads" (July 21, 1933), NUL-LC, Series 6, Box 89.

29. "Re: Colored Locomotive Firemen," (n.d.), 8–10, *FEPC Records,* Reel 10; Willard S. Townsend, "One American Problem and a Possible Solution," in Rayford Logan, ed., *What the Negro Wants* (Chapel Hill: University of North Carolina Press, 1944), 180–181; Daniel Benjamin, "'I've Been Working on the Railroad' . . ." *March of Labor* 2 (September 1950), 9.

30. Willard S. Townsend, "Townsend Hits Railroads Defiance of the FEPC," *Sunday Chicago Bee,* December 26, 1943; Townsend, "One American Problem," 181.

31. Colored Trainmen of America, "Ritual and All Secret Works. Effective Sept. 23, 1929 (n.p., n.d.), in Colored Trainmen of America Papers, Houston Metropolitan Research Center, Houston Public Library, Houston, Texas (hereafter CTA-HMRC).

32. B. G. McCullough to J. E. Callahan, April 5, 1923; T. P. Mock to Will Childs, April 24, 1923, and Mock to Jim Burnett, April 24, 1923, Box 2580, Folder 4; "Investigation Conducted at Harlingen, Texas, April 22, 1934, in connection with improper flagging on part of Brakeman Nelson Moore . . . ," Box 2580, Folder 8, in Colored Trainmen of America Collection, Southern Labor Archives/Special Collections Department, Pullen Library, Georgia State University (hereafter CTA-GSU); Damon McCrary to J. G. Irvin, February 24, 1939, in Box 1, CTA-HMRC. For similar efforts by the Association of Colored Railway Trainmen, see S. H. Clark to R. A. Nelson, September 10, 1946; Clark to A. J. Graham, September 20, 1946; Clark to Mr. Johnson, January 25, 1949, in Samuel H. Clark Papers, Library of Congress, Washington, D.C.

33. Superintendent to J. H. Morrison, December 6, 1918, Box 2580, Folder 1; Assistant Superintendent to J. D. Patrick, November 2, 1921, Box 2580, Folder 2; James Johnston to A. Moseley, February 16, 1922, Box 2580, Folder 3, CTA-GSU; Rufus Reed to Willie Jefferson, March 2, 1936, in Box 1940s, CTA-HMRC.

34. J. D. Patrick to W. H. Jefferson, November 17, 1937, in Box 1, Folder 1937, CTA-HMRC.

35. *Grand Lodge Proceedings of the Twelfth Annual Convention of the Association of Colored Railway Trainmen Held at Knoxville, Tennessee, July 15, 1929* (n.p., n.d.), 9–10, in the Department of Labor Library, Washington, D.C.

36. Local no. 36, NFRR Workers to J. F. Porterfield, August 12, 1931, Box 8, Folder 3, IC Papers.

37. Thomas D. Redd to Walker D. Hines et al. February 9, 1920, in James Gross

man, ed., *Black Workers in the Era of the Great Migration, 1916–1929* (Frederick, Md.: University Microfilms of America, 1985), Reel 10. In IC papers, Box 8, see: J. M. Egan to A. E. Clift, October 8, 1922 (Folder 3); Memorandum: Conference, Tuesday, July 15, 1924 (Folder 3); J. M. Egan to G. E. Patterson, January 23, 1929 (Folder 1).

38. In IC Papers, Box 8: Thomas D. Redd to A. E. Clift, July 30, 1920 (Folder 1); Redd to Clift, May 6, 1921 (Folder 1); "Memorandum: Conference, Tuesday, July 15, 1924 (Folder 3); J. M. Egan to Clift, October 8, 1922 (Folder 3); L. W. Fairchild to W. Atwill, November 21, 1931 (Folder 5); Atwill to Fairchild, November 23, 1931 (Folder 5). See also "Association of Colored Railway Trainmen and Locomotive Firemen," in Florence Murray, ed., *The Negro Handbook* (New York: Wendell Malliot and Co., 1942), 138–139.

39. Thomas D. Redd to Charles H. Markham, June 13, 1924; Redd to J. J. Pelley, February 22, 1924; J. M. Egan to A. E. Clift, October 8, 1922, in IC Papers, Box 8, Folder 3.

40. In IC Papers, Box 8: J. M. Egan to G. E. Patterson, January 23, 1929 (Folder 1); Memorandum Conference, July 21, 1930 (Folder 3); "Subjects for Discussion at Conference, Mr. Atwill with Brakeman T. D. Redd, Monday, July 21, 1930" (Folder 3); Redd to W. Atwill, June 27, 1930 (Folder 3); Redd to L. A. Downs, January 22, 1932 (Folder 3); IC Kentucky division colored trainmen and switchmen, Petition, May 18, 1928 (Folder 1).

41. Thomas Redd to Chas. Markham, August 25, 1922, in IC Papers, Box 8, Folder 3.

42. Claude A. Barnett to T. Arnold Hill, February 6, 1935, NUL-LC, Series 4A, Box 2; *Chicago Defender*, February 17, 1934.

43. Thomas D. Redd, "Get Together Meeting In Chicago, Illinois, Louisville, Ky., July 6th, 1934," in CTA-GSU, Box 2580, Folder 9; "Proceedings of the 'Get Together Gathering' of Representatives of the Organized Groups of Colored Railway Workers of America," September 18, 1934, in *Claude A. Barnett Papers, Subject Files on Black Americans, 1918–1967, Series C, Economic Conditions, 1918–1966, Part 3* (Frederick, Md.: University Publications of America, 1986), Reel 9; *Chicago Defender*, February 17, September 1, 8, 15, 1934.

44. John Clark to T. Arnold Hill, October 31, 1934, NUL-LC, Series 4A, Box 2; "The International Association of Railway Employees. Action in Washington, D.C., Nov. 5, 1934. To the Honorable J. B. Eastman," in "Minutes. Colored Trainmen of America . . . January 13th, 1935," in CTA-GSU, Box 2580, Folder 10; *California Eagle*, September 28, November 2, 1934; *Chicago Defender*, September 1, 8, 22, November 10, 1934; *Seattle Northwest Enterprise*, November 22, 1934. The initial name, the National Association of Railway Employees, was changed to International Association of Railway Employees as the result of the affiliation of a Canadian organization.

45. *Chicago Defender*, September 15, 1934; *Detroit Tribune Independent*, September 29, 1934; *Pittsburgh Courier*, September 29, 1934; Claude A. Barnett to T. Arnold Hill, March 25, 1936, in *Claude A. Barnett Papers*, Series C, Part 3, Reel 9.

46. *Pittsburgh Courier*, September 29, 1934; Leyton Weston, "Railway Employees'

Convention," *Catering Industry Employee* 43 (December 12, 1934), 27; *Chicago Defender*, November 10, 1934; "Minutes of the Meeting of the National Association of Railway Employees, Washington, D.C., November 5, 1934," pp. 6–8, in CTA-GSU. On Oxley, see *Baltimore Afro-American*, April 2, 1938.

47. *Chicago Defender*, January 26, 1935.

48. *Chicago Defender*, April 27, 1935.

49. *Detroit Tribune-Independent*, December 29, 1934.

50. *Black Dispatch*, August 13, 1936.

51. Thomas D. Redd to W. H. Davis, June 9, 1933; Redd to T. S. Jackson, July 7, 1933; Jackson to Redd, July 27, 1933, Nelson M. Willis to W. Atwill, April 16, 1934; Redd to T. A. Downs, March 2, 1934; Willis to G. E. Patterson, May 18, 1934; Willis to Atwill, April 16, 1934; Patterson to Willis, May 21, 1934; Office Memorandum—Petition for Mandamus, September 19, 1936; *Louisville Lodge no. 10, Association of Colored Railway Trainmen, vs. National Railroad Adjustment Board, First Division, no. 45687, In the District Court of the United States for the Northern District of Illinois, Eastern Division*, Petition for Mandamus, August 29, 1936, in IC Papers, Box 8, Folder 11.

52. Nelson M. Willis to National Railroad Adjustment Board, First Division, June 7, 1935; Office Memorandum—Petition for Mandamus, September 19, 1936, in IC Papers, Box 8, Folder 11.

53. Petition for Mandamus, August 29, 1936, and Brief for Petitioner, January 21, 1937, Case no. 45687, *Louisville Lodge no. 10, Association of Colored Railway Trainmen, vs. National Railroad Adjustment Board, First Division*, Records of the District Courts of the United States, Northern District of Illinois Eastern Division at Chicago, Record Group 21, National Archives and Records Administration, Great Lakes Region, Chicago; *Chicago Defender*, January 16, 1937.

54. Motion to Dismiss, November 9, 1936, and Memorandum, February 8, 1937, Case no. 45687, *Louisville Lodge no. 10, Association of Colored Railway Trainmen, vs. National Railroad Adjustment Board, First Division*, RG 21.

55. Roy Wilkins to Walter White, April 26, 1939; Wilkins to Thurgood Marshall, May 12, 1939, and Memorandum: Wilkins to Marshall, May 5, 1939; Memorandum: White to Marshall, May 18, 1939; Leyton Weston to White, May 31, 1939, *NAACP Papers*, Part 10, Reel 7; *Oklahoma City Black Dispatch*, May 14, 1938; *Houston Informer and Texas Freeman*, July 22, 1939; *Negro Labor News*, May 27, 1939.

56. A. Philip Randolph to Sir and Brother, August 20, 1941, in BSCP-LC, Box 66; "Unions Causing Negroes to Lose Jobs," *Claude A. Barnett Papers*, Series C, Part 3, Reel 9; W. S. Gandy to Louis Nelson, W. H. Jefferson, and C. L. Williams, April 7, 1939, in Box 1, Folder 1939, and Damon McCrary to F. C. Caldwell, March 30, 1939, in Box 1, Folder 1937, CTA-HMRC.

57. Hobart T. Taylor, Jr., "C. W. Rice—Labor Leader" (BA thesis, Prairie View State Normal and Industrial College, Prairie View, Texas, May 1939), 21–24; *Negro Labor News*, March 2, 1940. On black protest during the World War I era, see Steven A. Reich, "Soldiers of Democracy: Black Texans and the Fight for Citizenship, 1917–1921," *Journal of American History* 82 (March 1996), 1482, 1490, 1504.

58. C. W. Rice, "As I See It," *Negro Labor News,* November 12, 1938, March 18, 1939; Taylor, "C. W. Rice," 25–31.

59. C. W. Rice, "As I See It," *Negro Labor News,* July 17, 1934, July 31, 1937, February 13, 1943, July 30, 1938, September 11, 1937; Taylor, "C. W. Rice," 34–35.

60. C. W. Rice, "As I See It," *Negro Labor News,* December 20, 1941, May 18, July 27, 1940; Rice to Paul Kayser, February 8, 1954, in C. W. Rice Papers, Box 1, Folder 4, Houston Metropolitan Research Center, Houston Public Library.

61. C. W. Rice, "As I See It," *Negro Labor News,* October 23, 1937, April 23, 1938.

62. C. W. Rice, "As I See It," *Negro Labor News,* October 1, 1938, February 3, 1940, April 6, 1940, September 3, 1938, June 26, 1937; *Negro Labor News,* October 9, 1937; Taylor, "C. W. Rice," 55.

63. Taylor, "C. W. Rice," 28, 31, 37, 55; *Houston Informer and Texas Freeman,* May 29, 1937.

64. C. W. Rice, "As I See It," *Negro Labor News,* March 6, 1943, April 6, 1940; *Houston Informer and Texas Freeman,* April 17, May 17, 29, 1937, May 6, 1939, August 21, 1943. On black opposition to Rice, see Ernest Obadele-Starks, *Black Unionism in the Industrial South* (College Station: Texas A&M University Press, 2000), 28–29, 32, 90.

65. *Negro Labor News,* April 9, November 12, 1938, December 23, 1939; *Houston Informer and Texas Freeman,* May 16, 1936.

66. "Outstanding Labor Events 1940–41: Texas Railroad Coach Cleaners' Case: 1940," in Florence Murray, ed., *The Negro Handbook* (New York: Wendall Malliot and Co., 1942), 139–140; *Negro Labor News,* December 18, 1937, April 9, September 17, December 10, 1938, November 11, 1939, January 20, April 6, 1940; *Oklahoma City Black Dispatch,* August 6, September 3, 10, 1938; *Houston Informer and Texas Freeman,* April 9, 13, 1938; *Baltimore Afro-American,* June 11, 1938.

67. *Houston Informer and Texas Freeman,* December 17, 1938; "Outstanding Labor Events 1940–41," 139–140; court decision quoted in "Memorandum re: Rights of Colored Railway Employees against Discriminatory . . . ," in Charles Hamilton Houston Papers, Moorland Spingarn Research Center, Howard University, Washington, D.C. (hereafter CHH Papers), Box 163–21, Folder 18, p. 25.

68. *Houston Informer and Texas Freeman,* April 13, 1938.

69. *Negro Labor News,* October 9, 1937, July 16, 1938; *Houston Informer and Texas Freemen,* July 9, 1938.

70. *Negro Labor News,* May 13, December 23, 1939; *Houston Informer and Texas Freeman,* June 24, December 23, 1939; *Negro Labor News,* November 25, 1928.

71. *Negro Labor News,* September 11, 1937, November 12, 1938; *Houston Informer and Texas Freeman,* October 28, 1939, December 16, 1950; Gilbert Mers, *Working the Waterfront: The Ups and Downs of a Rebel Longshoreman* (Austin: University of Texas Press, 1988), 88–149.

72. Statement of C. W. Rice, "Proposed Amendments to the National Labor Relations Act," *Hearings before the Committee on Labor,* House of Representatives,

76th Congress, 1st sess., vol. 4 (Washington, D.C.: GPO, 1939), 1441–1442; *Negro Labor News,* June 24, July 8, 1939, March 6, 1943; *Black Worker* 10 (December 1944), 1, 4. On earlier advocacy of minority representation, see J. A. Reynolds to Walter White, December 18, 1936, in *NAACP Papers,* Part 10, Reel 7.

73. *Chicago Defender,* February 1, 1930; *Black Worker* 10 (December 1944), 4; *Seattle Northwest Enterprise,* November 3, 1939.

74. C. W. Rice, "As I See It," *Negro Labor News,* April 20, 1940; Randolph, "Crisis of Negro Railroad Workers," 818–819.

75. Randolph, "Crisis of Negro Railroad Workers," 815; Houston and Waddy to Committee on Fair Employment Practices, March 30, 1942, in *NAACP Papers,* Part 13-A, Reel 10; *Black Worker* 9 (October 1943), 1, 4.

76. *Houston Informer and Texas Freeman,* March 25, 1939; *Negro Labor News,* April 1, 1939; Ernest Calloway, "Negro Railroad Workers to Meet in Washington," *Chicago Defender,* May 6, 1939; *Washington Afro-American,* May 13, 27, 1939; Calloway, "Attend National Conference of Negro Railroad Workers," *Chicago Defender,* May 27, 1939; *Negro Labor News,* May 27, 1939; *Michigan Chronicle,* June 1, 1939; Calloway, "Rail Labor Prepares for the Future," *Chicago Defender,* June 30, 1939.

77. *Chicago Defender,* April 12, 1941; "Report of Proceedings of the Conference for Colored Locomotive Firemen," March 28 and 29, 1941, in CHH Papers, Box 163-22, Folder 22, p. 8.

78. A. Philip Randolph, "To the American People," March 22, 1941, *NAACP Papers,* Part 13, Reel 10; "Report of Proceedings of the Conference for Colored Locomotive Firemen," 9, 22, 24, 28, 31, 46; *Black Worker* 7 (March 1941), 1.

79. Virginia Blanton, "The Negro—Friend or Foe of Organized Labor?" *Catering Industry Employee* 44 (June 12, 1935), 22.

5. The Rise of the Red Caps

1. *Bags & Baggage* 3 (December 1940), 4; Frank Crosswaith, "Trade Unionism and the Negro," *Bags & Baggage* 4 (January 1941), 4.

2. *Bags & Baggage* 3 (December 1940), 4.

3. Ibid.; 4 (January 1941), 1, 2, 4.

4. *Baltimore Afro-American,* October 12, 1940; *Bags & Baggage* 3 (November 1940), 1–3; 4 (January 1941), 2; on additional cases, see *Bags & Baggage* 4 (May 1941), 1; 4 (July 1941), 3; 5 (March 1942), 4; 5 (October 1942), 4; *CIO News* (UTSEA ed.) 6 (May 10, 1943), 2; see also Tom O'Connor, "Redcaps Fight for End of Check System," *PM,* September 30, 1940.

5. *Bags & Baggage* 1 (September 1937), 4.

6. George W. Stevens, *The Land of the Dollar* (1897; rpt. Freeport, N.Y.: Books for Libraries Press, 1971), 48; William Chambers, *Things as They Are in America* (1854; rpt. New York: Negro Universities Press, 1968), 333–334.

7. George Augustus Sala, *America Revisited: From the Bay of New York to the Gulf of Mexico and from Lake Michigan to the Pacific,* 3rd ed. (London: Vizetelly & Co., 1883), vol. 2, 25–27, 104–106, 115, 153; Jeffrey Richards and John M.

MacKenzie, *The Railway Station: A Social History* (Oxford: Oxford University Press, 1986), 234–235; Max O'Rell, *A Frenchman in America: Recollections of Men and Things* (New York: Cassell Publishing Co., 1891), 86.

8. *Railroad Gazette,* May 15, 1896, 342; "Free Attendant Service" (Chicago, 1899), quoted in H. Roger Grant, "Experiencing the 'Best of Everything': Passenger Service on the Chicago and Northwestern Railway," *Railroad History,* Bulletin 169 (Autumn 1993), 40; James H. Hogans, "Among Railroad and Pullman Workers: Personality of the Week," *Baltimore Afro-American,* October 9, 1937 (Hogans' column is hereafter referred to as Hogans, "ARPW"); *Washington Afro-American,* October 22, 1938.

9. *Washington Afro-American,* November 26, 1938; *Baltimore Afro-American,* March 26, 1938; David Marshall, *Grand Central* (New York: Whittlesey House/McGraw-Hill Book Co., 1946), 88–91; T. Wilbur Winchester, "History of Red Cap," *Bags & Baggage* 1 (August 1937), 6; Reginald A. Johnson, "Red Caps Seek a Living Wage," *Opportunity* 17 (April 1939), 105; Ann Ford, "Ph.D.s Carry Your Bags," *Ken Magazine,* August 15, 1938, reprinted in Ernest Calloway, ed., "The Birth of a Union: What the Press of the Nation Has to Say about the New Red Cap" (Chicago: Educational Department, UTSEA, October 1, 1940); Leonard J. Kane, "America's First Red Cap," *Negro Digest* 5 (March 1947), 22; *Michigan Chronicle,* November 16, 1946; *Nashville Globe,* May 22, 1936, in *Tuskegee Institute News Clippings File* (Tuskegee, Ala.: Division of Behavioral Science Research, Carver Research Foundation, Tuskegee Institute, 1976) (hereafter *TINCF*), Reel 52; John L. Yancey, "Red Caps' Struggle for Employee Status," *American Federationist* 46 (March 1939), 259; Testimony of Willard S. Townsend, in the Supreme Court of the United States, October Term, 1944, no. 171, *Willard Saxby Townsend, et al., vs. The New York Central Railroad Company, et al.,* "Petition for a Writ of Certiorari to the United States Circuit Court of Appeals for the Seventh Circuit and Brief in Support Thereof," 7; St. Clair Drake and Horace R. Cayton, *Black Metropolis: A Study of Negro Life in a Northern City* (1945; rpt. New York: Harcourt, Brace & World, 1970), vol. 1, 237; "Red-Cap Chief's Career Ends," *Negro Railway Labor News* 1 (June–July, 1948), 2, in *Blacks in the Railroad Industry: Papers, 1946–1954* (New York: Schomburg Center for Research in Black Culture, New York Public Library, 1995); Before the Interstate Commerce Commission, no. 28842, In the Matter of Filing of a Tariff by the Dayton Union Railway Company Covering Its Charges for Red Cap Service, Brief of Respondent (December 14, 1942), 6.

10. *William* [sic] *Saxby Townsend, et al., vs. The New York Central Railroad Company, et al.,* U.S. Circuit Court of Appeals, Seventh Circuit, no. 8177, December 16, 1942, Transcript of Record (hereafter *Townsend v. New York Central,* Transcript), 129, 76–77; *Bags & Baggage* 2 (May 1938), 3; *New York Age,* August 9, 1919, July 21, 1923; *Louisiana Weekly,* October 1, 1927; Hogans, "ARPW," *Baltimore Afro-American,* August 15, 1936; *Baltimore Afro-American,* October 9, 1937; "PRR, Part Two," *Brown American* 1 (December 1936), 8.

11. U.S. Department of Labor, Wage and Hour Division, Research and Statistics

Branch, "Redcaps in Railway Terminals under the Fair Labor Standards Act, 1938–1941," April 1942, 5, 7 (Transcript at Department of Labor Library, Washington, D.C.).

12. U.S. Department of Labor, Wage and Hour Division, "Wages, Hours and Working Conditions of Recaps in Western Railway Terminals" (hereafter "Redcaps in Western Railway Terminals"), November 1941, 24 (typescript at Department of Labor Library); Howard A. Kroker, "Seattle Race Relations during the Second World War," *Pacific Northwest Quarterly* 67 (October 1976), 163; *Northwest Enterprise,* December 2, 1942; Hogans, "ARPW," *Baltimore Afro-American,* March 7, 1942; *Black Dispatch,* January 28, 1937; "Redcaps in Railway Terminals, 1938–1941," 12. See also *Bags & Baggage* 2 (April 1938), 1; 3 (December 1940), 1; 5 (February 1942), 1.

13. No title, *Crisis,* 2 (July 1911), 98; *New York Age,* December 30, 1915; "Redcaps in Railway Terminals, 1938–1941," 12.

14. *New York Age,* July 6, 1918, July 21, August 14, 1923; Drake and Cayton, *Black Metropolis,* 239; Horace Cayton, "The UTSEA in Action and Problems Facing the Freight Handlers," *Bags & Baggage* 4 (June 1941), 4; "Redcaps in Railway Terminals, 1938–1941," 10; Ford, "Ph.D.s Carry Your Bags"; *Chicago Defender,* October 20, 1934; Marshall, *Grand Central,* 89.

15. Drake and Cayton, *Black Metropolis,* 242; Hogans, "ARPW," *Baltimore Afro-American,* October 9, 1937; *Baltimore Afro-American,* January 6, 1945.

16. Drake and Cayton, *Black Metropolis,* 239; author's interview with Leon Despres, December 20, 1994, Chicago.

17. "Redcaps in Railway Terminals, 1938–1941," 12–13.

18. *Nashville Globe,* May 22, 1936, in *TINCF,* Reel 52; *New York Age,* August 14, 1923.

19. "PRR, Part Two," *Brown American* 1 (December 1936), 7; E. C. Robinson, "Railroads Share Red Caps' Tips," *Bags & Baggage* 4 (July 1941), 8; *Boston Guardian,* July 6, 1946.

20. Johnson, "Red Caps Seek a Living Wage," 105; *New York Age,* December 30, 1915, August 9, 1919.

21. Allan S. A. Titley, "Red Caps, Old and New," *Messenger* 10 (January 1928), 8, 22; Allan S. A. Titley, "Slaves of Grand Central Terminal," *Messenger* 9 (October 1927), 295–296; *Louisiana Weekly,* October 1, 1927; *Townsend v. New York Central,* Transcript, 245–246. On comparable conditions in the West, see Charles L. Upton, "Railroad Clatter," *California Eagle,* December 12, 1930.

22. *Townsend v. New York Central,* Transcript, 142, 75; *Detroit Tribune,* September 4, 1937; *Negro Labor News,* September 11, 1932; *Washington Afro-American,* October 22, 1938; Johnson, "Red Caps Seek a Living Wage," 105; *Bags & Baggage* 4 (July 1941), 8; 1 (August 1937), 1.

23. *New York Age,* August 9, 1919; Patricia W. Romero, "Willard Townsend and the International Brotherhood of Red Caps" (master's thesis, Miami University, Oxford, Ohio, 1965), 39–40; Labor Union Survey, January 17, 1928, National Urban League Records (hereafter NUL-LC), Series 6, Research Department, Early Surveys, Box 80; *Baltimore Afro-American,* October 16, 1920, in *TINCF,* Reel 26.

24. *Baltimore Afro-American,* October 16, 1926, in *TINCF,* Reel 26; Allan S. A. Titley, "Red Caps, Old and New," *Messenger* 10 (January 1928), 8, 22; Titley, "Slaves of Grand Central Terminal," *Messenger* 9 (October 1927), 295–296; *Louisiana Weekly,* October 1, 1927; *Townsend v. New York Central,* Transcript, 245–246; George S. Schuyler, "Meet a New CIO Union," *Bags & Baggage* 5 (August 1942), 2; *Bags & Baggage* 5 (July 1942), 4.

25. *New York Age,* July 6, 1918, July 13, 1916, July 21, 1923, March 15, 1917; *Chicago Defender,* October 17, 1914, January 25, 1930; *Washington Tribune,* July 16, August 13, 1921.

26. *New York Age,* July 21, 1923; *Chicago Defender,* February 13, 1926, January 8, May 28, 1927, May 24, December 13, 27, 1930, October 20, 1934, July 6, 1935, February 22, 29, 1936.

27. In *Illinois Central Magazine:* 22 (December 1933), 8; 22 (November 1933), 5; 23 (April 1936), 12; 24 (October 1938), 8.

28. In *Illinois Central Magazine:* 28 (May 1, 1940), 11–12; 23 (July 1934), 18; *Chicago Defender,* October 20, 1934; *Black Dispatch,* February 26, 1938; *Chicago Defender,* June 18, 1938; *Bags & Baggage* 1 (August 1937), 1; 1 (September 1937), 1.

29. *Bags & Baggage* 3 (January 1940), 3; *Townsend v. New York Central,* Transcript, 299; *Washington Afro-American,* October 22, 1938; "Redcaps in Railway Terminals, 1938–1941," 18; Lester B. Granger to Earl A. Williams, December 1, 1934; Martin L. Sweeney to Joseph B. Eastman, August 21, 1933; Red Caps Association to Frances Perkins, November 20, 1933, in NUL-LC, Series IV, Industrial Relations Department, General Department File, Box 8.

30. Kenyon T. Burke to T. Arnold Hill, October 13, 1934; Burke to T. Arnold Hill, November 11, 1934, in NUL-LC, Series IV, Industrial Relations Department, General Department File, Box 3; "This Is the Story," *8th Biennial Convention of the United Transport Service Employees Convention Journal, June 22–23–24–25, 1952, Hotel Manse, Cincinnati, Ohio* (n.d., n.p.); Hogans, "ARPW," *Baltimore Afro-American,* October 16, 1937, February 12, 1938.

31. *Black Dispatch,* January 28, 1937; "Chicago Red Caps Form Interracial Body . . ." *Claude A. Barnett Papers, Subject files on Black Americans, 1918–1967: Series C, Economic Conditions, 1918–1966, Part Three* (Frederick, Md.: University Publications of America, 1986) (hereafter *CAB Papers,* Series C, Part 3), Reel 9); *Houston Informer and Texas Freeman,* January 30, 1937; Samuel Enders Warren, "The Negro in the American Labor Movement" (Ph.D. diss., University of Wisconsin, 1941), 490.

32. J. T. Whitney, "Red Caps of Nation Convene in Chicago," *CAB Papers,* Series C, Part 3, Reel 9; *Houston Informer and Texas Freeman,* May 29, 1937; *Bags & Baggage* 1 (September 1937), 3; Gene Morgan, "Red Cap Brotherhood Meets, Laments Decline of Tipping," *Chicago Daily News,* May 19, 1937; Drake and Cayton, *Black Metropolis,* 238.

33. "Chicago Red-caps Look to Future," *Railway Clerk* 40 (January 1941), 28; *Chicago Labor Leader* (March 1941); author's interview with Leon Despres; Cayton and Drake, *Black Metropolis,* 240–242; "This Is the Story."

34. Author's interview with Leon Despres; *Bags & Baggage* 1 (September 1937), 3, 4; Warren, "The Negro in the American Labor Movement," 491.

35. Herbert R. Northrup, *Organized Labor and the Negro* (New York: Harper & Brothers Publishers, 1944), 83; *Bags & Baggage* 1 (September 1937), 4; Willard Townsend, John Yancey, Jr., and Ernest Calloway, "'We Accuse!' An Open Letter to President William Green," July 1, 1940, in Papers of the Brotherhood of Sleeping Car Porters, Library of Congress, Washington, D.C., Box 138.

36. *Bags & Baggage* 1 (October 1937), 1; 1 (December 1937), 1; 2 (May 1938), 1, 3; "This Is the Story"; Romero, "Willard Townsend," 55.

37. Author's interview with Leon Despres; Brailsford R. Brazeal, *The Brotherhood of Sleeping Car Porters: Its Origin and Development* (New York: Harper & Brothers, 1946), 226–227; Romero, "Willard Townsend," 49; *Washington Afro-American*, May 29, 1937.

38. "This Is the Story." Townsend quoted in P. L. Prattis, "Labor Everywhere," *Pittsburgh Courier*, September 14, 1946.

39. P. L. Prattis, "Labor Everywhere," *Pittsburgh Courier*, September 14, 1946; author's interview with Leon Despres; author's interview with Truman Gibson, December 15, 1994; author's interview with Ike Golden, April 13, 1995, Washington, D.C.; "This Is the Story"; *Negro Labor News*, September 13, 1947; Horace R. Cayton, "Railroadmen: Besieged by Two Rival Unions—Randolph, Townsend Should Agree," *Pittsburgh Courier*, July 26, 1941, in *CAB Papers*, Series C, Part 3, Reel 9; Romero, "Willard Townsend," 130, 61; "Report of the International Executive Board Rendered at the Fourth Biennial Convention of the Brotherhood of Sleeping Car Porters . . . held at Cleveland, Ohio, September 17 to 22, Inclusive, 1944," 35 (copy in Department of Labor Library, Washington, D.C.).

40. *Chicago Defender*, December 11, 1937; *Black Dispatch*, December 18, 1937; *Bags & Baggage* 1 (December 1937), 1; Hogans, "ARPW," *Baltimore Afro-American*, January 15, 1938.

41. *Bags & Baggage* 1 (December 1937), 3; 2 (April 1938), 1; *Chicago Defender*, January 22, 1938; *Detroit Tribune*, January 29, 1938; *Black Dispatch*, February 5, 1938; "Proceedings National Conference of Red Caps. Chicago, Illinois. January 14, 15, 16, 1938," in *The Papers of A. Philip Randolph* (Bethesda, Md.: University Publications of America, 1990), Reel 11; Hogans, "ARPW," *Baltimore Afro-American*, January 29, 1938. For a biographical sketch of Lee, see Hogans, "For Railroad Workers," *Baltimore Afro-American*, January 30, 1943.

42. *Chicago Tribune*, March 3, 1940; "Willard Saxby Townsend" in Gary Fink, ed., *Biographical Dictionary of American Labor* (Westport, Conn.: Greenwood Press, 1984), 554–555; *Baltimore Afro-American*, November 28, 1942; *Proceedings of the Fourth Biennial Convention of the United Transport Service Employees of America, CIO, May 17, 18, 19, 1944, Chicago, Illinois* (n.p., n.d.), 69; author's interview with Ike Golden, April 13, 1995. On the displacement of black dining car waiters on the Canadian National Railway, see *St. Paul Echo*, July 17, 1926, in *TINCF*, Reel 26; Hogans, "Things Seen, Heard and Done among Pullman Employees," *New York Age*, Aug. 14, 1926, in *TINCF*, Reel 26.

43. Harold L. Keith, "Willard S. Townsend, Boss of the Redcaps," *Pittsburgh Courier*, February 16, 1957; Lester B. Granger, "Phylon Profile, II: Willard S. Townsend," *Phylon* 5 (1944), 331; Rayford W. Logan and Michael Winston, *Dictionary of American Negro Biography* (New York: W. W. Norton Co., 1982),

600; "Willard Townsend Dies," *American Federationist* 64 (March 1957), 19; author's interview with Leon Despres.

44. "Willard S. Townsend, Red-Cap's President, Elected to CIO Executive Board Membership," *Railroad Review* 3 (July 1942), 1, in *Records of the Committee on Fair Employment Practice, 1941–1946* (hereafter *FEPC Records*) (Glen Rock, N.J.: Microfilming Corporation of America, 1971), Reel 10; *Sunday Chicago Bee,* May 6, June 3, 1945, July 13, 1947; *Pittsburgh Courier,* December 22, 1945; *Chicago Tribune, March 3, 1940; Pittsburgh Courier,* May 3, 1947, May 13, 1950; *Chicago Defender,* August 30, September 6, 1952; *Atlanta Daily World,* December 25, 1944; "Willard Townsend Dies," *American Federationist* 65 (March 1957), 19.

45. John L. Yancey, "A Human Document," *Interracial Review* 17 (December 1944), 183–184; *Sunday Chicago Bee,* March 16, May 4, 1947; *Bags & Baggage* 2 (October 1938), 4; *Fourth Biennial Convention,* 126.

46. Yancey, "Human Document," 184; *Sunday Chicago Bee,* April 8, September 3, 1945; *Negro Labor News,* April 30, 1949; Yancey, "Anti-Discrimination in C.I.O.," *Interracial Review* 18 (June 1945), 88–90.

47. Biographical sketch in "Introduction to the Papers of Ernest Calloway (1909–1989), Addenda, 1932–1980," Western Historical Manuscript Collection, University of Missouri–St. Louis.

48. Ernest Hays Calloway, "The Negro in the Kentucky Coal Fields," *Opportunity* 12 (March 1934), 84–86; Calloway, "A Labor Study (South)," *Opportunity* 12 (June 1934), 181–182.

49. *Bags & Baggage* (July 1942), 2; (June 1941), 2; author's interview with Leon Despres.

50. *Bags & Baggage* 1 (August 1937), 1, 7.

51. Ernest Calloway, "The Red Caps' Struggle for a Livelihood" (Part 1), *Opportunity* 18 (June 1940), 175; *Bags & Baggage* 1 (August 1937), 1; "Redcaps in Railway Terminals, 1938–1941," 15; Warren, "The Negro in the American Labor Movement," 494.

52. *Bags & Baggage* 1 (August 1937), 7; 1 (December 1937), 1; 2 (April 1938), 2; *Chicago Defender,* December 4, 1937; Johnson, "Red Caps Seek a Living Wage," 106; *Black Dispatch,* December 18, 1937.

53. "Redcaps in Railway Terminals, 1938–1941," 15–17; *Black Dispatch,* December 18, 1937; *Bags & Baggage* 1 (December 1937), 1; 2 (April 1938), 2; 2 (October 1938), 1; *Chicago Defender,* December 4, 1937, February 26, June 25, October 15, 1938, April 22, 1939; *Minneapolis Spokesman,* July 1, October 21, 1938; John Yancey, "Our Right to Live" (mimeograph, Educational Department, UTSEA) in Department of Labor Library, Washington, D.C.; Calloway, "Red Caps' Struggle for a Livelihood," 176. The 1938 ICC decision applied to red caps working in cities with a population over 100,000; in April 1939, the ICC extended the definition to include those in cities of fewer than 100,000. *Chicago Defender,* April 22, 1939.

54. Author's interview with Leon Despres; Calloway, "Labor" column, *Chicago Defender,* May 27, 1939; *Bags & Baggage* 1 (August 1937), 1–2; 1 (October 1937), 1; Calloway, "Red Caps' Struggle for a Livelihood," 175–176.

55. *California Eagle,* July 2, 1937; *Bags & Baggage* 1 (August 1937), 3; *Black Dis-*

patch, July 22, 1937. See also "Redcaps in Railway Terminals, 1938–1941," 18; Ernest Calloway's "Labor" column in the *Chicago Defender,* May 20, July 1, September 16, 1939; *Bags & Baggage* 3 (August 1939), 1.

56. *Bags & Baggage* 1 (September 1937), 1–2.

57. *Townsend v. New York Central,* Transcript, 159–162; *Black Dispatch,* February 26, 1938; *Chicago Defender,* June 18, 1938, July 8, 15, 1939; *Illinois Central Magazine* 28 (March 1940), 13; author's interview with Leon Despres; Warren, "The Negro in the American Labor Movement," 498.

58. On the FLSA, see "The Fair Labor Standards Act of 1938," *Labor Information Bulletin* 5 (July 1938), 1–5; "Backers of Wage-Hour Bill Ready for Fight to Force Its Passage," *Bags & Baggage* 2 (May 1938), 4; Elmer F. Andrews, "A New Deal for Negro Workers," *Opportunity* 17 (June 1939), 166–167.

59. *Townsend v. New York, Central,* Transcript, 80–82, 282, 575–576; "Redcaps in Railway Terminals, 1938–1941," 19–21; *Bags & Baggage* 3 (January 1940), 5; "Red Caps," *Brown American* 3 (August 1939), 7–8; *Chicago Bee,* November 13 1938, in *TINCF,* Reel 58; *Minneapolis Spokesman,* November 11, 1938; *Washington Afro-American,* November 5, 19, 1938.

60. *Townsend v. New York Central,* Transcript, 38; *Black Dispatch,* November 12, 26, 1938; *Baltimore Afro-American,* November 22, 1938; *Atlanta Daily World,* November 14, 1938; *Chicago Defender,* December 3, 1938, June 24, July 8, 1939; John L. Yancey, "Red Caps' Struggle for Employee Status," *American Federationist* 46 (March 1939), 260–263; Johnson, "Red Caps Seek a Living Wage," 106–107; *Minneapolis Spokesman,* February 10, 1939; *California Eagle,* March 3, 1939; *Northwest Enterprise,* June 16, 1939; *Houston Informer and Texas Freeman,* July 8, 1939; *Washington Afro-American,* July 8, 1939.

61. *Bags & Baggage* 3 (January 1940), 5; *Washington Afro-American,* November 5, 1938; *Townsend v. New York Central,* Transcript, 733–734, 738–739.

62. *Townsend v. New York Central,* Transcript, 97, 118, 130, 599, 730–732, 736–737; *Chicago Defender,* January 25, 1941; *Bags & Baggage* 4 (February 1941), 1; *Negro Labor News,* November 12, 1938, November 25, 1939; *Black Dispatch,* November 5, 1938; *Detroit Tribune,* August 19, 1939.

63. Harry Weiss and Philip Arnow, "Recent Transition of Redcaps from Tip to Wage Status," *American Labor Legislation Review* 32 (September 1942), 136; *Chicago Defender,* July 8, 1939; *Michigan Chronicle,* June 17, 1939; *Houston Informer and Texas Freeman,* July 8, 1939; Calloway, "Red Caps' Struggle for a Livelihood," Part 1, 205–206; *Chicago Defender,* April 20, 1940, April 5, 1942; "United Transport Service Employees of America," in Florence Murray, ed., *The Negro Handbook* (New York: Wendell Malliet & Co., 1942), 136–137; *Bags & Baggage* 3 (January 1940), 5.

64. *Bags & Baggage* 3 (January 1940), 7; 3 (November 1940), 1–2; 3 (December 1940), 1; *Michigan Chronicle,* November 18, 1939; *Detroit Tribune,* November 11, 1939; *Chicago Defender,* April 13, July 6, 1940, January 25, 1941.

65. Joseph A. Padway, "Legal Department: The Court Holds that Tips Given Red Caps Constitute Wages under the Wage and Hour Law," *Catering Industry Employee* 50 (August 1941), 16–17; Northrup, *Organized Labor and the Negro,* 87; *Minneapolis Spokesman,* June 27, 1941, *Chicago Defender,* March 1, 11,

1942. In *Bags & Baggage* see 3 (November 1940), 2; 4 (March 1941), 1; 4 (June 1941), 1; 4 (July 1941), 1; 4 (November 1941), 1; 5 (January 1942), 2; 5 (March 1942), 1; 5 (April 1942), 4; 5 (August 1942), 2.

66. "Facts behind the Railroad's 10-cent Bag Fee," typescript pamphlet issued by the Educational Department of UTSEA, 1940; "Redcaps in Railway Terminals, 1938–1941," 29; *Michigan Chronicle,* February 3, 1940; *Chicago Defender,* March 23, April 6, 27, August 17, September 7, 1940; *Pittsburgh Courier,* September 12, 1942; *Baltimore Afro-American,* August 16, 1941; Before the Interstate Commerce Commission. Ida M. Stopher vs. The Cincinnati Union Terminal Company, Inc., no. 28495, Brief of United Transport Service Employees of America, Intervenor, and Ida M. Stopher, Complainant (November 1, 1940).

67. *Pittsburgh Courier,* September 12, 1942; *Baltimore Afro-American,* October 17, 1942.

68. Interstate Commerce Commission, no. 28495, Ida M. Stopher v. Cincinnati Union Terminal Company, Incorporated. Decided June 25, 1941, p. 47; *Pittsburgh Courier,* September 19, 1942; *Norfolk Journal and Guide,* November 15, December 6, 1947; *Chicago Defender,* February 14, 1948; *Pittsburgh Courier,* August 20, 1949, April 1, 1950; *Bags & Baggage* 5 (September 1942), 1.

69. "This Is the Story"; *Bags & Baggage* 5 (August 1942), 2; *Railroad Workers' Link* 2 (January 1948); *Chicago Defender,* May 18, 1940, October 3, 1942; *Seattle Northwest Enterprise,* April 4, 1941; *Norfolk Journal and Guide,* October 31, 1942, March 4, 1944, May 24, 1945; *Michigan Chronicle,* October 13, 1945; *Boston Guardian,* September 13, 1947; *New York Times,* December 1, 1950, March 18, 1951; *Baltimore Afro-American,* September 13, 1947; *Pittsburgh Courier,* August 20, 1949.

70. Lawrence O'Kane, "Few Answer Call of 'Red Cap' Today," *New York Times,* September 25, 1955, 75; *Railroad Workers' Link,* June 1950; Freeman Hubbard, *Railroad Avenue: Great Stories and Legends of American Railroading* (1945; rpt. San Marino, Calif.: Golden West Books, 1964), 424.

71. UTSEA v. NMB: Complaint for Injunctive Relief, U.S. District Court for the District of Columbia, in *NAACP Papers,* Part 13-A, Reel 10.

72. Ibid. Alfred Baker Lewis to Thurgood Marshall, January 22, 1941; Alfred Baker Lewis to Roy Wilkins, January 8, 1941; Willard S. Townsend to Walter White, March 20, 1941, in *NAACP Papers,* Part 13-A, Reel 10. See also *Northwest Enterprise,* April 4, 1941; *Bags & Baggage* 3 (November 1940), 3; 3 (April 1941), 2.

73. Alfred Baker Lewis to Ralph Ingersoll, March 8, 1941, in *NAACP Papers,* Part 13-A, Reel 10.

74. "Rump Union Pulls a Boner," *Railway Clerk* 41 (September 1942), 358.

75. *Pittsburgh Courier,* July 25, 1942; *Bags & Baggage* 5 (July 1942), 1; 6 (January 1943), 1; 4 (March 1941), 1; 5 (June 1942), 2; 5 (July 1942), 1; *CIO News* (UTSEA ed.) 6 (August 30, 1943), 12; *Pittsburgh Courier,* August 14, 1943; *Minneapolis Spokesman,* August 13, 1943; *Michigan Chronicle,* August 14, 1943.

76. *Norfolk Journal and Guide,* December 11, 1943. The court refused to recon-

sider in January 1944. *Washington Tribune,* January 15, 1944; *Sunday Chicago Bee,* January 16, 1944; *Chicago Daily Tribune,* January 11, 1944, in *TINCF,* Reel 87; Northrup, *Organized Labor and the Negro,* 88–91; *Minneapolis Spokesman,* January 14, 21, 1944; *Baltimore Afro-American,* December 8, 1943, January 15, 22, 1944.

77. Northrup, *Organized Labor and the Negro,* 83; George M. Harrison to John R. Hoskins, December 31, 1940, in *NAACP Papers,* Part 13-A, Reel 10; Ernest Calloway, "Their World and Ours: Victory over Jim Crow," *Bags & Baggage* 4 (October 1941), 4; "This Is the Story." See also George McCray, "The Labor Movement: Gains in Union Membership," in Florence Murray, ed., *The Negro Handbook 1944* (New York: Current Reference Publications, 1944), 205.

78. *Report of the Proceedings of the Sixtieth Annual Convention of the American Federation of Labor Held at New Orleans, Louisiana, November 18 to 29, Inclusive, 1940* (Washington, D.C.: Randsdell, 1940), 644–649; Jerry Orr, "Freight Handlers and Store Keepers, Louisville and Nashville Railroad," n.d., *FEPC Records,* Reel 10; M. J. Richmond to A. Philip Randolph, August 20, 1940; Arthur Williams and Herbert Bane to George M. Harrison, September 24, 1940, in Records of the Brotherhood of Sleeping Car Porters, Library of Congress, Box 7; Hogans, "ARPW," *Baltimore Afro-American,* April 5, 1941.

79. *Minneapolis Spokesman,* September 27, 1940; *Bags & Baggage* 3 (November 1940), 2; 4 (July 1941), 8; (December 1941), 5; 5 (February 1942), 1; Northrup, *Organized Labor and the Negro,* 84–85; Orr, "Freight Handlers." Those freight handlers who remained in auxiliaries of the Clerks continued to have much cause for complaint. See Erven White to FEPC, September 6, 1943, in *FEPC Records,* Reel 11.

80. Walter White to C. M. Dickson, April 29, 1941, in *NAACP Papers,* Part 13-A, Reel 10, *Bags & Baggage* 3 (November 1940), 4.

81. *Bags & Baggage* 4 (March 1941), 1, 3, 4; *Fourth Biennial Convention,* 38.

82. *Bags & Baggage* 4 (April 1941), 1; 4 (May 1941), 2; 4 (July 1941), 3; 4 (October 1941), 2; 4 (December 1941), 1; 5 (February 1942), 1; see also Calloway, "Their World and Ours."

83. Weiss and Arnow, "Recent Transition of Redcaps," 142; *Bags & Baggage* 5 (May 1942) 2; 3 (November 1940), 4. See also "Red Caps—They Have Come a Longways," *Pulse* 5 (December 1947), 7.

84. *Chicago Defender,* April 18, May 30, June 6, 1942; *Pittsburgh Courier,* August 29, 1942; Willard S. Townsend, "The CIO and the Race Question," *Sunday Chicago Bee,* January 2, 1944; *Sunday Chicago Bee,* October 27, 1946.

85. *Sunday Chicago Bee,* August 11, 1946; *Fourth Biennial Convention,* 41–42; "Report of the International President of the United Transport Service Employees, CIO, Chicago, June 18, 1950, to the . . . Seventh Biennial Constitutional Convention," in United Transport Service Employees Collection, Box 1, Archives of Labor and Urban Affairs and University Archives, Wayne State University; *CIO News* (UTSEA ed.) 8 (February 26, 1945), 1.

86. Hogans, "ARPW," *Baltimore Afro-American,* March 8, 1941; *Chicago Defender,* March 10, 1941; George F. McCray, "The Labor Front" column, *Chi-*

cago Defender, April 19, 1941; *Baltimore Afro-American,* January 17, 1942; *Sunday Chicago Bee,* January 12, 1947; George M. Harrison to Robert F. Cole, March 8, 1941, and Harrison to Frances Perkins, March 17, 1941, in *NAACP Papers,* Part 13-A, Reel 10; "From Challenge to Victory: Highlights of UTSEA History," in *Souvenir Journal: Proceedings, Third Biennial Convention, United Transport Service Employees of America, Cincinnati, Ohio, May 17, 18, 19, 1942* (n.p., 1942), 17.

6. The Politics of Fair Employment

1. *Atlanta Daily World,* September 12, 1943; *Pittsburgh Courier,* September 11, 1943; *Baltimore Afro-American,* September 4, 1943; Bartley C. Crum to Arthur Lewis, August 23, 1943, and Winthrop Martin to Barney, September 6, 1943, in *Records of the Committee on Fair Employment Practice, 1941–1946* (Glen Rock, N.J.: Microfilming Corporation of America, 1971) (hereafter *FEPC Records),* Reel 10.
2. *Black Worker* 9 (November 1943), 2.
3. The best and most extensive coverage in the African-American press can be found in the numerous articles on the hearings in the *Baltimore Afro-American,* September 25, 1943. See also Chas. H. Thompson, "FEPC Hearings Reduce Race Problem to Lowest Terms—Equal Economic Opportunity," *Journal of Negro Education* 11 (Fall 1943), 585–588; *Chicago Defender,* September 18, 25, 1943; *Houston Informer and Texas Freeman,* September 18, 1943; *Pittsburgh Courier,* September 25, 1943; *New York Age,* September 11, 18, 25, 1943; *Norfolk Journal and Guide,* September 25, 1943; "Discrimination in R.R. Employment," *Traffic World* 72 (September 11, 1943), 587, and (September 25, 1943), 734.
4. Reprinted in *Norfolk Journal and Guide,* September 2, 1943.
5. "Material on the Railroad Case," *FEPC Records,* Reel 10. In *FEPC Records,* Reel 10, see the "Summary, Findings and Directives" for the Jacksonville Terminal Company and the Brotherhood of Locomotive Firemen and Enginemen, the Missouri-Kansas-Texas Railroad, the Illinois Central Railroad, and parties to the Southeastern Carriers Conference, all issued in November 1943. See also *Minneapolis Spokesman,* December 3, 1943; *Pittsburgh Courier,* November 27, 1943.
6. H. Roger Grant, *Erie Lackawanna: Death of an American Railroad, 1938–1992* (Stanford: Stanford University Press, 1994), 34; John F. Stover, *History of the Baltimore and Ohio Railroad* (West Lafayette, Ind.: Purdue University Press, 1987), 309; H. Roger Grant, *The North Western: A History of the Chicago and North Western Railway System* (De Kalb: Northern Illinois University Press, 1996), 171.
7. Maury Klein, *Union Pacific: The Rebirth, 1894–1969* (New York: Doubleday, 1987), 414–415.
8. Carey McWilliams, "Report on Importation of Negro Labor to California," August 10, 1942, in *FEPC Records,* Reel 11; T.W.H. to J.M.S., February 22, 1943, Records of the Pennsylvania Railroad, Box 309, VP-Operations, General,

Folder 13, Hagley Museum and Library, Wilmington, Del.; *Baltimore Afro-American*, November 14, 1942.

9. Office of Defense Transportation, "Summary—Report, Conference on Womanpower in Transportation" (typescript, March 18–19, 1943), in Department of Labor Library, Washington, D.C. (hereafter DOL); *Baltimore Afro-American*, October 10, 1942, December 11, 1943, December 18, 25, 1943; Stover, *Baltimore and Ohio Railroad*, 307–309; "To Elizabeth Gurley Flynn From a Woman Brakeman," *The Worker*, August 13, 1944; "Make Way for (Miss) Casey Jones," *Santa Fe Magazine* 37 (August 1943), 9–15; "Of Particular Interest to the Women of the Santa Fe," *Santa Fe Magazine* 38 (June 1944), 14–16.

10. Cornelius C. Hill to Lawrence W. Cramer, September 24, 1942, in *FEPC Records*, Reel 10.

11. In *FEPC Records*, Reel 12: "Latest Facts," September 30, 1942 (unknown author; likely a black Memphis railroader); B. H. Russell to Lawrence Cramer, December 3, 1942; affidavit of Wade Lee Jackson, August 1943. See also *Michigan Chronicle*, June 6, 1942.

12. B. G. Gray to Malcolm S. McClean, December 1, 1942, in *FEPC Records*, Reel 12; "Summary of Complaints against Chesapeake and Ohio Railway, and International Association of Machinists" and "Response of the Chesapeake and Ohio Railway Company on Summary of Complaints Attached to Letter of August 30, 1943," in *FEPC Records*, Reel 9. See also Irven White to FEPC, September 6, 1943; Carroll R. Jackson to Johnny Franks, December 2, 1942; Memorandum: William T. McKnight to Will Maslow, December 16, 1944; Complaint of Coach Cleaners Employed by the Chicago & North Western Railway Company, November 19, 1942, in *FEPC Records*, Reel 11.

13. Jesse J. Gonzalez to Leo P. Grant et al., June 11, 1942, in *FEPC Records*, Reel 9; see also *Baltimore Afro-American*, July 7, 1943. On the resistance to the upgrading of black Pullman shop workers and persistent corporate discrimination against blacks and women, see Susan E. Hirsch, "No Victory at the Workplace: Women and Minorities at Pullman during World War II," *Mid-America* 75 (October 1993), 290–295.

14. *Baltimore Afro-American*, January 9, 1943; *Sunday Chicago Bee*, August 27, 1944; *Pittsburgh Courier*, December 5, 1942, November 6, 1943; *New York Age*, August 7, 1943; "The Brown Railroader: 'Ladies of the Steel Road,'" *Brown American* (Summer 1944), 10; Kathryn Blood, "Negro Women War Workers," U.S. Department of Labor, *Women's Bureau Bulletin* no. 205 (1945), 9; Ruthe Winegarten, *Black Texas Women: One Hundred Fifty Years of Trial and Triumph* (Austin: University of Texas Press, 1995), 226.

15. Mildred Johnson to George M. Johnson, November 16, 1942, in *FEPC Records*, Reel 11.

16. Office of War Information report cited in "Working on the Railroad," *Sunday Chicago Bee*, Monthly Picture Section, May 1943, and *Michigan Chronicle*, May 1, 1943; *Pittsburgh Courier*, March 18, 1944; Chester W. Gregory, *Women in Defense Work during World War II: An Analysis of the Labor Problem and Women' Rights* (New York: Exposition Press, 1974), 135–136, 148–149.

17. *Minneapolis Spokesman,* February 23, 1945; ODT and the Children's Bureau of the Department of Labor, "Federal and State Legislation and Regulations Affecting the Employment of Young People in Transportation," typescript, June 1943, DOL; *London, Canada, Dawn of Tomorrow,* March 4, 1944.

18. Quote in Claude Moore Fuess, *Joseph B. Eastman: Servant of the People* (New York: Columbia University Press, 1952), 332; *Baltimore Afro-American,* March 25, 1944; Office of Defense Transportation, "Annual Report to the President for the Year 1943," in OF4700a, Box 1, Franklin Delano Roosevelt Papers, Franklin Delano Roosevelt Presidential Library, Hyde Park, New York (hereafter FDR Papers); *Pittsburgh Courier,* January 1, 1944; Barbara A. Driscoll, *Tracks North: The Railroad Bracero Program of World War II* (Austin, Tex.: Center for Mexican American Studies Books, 1999), ix, 61–66, 137–149.

19. *Baltimore Afro-American,* December 25, 1943, January 8, 1944; *Norfolk Journal and Guide,* January 8, 1944; *New York Age,* January 1, 1944; Horace R. Cayton, "Railroadmen: Besieged by Two Rival Unions—Randolph, Townsend Should Agree," *Pittsburgh Courier,* July 26 1941. The federal takeover lasted from December 27, 1943 to January 18, 1944. Grant, *The North Western,* 174–175.

20. *Minneapolis Spokesman,* December 8, 1944, January 5, July 27, August 3, 1945; U.S. War Manpower Commission, "Employment Trends in Urgent War Production, June 1945," typescript, DOL, 30–32.

21. *Chicago Defender,* August 7, 1945.

22. Quoted in Jervis Anderson, *A. Philip Randolph: A Biographical Portrait* (New York: Harcourt Brace Jovanovich, 1972), 248–249; *Boston Guardian,* June 7, 1941.

23. *Michigan Chronicle,* June 28, 1941; *Chicago Defender,* June 7, 21, 1941.

24. Ira De A. Reid, "A Critical Summary: The Negro on the Home Front in World Wars I and II," *Journal of Negro Education* 12 (Summer 1943), 511–520; *Pittsburgh Courier,* January 31, 1942, cited in Lee Finckle, *Forum for Protest: The Black Press during World War II* (Rutherford, N.J.: Fairleigh Dickinson University Press, 1975), 112; Charles S. Johnson and Associates, *To Stem This Tide: A Survey of Racial Tension Areas in the United States* (1943; rpt. New York: AMS Press, 1969), 91.

25. Numbers from Robert Korstad and Nelson Lichtenstein, "Opportunities Found and Lost: Labor, Radicals, and the Early Civil Rights Movement," *Journal of American History* 75 (December 1988), 787; Steven F. Lawson, *Running for Freedom: Civil Rights and Black Politics in America since 1941* (New York: McGraw-Hill, 1991), 8. On black trade union membership, see George McCray, "The Labor Movement: Gains in Union Membership," in Florence Murray, ed., *The Negro Handbook 1944* (New York: Current Reference Publications, 1944), 202–208.

26. Johnson, *To Stem,* 107; George B. Tidal, *The Emergence of the New South, 1913–1945* (Baton Rouge: Louisiana State University Press, 1967), 716; Lawson, *Running for Freedom,* 20. See also Richard M. Dalfiume, "The 'Forgotten Years' of the Negro Revolution," *Journal of American History* 55 (June 1968), 90–106.

27. On the alliance between the NAACP and Randolph, see John H. Bracey, Jr.,

and August Meier, "Allies or Adversaries? The NAACP, A. Philip Randolph and the 1941 March on Washington," *Georgia Historical Quarterly* 75 (Spring 1991), 1–17; John Egerton, *Speak Now against the Day: The Generation before the Civil Rights Movement in the South* (Chapel Hill: University of North Carolina Press, 1994), 214–217. See also Bernard C. Nalty, *Strength for the Fight: A History of Black Americans in the Military* (New York: The Free Press, 1986), 138–141; *Northwest Enterprise,* June 21, 1941.

28. On the MOWM and the negotiations leading to the issuance of Executive Order 8802, see Anderson, *A. Philip Randolph,* 243–261; Herbert Garfinkel, *When Negroes March: The March on Washington Movement in the Organizational Politics for FEPC* (1959; rpt. New York: Atheneum, 1969), 34–61; Paula F. Pfeffer, *A. Philip Randolph, Pioneer of the Civil Rights Movement* (Baton Rouge: Louisiana State University Press, 1990), 46–55; *Northwest Enterprise,* July 11, 1941.

29. "President's Committee on Fair Employment Practice," in Murray, ed., *Negro Handbook 1944,* 211; George F. McCray, "The Labor Front," *Chicago Defender,* August 9, 1941.

30. Mark Ethridge to Stephen Early, December 23, 1941, OF4245g, Box 3, FDR Papers.

31. Confidential Memorandum: Lawrence W. Cramer to All Committee Members, August 5, 1942, in William H. Harris, ed., *Records of the Brotherhood of Sleeping Car Porters, Series A, Holdings of the Chicago Historical Society and the Newberry Library, 1925–1969.* Part 1: *Records of the BSCP, 1925–1969* (Bethesda, Md.: University Publications of America, 1990) (hereafter *BSCP Records),* Reel 20; Clete Daniel, *Chicano Workers and the Politics of Fairness: The FEPC in the Southwest, 1941–1945* (Austin: University of Texas Press, 1991), 24–25; *Minneapolis Spokesman,* November 13, 1942; *Baltimore Afro-American,* August 22, 29, 1942.

32. *Baltimore Afro-American,* August 22, 29, September 5, 1942. See also George F. McCray, "FEPC Shift Damaging," *Baltimore Afro-American,* September 5, October 31, December 5, 1942.

33. Ethridge quoted in Denton L. Watson, *Lion in the Lobby: Clarence Mitchell, Jr.'s Struggle for the Passage of Civil Rights Laws* (New York: William Morrow and Co., 1990), 133; Louis C. Kesselman, "The Fair Employment Practice Commission Movement in Perspective," *Journal of Negro History* 31 (January 1946), 38–39.

34. On the FEPC's limitations, see Kesselman, "Fair Employment Practice Commission," 39. The most comprehensive account of the agency is Merl E. Reed, *Seedtime for the Modern Civil Rights Movement: The President's Committee on Fair Employment Practice, 1941–1946* (Baton Rouge: Louisiana State University Press, 1991).

35. Milton P. Webster to St. Clair Crutcher, December 17, 1942, in *BSCP Records,* Reel 21; Webster to Thomas D. Redd, September 1, 1942, Box 130, Folder 130–10, Papers of the Brotherhood of Sleeping Car Porters, Chicago Historical Society (hereafter BSCP Papers–CHS); "Material on the Railroad Cases," *FEPC Records,* Reel 10; *Baltimore Afro-American,* September 5, 1942.

36. For a selection of examples, see W. H. Johnson to Milton P. Webster, November

9, 1942, and "Complaint of Coach Cleaners Employed by the Chicago & North Western Railway Company," November 19, 1942, both in *BSCP Records,* Reel 21; S. E. Adkins to Webster, November 8, 1943, *BSCP Records,* Reel 23; "Complaint Alleging Refusal of Brotherhood of Railway Trainmen to Admit a Negro to Membership," September 28, 1944, *BSCP Records,* Reel 24; Otis Ogletree to Harold A. Stevens, August 11, 1942, Box 130, Folder 130–8, BSCP Papers–CHS; J. W. Crawford to Webster, July 28, 1942, Box 130, Folder 130–7, BSCP Papers–CHS. See also *Baltimore Afro-American,* October 10, 1942.

37. Arthur Lewis and H. L. Leonard to Paul V. McNutt, July 21, 1943, in *FEPC Records,* Reel 10; Charles Hamilton Houston and Joseph C. Waddy, "Evidence and Supplementary Material Re Discrimination . . . June 3, 1942," in *FEPC Records,* Reel 10; Waddy to FEPC, August 27, 1943, in *FEPC Records,* Reel 12.

38. In *BSCP Records:* Harold A. Stevens to Milton P. Webster, July 2, 1942, and Lawrence W. Cramer to Webster, July 15, 1942, Reel 20; Dred Montgomery to Webster, August 20, 1943, Reel 22. In BSCP Papers–CHS: Webster to Thomas D. Redd, September 1, 1942, and Redd to Webster, September 20, 1942, in Box 130, Folder 130–10; Emmett N. Brooks to Webster, August 23, 1942, Box 130, Folder 130–8. In FEPC Records, Reel 10: Chicago Committee on Railroad Employment, "Brief Setting Forth the Discriminatory Practices against Negro Workers in the Railroad Industry . . ."; "Chicago Negro Labor Win the War Conference Committee on Railroad Manpower, Petition"; Charles Hamilton Houston and Joseph C. Waddy to FEPC, May 9, 1942. See also *Chicago Defender,* August 1, 8, September 5, 12, 1942; *Baltimore Afro-American,* August 29, 1942.

39. Milton P. Webster to Lawrence W. Cramer, October 10, 1942; Cramer to Webster, October 14, 1942; Maceo W. Hubbard to Webster, October 21, 1942, in *BSCP Records,* Reel 20; "Advance Release," Office of War Information, War Manpower Commission, for October 5, 1942, *FEPC Records,* Reel 10; *Norfolk Journal and Guide,* December 12, 1942; *Seattle Northwest Enterprise,* January 20, 1943. Investigations continued long after the 1943 hearings. See Jordan Jefferson Report, November 2, 1944, in Colored Trainmen of America Papers, Houston Metropolitan Research Center, Houston Public Library, Houston, Texas.

40. "The Negro in Industry," *New Republic* 109 (October 18, 1943), 539; Harrison quote in Daniel, *Chicano Workers,* 108; James H. Hogans, "Among Railroad and Pullman Workers," *Baltimore Afro-American,* January 23, 1943; *Baltimore Afro-American,* January 23, 30, 1943.

41. "Negro in Industry," 539; *Pittsburgh Courier,* January 16, 1943; *PM,* January 12, 1943; *Baltimore Afro-American,* January 16, 1943; Reed, *Seedtime,* 90–91; Daniel, *Chicano Workers,* 109–110.

42. *Minneapolis Spokesman,* January 15, 1943; "President's Committee on Fair Employment Practice," in Murray, ed., *Negro Handbook 1944,* 211; "The FEPC," *Interracial Review* 16 (January 1943), 5; Louis Ruchames, *Race, Jobs, and Politics: The Story of FEPC* (New York: Columbia University Press, 1953), 50–53; *Pittsburgh Courier,* December 12, 1942; *Baltimore Afro-American,* December 12, 1942; January 9, 1943.

43. Harry Epstein to Malcolm S. MacLean, January 12, 1943; Epstein to Milton P. Webster, January 14, 1943; Charles H. Houston to MacLean, January 16, 1943; Harold A. Stevens to MacLean, January 15, 1943, in *BSCP Records*, Reel 21; *Journal and Guide*, January 23, 1943; *Baltimore Afro-American*, January 16, March 13, 1943, July 15, 1944.

44. "Negro in Industry," 539; Reed, *Seedtime*, 92; *Houston Informer and Texas Freeman*, February 13, 1943; *Minneapolis Spokesman*, January 22, 1943; *Baltimore Afro-American*, January 23, 30, February 27, 1943; *Norfolk Journal and Guide*, January 23, 1943. In *BSCP Records*, Reel 21, see *Chicago Sun*, January 14, 1943; *Pittsburgh Courier*, February 20, 1943; *Norfolk Journal and Guide*, March 6, 1943.

45. *Norfolk Journal and Guide*, January 30, 1943; Alexander Saxton to Milton P. Webster, January 19, 1943, in *BSCP Records*, Reel 21; *Pittsburgh Courier*, July 11, 1942; author's telephone interview with Alexander Saxton, July 13, 1999. The Chicago Negro Labor Win the War Conference allied many of that city's railroad unions, including the AFL's Joint Council of Dining Car Employees; the CIO's UTSEA; railroad carmen, firemen and oilers; and a Clerks' auxiliary. Saxton, a Communist party member, would become a novelist and eventually a historian of race and labor in the United States.

46. *Baltimore Afro-American*, January 30, 1943. In *BSCP Records:* "Resolution Adopted by the Save the FEPC Conference," February 4, 1943: News Release," February 5, 1943. See also *Black Worker* 9 (January 1943), 1, 4; 9 (February 1943), 1, 4; 9 (April 1943), 2; *Baltimore Afro-American*, January 23, February 13, 20, March 31, 1943. In OF4245g, FDR Papers, see Benjamin V. Armstead and Aeoloiah Lee to Roosevelt, August 13, 1942; Norman Thomas to Roosevelt, August 25, 1942; Morris Milgarm to Roosevelt, August 22, 1942; Louis E. Schotz to Gordon Canfield, January 20, 1944; Walter White, Memorandum for the President, January 29, 1943.

47. Jonathan Daniels, Memorandum for Marvin McIntyre, January 26, 1943, OF4245g, Box 3, and Daniels, Memorandum for Marvin McIntyre, December 14, 1942, OF4245g, Box 6, FDR Papers; Daniel, *Chicano Workers*, 115, 134–135; *Baltimore Afro-American*, February 6, 13, 27, June 5, 1943; *Black Worker* 9 (July 1943), 4; *Pittsburgh Courier*, July 17, 1943.

48. *Pittsburgh Courier*, September 25, 1943; *New York Age*, September 18, 1943. On the hearings, see Alexa B. Henderson, "FEPC and the Southern Railway Case: An Investigation into the Discriminatory Practices of Railroads during World War II," *Journal of Negro History* 61 (April 1976), 173–187.

49. Memorandum, Francis X. Riley to Lawrence W. Cramer, November 1942, in *FEPC Records*, Reel 10; George F. McCray, "The Labor Movement, 1944–1945. Locomotive Firemen Case," in Florence Murray, ed., *The Negro Handbook 1946–1947* (New York: Current Books, 1947), 121–122; "Concerted Movement—Southeastern Railroads: Employment and Assignment of Promotable Firemen," *Report of Grand Lodge Officers of the Brotherhood of Locomotive Firemen and Enginemen to the Thirty-Fourth Convention* (Denver, July 1941), 549–552; "Re: Colored Locomotive Firemen" and untitled report 1942, in *BSCP Records*, Reel 21.

50. *Chicago Defender*, November 15, 1941; Report of Joseph C. Waddy in re trip to

Pensacola, Florida, July 23, 1941, to August 1, 1941, in Box 163-23, Folder 2, Charles Hamilton Houston Papers, Moorland Spingarn Research Center, Howard University, Washington, D.C.

51. Quotes and further narrative in Bester William Steele v. Louisville & Nashville Railroad Company, Brotherhood of Locomotive Firemen and Enginemen, et al., U.S. Supreme Court, Docket no. 45, October term, 1944, December 18, 1944 (323 U.S. 192, 65 S. Ct. 226), in *9 Labor Cases* 51482–91; Bester William Steele: Questionnaire Re Discrimination in the Railroad Industry, in *FEPC Papers*, Reel 12.

52. *Baltimore Afro-American*, September 25, 1943.

53. *Chicago Defender*, September 18, 25, 1943; *Minneapolis Spokesman*, September 24, 1943; Herbert Northrup, "The Negro in the Railway Unions," *Phylon* 5 (Second Quarter 1944), 159–164.

54. Malcolm Ross, *All Manner of Men* (New York: Reynal & Hitchcock, 1948), 126; Winifred Raushenbush, "Green Light for the FEPC," *Survey Graphic* 32 (December 1943), 500–501; "The Elimination of the Negro Firemen on American Railways . . . ," *Lawyers Guild Review* 4 (March–April 1944), 32–37; *Pittsburgh Courier*, September 25, 1943.

55. Malcolm Ross to the President, December 27, 1943, in OF4245g, Box 4, FDR Papers; Atlantic Coast Line Railroad Company et al. to President's Committee on Fair Employment Practice, December 13, 1943, in *FEPC Records*, Reel 9; *Baltimore Afro-American*, December 18, 1943; "Discrimination in R.R. Employment," *Traffic World* 62 (December 18, 1943), 1535; *Minneapolis Spokesman*, December 17, 1943; *New York Age*, December 18, 25, 1943; *Pittsburgh Courier*, December 18, 1943; *Seattle Northwest Enterprise*, December 15, 1943; *Norfolk Journal and Guide*, December 25, 1943.

56. *Chicago Defender*, September 11, 1943; *Pittsburgh Courier*, September 11, 1943.

57. Memorandum, Francis X. Riley to Lawrence W. Cramer, November 16, 1942, in *FEPC Records*, Reel 10.

58. Office memorandum: Francis X. Riley to Lawrence W. Cramer, October 30, 1942, in *FEPC Records*, Reel 10.

59. Memorandum, Francis X. Riley to Lawrence W. Cramer, November 16, 1942, in *FEPC Records*, Reel 10.

60. In *FEPC Records*, Reel 10: Thomas W. Davis, "Answer of Atlantic Coast Line Railroad Company . . . "; W. E. Smith, "Answer of Louisville & Nashville Railroad . . . ," September 13, 1943.

61. Smith, "Answer"; Davis, "Answer"; *Baltimore Afro-American*, December 18, 1943; *Norfolk Journal and Guide*, March 18, 1944.

62. *Chicago Defender*, December 25, 1943; *Norfolk Journal and Guide*, December 25, 1943, January 8, 1944; *Baltimore Afro-American*, September 25, December 11, 1943, January 1, 15, 1944, March 11, 1944; *Pittsburgh Courier*, January 22, February 5, March 11, 1944; *Atlanta Daily World*, January 30, 1944; *Minneapolis Spokesman*, May 12, 1944; *Michigan Chronicle*, August 19, 1944; *New York Age*, March 11, 1944; *Hearings before the Special Committee to Investigate Executive Agencies*, House of Representatives, 78th Congress, 1st and 2nd sess. Pursuant to H. Res. 102, Part 2, March 2, 1944, 2160.

63. *Pittsburgh Courier,* December 25, 1943, January 8, 1944; *Chicago Defender,* January 1, 1944; *New York Age,* January 8, 1944; "Interpreter Releases, President's Committee on Fair Employment Practice," December 23, 1943, in *FEPC Records,* Reel 10.

64. Franklin D. Roosevelt to Walter P. Stacy, January 1, 1944, in OF4245, Box 8, FDR Papers; *Chicago Defender,* January 8, 1943; *Atlanta Daily World,* January 4, 1944; *Sunday Chicago Bee,* January 9, 1944; *Pittsburgh Courier,* January 8, 1944; *Baltimore Afro-American,* January 8, 1944.

65. *Chicago Defender,* January 15, 1944; *Baltimore Afro-American,* March 4, May 27, 1944. For biographical sketches of the committee's members, see J.F.D. "Confidential" Memorandum, January 4, 1944, Box 309, VP-Operations, General, Folder 13, Records of the Pennsylvania Railroad, Hagley Museum and Library, Wilmington, Delaware.

66. Memorandum for the President, from Jonathan Daniels, February 25, 1944; Walter P. Stacy to Jonathan Daniels, February 5, 1945; Report of Special Committee appointed by the President, January 1, 1944, to consider cases of Racial Discrimination in Railroad Employment, December 5, 1944, in OF4245, Box 8, FDR Papers; *Atlanta Daily World,* February 26, 1944; *Pittsburgh Courier,* March 18, 1944; *New York Age,* June 3, 1944; *Norfolk Journal and Guide,* March 4, 1944.

67. Walter P. Stacy to Charles Hamilton Houston, January 22, 1945, and Philleo Nash to Jonathan Daniels, February 19, 1945, in OF4245g, Box 8, FDR Papers; *Baltimore Afro-American,* January 27, 1945; *Norfolk Journal and Guide,* January 27, 1945; *Michigan Chronicle,* February 3, 1945; *Minneapolis Spokesman,* August 3, 1945; *Chicago Defender,* October 20, 1945; *Pittsburgh Courier,* November 3, 1945.

68. U.S. Committee on Fair Employment Practice, *Final Report,* June 28, 1946 (Washington, D.C.: Government Printing Office, 1947), 12.

69. Willard S. Townsend, "Townsend Hits Railroads Defiance of the FEPC," *Sunday Chicago Bee,* December 26, 1943.

70. Reed, *Seedtime,* 110–113, 116; Will Maslow, "FEPC—A Case History in Parliamentary Maneuver," *University of Chicago Law Review* 13 (June 1946), 410–411; "President's Committee on Fair Employment Practice," in Murray, ed., *Negro Handbook 1944,* 211; Pfeffer, *A. Philip Randolph,* 92–93; *Black Worker* 9 (July 1943), 4.

7. The Politics of Fair Representation

1. U.S. Committee on Fair Employment Practice, *Final Report,* June 28, 1946 (Washington, D.C.: Government Printing Office, 1947), 13.

2. *Savannah Tribune,* January 17, 1920; *Detroit Tribune Independent,* July 27, 1935; *New York Age,* July 27, 1935; William H. Hastie, "Charles Hamilton Houston (1885–1950)," *Crisis* 57 (June 1950), 364–365, 405–406; *Black Dispatch,* July 23, 1938. On Houston's life, see Genna Rae McNeil, *Groundwork: Charles Hamilton Houston and the Struggle for Civil Rights* (Philadelphia: University of Pennsylvania Press, 1983).

3. James M. Hubila, Jr., "Houston Speaked High for Labor," *Pittsburgh Courier*

June 30, 1950; Conference, Richmond Va., June 29, 1939, in John H. Bracey, Jr., and August Meier, eds., *Papers of the NAACP, Part 10: Peonage, Labor, and the New Deal, 1913–1939* (Frederick, Md.: University Publications of America, 1990) (hereafter *NAACP Papers*, Part 10), Reel 7; *Ed Teague vs. BLFE and Gulf, Mobile, and Northern Railroad Company*, Complaint for Injunction and Damages . . . in John L. LeFlore Papers, Series I, Box 4, NAACP Files, at University of South Alabama Archives; NAACP and IARE, "Memorandum of Conference at Mobile, Alabama, March 21, 1939 . . . ," in *NAACP Papers*, Part 10, Reel 7; "Conference," June 29, 1939, in *NAACP Papers*, Part 10, Reel 12; "Complaint and Affidavit of Ed Teague," in *Records of the Committee on Fair Employment Practice, 1941–1946* (Glen Rock, N.J.: Microfilming Corporation of America, 1971) (hereafter *FEPC Records*), Reel 13; "Gulf, Mobile and Northern Railroad Company, Memorandum of Agreement," January 5, 1938; L. R. Moloy to Robert F. Cole, December 6, 1938; Moloy to G. P. Brock, September 23, 1938; Moloy to H. S. Myers, October 16, 1939; and Charles Hamilton Houston and Joseph C. Waddy to G. P. Brock, October 5, 1939, in *FEPC Records*, Reel 9; John L. LeFlore Interview (1970–1972), in Melton McLaurin Collection, University of South Alabama Archives.

4. In the Charles Hamilton Houston Papers, Moorland Spingarn Research Center, Howard University, Washington, D.C. (hereafter CHH Papers): Charles Hamilton Houston to Miles Jackson, May 12, 1941, Box 163–22, Folder 22; Miles Jackson, Jim Caldwell, Bester Steele, and Arthur Willingham to Walter White, April 22, 1941, Box 163–22, Folder 2; Report of the General Committee, I.A. of R.E. Local 41 L&N Railroad Company, May 16, 1941, Box 163–23, Folder 2; Report of Meeting, Louisville, Kentucky, July 31, 1941, Box 163–23, Folder 2.

5. Memorandum for Brothers F. C. Caldwell, Samuel H. Clark, Bester William Steele and Locals 41 and 33, International Association of Railway Employees, August 6, 1941, by Charles Houston and Arthur Lewis, CHH Papers, Box 163–23, Folder 2.

6. In CHH Papers: "Knoxville Conference, July 23, 1941, 10 A.M., Bester William Steele," Box 163–23, Folder 2; "Interview Steele," Box 163–23, Folder 7; Steele to J. Caldwell and Charles Houston, August 24, 1941; J. T. Settle to Houston, August 24, 1941, Box 163–23, Folder 3; Settle to Houston, February 9, 1942, Box 163–23, Folder 8; Steele to Caldwell, October 29, 1941, Box 163–23, Folder 4; Steele to Board Members and Officers of IARE and ACRT April 16, 1944, Box 163–37, Folder 4. In *FEPC Records*, Reel 12: "Questionnaire Re Discrimination in the Railway Industry: Bester William Steele"; Steele to Bartley C. Crum, August 24, 1943. Lynda Dempsey Cochran, "Arthur Davis Shores: Advocate for Freedom" (master's thesis, Georgia Southern College, 1977), 54–58.

7. *Steele v. Louisville & N. R. Co. et al.*, 6 Div. 153, January 13, 1944, 16 *Southern Reporter*, Second Series, 416–423; *Norfolk Journal and Guide*, December 4, 1943; *Baltimore Afro-American*, January 22, 1944; Arthur Davis Shores to Charles Hamilton Houston, July 21, August 9, 1941, CHH Papers, Box 163–23, Folder 3; Arthur Lewis, Memorandum, September 2, 1941, CHH Papers, Box 163–23, Folder 4.

8. *Pittsburgh Courier,* August 29, 1942; *Norfolk Journal and Guide,* November 13, 1943. Also see Tom Tunstall, Supplemental Questionnaire, Railroad Hearings; Tunstall to Guy M. Dodson, March 31, 1942; and "Complaint and Affidavit of Tom Tunstall," May 29, 1942, in *FEPC Records,* Reel 12; *Norfolk Journal and Guide,* March 13, April 24, May 1, 1943, January 15, 1944; *Baltimore Afro-American,* January 29, 1944; *Tom Tunstall v. Brotherhood of Locomotive Firemen and Enginemen, et al.,* U.S. Circuit Court of Appeals, Fourth Circuit, no. 5125, January 10, 1944, in 7 *Labor Cases* 65,657–9.

9. *Atlanta Daily World,* May 30, December 1, 1944; *Baltimore Afro-American,* June 10, 17, 1944; *New York Age,* November 25, 1944; *Minneapolis Spokesman,* November 24, 1944; *Pittsburgh Courier,* November 18, 1944; *Northwest Herald,* November 28, 1944; *Steele v. Louisville & Nashville Railroad Company, Brotherhood of Locomotive Firemen and Enginemen, et al.,* 323 U.S. 192, 65 S. Ct. 226 (hereafter *Steele v. L&N* (1944)); *Tom Tunstall v. Brotherhood of Locomotive Firemen and Enginemen, Ocean Lodge No. 76, Port Norfolk Lodge No. 775, et al.,* 323 U.S. 210, 65 S. Ct. 235.

10. *Steele v. L&N* (1944).

11. Ibid.

12. Charles Hamilton Houston, Memorandum to ACRT, IARE, et al., December 20, 1944, CHH Papers, Box 163–23, Folder 14.

13. Ibid.; *Atlanta Daily World,* December 30, 1944; *Minneapolis Spokesman,* December 22, 1944; *Baltimore Afro-American,* December 23, 1944; *Chicago Defender,* December 30, 1944; *Pittsburgh Courier,* December 30, 1944.

14. Houston quote in McNeil, *Groundwork,* 162; Mark Tushnett, *Making Civil Rights Law: Thurgood Marshall and the Supreme Court, 1936–1961* (New York: Oxford University Press, 1994), 70; Richard Kluger, *Simple Justice: The History of Brown v. Board of Education and Black America's Struggle for Equality* (New York: Vintage Books, 1975), 234–235.

15. *Birmingham World,* January 5, 1945; *Baltimore Afro-American,* January 13, 1947; "Report of the Proceedings of the Firemen's Conference . . . held at Birmingham, Alabama, October 22, 23, 24, 1946," in William H. Harris, ed., *Records of the Brotherhood of Sleeping Car Porters, Series A, Holdings of the Chicago Historical Society and the Newberry Library, 1925–1969,* Part 1: *Records of the BSCP, 1925–1969* (Bethesda, Md.: University Publications of America, 1990) (hereafter *BSCP Records*), Reel 9, 9; C. A. Chick, "Some Recent United States Supreme Court Decisions Affecting the Rights of Negro Workers," *Journal of Negro Education* 16 (Spring 1947), 177.

16. Marjorie McKenzie, "Pursuit of Democracy: NLRB Case and Not Rail Brotherhood Case Goes to Heart of Issue Facing Negroes," *Pittsburgh Courier,* December 30, 1944; *Baltimore Afro-American,* December 30, 1944. See also FEPC, Memorandum: "Analysis of Cases Involving Negro Firemen Decided by the United States Supreme Court December 18, 1944," February 9, 1945, in *BSCP Records,* Reel 25. For an overview of the strengths and limits of black railroaders' litigation, see Neil M. Herring, "The 'Fair Representation' Doctrine: An Effective Weapon against Union Racial Discrimination?" *Maryland Law Review* 24 (Spring 1964), 113–165.

17. Houston Memorandum to ACRTLF, IARE, et al., December 20, 1944, in CHH Papers, Box 163–23, Folder 14.

18. Houston, "Foul Employment Practices of the Railroads," speech before the National Urban League Annual Conference, September 6, 1949, in *Papers of the NAACP, Part 13: The NAACP and Labor, 1940–1955, Series C* (Bethesda, Md.: University Publications of America, 1992), Reel 7; *Salvant v. Louisville & N. R. Co. et al.*, No. 1441, U.S. District Court, W. D. Kentucky, Louisville Division, February 1, 1949, 83 F.Supp. 391

19. W. E. Mitchell to S. G. Davenport, September 14, 1942, in Papers of the Brotherhood of Locomotive Firemen and Enginemen, Kheel Center for Labor-Management Documentation and Archives, Cornell University (hereafter BLFE Papers), Box 160.

20. Harold C. Heiss to D. B. Robertson, November 28, 1947; William Maupin to Robertson, January 12, 1948; Acting General Chairman to all Local Chairmen, December 27, 1947, BLFE Papers, Box 160; *Hinton v. Seaboard Air Line Railroad*, 170 F.2d 892 (4th Cir. 1948); *Graham v. Southern Railway*, 74 F. Supp. 663 (D.D.C. 1947); *Brotherhood v. Graham*, 175 F.2d 802 (D.C. Cir. 1948), *Graham v. BLFE*, Supreme Court, No. 16, November 7, 1949, in 9 *FEP Cases* 399.

21. Memorandum, Charles Hamilton Houston and Joseph C. Waddy to S. H. Clark, Arthur Lewis, and Jordan J. Jefferson, September 27, 1948, Colored Trainmen of America Papers, Houston Metropolitan Research Center, Houston Public Library (hereafter CTA-HMRC); W. E. Mitchell to D. B. Robertson, October 16, 1947, in BLFE Papers, Box 160.

22. *Chicago Defender,* February 14, 1948; *Norfolk Journal and Guide,* February 7, 1948; *Railroad Workers' Link,* February 1948, March 1948, October 1949. Houston had earlier raised the issue of promotions in negotiations with the BLFE but had insisted on giving those eligible "reasonable time" to prepare for the qualifying examinations. Charles Hamilton Houston and Joseph C. Waddy to Harold Heiss, Russell Day, and Ralph Hoyt, February 15, 1947, in BLFE Papers, Box 160.

23. *Norfolk Journal and Guide,* January 31, April 24, 1948; *Black Worker* 8 (February 1948), 1, 4. (Note: Volume numbers for the *Black Worker* in the late 1940s and 1950s are inconsistent; I have cited the volume listed on each issue).

24. *Norfolk Journal and Guide,* February 1, 1947.

25. *Willie J. Rolax, et al., v. Atlantic Coast Line Railroad Company, et al.,* U.S. District Court, Eastern District of Virginia, Richmond Division. Civil No. 670, February 23, 1950, 18 *Labor Cases* 77683–90 (hereafter *Rolax v. ACL*); *Pittsburgh Courier,* March 4, 1950; *Railroad Workers' Link,* May 1950; *Black Worker* 7 (March 1950), 1–2; 7 (April 1950), 1, 3.

26. *Rolax v. ACL.*

27. *Matt Mitchell, James Harris and George Sams, et al., v. Gulf, Mobile and Ohio Railroad Company, Brotherhood of Locomotive Firemen and Enginemen, an Unincorporated Association, Local Lodge No. 769, Brotherhood of Locomotive Firemen and Enginemen, and George E. Cox,* U.S. District Court, Northern District of Alabama, Civil No. 537, May 2, 1950, 18 *Labor Cases* 77582–89; *BLFE*

v. Mitchell, U.S. Court of Appeals (New Orleans), July 11, 1951, 9 *FEP Cases* 409–413.

28. *Mitchell et al., v. Gulf, Mobile and Ohio Railroad Company, BLFE, et al.* (1950).

29. Ibid.; *BLFE v. Mitchell* (1951); author's interviews with Jerome A. ("Buddy") Cooper, Birmingham, October 22, 1993, and November 13, 1998; *Pittsburgh Courier,* February 4, 1950; *Northwest Enterprise,* April 5, 1950; *Black Worker* 7 (April 1950), 1; 7 (May 1950), 1–2; 7 (June 1950), 1–2; *Louisiana Weekly,* May 13, 1950; *Pittsburgh Courier,* May 13, 1950, July 28, 1951.

30. Press release, January 15, 1942, in *BSCP Records,* Reel 26; "Agreement of Settlement," December 28, 1951, in Records of the Brotherhood of Sleeping Car Porters, Library of Congress (hereafter BSCP-LC), Box 66; *Black Worker* 7 (January 1952), 1; 7 (June 1952), 1.

31. BSCP and Provisional Committee, "A Call to Conference, October 22–23, 1954," BSCP-LC, Box 68. For other, related legal cases, see: *Graham v. Brotherhood of Locomotive Firemen and Enginemen,* 338 U.S. 232, 234 (1949); Petition for a Writ of Certiorari, *Al Marshall, et al., v. Brotherhood of Locomotive Firemen and Enginemen, et al.,* in the Supreme Court of the United States, October Term, 1959, no. 542, 4, in BSCP-LC, Box 124.

32. "Eleventh Annual Conference of the Brotherhood of Sleeping Car Porters Provisional Committee for the Organization of Colored Locomotive Firemen and Enginemen held May 23 and 24, 1952," 1, 10, in *BSCP Records,* Reel 26; *Chicago Defender,* June 7, 1952; BSCP, "Call to the Fourteenth Annual Conference, September 16–17, 1955," BSCP-LC, Box 68.

33. *New York Times,* October 24, 1945; press release, "Brotherhood Saves Colored Locomotive Firemen's Jobs, January 15, 1952," in *BSCP Records,* Reel 26; Georgia Firemen to B. F. McLaurin, February 28, 1953, BSCP-LC, Box 125; Joseph Goldstein, "Report on Negro Firemen," April 20, 1954, and Joseph Rauh to A. Philip Randolph, April 20, 1954, in Joseph L. Rauh Papers, Library of Congress, Washington, D.C.

34. On the campaign for a permanent FEPC, see Paula F. Pfeffer, *A. Philip Randolph, Pioneer of the Civil Rights Movement* (Baton Rouge: Louisiana State University Press, 1990), 97–108.

35. *Black Worker* 7 (November 1951), 1, 3, 8.

36. *Black Worker* 7 (January 1951), 1; 7 (February 1951), 1; 7 (June 1951), 1, 3; 7 (September 1951), 1, 3; 7 (October 1951), 1, 3.

37. *Railway Labor Act Amendments, Hearings before the Committee on Interstate and Foreign Commerce on H.R. 7789,* May 9–12, 25, 26, June 7, 1950, 81st Congress, 2nd sess. (Washington, D.C.: Government Printing Office, 1950), 49, 66–67, 280, 282, 294–95; *To Amend the Railway Labor Act . . . : Hearings before a Subcommittee of the Committee on Labor and Public Welfare on S.3295,* May 1, 4, 5, 15, 17, 18, and 23, 1950, 81st Congress, 2nd sess. (Washington, D.C.: Government Printing Office, 1950), 129–147, 230–303; *Pittsburgh Courier,* August 12, 1950.

38. *Black Worker* 7 (February 1949), 1; 7 (June 1950), 2; 7 (August 1950), 1; 7 (November 1950), 2; 7 (December 1950), 3.

39. *Black Worker* 7 (December 1950), 3; *Black Worker* 7 (January 1951), 1.

40. *New York Times,* January 29, 1948; *Black Worker* 8 (February 1948), 1; *Chicago Defender,* February 14, 1948.

41. *Lee Oliphant et al. v. Brotherhood of Locomotive Firemen and Enginemen et al.,* U.S. District Court, Northern District, Ohio, September 27, 1957, Civ. no. 314654, 33 *Labor Cases* 95,024–27.

42. *Oliphant v. BLFE* (1957); Joseph Rauh, "Civil Rights and Liberties and Labor Unions," *Labor Law Journal* (December 1957), 875–876; "Rail Union Sued to Stop Jim Crow Rule," *March of Labor* 7 (February 1955), 9.

43. *Oliphant et al. v. BLFE, et al.,* U.S. Court of Appeals, Sixth Circuit (Cincinnati), no. 13387, November 26, 1958, cited in 9 *FEP Cases* 446–449.

44. A. Philip Randolph to Milton P. Webster, December 16, 1958, and Joseph Rauh to Randolph, November 28, 1958, *BSCP Records,* Reel 26; Rauh to Randolph, March 10, 1959, BSCP-LC, Box 26; Randolph and B. F. McLaurin to Provisional Committee Members, December 10, 1958, BSCP-LC, Box 66.

45. Karl E. Klare, "The Quest for Industrial Democracy and the Struggle against Racism: Perspectives from Labor Law and Civil Rights Law," *Oregon Law Review* 61 (December 1982), 188–190; Lester Ashe, "Comment on the Rauh Paper," *Labor Law Journal* (December 1957), 892–893.

46. B. W. Steele, IARE Circular Letter 1, January 1949, BSCP-LC, Box 127.

47. Charles Hamilton Houston, memorandum to Samuel H. Clark, Arthur Lewis, and Jordan J. Jefferson, October 6, 1947; Minutes of First Meeting of Negro Railway Labor Executives Committee, March 6, 1948; Minutes of Second Meeting of Negro Railway Labor Executives Committee, April 14, 1948, CTA-HMRC; *Pittsburgh Courier,* July 3, 1948; Daniel Benjamin, "'I've Been Working on the Railroad' . . . " *March of Labor* 2 (September 1950), 10.

48. Minutes of First Meeting, March 6, 1948, and Minutes of Second Meeting, April 14, 1948, CTA-HMRC. Copies of the *Negro Railway Labor News* for 1949 and 1950 can be found in the CTA-HMRC and in *Blacks in the Railway Industry: Papers, 1946–1954* (New York: New York Public Library, Schomburg Center for Research in Black Culture, 1995).

49. *Negro Railway Labor News* 1 (June–July 1949); Charles Hamilton Houston address to Meeting of Representatives of ACRT, IARE, and CTA, October 2, 1948; Houston Notes of Conference with Archibald Bromsen, February 2, 1948, in CTA-HMRC.

50. J. O. McDonald to the FEPC Committee, September 12, 1943, in *BSCP Records,* Reel 23; "Addenda to Statement of L. W. Fairchild," in *FEPC Records,* Reel 10; *Hearings before a Special Subcommittee of the Committee on Education and Labor on H.R. 4453 and Companion Bills to Prohibit Discrimination in Employment,* 81st Congress, 1st sess. (Washington, D.C.: Government Printing Office, 1949), 199 (hereafter *1949 Hearings on Federal FEP Act*).

51. Statement of L. W. Fairchild to FEPC, January 25, 26, 27, 1943, in *BSCP Records,* Reel 21.

52. Cited in *Hunter et al. v. Atchison, T. & S. F. Ry. Co.,* Civ. No. 44-C-971, February 6, 1948, in 78 Federal Supplement, 984; C. C. Smith to R. B. Ball, August 2, 1944; Ball to Smith, August 19, 1944, in *FEPC Records,* Reel 11. Also see M. P. Webster to Mark Ethridge, November 7, 1942, in *BSCP Records,* Reel 21;

Richard Westbrooks to C. C. Smith, January 15, 1945; National Railroad Adjustment Board, First Division, Award no. 6640, Docket no. 7400; office memorandum, W. Don Ellinger to Will Maslow, November 8, 1944; Richard Westbrooks, "Complaint of Train Porter Brakemen," July 1, 1944, in *FEPC Records,* Reel 11.

53. "Report of Proceedings of the Sixth Biennial Convention and Twenty-Third Anniversary Celebration of the Brotherhood of Sleeping Car Porters, Held at Detroit, Michigan, September 12th to 17th, Inclusive, 1948," in *The Papers of A. Philip Randolph* (Bethesda, Md.: University Publications of America, 1990), Reel 4 (hereafter "1948 BSCP Proceedings"), 126, 128; *Black Worker* 9 (March 1945), 1–2.

54. Statement of L. W. Fairchild to FEPC, 5; *Randolph et al. v. Missouri-Kansas-Texas R. Co. et al.* No. 4211 (October 28, 1946), 68 F. Supp. 1007; *Pittsburgh Courier,* June 22, 1946; *Norfolk Journal and Guide,* July 6, 1946; *Black Worker* 7 (November 1948), 3; George F. McCray, "The Labor Movement and Employment: Court Decisions: Porter-Brakemen Case and Similar Cases," in Florence Murray, ed., *The Negro Handbook 1949* (New York: Macmillan, 1949), 164–165; *Pittsburgh Courier,* March 2, 1946; *Norfolk Journal and Guide,* May 3, 1952; *1949 Hearings on Federal FEP Act,* 186.

55. *Black Worker* 7 (May 1951), 6; *Northwest Enterprise,* November 22, 1944; *Sunday Chicago Bee,* November 19, December 3, 1944; *Chicago Defender,* November 4, 11, December 9, 1944, March 3, 1945, February 14, 1948; *Atlanta Daily World,* December 9, 1944; *Norfolk Journal and Guide,* September 21, November 16, 1946; *Seattle Northwest Enterprise,* December 29, 1948; *Pittsburgh Courier,* November 11, 1944, January 1, 1949, July 15, 1950; *Negro Labor News,* June 11, 1949; *Black Worker* 7 (January 1949).

56. *Pittsburgh Courier,* June 22, 1946, March 1, 1947, July 8, 1950; *Norfolk Journal and Guide,* July 6, 1946, May 29, October 9, 1948; *Negro Labor News,* September 10, 1949; *Boston Guardian,* November 16, 1946; "1948 BSCP Proceedings," 10–11, 29, 107; *Black Worker* 8 (October 1948), 1–2; (November 1948), 1; *Black Worker* 7 (July 1950), 1.

57. Charles Hamilton Houston and Joseph Waddy to S. H. Clark, Arthur Lewis, and Jordan J. Jefferson, Memorandum, September 27, 1948, CTA-HMRC.

58. *Simon L. Howard, Sr. v. St. Louis–San Francisco Railway Company, Brotherhood of Railroad Trainmen . . . and C. O. Carnahan, General Chairman, Brotherhood of Railroad Trainmen,* U.S. Court of Appeals, Eighth Circuit, September 11, 1951, 191 F. (2d) 442; E. Larry Eberlein, "Judicial Regulation of the Railway Brotherhoods' Discriminatory Practices," *Wisconsin Law Review* (May 1953), 525–534.

59. *Brotherhood of Railroad Trainmen, et al. v. Simon L. Howard, Sr., and St. Louis–San Francisco Railway Company,* U.S. Supreme Court, October Term, 1951. Docket No. 458, June 9, 1952 (343 U.S. 768).

60. "Labor Law—Collective Bargaining Agent—Racial Discrimination," *New York University Law Review* 27 (October 1952), 713–719.

61. Stymied by legal rulings blocking their predatory advances on the train porters' positions, the BRT resorted to advocating the passage of state full-crew laws de-

signed to exclude black porter brakemen. Opposed by black railroaders and railroad companies, they failed. See A. Philip Randolph, "The Crisis of Negro Railroad Workers," *American Federationist* 46 (August 1939), 817–818; *Houston Informer and Texas Freeman,* July 14, 1937; *Black Worker* 7 (April 1949), 1–2; 7 (May 1949), 5; 7 (June 1949), 1–2, 4; 7 (July 1949), 6, 8; 7 (August 1949), 1, 3, 8; 7 (May 1951), 1, 6; 7 (June 1951), 1; testimony of Theodore E. Brown, *To Amend the Railway Labor Act . . . Hearings on S.3295,* 239.

62. "BLFE Phony 'Equality' Brings New Court Test," *Railroad Workers' Link* 2 (March 1948).

63. *Railroad Workers' Link* 2 (March 1948); Samuel H. Clark, "Pres. Report, Biennial Convention, Chicago, Summer 1958," Samuel H. Clark Papers, Library of Congress.

64. APR and Provisional Committee to Sirs and Brothers, "Eighteenth Annual Conference, May 22–23, 1959," BSCP-LC, Box 68; Randolph to J. A. Howard, Jr., October 11, 1960, CTA-HMRC.

65. John F. Stover, *The Life and Decline of the American Railroad* (New York: Oxford University Press, 1970), 192–193; Stover, *American Railroads,* 2nd ed. (Chicago: University of Chicago Press, 1997), 192–225; Maury Klein, *Union Pacific: The Rebirth, 1984–1969* (New York: Doubleday, 1989), 489; H. Roger Grant, *The Northwestern: A History of the Chicago and North Western Railway System* (De Kalb: Northern Illinois University Press, 1996), 201–202; Howard W. Risher, Jr., "The Negro in the Railroad Industry," in Herbert R. Northrup et al., *Negro Employment in Land and Air Transport: A Study of Racial Policies in the Railroad, Airline, Trucking, and Urban Transit Industries,* vol. 5, *Studies of Negro Employment* (Philadelphia: Industrial Research Unit, Wharton School of Finance and Commerce, 1971), 76; *New York Times,* January 9, 1965; see also J. F. Little, Jr., to James A. Howard, January 9, 1961, CTA-HMRC.

8. Black Railroaders in the Modern Era

1. *Hearings before the Special Subcommittee on Labor of the Committee on Education and Labor, House of Representatives,* 87th Congress, 2nd sess., January 15–19, 24, 1962 (Washington, D.C.: Government Printing Office, 1962), 852–853, 722; "Eleventh Annual Conference of the BSCP Provisional Committee . . . May 23 and 24, 1952" (typescript), p. 3 in William H. Harris, ed., *Records of the Brotherhood of Sleeping Car Porters, Series A, Holdings of the Chicago Historical Society and the Newberry Library, 1925–1969,* Part 1, *Records of the BSCP, 1925–1969* (Bethesda, Md.: University Publications of America, 1990) (hereafter *BSCP Records*), Reel 26.

2. Author's telephone interview with James A. Reed, Jackson, Mississippi, August 26, 1996; on family ties and hiring, author's telephone interview with Samuel M. Ledford, Jr., April 8, 1997.

3. Author's interview with Reed.

4. Ibid.

5. Ibid.

6. *Chicago Defender*, October 11, 1952; Morroe Berger, "The New York State Law against Discrimination: Operation and Administration," *Cornell Law Quarterly* 35 (Summer 1950), 747–796.

7. *Norfolk Journal and Guide*, January 19, 1946, January 11, 1947, January 24, 1948; *Interracial Review* 20 (January 1947), 16; *New York Age*, February 10, 1945.

8. Jacob Wittner and Milton Rosenberg, "Report of the Conference on Employment of Negroes in Operating Crafts . . . on September 9, 1953," and Henry Spitz to Elmer A. Carter, October 5, 1953, Memorandum, in State Commission against Discrimination Records, New York State Archives, Albany (hereafter SCAD Records), Box 5; *New York Times*, September 13, 1953, December 11, 12, 1956.

9. Complaint no. C-3262-53, Louis Tribble against Pennsylvania Railroad, April 27, 1953; Determination after Investigation and Conference, Case no. C-3272-53: Leroy L. Hall vs. Pennsylvania Railroad, January 29, 1954; Notes on Case no. C-3262-53, May 13, 953; Jacob Wittner, Field Representative, Notes on Case no. C-3252–52, June 22, 1953; Elmer A. Carter, memorandum re Address before the Railroad Employees Association against Discrimination . . . February 14, 1954, March 8, 1954, SCAD Records, Box 5. See also Brooklyn NAACP Labor Committee, "Attention—Negro Men and Women!" (1954), *Papers of the NAACP, Part 13: The NAACP and Labor, 1940–1955, Series A* (Bethesda, Md.. University Publications of America, 1992) (hereafter *NAACP Papers*, Part 13-A), Reel 13.

10. Determination after Investigation and Conference, Case no. C-3280-53: Charles Morris vs. Pennsylvania Railroad, January 29, 1954; Determination after Investigation and Conference, Case no. C-3272-53: Leroy L. Hall vs. Pennsylvania Railroad, January 29, 1954; Jacob Wittner, notes on conference between SCAD and Pennsylvania Railroad officials, Case no. C-3262-53, September 29, 1953; Wittner to Elmer A. Carter, Memorandum re Case no. C-3280-53, November 25, 1953, in SCAD Records, Box 5; Theodore Leskes and Sol Rabkin, American Jewish Committee, memorandum, October 28, 1953, re: "First Negro brakeman employed by Pennsylvania R.R." *NAACP Papers*, Part 13-A, Reel 13; *New York Times*, October 21, 1953.

11. I. R. Korbliet to J. Edward Conway, memorandum re Case no. C-3494-54, Conference with Respondent, December 2, 1954; Korbliet to Conway, memorandum re Case no. C-3494-54, Conference with Respondent, January 14, 1955; Decision and Determination after Investigation and Conference, Case no. C-3494-54, Howard Willis vs. Long Island Railroad, May 11, 1955, in SCAD Records, Box 6.

12. "Railroad Employment in New York and New Jersey: A Joint Study by the New York State Commission against Discrimination and the New Jersey Division against Discrimination" (1959) (copy in Department of Labor Library, Washington, D.C.). The railroad employing the most black brakemen was the Pennsylvania, which employed 140 black brakemen between November 1953 and May 1956, of which 114 remained in service by May 1956. Elmer Carter to A. Philip Randolph, June 13, 1956, in *The Papers of A. Philip Randolph*

(Bethesda, Md.: University Publications of America, 1990) (hereafter *APR Papers*), Reel 6.

13. Harry Fleischman, "Equality and the Unions," Golden Anniversary Conference, National Urban League, typescript, (in Department of Labor Library), 4; Herbert Hill, "The Racial Practices of Organized Labor: The Contemporary Record," in Julius Jacobson, ed., *The Negro and the American Labor Movement* (New York: Anchor Books, 1968), 291; *Chicago Courier,* January 30, 1960, in *BSCP Records,* Reel 29.

14. A. Philip Randolph to John Whitaker, April 21, 1960, Colored Trainmen of America Papers, Houston Metropolitan Research Center, Houston Public Library, Houston, Texas (hereafter CTA-HMRC); "Report of Proceedings of the [BSCP's] Fourth Triennial Convention and Thirty-Seventh Anniversary," 1962, typescript, 160, in *APR Papers,* Reel 11.

15. A. Philip Randolph to J. A. Howard, Jr., October 1, 1960, CTA-HMRC.

16. Ibid.; "Introduction of Proposed Plan for Merger" (n.d.); Joseph C. Waddy to J. A. Howard, January 3, 1961; Jordan Jefferson, President, to Louis Nelson and Aubry Harris, September 15, 1950; A. Philip Randolph to John Whitaker, April 21, 1960; "Minutes of the Fourteenth Annual Grand Lodge Session of the Colored Trainmen of America, Kingsville, Texas, September 11–13, 1960," all in CTA-HMRC. Report of Proceedings of the Fourth Triennial Convention and Thirty-Seventh Anniversary of the Brotherhood of Sleeping Car Porters, 1962, typescript, 144–145, 157, in *APR Papers,* Reel 11; Whitaker to Randolph, January 6, 1961, and "Report of Merger Committee," October 4, 1960, in *BSCP Records,* Reel 29.

17. Isaac Hollis, Jr., to CTA, July 26, 1966; Equal Employment Opportunity Commission, Henry Hudson vs. Missouri Pacific Railroad Company, Case no. 6-6-5834, Decision, April 14, 1967, in CTA-HMRC.

18. James R. Watson, Jr., to James Gough, December 19, 1966; R. R. Green to Brakemen, June 8, 1966; Mediator's Report, Case no. R-3941, BRT vs. Colored Trainmen of America on Mo Pac RR; Truett V. Tillmon to Ralph W. Yarborough, August 10, 1967; C.T. of A. Minutes, March 30, 1969, in CTA-HMRC.

19. "Transport Service Employees Merge with BRAC," *Railway Clerk Interchange* 71 (October–November 1972), 8.

20. C. L. Dellums to Randolph, January 13, 1969, and "Train Porters Eye Amtrak," September 19, 1971, uncited publication, in *APR Papers,* Reel 6; *New York Times,* January 9, 1965. See also David D. Perata, "George Doesn't Work Here Anymore," *Trains* (June 1991), 54–57.

21. Hugh Davis Graham, *The Civil Rights Era: Origins and Development of National Policy, 1960–1972* (New York: Oxford University Press, 1990), 146–149; Judith Stein, *Running Steel, Running America: Race, Economic Policy, and the Decline of Liberalism* (Chapel Hill: University of North Carolina Press, 1998), 81–88; Alfred W. Blumrosen, *Black Employment and the Law* (New Brunswick: Rutgers University Press, 1971), 3–9, 226.

22. Stein, *Running Steel,* 87; Howard W. Risher, Jr., "The Negro in the Railroad Industry," in Herbert R. Northrup et al., *Negro Employment in Land and Air*

Transport: A Study of Racial Policies in the Railroad, Airline, Trucking, and Urban Transit Industries, Vol. 5, *Studies of Negro Employment* (Philadelphia: Industrial Research Unit, Wharton School of Finance and Commerce, 1971), 88, 96; Timothy J. Minchin, "Federal Policy and the Racial Integration of Southern Industry, 1961–1980," *Journal of Policy History* 11 (1999), 147–178; "Rail Industry Talks Equal Opportunity Commitment but Doesn't Follow Through, EEOC Chairman Holds," *Daily Labor Report,* December 9, 1970, A6–A7. See also Tom Shedd, "Where Do Railroads Stand on EEO?" and "Railroads and the Negro: Renewing the Reservoir of Good Will," *Modern Railroads* 24 (February 1969), 40–42, 44–45; Frank E. Shaffer, "The Open Door," *Modern Railroads* 34 (January 1979), 58–61.

23. Author's telephone interview with Joe Vernon Sears, June 29, 1999; Joe Vernon Sears v. Atchison, Topeka and Santa Fe Railway Company, and United Transportation Union, Civ. A. No. W-4963, U.S. District Court, D. Kansas, in 454 F. Supp. 158 (1978); Sears v. Santa Fe Ry. Co., U.S. Court of Appeals, Tenth Circuit, Denver, March 11, 1981, in 25 FEP Cases 337; Jon Roe, "Long Ride to Justice," pamphlet of articles reprinted from the *Wichita Eagle,* November 25–27, 1993.

24. Author's interview with Sears; Roe, "Long Ride to Justice."

25. Roe, "Long Ride to Justice"; "A Look at Love v. Pullman," *University of Chicago Law Review* 37, 181–195.

26. Agnes Calliste, "The Struggle for Employment Equity by Blacks on American and Canadian Railroads," *Journal of Black Studies* 25 (January 1995), 303–307; Jennifer E. Baniewicz, "The Pullman Porter-in-Charge" (seminar paper, University of Illinois at Chicago, May 1996). In Pullman Company Archive, Record Group no. 4, Law Department Records, Series 2, Court Case Records, Newberry Library, Chicago (hereafter Pullman Court Records) see: In the Supreme Court of the United States, October Term, 1970, no. 967, *Earl A. Love, USA, and EEO vs. Pullman Company,* on Writ of Cert to the United States Court of Appeals for the Tenth Circuit, Motion for Leave to File Brief Amicus Curiae and Brief for the NAACP as Amicus Curiae (Box 10, Folder 112), and Joe L. Black to Director of Compliance, Final Investigation Report, re: Earl A. Love, Case no. 6-5-5042, July 23, 1966 (Box 10, Folder 114).

27. Calliste, "Struggle for Employment Equity," 303–307. In Pullman Court Records, see In the U.S. District Court for the District of Colorado, Civil Action C-899, *Earl A. Love v. Pullman Co.* Memorandum Opinion and Order, February 9, 1976 (Box 10, Folder 116), and U.S. Court of Appeals, nos. 76-1993-4-5, *Earl A. Love v. Pullman,* January 26, 1978 (Box 12, Folder 179).

28. *United States of America v. Jacksonville Terminal Company, Brotherhood of Railroad Trainmen, et al.,* No. 30448, U.S. Court of Appeals, Fifth Circuit, 451 F2d 418 (1971); Risher, Jr., "Negro in the Railroad Industry," 158–163.

29. *U.S. v. Jacksonville Terminal Company, et al.,* 451 F2d 418 (1971).

30. *Robert Rock et al. v. Norfolk & Western Railway Company,* U.S. Court of Appeals, Fourth Circuit, 473 F.2d 1344 (1973); *Rock et al. v. Norfolk & Western Railway Company,* U.S. District Court, Eastern District of Virginia, 1974, 11 FEP Cases 407.

31. On railroad company efforts to comply with Title VII, see Tom Shedd, "Where Do Railroads Stand on EEO?" and "Railroads and the Negro Renewing the Reservoir of Good Will," *Modern Railroads* 24 (February 1969), 40–42, 44–45; Frank E. Shaffer, "The Open Door," *Modern Railroads* 34 (January 1979), 58–60; Beverly Rabner Silverberg, "Putting a New Face on the Northeast Corridor," *Transportation USA* 4 (Spring 1978), 15–16.

32. Author's interview with Herman Autry, Houston, Texas, June 26, 1996. The following narrative of Autry's experience is based on this interview.

33. Author's telephone interview with Eddie Lee Jenkins III, Barnwell, South Carolina, September 17, 1997.

34. Ibid. On the problem of black workers and accommodations, see also Carl Ryant, "'Where the Railroad Was, the River Is': Oral History from L&N Workers," *Register of the Kentucky Historical Society* 82 (Winter 1984), 66.

35. Author's interview with Dave Leftridge, Calumet City, Illinois, June 16, 1996.

36. Author's interview with Reed; author's interview with Leftridge.

37. Sarah McNaught, "Hate Train," *Boston Phoenix,* October 10–17, 1996; McNaught, "Train Reaction," *Boston Phoenix,* October 24–31, 1996; McNaught, "Sending a Message," *Boston Phoenix,* January 21–28, 1999; Stephen Franklin, "Amtrak Faces Discrimination Suit," *Chicago Tribune,* August 21, 1998; *New York Times,* August 1, 1999; author's telephone interview with Samuel M. Ledford, Jr., Phoenix, Arizona, April 8, 1997; author's interview with Anthony Smith, Bellwood, Illinois, May 14, 1999; *New York Times,* August 1, 1999. For a positive view of integration in the railway labor force, see Beverly Rabner Silverberg, "Putting a New Face on the Northeast Corridor: Minorities, Women Are among Workers on Railroad Crews," *Transportation USA* 4 (Spring 1978), 15–16.

Acknowledgments

Over the years, numerous scholars have provided criticism and commentary on various drafts of the book's chapters. Alex Lichtenstein, Beth Bates, Joseph McCartin, Colin Davis, and Michael Honey generously subjected significant portions of the book to their careful scrutiny. I depended on the insights and guidance of a number of legal scholars and lawyers—Leon Letwin, Risa Goluboff, Sarah deLone, and Gwen McNamee—who gave careful readings to the book's sections on the role of labor law in shaping black workers' experiences. John Lyons, Robert Zieger, Leon Fink, and Judith Stein read the completed manuscript near its final stages, providing the big-picture criticisms that prompted needed recrafting. I also want to express my thanks to Bruce Laurie, Julie Greene, Kimberley Phillips, David Montgomery, Daniel Letwin, Merl Reed, Eileen Boris, Thomas Sugrue, Bruce Nelson, Gareth Canaan, Jason Digman, Margaret Strobel, Victor Ortiz, James Grossman, David Roediger, and Paul Taillon, who read drafts of various sections. I have had the privilege of presenting portions of the book at a variety of seminars and workshops. In particular, I benefited greatly from the observations of the participants in the American Bar Foundation Seminar, the Penn State University Labor History Workshop, the Newberry Library Seminar in American Social History, the Workshop in Social History at the University of Chicago, and the Arts and Sciences Forum at Chicago State University.

Archivists and reference librarians are an indispensable resource, without whom historians would find it impossible to carry out their research. In Chicago, Martin Tuohy offered expert guidance through the holdings of the Great Lakes Region office of the National Archives and Records Administration. In addition, I offer my appreciation to Archie Motley of the Chicago Historical Society; Robert C. Dinwiddie at the Southern Labor Archives at Georgia State University; Tara Wenger at the Houston Metropolitan Research Center of the Houston Public Library; Richard Strassberg, Hope

Nisley, and Patrizia Sione at the Kheel Center for Labor-Management Documentation and Archives at Cornell University; James D. Folts of the New York State Archives; Gerald Saxon and Shirley Rodnitzky of the University of Texas at Arlington Special Collections Division; Kay Bost of the DeGoyler Library at Southern Methodist University; Elisa Baldwin of the University Archives of the University South Alabama; James Cassedy at the Washington National Records Center and Ken Hall and Bill Creech of the National Archives; and Denise Conklin of the Historical Collections and Labor Archives at Pennsylvania State University. In addition, I relied heavily on the support of archivists and reference librarians at the Hagley Museum and Library; the Newberry Library; Carter G. Woodson Regional Library of the Chicago Public Library; the Moorland Spingarn Research Center at Howard University; the Walter P. Reuther Library at Wayne State University; the Bancroft Library at the University of California at Berkeley; the AFL-CIO's George Meany Memorial Archives; the Schomberg Center for Research in Black Culture of the New York Public Library; the Transportation Library of Northwestern University; the Archives and Special Collections of the Healey Library, University of Massachusetts, Boston; and the Franklin Delano Roosevelt Presidential Library. Journalist Sarah McNaught pointed me in fruitful directions for exploring recent protests against discriminatory treatment in the railroad industry; James C. Juhnke directed me to events and sources regarding the 1950s through the 1980s; Greg Leroy, a former Pullman porter and union leader turned historian turned labor researcher, shared his insights and his own earlier writings with me; Greg Simmons provided valuable research assistance.

One of the most important sources for this book were the many former and current railroad workers and union activists and supporters who agreed to participate in oral histories, taking the time not only to remember and reflect on the past but also to teach me about their world, their aspirations, and their struggles. From more than any other source, I learned of railroaders' worlds, aspirations, determination, and struggles from Ishmael Flory, Alexander Saxton, Ike Golden, Leon Despres, James A. Reed, Dave Leftridge, Eddie Lee Jenkins III, Jerome "Buddy" Cooper, Molly West, Donald "Sisi" Mosby, Samuel Ledford, Jr., Roosevelt Thompson, Winetta A. Frazier, Anthony Berry, Timuel Black, Truman Gibson, Jr., Randolph Purnell, Jr., Bennie Brunson, Hugh L. Porter, Larry Minter, Anthony W. Smith, T. O. Wilson, Ralph Stevens, George Williams, Herman Autry, Henry Hines, Leroy Shackelford, Patrick Simmons, Grace Manuel, Joe V. Sears, John Williams, Sam Currie, Preston Steiner, John Fite III, Jaqueline A. Whalum, Arthur Maxwell, Saul Slapikoff, Leland Cain, Jr., Andrew Walton, Carl

Meacham, Arthur Eiland, and the members of the Black Railroad Workers' Association of the Burlington Northern Santa Fe Railroad.

The generous support of a number of institutions allowed me the time to research and write this book. I am grateful to the Charles Warren Center at Harvard University, the Institute for the Humanities and the Great Cities Program at the University of Illinois at Chicago (UIC), and the National Endowment for the Humanities for research fellowships. Research and transcription funds were also provided by the Institute for the Humanities and the Office of Social Science Research at UIC. Tom Ryan of UIC's Office of Public Affairs enthusiastically publicized the project, allowing me to make contact with many current and former railroad employees. The University of Illinois Press and the *American Historical Review* kindly allowed me to use portions of essays I had previously published. I also had the considerable fortune to meet and work with Joyce Seltzer, who was everything one could want an editor to be; Joyce, David Lobenstine, and Donna Bouvier of Harvard University Press nurtured and shaped the project in decisive ways.

And finally, my family. My parents, Alice and Jack Arnesen, provided more than moral support; they read and critiqued the manuscript and located specific materials for me at various Washington, D.C., libraries and archives when I needed them on very short notice. Rachel joined Katrin Schultheiss and myself about midway through the process of writing this book, although she likely won't recall the early visits to railroad museums we made; Samuel and William arrived together as the project was nearing its conclusion (they'll get to those museums soon). In no way did Rachel, Sam, and Will facilitate the research and writing, their appreciation of trains notwithstanding. But they taught me to work more efficiently and they put the book in its proper perspective, reminding me each day of far more important things. Perhaps someday they will understand how and why history animates Katrin and me so much. Katrin has been with the project since its inception (she reminds me that I initially promised that this would be a very short book). As a historian herself, she has been an unsparing editor and critic, subjecting every chapter to the closest of readings and challenging me to sharpen arguments at every turn. Our almost daily conversations about history and our research over the years have proven the most valuable and rewarding of all. Her friendship, support, and love have enabled me to write this book. *Brotherhoods of Color* is dedicated to her.

Index